500 BEST USA VACATIONS

Edited by R. Alan Fox

VACATION PUBLICATIONS

HOUSTON

500 BEST USA VACATIONS

Edited by: R. Alan Fox

Art Direction and Cover Design: Fred W. Salzmann

Editorial Assistants: Jennifer Hunt, Jill Boxrud, Alison Nesmith

Front cover photos, from top: Dick Hamilton, White Mountain News Bureau; White Mountain News Bureau; St. Louis Convention & Visitors Commission; Tom Darden, Maryland Office of Tourism Development; Hot Springs Convention & Visitors Bureau.

Published by Vacation Publications, Inc.
1502 Augusta Drive, Suite 415
Houston, TX 77057

Library of Congress Catalog Card Number: 96-60038
ISBN 0-9644216-4-X

Printed in the United States of America

VACATION
PUBLICATIONS

THE CONTRIBUTORS

Carol Barrington of Houston, TX, is a contributing editor of *Vacations* magazine and a winner of the Lowell Thomas Travel Journalist of the Year award.

Jay Clarke is travel editor at *The Miami Herald* and an award-winning travel journalist.

Steve Cohen of Hesperus, CO, is a free-lance writer and photographer and author of several guidebooks.

Anne Z. Cooke and **Steve Haggerty** are free-lance writers and photographers from Marina del Rey, CA.

Judi Dash is a free-lance writer living in Beachwood, OH.

Lee Foster of Berkeley, CA, is a free-lance writer and photographer.

Mary Ann Hemphill of Newport Beach, CA, writes a travel shopping column for *Vacations* magazine.

Dave G. Houser of Ruidoso, NM, is a contributing editor at *Vacations* and an award-winning travel photographer.

Carole Jacobs of Altadena, CA, is a contributing editor of *Vacations* magazine and is travel editor at *Shape* magazine.

Evelyn Kanter is a free-lance writer who lives in New York City.

Kathy Kincade of Portsmouth, NH, has written several books about festivals.

Katy Koontz, formerly travel and features editor of *McCall's* magazine, is a contributing editor of *Vacations* magazine living in Knoxville, TN.

Sylvia McNair of Evanston, IL, is the author of a dozen books, including a series of children's travel publications and "Vacation Places Rated."

Jennifer Merin of New York City writes frequently about health and is the author of several shopping guides.

Everett Potter of Pelham, NY, is a syndicated travel columnist and a winner of Lowell Thomas Travel Journalism awards in 1993 and 1994.

Gail Rickey of Houston, TX, is author of *Best Places to Stay in the Southwest*.

June Naylor Rodriguez of Fort Worth, TX, a features writer for the *Fort Worth Star-Telegram*, contributes frequently to *Vacations* magazine.

George L. Rosenblatt of Houston, TX, is a free-lance travel writer.

Shirley Slater of Los Angeles writes frequently about cruise, ski and RV vacations.

Candyce H. Stapen of Washington, DC, writes frequently for *Vacations* magazine and is the author of two books on family vacations.

Yvonne Vollert of Agoura, CA, is a free-lance writer specializing in RV travel.

TABLE OF CONTENTS

MAPS

INTRODUCTION

You just can't beat the USA for the number, variety and quality of vacation opportunities. From Denali National Park, AK, to St. Croix, U.S. Virgin Islands, there are dozens (hundreds!) of tempting options for every taste and budget.

So why do so many Americans return to the same destination year after year? Tradition, no doubt, plays a key role, and to many, it's simply less risky to trust your important (and expensive) vacation to a familiar and well-liked town, beach or hotel.

But millions of us seek new ventures with our scarce leisure time — something different, challenging, relaxing or rewarding. Our hurdle is finding the right place for the right price without spending months in the search process.

That's why *500 Best USA Vacations* was published.

If you have a wanderlust, a yearning for new places and new experiences, this is the one travel resource you'll need. Here, under one cover, is a lifetime of new vacation ideas — something special for every traveler. Organized by category, with ideas to suit every interest and whim, these are the vacation picks voted best by our slate of top travel writers. Here's how they were compiled.

As the publisher of *Vacations* magazine since its inception in 1987, I've followed the rapid growth and development of vacation alternatives in this country and abroad. With over 100 contributing writers and editors in the field visiting up-and-coming locations, sampling new lodging, sailing new riverboats and cruise ships and making suggestions about which to feature, it's been possible to highlight in our magazine the very best of what America has to offer. And so we have, for each of the past 7 years, in our annual special issue entitled "100 Best USA Summer Vacations."

From the 700 Vacations featured in those issues, we have selected and updated approximately 350 as the core of this book. Then we added vacation spots that truly shine in Fall, Winter or Spring, and non-traditional categories, such as Great River Towns, Haunted Hideaways and Streets of Dreams. Some of our recommendations were based on a survey of *Vacations* magazine's more than one million readers, who offered up nearly 3,000 vacation ideas for our consideration.

Each of the fine writers who contributed to this book was given two guidelines to follow: Get a good geographic mix in your selection, and look for vacations that offer particularly good value for the money spent, whatever the cost. So while most of our listings are budget or moderate in cost, even our splurge suggestions are well worth the price.

Speaking of price, it's important to note that all of the prices in this book were supplied by the featured companies within two months of going to press. All of the rates are subject to change without notice, and in these days of sophisticated inventory control systems, it's not at all uncommon for prices to fluctuate up or down on a daily basis. So use the prices shown as a general indicator only, and always reconfirm the actual price before making a reservation.

Now turn the page to see our guide to America's travel treasures — and have a great trip.

Alan Fox
Editor

GREAT RIVER TOWNS

There's something about water that attracts vacationers like a magnet. For many, the pull draws them right to the ocean, with its promise of warm sun, soft sand and colorful shells (not to mention saltwater taffy).

Others prefer streams and rivers where the movement, the sense of constant flow, is soothing and engaging.

The best known river town of them all is New Orleans (or N'awlins, as the locals say) where you can walk the colorful streets of the French Quarter surrounded by swirls of jazz notes from street musicians.

During the 1800s, the riverfront here was so choked with steamboats that you could walk a mile on their decks without setting foot ashore. Today you'll find only a few such boats, toting tourists instead of cotton, yet the old-fashioned ambience remains as strong as ever.

You can cruise from New Orleans on the antique Delta Queen, the larger and more modern Mississippi Queen or the new American Queen, three paddle-wheel steamboats that offer a fascinating journey in time as well as distance.

Many other U.S. towns, big and small, owe their atmosphere — from modern-day water sports to the old-fashioned spirit of Mark Twain — to the river. Here are some of the best, each packed with plenty of river flavor. Room rates are per night, double occupancy.

New Orleans, Louisiana

This gracious Southern city exudes Old World charm, most of it emanating from its historic heart — the 13-block French Quarter. Here you'll find historic homes with fancy wrought-iron balconies, delightful antique shops and boutiques and memorable restaurants showcasing spicy Cajun and Creole cuisine.

Spend time just hanging out along the Mississippi River in Jackson Square, where street-corner musicians, mimes and magicians will entertain you for hours. Stroll along the river until you come to the Aquarium of the Americas, where a Plexiglas tunnel takes you through a re-created Caribbean reef without your getting wet.

The city's historic streetcars, the oldest continuously operating street railway system in existence, also are worth a ride. Take the St. Charles Avenue trolley from the French Quarter through the grand mansions of the Garden District. This route brings you to Audubon Park and the Audubon Zoo, also on the river, where a simulated Louisiana swamp exhibit (complete with black bears and alligators) is one of the most unusual attractions.

For a short sightseeing or dinner cruise on the Mississippi, try the paddle wheelers Creole Queen and Cajun Queen. For an overnight steamboat experience, book a cabin on any of the three steamboats owned by Delta Queen Steamboat Co.

Accommodations: Le Richelieu, an 86-room, European-style inn in the French Quarter, starts at $95, including free parking, 1234 Chartres, New Orleans, LA 70116, (800) 535-9653.

Information: New Orleans Metropolitan Convention and Visitors Bureau, 1520

Sugar Bowl Drive, New Orleans, LA 70112, (800) 345-1187.

Memphis, Tennessee

This city celebrates the Mississippi River by devoting a whole island to it. The crown jewel of Mud Island, accessible by tram from downtown, is its Riverwalk — a three-quarter-mile scale model of the Mississippi. The intriguing Mississippi River Museum, which details river legends and folklore, also can be found on the island, along with shops, restaurants and an amphitheater for summer concerts.

Memphis is where W.C. Handy first wrote the blues, and Beale Street Historic District, which includes the site of Handy's house, is chockablock with nightclubs where you can sample jazz and rock as well. Beale Street also is known for the offbeat A. Schwab's Dry Goods Store, dating from 1876, and the Center for Southern Folklore, a sort of cultural museum of the South.

Graceland, the estate of the late Elvis Presley, is one of the most popular attractions in town. Guided tours of the mansion are just part of the package. The Trophy Room, the Hall of Gold (the largest privately owned collection of gold records in the world), Presley's grave, his two private jets, a museum of his cars and another of personal effects round out the offerings.

A poignant landmark is the National Civil Rights Museum, on the site of the former Lorraine Motel, where Martin Luther King Jr. was assassinated. The museum provides an outstanding overview of the history of the civil rights movement with video and interactive exhibits.

Accommodations: The Peabody Hotel, an elegant historic hotel famous for its resident marching ducks, starts at $125 with the "Boogie Your Blues" package, 149 Union Ave., Memphis, TN 38103, (800) PEABODY.

Information: Memphis Convention and Visitors Bureau, 47 Union Ave., Memphis, TN 38103, (901) 543-5300.

St. Louis, Missouri

With a top-rate zoo, a hard-hitting baseball team and an eye-popping national monument among its attractions, St. Louis is a river town made for low-cost family fun.

The down-to-earth Heartland city on the Mississippi River is just the right size, large enough to offer a variety of day and night activities but still easy to get around.

Free attractions include the zoo, the St. Louis Science Center and Grant's Farm—a historic farm, wild game preserve and home of the Anheuser-Busch Clydesdales.

Ride to the top of the spectacular landmark, the 630-foot-tall Gateway Arch commemorating America's westward movement. Visit the Dog Museum in historic Jarville House, and ride on a restored, 1920s hand-carved St. Louis carousel in suburban Faust County Park.

Other options include riverboat cruises, Six Flags amusement park, Bob Kramer's Marionettes (where you learn about the puppets in addition to seeing performances), the hands-on exhibits at the Magic House and National Bowling Hall of Fame and Museum.

St. Louis is home to the Cardinals baseball team, and children can visit with the team mascot, Fredbird, during the game in the special Kids Corner.

Accommodations: Regal Riverfront Hotel, from $137, 200 S. Fourth St., St. Louis, MO 63102, (800) 325-7353.

Information: St. Louis Convention & Visitors Commission, 10 S. Broadway, Suite

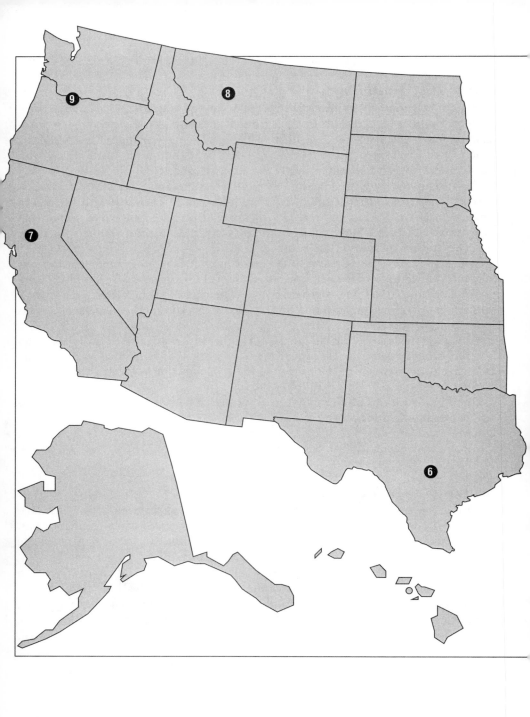

GREAT RIVER TOWNS

1 New Orleans, Louisiana
2 Memphis, Tennessee
3 St. Louis, Missouri

4 Hannibal, Missouri
5 Cold Spring, New York
6 San Antonio, Texas

7 Sacramento, California
8 Great Falls, Montana
9 Hood River, Oregon

300, St. Louis, MO 63102, (800) 247-9791.

Hannibal, Missouri

This quaint little town 100 miles north of St. Louis was the boyhood home of Samuel Langhorne Clemens — better known as Mark Twain, a pen name he took from riverboat slang. The famous author and river captain used the town as the setting for his classic "The Adventures of Tom Sawyer."

You'll find plenty of Twain in this town, starting with the Mark Twain Boyhood Home and Museum. It contains Norman Rockwell paintings for editions of "The Adventures of Tom Sawyer" and "The Adventures of Huckleberry Finn," a slide presentation about Twain and photos of townspeople who inspired his characters.

You also can visit 400-acre Riverview Park, with its two scenic overlooks of the Mississippi River and its Mark Twain statue. At the base of Cardiff Hill is a statue of Tom Sawyer and Huckleberry Finn, believed to be the first statue of fictional characters erected in the United States. At Mark Twain Cave, you can take a one-hour guided tour. The Becky Thatcher Bookshop is located in the house where Laura Hawkins, Twain's childhood sweetheart and the model for Becky Thatcher, grew up.

Twain-themed tours include riverboat excursions and narrated train and trolley rides. "The Reflections of Mark Twain" is a two-hour pageant telling the story of Twain and his characters, including tales from his days as a riverboat captain.

Betwixt the Twain memorabilia you'll find the Optical Museum, Light Show and Discovery Center with its interactive exhibits and theater and the Molly Brown Dinner Theater (named for the "Unsinkable Molly Brown," another Hannibal hero).

Accommodations: Garth Woodside Mansion, an antique-filled 1871 Victorian country estate, starts at $65, including full breakfast and your own nightshirt, R.R. 1, Box 304, Hannibal, MO 63401, (314) 221-2789.

Information: Hannibal Visitors and Convention Bureau, 505 N. Third, Hannibal, MO 63401, (314) 221-2477.

Cold Spring, New York

George Washington may not have slept here, but legend says he did drink here. This spot along the Hudson River north of New York City was known as Cold Spring as early as 1772, when the story goes that our founding father sipped water from a stream in the area. Finding it chilly indeed, he supposedly gave Cold Spring its name.

Whether or not the story holds water, Cold Spring remains a delightful historic jewel. The focal point of town is the old-fashioned Main Street on the banks of the Hudson. The street is filled with quaint specialty shops, intimate restaurants and 19th-century storefronts.

The town had its heyday in the last century when the West Point Foundry was in full operation, manufacturing the Parrott cannon, which some historians claim assured the Union's victory in the Civil War. Visitors can learn about this history in the Foundry School Museum, which houses a reconstruction of the original foundry schoolroom as well as a 19th-century kitchen.

The surrounding area of upstate New York along the Hudson River, known as the Hudson Highlands, is well worth exploring. The region boasts many buildings, bridges and roads listed on the National Register of Historic Places.

One of the most notable is Boscobel, a 19th-century estate considered one of the nation's leading museums of the decorative arts of the Federal period. From the grounds, graced by an apple orchard and several lovely gardens, you'll enjoy a stunning view of the Hudson.

The U.S. Military Academy and Museum, just across the river, displays the largest collection of military memorabilia in the Western Hemisphere.

Accommodations: Plumbush Inn, a historic Victorian B&B and highly acclaimed Swiss restaurant, starts at $95, Route 90, Cold Spring, NY 10516, (914) 265-3904.

Information: Cold Spring Chamber of Commerce, P. O. Box 342, Cold Spring, NY 10516, (914) 265-9060.

San Antonio, Texas

The San Antonio River is a star attraction in this city's business district, but don't look for it among the banks, department stores and offices downtown. Instead, you'll find it 20 feet below street level, accessible by various flights of stairs leading to the beautiful and romantic River Walk (Paseo del Rio).

Cobblestone and flagstone paths flank the river on both sides for two and one-half miles, leading you past small parks, an open-air theater, European-style sidewalk cafes, upscale bars and nightclubs and lots of quaint shops and galleries. You can explore the River Walk on foot or hop aboard a river barge for a narrated tour. At night, reserve a spot on a candlelight dinner barge for a memorable moveable feast.

La Villita, San Antonio's original settlement, is worth a stop along the route. Now a shopping area specializing in the work of local artists, its galleries are housed in the settlement's original buildings.

Other stops should include Market Square and its colorful Mexican market (El Mercado), The Institute of Texan Cultures (a museum detailing cultures of various ethnic groups with ties to Texas) and the Buckhorn Hall of Horns, Fins & Feathers, which boasts the world's largest collection of antlers among its mounted specimens of Texas wildlife.

The unusual Hertzberg Circus Collection, a museum of circus memorabilia dating from the time of King Charles II, makes a delightful diversion, as does the King William Historic District, a residential neighborhood of Victorian mansions (some open for touring) built by the city's early German merchants.

And, of course, in the thick of downtown you'll find the famed Alamo, where you can hear the dramatic stories of the heroes who fought here for independence from Mexico.

Four other Spanish missions dating from the 18th century are still in use as churches today. Follow the river south outside the city to San Jose Mission, the largest and most elaborate of the four. It conducts a mariachi mass each Sunday.

Accommodations: On the river, Holiday Inn Riverwalk, from $169, 217 N. Saint Mary's, San Antonio, TX 78205, (800) HOLIDAY or (210) 224-2500. For luxury and wide-open spaces a few miles from town, try the Hyatt Regency Hill Country, from $230, 9800 Hyatt Resort Drive, San Antonio, TX 78251, (800) 223-1234 or (210) 647-1234.

Information: San Antonio Convention and Visitors Bureau, P.O. Box 2277, San Antonio, TX 78298, (800) 447-3372.

Sacramento, California

Sacramento's American River more or less put California on the map when gold was discovered here in 1848. The following year, the rush was on and sleepy little Sacramento became the gateway to the mother lode.

It grew in size and importance, also becoming the site where the first transcontinental railroad was planned and the place where the first transcontinental telegraph was sent.

Today, Old Sacramento is a 28-acre state historic park along the Sacramento River, boasting the greatest concentration of historic buildings in the state. The boardwalks, cobblestone streets, gas lights and brick buildings of this waterfront district recall another era, when gold dust was the currency of choice.

Although the area is just a few blocks long, it houses more than 120 shops and almost two dozen restaurants, including the Pilothouse aboard the newly restored Delta King riverboat, which operated between Sacramento and San Francisco from 1927 to 1940.

In this historic district, you'll also find the Eagle Theater, the first building west of the Mississippi built specifically as a theater, and the California State Railroad Museum, the largest interpretive museum of its kind in North America. The museum contains 21 restored locomotives and many railroad cars from the 1860s to the 1960s. One car, a 1929 Canadian National Pullman, sways and hisses as though in motion, scenery flashing past the windows. The museum also offers an excursion ride on a steam train that chugs along the river.

For a different perspective, take a spin on one of the steamboats tied up among the sailboats at the dock, or try a horse-drawn carriage ride.

For some pre-gold rush history, take a self-guided tour of Sutter's Fort, Sacramento's first settlement, dating from 1839. The State Indian Museum next door also is worth a visit.

Accommodations: The Delta King, an authentic 1927 riverboat that stays tied at its dock in Old Sacramento, starting at $99, 1000 Front St., Old Sacramento, CA 95814, (800) 825-5464.

Information: Sacramento Convention and Visitors Bureau, 1421 K St., Sacramento, CA 95814, (916) 264-7777.

Great Falls, Montana

This river town is known for two notable rivers, the Missouri River being the most obvious.

The second river, called the Roe, is a little easier to miss. It's only 240 feet long and has the grand distinction of being listed in the Guinness Book of World Records as the shortest river in the world.

You can find the Roe River in 218-acre Giant Springs State Park, named for one of the largest freshwater springs in the country, thanks to its flow of 134,000 gallons per minute.

To see more of the Missouri River, take a self-guided driving tour of the portage route explorers Lewis and Clark took in the early 1800s around the great falls that gave the town its name. Although today's drive takes less than an hour, Lewis and Clark needed 10 days to cover the 18 miles, one of the greatest ordeals they endured on their two-year, 6,000-mile journey across the continent.

For a closer look, set off on the River's Edge Trail, a paved biking and hiking trail following the river. For in-your-face river experiences, go water-skiing, windsurfing or canoeing, or join a guided float trip.

Nearby is Fort Benton, once a trading post, military fort and the world's innermost port. As many as 50 steamboats a season docked here in the late 1800s. One of them sank before it could chug away, leaving its remains just below the surface of the water.

Accommodations: The Chalet, a former governor's Victorian chalet, starts at $40,

1204 Fourth Ave. N., Great Falls, MT 59401, (406) 452-9001 or (800) 786-9002.

Information: Great Falls Area Chamber of Commerce, P.O. Box 2127, Great Falls, MT 59403, (406) 761-4434.

Hood River, Oregon

The beautiful and rugged Columbia River Gorge may be part of the wild territory that Lewis and Clark explored from 1804 to 1805, but the craft plying the waters around Hood River today are vastly different from your average birch-bark canoe.

Known as the sailboarding capital of the world now, the town of Hood River annually draws about 10,000 sailboarders from all parts of the globe. The best vantage point to watch colorful sails whipping across the water is the Columbia Gorge Sailpark at Hood River's Port Marina Park. If you're not content to watch, join the fun yourself and take a lesson.

For a broader perspective, explore the Hood River Valley aboard the Mount Hood Railroad, dating from 1906. The ride will take you from the gorge to the foothills of majestic Mount Hood.

Hood River also is known as one of the country's most productive fruit baskets, thanks to its fertile volcanic soil. A drive on Hood River County's Fruit Loop takes you past numerous local farm stands where apples, cherries, peaches, pears, blueberries and vegetables are sold.

Beer is another of Hood River's notable products. Take a self-guided tour and then sample all you want at the Full Sail Brew Pub. Just west of Hood River, at the Marine Park in Cascade Locks, you can take a two-hour stern-wheeler cruise to view the fabulous gorge scenery.

Back in your car, tour the Columbia River Gorge National Scenic Area via the Historic Columbia River Highway, where you'll see Multnomah Falls — a 620-foot waterfall that's the fourth-highest in the United States.

Accommodations: The Hood River Hotel, an inn with views of the river, starts at $59, 102 Oak St., Hood River, OR 97031, (800) 386-1859 or (503) 386-1900.

Information: Hood River County Chamber of Commerce, Port Marina Park, Hood River, OR 97031, (800) 366-3530.

UNDISCOVERED PLACES

Although nothing worth visiting remains truly "undiscovered," countless wonderful travel experiences seldom get to preen in the spotlight of publicity.

It's a good thing, too. Popularity often destroys the very pleasures that attracted visitors in the first place.

But legions of travelers are desperate to avoid the crowds, willing to wander that "road less traveled" even if it isn't paved. The recommendations herein are for people who delight in the serendipity of finding that perfect little inn or charming cafe, who love licking homemade ice cream or wading barefoot in ocean surf or a mountain stream.

But there's a catch. If you really enjoy one of our treasures, be careful whom you tell. To paraphrase that old World War II slogan, "Loose lips sink great trips!" You may return to find the crowds you were originally trying to flee.

Accommodation prices noted are for two persons per night and do not include tax.

Bandera, Texas

If you'd rather hear jingling spurs than ringing telephones, you're probably ready to be a dude. The place for you may be Bandera, a Texas town that claims to be the "cowboy capital of the world."

Only 45 minutes west of San Antonio, Bandera boasts a long tradition of ranching, and many national rodeo champions hail from the area. It's a lifestyle that city slickers can sample at one of seven dude ranches, all offering family lodging in bunkhouses or cabins, horseback and hay rides, trick roping and snake-handling (!) demonstrations, rodeos and country-western dancing, golfing, and fishing and tubing on the mellow Medina River.

A fine choice is Dixie Dude Ranch, in business for more than 50 years and family-operated by the fourth generation. The 800-acre spread is nothing if not homey, and guests find themselves making friends during fried-chicken suppers, poolside cookouts and Saturday-night barbecues.

Bandera Downs, east of town, has parimutuel racing of thoroughbreds and quarter horses from early March through late October, and you can find plenty of sweets and Texas eats at the midsummer Texas International Apple Festival.

Accommodations: Dixie Dude Ranch, from about $80, P.O. Box 548, Bandera, TX 78003, (800) 375-9255.

Information: Bandera Convention & Visitors Bureau, P.O. Box 171, Bandera, TX 78003, (800) 364-3833.

Cedar Key, Florida

Despite its name, you won't find this island in the Florida Keys. It's more than 300 miles north, in the Gulf of Mexico, but it's got the same funky feel of better-known Key West.

Weather-worn buildings sit on pilings on the waterfront; metal roofs and second-story overhangs mark the buildings on Second Street, the main drag. And when one of the bars here boasts it carries 20 different brands of beer, you know the place is starting to get trendy. Not like overcrowded Key West, to be sure, but it wouldn't be a bad idea to visit before too many more people hear of the place.

What's to do in Cedar Key? Not much, which is just fine with most visitors. You feed on seafood, take a waterfront stroll, or sit in a rocking chair on an upstairs porch and watch pelicans dive for dinner. When the spirit moves you, you might visit the state's Cedar Key Museum.

There, you'll find that Cedar Key thrived in the 19th century in a variety of roles — successively as a center of lumbering, shipbuilding, sponge fishing, commercial fishing and oyster canning. Tourism now is the big money-earner. Behind the waterfront's weather-beaten exteriors are modern bars, cafes and boutiques, making it not as rustic as it looks.

Accommodations: The Island Hotel, $85-$95, including breakfast, P.O. Box 460, Cedar Key, FL 32625, (904) 543-5111.

Information: Florida Division of Tourism, 126 W. Van Buren St., Tallahassee, FL 32399, (904) 487-1462.

Caprock Canyons, Texas

This 13,950 acres of rugged, rusty red sandstone in the heart of the Texas Panhandle looks like it's waiting for the next Wells Fargo stage.

Sedentary travelers can stick to what they can see from the air-conditioned comfort of their cars; there's a six-mile scenic drive that also accesses several camping areas. But the best way to see these hoodoos, cliffs and canyons is astride a horse. A local wrangler runs a good string of cayuses daily in summer, on weekends in spring and fall.

Don't forget your camera — red-hot sunset shots nearly burn your film — and binoculars help spot abundant wildlife ranging from aoudad sheep to more than 175 species of birds. If the rain gods have smiled, you'll find swimming and fishing in 120-acre Lake Theo.

Accommodations: Quitaque Quail Lodge, $69-$79, P.O. Box 36, Quitaque, TX 79255, (806) 455-1261.

Information: Caprock Canyons State Park, P.O. Box 204, Quitaque, TX 79255, (806) 455-1492.

Gulf Seashore, Mississippi

When the real world is too much for you, dodge those stress bullets by running away to the Gulf Islands National Seashore off the Mississippi coast. Just getting to West Ship Island, the most accessible, on the 40-minute ferry ride from Gulfport helps you downshift from the fast lane.

First stop is Fort Massachusetts, built in the 1860s and obsolete before the cement dried on its red bricks. After a free tour led by a ranger, follow the long boardwalk to the concession area and official swimming beach. Hats, shoes and sunscreen are essentials, but swimsuits tend to be optional if you hike to secluded bays.

Accommodations: Sleep Inn, from $50, 7412 Tucker Road, Ocean Springs, MS 39565, (601) 872-0440 or (800) 627-5337.

Information: Gulf Islands National Seashore, 3500 Park Road, Ocean Springs, MS 39564, (601) 875-9057.

West Okoboji, Iowa

Folks who study such things say the world has only three truly blue lakes, and Iowa's

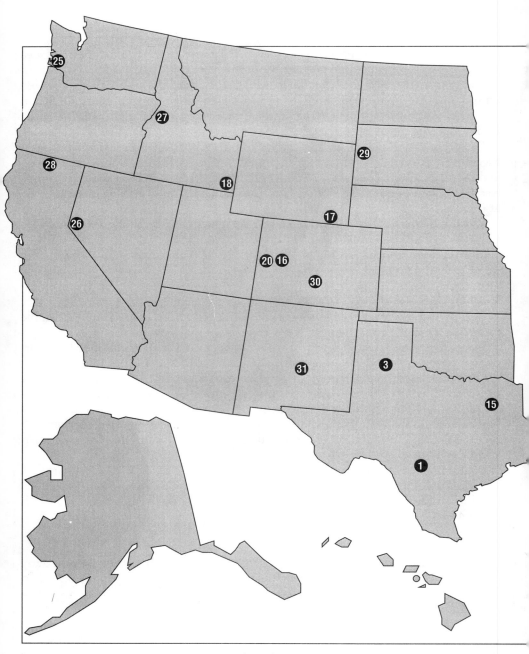

1 Bandera, Texas	8 Magnolia, Arkansas	15 Mineola, Texas
2 Cedar Key, Florida	9 St. Francisville, Louisiana	16 Redstone, Colorado
3 Caprock Canyons, Texas	10 West Point, Kentucky	17 Laramie, Wyoming
4 Gulf Seashore, Mississippi	11 Litchfield Hills, Connecticut	18 Lava Hot Springs, Idaho
5 West Okoboji, Iowa	12 Lewes, Delaware	19 Minnesota to South Dakota
6 Beaver Island, Michigan	13 Edisto Island, South Carolina	Pilgrimage*
7 Eagles Mere, Pennsylvania	14 Cabbage Key, Florida	20 Mesa County, Colorado

UNDISCOVERED PLACES

3,850-acre West Okoboji is one of them. It keeps good company; Switzerland's Lake Geneva and Canada's Lake Louise are the other two.

Sorry — there are no majestic mountains in Iowa, but hey, you can't have everything. However, West Okoboji is just one of more than a dozen freshwater lakes scattered over 15,000 acres of grassland prairie in the northwestern corner of this farming state.

Vacationers can wet a fishing line or engage in extensive water sports, golf, summer theater and family-focused amusements, including a vintage wooden roller coaster.

Accommodations: Village East Resort, $115-$160, P.O. Box 499, Okoboji, IA 51355, (800) 727-4561 or (712) 332-2161.

Information: Iowa Great Lakes Area Chamber of Commerce, Box 9, Arnold's Park, IA 51331, (800) 839-9987 or (712) 332-2107.

Beaver Island, Michigan

Loners love this bit of richly forested land isolated from modern life by 32 miles of open water and decades of attitude. Those who want to commune with nature find plenty of solitude and natural beauty on this Michigan island.

Stargazers also love this spot. Because of its lack of artificial light, the heavens seem close enough to touch, and the aurora borealis often dances across the night skies.

Called "a different world" by its 400 full-time residents, the 53 square miles of Beaver Island first were settled by Irish fishermen in the early 1800s because the green forests and dune-rimmed bays reminded them of home. After you've hoisted a pint or two at the Shamrock Pub in tiny St. James, ask about the Bloomer Revolt of 1856.

Accommodations: Beaver Island Lodge, from $62, P.O. Box 215, Beaver Island, MI 49782, (616) 448-2396.

Information: Beaver Island Chamber of Commerce, P.O. Box 5, Beaver Island, MI 49782, (616) 448-2505 May 15-Oct. 15, (616) 547-2101 the rest of the year.

Eagles Mere, Pennsylvania

Wealthy Victorian property owners from Philadelphia knew beauty and peace when they found it, so much so that they placed much of their favorite resort village under the protective and perpetual care of a non-profit association. The result is a bit of authentic Victoriana in the rolling mountains of northeastern Pennsylvania.

There are paths for strolling, a lake for swimming, and tea shops when one feels peckish, as the Brits say when they need a bite to eat. You can cruise around tree-edged Eagles Mere Lake aboard the "Hardly Able" motor launch and explore nearby Ricketts Glen, one of Pennsylvania's most beautiful state parks.

Accommodations: Eagles Mere Inn, from $135, Box 356, Eagles Mere, PA 17731, (717) 525-3273.

Information: Endless Mountains Visitors Bureau, R.R. 6, Box 132A, Tunkhannock, PA 18657, (800) 769-8999 or (717) 836-5431.

Magnolia, Arkansas

Three old walls on the courthouse square boast smashing murals, and three more murals are under way. All depict the history of a thriving small town in southwest Arkansas replete with giant magnolia trees, antebellum homes, historic bed-and-breakfast inns, good shopping and challenging fishing in Lake Columbia.

For people who prefer their vacations off the tourist track, where hotel rates and meals tend to be less expensive, Magnolia is a charming option reminiscent of Andy Griffith's

Mayberry RFD.

Accommodations: Best Western Coachman's Inn, from $49, 420 E. Main St., Magnolia, AR 71753, (800) 237-6122 or (501) 234-6122.

Information: Magnolia-Columbia County Chamber of Commerce, P.O. Box 866, Magnolia, AR 71753, (501) 234-4352.

St. Francisville, Louisiana

If you enjoy the grace of the Old South, classical music and lovely gardens, add this early 19th-century town to your travel wish list.

St. Francisville, LA, less than an hour's drive north from Interstate 10 at Baton Rouge, has more than 140 structures with well-earned spots on the National Register of Historic Places.

A walking-tour brochure tells all. Seven of the historic homes welcome visitors, and more than a dozen offer traditional Southern hospitality overnight (the skittish should ask about ghosts).

There's also an Arnold Palmer-designed championship golf course nearby, and the Baton Rouge Symphony performs outdoor concerts in the area throughout summer.

Accommodations: Ramada Inn, from $65, P.O. Box 440, St. Francisville, LA 70775, (800) 523-6118 or (504) 635-3821.

Information: West Feliciana Parish Tourist Commission, P.O. Box 1548, St. Francisville, LA 70775, (504) 635-6330.

West Point, Kentucky

For historians and Civil War buffs, this tiny town is a real find. Back in the 1800s, West Point, KY, was a major ferry site, the beginning of the cobblestone Louisville-Nashville turnpike, and host to such notables as Jenny Lind, James Audubon, Andrew Jackson and Henry Clay.

Visitors now find a town barely there — but with more than 20 historic sites and buildings (including a 1797 inn that needs an angel, and General Sherman's 1861 headquarters), an old railroad hotel refreshed into an excellent restaurant, and a smattering of shops. Betsy the Bus valiantly totes visitors up to Fort Duffield, built by Yankee troops in 1861 on the bluffs above town at the confluence of the Salt and Ohio rivers.

Restoration of the fort is under way, and living-history programs usually operate the first weekend of every month.

Accommodations: Ditto House, from $69, including breakfast, 204 Elm St., West Point, KY 40177, (502) 922-4939.

Information: West Point Merchants Association, (502) 922-4560.

Litchfield Hills, Connecticut

This scenic northwestern corner of the Constitution State is happy hunting grounds for those in the know. Romantic inns (Washington did indeed sleep here), scenic rivers and forests, covered bridges, industrial-strength antiquing, country roads that wind through some of the most glorious scenery in America — it's all here and worth several weeks of rambling when you can spare the time.

A free auto-tour brochure details eight self-drive loops, including two of specific interest to antique buffs and one designed for photographers. Looking for "soft" adventure? Few summer experiences anywhere surpass a white-water rafting trip on the

Housatonic River or a quiet canoe paddle through a serene bird sanctuary known as Bartholemews Cobble. Many outfitters offer advice, takeout service, equipment and guides.

Accommodations: The Old Riverton Inn (B&B), a 1796 stage stop listed on the National Register of Historic Places, $75-$165, P.O. Box 6, Riverton, CT 06065, (800) EST 1796 or (203) 379-8678. Area lodging options also include many other inns, B&Bs, lakeside cottages, full-service resorts and name-brand hotels.

Information: Litchfield Hills Travel Council, P.O. Box 968, Litchfield, CT 06759, (203) 567-4506.

Lewes, Delaware

Settled by Dutch seafarers in 1631, Lewes (pronounced *Loo-is*) is the oldest and perhaps the most interesting town in Delaware. Its history includes Indian massacres and pirates, followed by British bombardments during the War of 1812. Many structures around the harbor date from the 17th to 19th centuries.

Don't miss Shipcarpenter Square, a large block of historic buildings restored to fresh use as museums, galleries or shops. For more of the same, catch the ferry to historic Cape May, NJ.

Lewes also is a sailing and charter fishing center, and 3,020-acre Cape Henlopen State Park, noted for its four-mile-long beach and Seaside Nature Center, is one mile east. Park fun includes a nine-hole Frisbee golf course and observation of the famous "walking dunes," the highest sand dunes between Cape Cod and Cape Hatteras.

Prime Hook National Wildlife Refuge, 10 miles northwest, offers excellent hunting, fishing, canoeing, boating and wildlife observation.

Accommodations: The Beacon Motel, $45-$150, 514 Savannah Road, P.O. Box 609, Lewes, DE 19958, (302) 645-4888 or (800) 735-4888.

Information: Lewes Chamber of Commerce and Visitors Bureau, P.O. Box 1, Lewes, DE 19958, (302) 645-8073. Delaware Development Office, 99 Kings Highway, Dover, DE 19903, (800) 441-8846 or (302) 739-4271.

Edisto Island, South Carolina

This unspoiled island and its single town is the exact opposite of over-franchised Myrtle Beach. And while Charleston is only a 45-minute drive north, it might as well be on a different planet.

A series of peninsulas laced with marshes and fishing creeks, bounded by bays and rivers and studded with moss-covered oaks, this historic island's three-mile-long beach abounds in shells and sand dollars. Water sports include body surfing and ocean fishing, and if you bring some crabbing gear or a shrimp net, you probably can catch a few free dinners.

Edisto Beach State Park offers nature and hiking trails, jogging and bike paths, interpretive programs, rustic cabins and ocean-front campsites. Elsewhere on the island, you'll find a par 71 championship golf course as well as fishing and sailing charters, miniature golf, horseback trail rides, river cruises, twice-a-week bingo and a new historical museum.

Accommodations: Cassina Point Plantation, $105, including breakfast, P.O. Box 535, Edisto Island, SC 29438, (803) 869-2535.

Information: Edisto Chamber of Commerce, P.O. Box 206, Edisto Island, SC 29438, (803) 869-3867.

Cabbage Key, Florida

Reached only by boat, this hideaway island five miles south of Boca Grande and 20 miles north of Fort Myers was once the winter estate home of Alan Rinehart, son of famous playwright and novelist Mary Roberts Rinehart. Their architecturally interesting family home, circa 1936-38, now is Cabbage Key Inn, the 100-acre island's only lodging and commercial venture.

"Old Florida" peace and tranquillity abound. Artists are in heaven here, and celebrities such as TV newsman Ted Koppel and folk singer Jimmy Buffet come here to recharge their batteries. Buffet's song "Cheeseburger in Paradise" was written about Cabbage Key.

Located at Marker 60 on the Intracoastal Waterway, the inn's marina offers fishing and sailing charters, plus swimming from assorted docks. For great beaches and shelling, however, you'll have to travel to one of several barrier islands nearby. Best bet: Explore by motorized skiff for a day or catch the all-day islands cruise that originates at the northern tip of Captiva Island.

Whether you come on a day trip or as an overnight guest, bring an extra buck or two. Some years back, a fisherman left a dollar in advance to reserve a cold beer upon his return, and the walls of the inn's dining room and lounge now are papered with autographed dollar bills.

Accommodations: Cabbage Key Inn has six rooms with private baths ($65 double), and six two-bedroom cottages that sleep six ($145, with a two-night minimum).

Information: Cabbage Key, P.O. Box 200, Pineland, FL 33945, (813) 283-2278. For regional information, contact Lee County Visitor and Information Bureau, P.O. Box 2445, Fort Myers, FL 33902, (800) 533-4753.

Mineola, Texas

Ever sipped a sarsaparilla? In Mineola (population 4,387), Kitchens Hardware & Delicatessen sells that time-honored beverage along with great Reuben sandwiches and all the nails you'll ever need. For those who love vintage Main Street America, this tiny town on U.S. Highway 80 midway between Dallas, TX, and Shreveport, LA, is a find.

At last count, 23 antique stores were within a two-mile drive (the majority on Commerce and Johnson streets in the heart of town), and local musicians plunk some mean tunes nearly every weekend at the Piney Woods Pickin' Parlour, a popular family-style music hall on Johnson Street. Guests staying at Mineola's bed-and-breakfast establishments can arrange to arrive at these "parlour concerts" via horse-drawn surrey.

There's excellent golf and fishing nearby, and if you are coming on the first weekend of the month, plan a detour to "First Monday at Canton." This oldest and largest antique market/swap meet in Texas is a 30-minute drive southwest.

Accommodations: Munzesheimer Manor, a restored "Princess Victorian" circa 1898, $75-$95 per night, including breakfast and Victorian nightwear, 202 N. Newsome, Mineola, TX 75773, (903) 569-6634.

Information: Mineola Chamber of Commerce, P.O. Box 68, Mineola, TX 75773, (800) MINEOLA or (903) 569-2087.

Redstone, Colorado

Once an almost forgotten blip of 19th-century civilization in gorgeous Crystal River Canyon, this tiny old mining town hasn't yet been tarted up to nearby Aspen's style or prices. Such "progress" seems inevitable though, so come soon.

In 1892 an entrepreneur named John Cleveland Osgood founded, with others, the Colorado Fuel and Iron Co. to mine high-grade coking coal in this area, and Redstone scrambled to life both as the site of the coke ovens and as Osgood's company town.

Demonstrating a social benevolence unusual for those Dickensian times, Osgood built 84 Swiss chalet-style homes to house his miners and their families, followed in 1902 by an elegant 20-room inn for his bachelor employees. Next came the completion of his own lavish Cleveholm Manor, a $2.5 million, 42-room Tudor mansion on a hillside south of town.

Today, a number of Osgood's "chalets" house high-quality shops and galleries. The Redstone Inn has just been nicely refurbished, offering good dining amid a great collection of Stickley Mission Oak furniture. And still-elegant Cleveholm Manor (also known as Redstone Castle) has become a hard-to-book B&B.

After wandering the town's single street, you can explore via mountain bike, horse or four-wheel drive or poke around the interesting old coke ovens. You can wade, fish or kayak in the Crystal River or just find a rocker and relax. Photographers and leaf peepers, take note: This is prime aspen territory during the first three weeks of September; reserve lodging (midweek suggested) as far in advance as possible.

Accommodations: The Redstone Inn, $52-$92, some shared baths, 0082 Redstone Blvd., Redstone, CO 81623, (800) 748-2524. If accommodations are available and your budget can stand a splurge, consider Cleveholm Manor, the "Hearst Castle" of Colorado, $95-$180 including breakfast (some rooms share baths), 0058 Redstone Blvd., Redstone, CO 81623, (800) 643-4837 or, in Colorado, (970) 963-3463.

Information: Redstone Community Association, care of Carbondale Chamber of Commerce, 0590 Highway 133, Carbondale, CO 81623, (970) 963-1890.

Laramie, Wyoming

Opened in mid-1991, Wyoming Territorial Park in Laramie is a 180-acre, $30 million Western heritage complex that makes 19th-century Wyoming come alive. Centered on an 1890s territorial prison (now a museum) that once clipped Butch Cassidy's wings, its "history is fun" theme also includes a rowdy frontier town full of cafes and shops. There are crafts demonstrations (including authentic period dolls and lace), on-going archaeological digs and summer dinner theater in what was an old horse barn.

Accommodations: Annie Moore's Guest House, a Queen Anne Victorian B&B three minutes from the park's entrance, $55-$65, 819 University Ave., Laramie, WY 82070, (800) 552-8992.

Information: Laramie Area Chamber of Commerce, 800 S. Third St., Laramie, WY 82070, (800) 445-5303.

Lava Hot Springs, Idaho

Once neutral R&R turf for rival Bannock and Shoshone Indian tribes and later a welcome stop on the tough Oregon Trail, this natural geothermal spa 37 miles south of Pocatello has evolved into a family-style resort where swimming and soaking reign supreme.

Backed by massive cliffs along the Portneuf River and beautifully landscaped with garden terraces, the resort's four natural mineral water pools test out at hot (two pools at 104 degrees), hotter (107-110 degrees) and hottest (112 degrees) year-round. All are odor-free and two have whirlpools.

While Lava Hot Springs officials make no official health or medical claims, locals say that a soak or two often greatly benefits those suffering from arthritis, rheumatism and temporary bone or muscle problems. For best results, follow up your soak with a massage by one of the spa's medically trained technicians.

In summer two additional swimming pools, including a diving complex with three platforms, are a short walk from the hot springs. If you don't know how to swim or dive, they'll teach you. You also can rent tubes for a river float, fish for trout or play golf.

Accommodations: Lava Hot Springs Inn, $54-$95 including breakfast (some rooms share baths), P.O. Box 670, Lava Hot Springs, ID 83246, (208) 776-5830. Other lodging choices include condominiums, motels and campgrounds.

Information: Lava Hot Springs Foundation, P.O. Box 669, Lava Hot Springs, ID 83246, (800) 423-8597.

Minnesota to South Dakota Pilgrimage

This do-it-yourself pilgrimage traces the route taken by the Ingalls family as they moved westward, as described by Laura Ingalls Wilder in her "Little House" books. The trek begins in Walnut Grove in the southwestern corner of Minnesota and then moves almost due west 100 miles to De Smet, SD, as it follows the pioneering adventures of the family between 1870 and 1900.

Along the way, the family's various homes and more than a dozen other sites have been refurbished to look as Laura Ingalls Wilder described them in her books.

Both towns offer Wilder museums and tour itineraries as well as outstanding mid-summer pageants based on her books. En route across these rich grassland prairies, make a short detour south to Pipestone National Monument, MN, a sacred Indian quarry of red-colored Sioux quartzite (catlinite) so outstanding it was mentioned by Longfellow in his epic 1855 poem, "The Song of Hiawatha." Visitors can watch American Indians quarry pipestone and make pipes that can be purchased at the Upper Midwest Indian Cultural Center on the grounds.

Accommodations: You too can sleep in a one-room soddy, as the Ingalls family did (no running water or electricity, toilet out back), at an authentically reconstructed B&B at Sod House on the Prairie, $75-$125, including breakfast. Reservations essential, Route 2, Box 75, Sanborn, MN 56083, (507) 723-5138.

Information: Minnesota Office of Tourism, 100 Metro Square, 121 Seventh Place East, St. Paul, MN 55101-2112, (800) 657-3700. Glacial Lakes Tourism Association of South Dakota, P.O. Box 244, Watertown, SD 57201, (605) 886-7305 or (800) 244-8860. Laura Ingalls Wilder Memorial Society, P.O. Box 344, De Smet, SD 57231, (800) 880-3383 or (605) 854-3383.

Mesa County, Colorado

The fruit of the vine on the sunset side of the Rockies? Yes, Mesa County is a mini-Napa Valley, and some of the nation's finest peaches, apples, pears, apricots and cherries also flourish here on "U-pick-'em" farms.

Make your touring base the small town of Palisade, 20 minutes east of Grand Junction via Interstate 70. From there, you can taste your way through five local wineries and relive the 1900s rural life at Cross Orchards Living History Farm in Grand Junction (kids love the display of narrow-gauge railway cars).

You also can explore the red-walled canyons of Colorado National Monument and enjoy all manner of recreation along the Colorado River. Raft trips are available May through September. Mountain biking also is popular, and trout fishing in nearby canyons is super. Dinosaur Valley Museum and on-going dinosaur digs are a short drive west.

Accommodations: The Orchard House, a bed-and-breakfast inn amidst peach and apricot trees, $80 for a two-bedroom suite with kitchen and living room ($30 for children ages 6-16), including a stupendous breakfast of your choice, 3573 E. 1/2 Road, Palisade, CO 81526, (303) 464-0529.

Information: Palisade Chamber of Commerce, P.O. Box 729, Palisade, CO 81526, (303) 464-7458. Grand Junction Visitor and Convention Bureau, 740 Horizon Drive, Grand Junction, CO 81501, (800) 962-2547.

Bluff Country, Minnesota

Named for the high bluffs that rise from the Mississippi River, this rolling and wooded terrain in the southeast corner of Minnesota is dotted with quaint turn-of-the-century towns and Amish farms.

Harmony is the center for the latter — guided tours help you sample Amish hospitality and crafts — and nearby Lanesboro's entire downtown area is listed on the National Register. There's a wonderful collection of B&B inns here, along with cozy cafes, a winery and summer stock theater.

The 28.5-mile Root River State Trail (it's paved) runs through Lanesboro for hiking and cycling, and the adjacent Root River offers canoeing and fishing. Nearby Spring Valley, the first Norwegian settlement in Minnesota, has a Methodist church with ties to Laura Ingalls Wilder, author of the "Little House on the Prairie" series of books. The stained-glass windows of the church date to 1715.

Accommodations: The Jail House B&B Inn, the county's 1869 Italianate jail transformed into lodging with antiques and private baths, $40-$105 weekdays (including "heavy" breakfast) and $69-$140 weekends (with full country breakfast), P.O. Box 422, Preston, MN 55965, (507) 765-2181.

Information: Historic Bluff Country, P.O. Box 609, Harmony, MN 55939, (507) 886-2230.

Lake Toxaway, North Carolina

Billed as "environmental thinking on a working farm," the unique family experience called Earthshine Mountain Lodge sits on a mountaintop surrounded by 70 acres of wilderness, midway between Brevard and Cashiers off U.S. 64.

Under the direction of owners Kim Maurer and Marion Boatwright (both are outdoor education and recreation professionals), Earthshine's guests participate in many "homestead" projects such as picking garden veggies and ripe berries, making jam, pressing apples for cider, making bread, gathering eggs, helping with meal preparation, pond explorations (complete with net, microscope and guidebook) and feeding farm stock.

There also are rivers for fishing and swimming, and nature trails for hiking and exploring. Only horseback riding ($20 per hour), the climbing wall ($30) and a "high ropes adventure course" ($40) cost extra.

Blue Ridge living at its natural best, Earthshine offers a "rustically elegant" lifestyle in tune with nature. Each of the ten guest rooms in the cedar log lodge has a private bath and handmade quilts on log beds. Eight include a loft straight out of "Little House on the Prairie."

Cost: $100 nightly for each adult, $15-$50 for each child, including three meals.
Information: Earthshine Mountain Lodge, Route 1, Golden Road, Lake Toxaway, NC 28747, (704) 862-4207.

Kelleys Island, Ohio

The largest American island in Lake Erie, 2,800-acre Kelleys Island also is one of the least developed. This means you'll find lush natural settings with plenty of things to do. But as locals say, there's no rat race here — just 10-K and 5-K runs in June. The island has a population of only 150.

Glacial Grooves State Memorial on the north shore preserves the largest glacial trail visible in the world, a deep trough and striations left by ice-age glaciers 30,000 years ago. Later history shows in dozens of archaeological sites, ranging from prehistoric to American Indian pictographs, and in more than 300 buildings dating from the 1830s through Victorian times. The entire island is listed on the National Register of Historic Places.

Visitors come by ferry from Marblehead on the mainland to walk miles of trails, putter around the quaint shopping area and historic winery, and enjoy the swimming, camping and naturalist programs at Kelleys Island State Park. No need to bring your car. Bikes, mopeds and golf carts can be rented, and there's a downtown shuttle service and narrated sightseeing by tram. Marinas abound — there's great fishing for walleye and small-mouth bass through November. Sailing classes and snorkeling trips also are available.

Accommodations: The Inn on Kelleys Island, with an old-fashioned front porch and private beach, seven-minute walk from downtown, starting at $65 (shared baths), P.O. Box 11, Kelleys Island, OH 43438, (616) 245-3358 (November-April) or (419) 746-2258 (April-October). The island has many cottages and condos, plus 13 B&Bs.
Information: Kelleys Island Chamber of Commerce, P.O. Box 783-F, Kelleys Island, OH 43438, (419) 746-2360. Also, Erie County Visitors & Convention Bureau, 231 W. Washington Row, Sandusky, OH 44870, (800) 255-ERIE.

'Currier and Ives' Land, New Hampshire

Known as the "Currier and Ives corner of New Hampshire," this rural ramble in the southwestern portion of the state centers on Keene. Don't miss Colony Mill Marketplace, a 19th-century woolen mill that's now home to more than 40 stores and eateries.

Nearby in the Monadnock region are three of the most picture-perfect towns in New England: Fitzwilliam, Harrisville and Peterborough. The latter was the model for Thornton Wilder's "Our Town."

Back-roads biking, lakes and ponds for swimming and fishing, good summer stock theater and lots of art galleries and antiques shops make Monadnock a great destination. Pickety Place Herb Farm and Restaurant in Mason is a must-see, a 200-year-old home that inspired the story of "Little Red Riding Hood." Reserve for the five-course lunch, P.O. Box 544, Greenville, NH 03048, (603) 878-1151.

Accommodations: The Inn at East Hill Farm, a working farm/resort at the base of Mount Monadnock, $45-$64 per person, including three meals daily, 460 Monadnock St., Troy, NH 03465, (800) 242-6495.
Information: Monadnock Travel Council, 48 Central Square, Keene, NH 03431, (603) 352-1303.

Long Beach Peninsula, Washington

A narrow, 60-mile lick of sand, bog and forest begins at the mouth of the Columbia River and stretches due north past the quiet village of Oysterville to a nature lover's paradise called Leadbetter Point. In between are picturesque lighthouses, beautiful state parks, wildlife refuges and birding areas, historic forts and museums, and one of America's longest open beaches.

On Long Beach Peninsula, five quaint communities offer everything from solitude and deep-sea fishing to sand-castle and kite-flying contests. A 2,300-foot nature boardwalk in Long Beach accesses and interprets the dunes, and all of tiny Oysterville is listed on the National Register of Historic Places.

Horses, mopeds and volleyball equipment can be rented in Long Beach, and deep-sea fishing is big in Ilwaco. Don't even wade in the surf, however; cold water, a vicious undertow and frequent rogue waves are spoilers. Fun to know: The 16 miles of sand between Seaview and Oysterville are an official Washington state highway.

Accommodations: Shelburne Country Inn & Shoalwater Restaurant in Seaview, one of America's best retreats, $95-$165, including full breakfast, P.O. Box 250, Seaview, WA 98644, (800) 466-1896 or (360) 642-2442.

Information: Peninsula Visitors Bureau, P.O. Box 562, Long Beach, WA 98631, (800) 451-2542 or (360) 624-2400.

Carson Valley, Nevada

Touristically overshadowed by Lake Tahoe 12 miles west, the small towns of Genoa and Minden-Gardnerville make great undiscovered getaways.

Genoa is the oldest non-Indian settlement in Nevada (1850). Its historic downtown district includes a great museum in an 1865 courthouse, the state's oldest saloon and an oasis called Mormon Station State Historic Park. The latter is a reconstruction of the town's original fort/trading post and a good spot for picnics.

Minden and Gardnerville offer antique shops, casinos and some great Basque restaurants; ballooning and biking also are popular here. Little Antelope Pack Station outfitters, 35 miles south in Coleville, CA, offer daylong horseback rides along Silver King Creek (you pass the oldest living thing in the Sierras, a 2,000-year old juniper). Or, they'll haul you into the magnificent Carson Iceberg Wilderness Area. Bring fishing gear; Tamarack Lake is the only known habitat of the rare Paiute trout. When you re-enter civilization, you'll no doubt enjoy a soak at Walley's Hot Springs Resort near Genoa, established in 1862 on what was the old Pony Express route and immigrant trail.

Accommodations: Walley's Hot Springs Resort near Genoa, historic cabins, $85-$120, P.O. Box 26, Genoa, NV 89411, (702) 782-8155; or the Genoa House Inn, an authentic Victorian on the national register, $115-$130, including breakfast, P.O. Box 141, Genoa, NV 89411, (702) 782-7075.

Information: Carson Valley Chamber of Commerce and Visitor Authority, 1524 Highway 395 N., No. 1, Gardnerville, NV 89410, (800) 727-7677.

McCall, Idaho

Love Alpine adventures by day and all the comforts of home by night? Try this scenic recreation area, some 90 driving minutes north of Boise via State Route 55.

Lush forests surround both Cascade and Payette lakes, and the Payette River's white water can be sampled on half-day or longer floats. Other rugged outdoor sports, including llama- and horse-packing expeditions, also are widely available.

The area is heaven for fishing enthusiasts. Cascade Lake is one of the best fisheries in the state, seven other major lakes are within a short drive, and 200 additional high mountain lakes are within a 30-mile radius of McCall.

McCall, a resort community at the edge of Payette Lake, makes a good base, with golfing, a summer music festival and Fourth of July fireworks over the water. Look for colorful wildflowers as you search out ghost towns via local back roads.

Accommodations: Hotel McCall, mountain and lake views, fresh flowers and afternoon wine parties, $82 ($57 with shared bath), including breakfast, P.O. Box 1778, McCall, ID 83638, (208) 634-8105.

Information: Southwest Idaho Travel Association, P.O. Box 2106, Boise, ID 83701, (800) 635-5240.

Dunsmuir, California

This charming, historic railroad town (population 2,300) sits on the edge of northern California's Trinity Alps area. Some 25 miles north of Lake Shasta and a jot off Interstate 5 on the upper Sacramento River, Dunsmuir offers year-round recreation in an Old West atmosphere.

Walking, cycling, hiking, rafting, kayaking, tubing, gold panning — all thrive here in spectacularly scenic surroundings. Stocked trout ponds, more than 50 secluded lakes and numerous creeks keep fishing lines wet, and massive granite spires (up to 6,000 feet) south of town form Castle Crags State Park.

The upper Sacramento River, which flows beneath buildings in downtown Dunsmuir, looks much as it did in its pre-settler days. Don't miss a hike or float to view Mossbrae Falls, artesian water carried by lava tubes to riverside cliffs alive with moss and wildflowers.

Best times to come include Railroad Days in mid-June and the annual Sacramento River Jazz Festival in July.

Accommodations: The 50-acre Railroad Park Resort and Campground, 100 Railroad Park Road, Dunsmuir, CA 96025, (916) 235-4440 or, in California, (800) 974-RAIL, has a 27-unit RV park, four cabins and 24 authentic cabooses that each sleep two to five persons. Room rates are $85 for two, $5 for each additional adult or child.

Information: Dunsmuir Chamber of Commerce, P.O. Box 17, Dunsmuir, CA 96025, (800) DUNSMUIR or (916) 235-2177.

Spearfish Canyon, South Dakota

One of America's National Forest Scenic Byways, U.S. 14A meanders through spectacular Spearfish Canyon for 20 miles, linking the town of Spearfish with tiny Cheyenne Crossing in the northern area of the Black Hills.

Six times more ancient than Arizona's Grand Canyon, Spearfish Canyon's pastel limestone walls often exceed 1,000 feet in height. An American Indian winter campsite for centuries, it played that role again in the Oscar-winning movie, "Dances With Wolves."

A favorite route for cyclists because of its easy 3 percent grade, the road through Spearfish Canyon accesses an incredibly beautiful trout stream, hiking trails, waterfalls, thickets of quaking aspens, nice picnic spots, a few old mines and the remains of communities they spawned.

Accommodations: Historic Lown House, 745 Fifth St., Spearfish, SD 57783, (605)

642-5663, a Queen Anne Victorian built in 1893, offers bed-and-breakfast lodging in four rooms with private baths, $65-$70.

Information: Spearfish Area Chamber and Convention and Visitors Bureau, P.O. Box 550, Spearfish, SD 57783, (800) 626-8013 or (605) 642-2626.

Mount Princeton, Colorado

Ideal for water-lovers who just want to relax, this inexpensive, comfortable resort features more than 20 hot springs welling up from deep in the earth. They supply odorless, crystal clear, 135-degree water for three outdoor pools and private indoor hot tubs in a century-old bathhouse. Facials, body scrubs and therapeutic massages are available.

Surrounded by peaks of the Collegiate Range, Mount Princeton offers fishing, hunting, hiking, white-water rafting and horseback riding in summer. Plan an exploration to the historic mining town of St. Elmo or a guided raft plunge through the rapids of Brown's Canyon on the Arkansas River, known as the "white-water capital of Colorado."

Accommodations: Lodge room rates at Mount Princeton, which include use of all hot springs pools, are $77-$95 for two. Pool fees for non-guests are $1-$6.

Information: Mount Princeton Hot Springs Resort, 15870 County Road 162, Nathrop, CO 81236, (719) 395-2361.

Salt Missions Trail, New Mexico

This driving trip explores the Indian and missions territory southeast of Albuquerque and Interstate 40/U.S. 66. Following prehistoric trade routes for much of the way, you'll tour ruined Anasazi pueblos and the mission churches of Las Salinas, visit Spanish land grant villages, fish for trout, wander apple orchards and old general stores, and wind along the east side of Sandia Mountain to three revived ghost towns now favored by artists and craftspersons.

Plan on spending some time at the three historic sites that make up the Salinas Pueblo Missions National Monument in Mountainair. Rooted in cultures some 7,000 years old, the villages remained active until around 1670, when they were abandoned suddenly — "cities that died of fear."

When history gets heavy, lighten up with a break at the Shaffer Hotel and Rancho Bonito in Mountainair. Built in 1923 by folk artist Pop Shaffer as lodging over his hardware store, Pop's eclectic hotel and Rancho Bonito are on the National Register of Historic Places.

Accommodations: Double rooms with full breakfast at the Shaffer Hotel, P.O. Box 130, Mountainair, NM 87036, (800) 293-2888 or (505) 847-2375, are $45; some rooms share baths.

Information: Salinas Pueblo Missions Visitor Center, P.O. Box 496, Mountainair, NM 87036, (505) 847-2585.

Eagle River, Wisconsin

Thriving in an unspoiled region of Wisconsin, the town of Eagle River is in the middle of the longest chain of freshwater inland lakes in the world — 28 separate bodies of water connected by canoeable rivers.

You can boat from one end to the other without getting lost. There are numerous spots along the forested shores to stop for supplies, shopping, lunch or a picnic.

Fishing is great here and you can water-ski, canoe, kayak or tube these generally quiet waters. Don't own even an inner tube? Not to worry; local marinas rent just about everything that floats.

Accommodations: Cabins, cottages and campgrounds abound. Cranberry Inn Resort, 1429 Silver Lake Road, Eagle River, WI 54521, (715) 479-2215, is typical, offering fully equipped housekeeping units at $145 for three nights, $395-$545 by the week. The inn also has B&B units for $88 a night.

Information: Eagle River Information Bureau, P.O. Box 218, Eagle River, WI 54521, (800) 359-6315.

Ohiopyle State Park, Pennsylvania

White-water rafting on the Youghiogheny River through Ohiopyle State Park is just one reason to bring a family to these rolling foothills of the Allegheny Mountains.

Some sections of the "Yock" river are safe enough for small children; others challenge go-for-broke teenagers. This 18,719-acre park also has great cycling (with rentals) along the Youghiogheny River Bike Trail, as well as outstanding fishing, camping and birding.

One of architect Frank Lloyd Wright's most famous home designs, Fallingwater, is open for tours in nearby Mill Run, a two-hour drive southeast from Pittsburgh. This is the only Wright house remaining with its original setting, furnishings and artwork intact.

There also are many golf courses in the area, which is Arnold Palmer's home territory. If you have tiny ones in tow, don't miss 400-acre Idlewild Park in Ligonier, an old-fashioned amusement park that includes Mr. Rogers' Neighborhood of Make-Believe and the Story Book Forest.

Accommodations: The Inn at Georgian Place, 800 Georgian Place Drive, Somerset, PA 15501, (814) 443-1043, an 11-room mansion finished in 1918, is the centerpiece of the 50-store Horizon Outlet Center Somerset. Doubles are $85-$165, including a full-service breakfast.

Information: Laurel Highlands, Town Hall, 120 E. Main St., Ligonier, PA 15658, (800) 925-7669 for a visitors guide and map, (800) 333-5661 for general information.

Helen, Georgia

Blatant tourism has its place, particularly when it's as well done as this bit of red-roofed Bavaria in Northwest Georgia's mountains. The setting is ideal — lots of alpine greenery and the handsome Chattahoochee River roaring through town — and they don't miss an architectural beat. Even the local factory outlet stores come dressed Bavarian-style.

More than 230 businesses lie under painted eaves. Shops sell beer steins and cuckoo clocks, restaurants serve German dishes, and musicians clad in lederhosen fill the air with polkas.

After roaming Helen's cobblestone streets, you can tube the Chattahoochee, view four states from the 4,784-foot summit of Brasstown Bald, pan for gold, and marvel at 1,100-foot-deep Tallulah Gorge. Unicoi State Park offers hiking, camping, swimming and picnicking, and if you have tots, don't miss Babyland General Hospital in nearby Cleveland. That's where Cabbage Patch dolls are "born."

Accommodations: Bavarian Brook Lodge and Rentals, P.O. Box 333, Helen, GA 30545, (800) 422-6355, offers rooms and riverfront condos, $60-$250.

Information: Helen Welcome Center, P.O. Box 730, Helen, GA 30545, (800) 833-0549.

St. Joseph Peninsula, Florida

St. Joseph Peninsula juts into the Gulf of Mexico about 30 miles west of Apalachicola, a part of the Sunshine State's Panhandle that refers to itself as the Forgotten Coast.

In marked contrast to the strip development that mars Panama City's beautiful beaches, Cape San Blas has miles of open sand, surf and scrub with only a smattering of second-home and condo developments.

People come here for the quiet, to dig in the scallop beds just offshore in St. Joseph Bay and to enjoy St. Joseph Peninsula State Park. Charters offer snorkeling, shelling and deep-sea fishing, and there's an 18-hole golf course and driving range nearby.

Accommodations: The Old Saltworks Cabins, P.O. Box 526, Port St. Joe, FL 32457, (904) 229-6097, help make this cape special. Airy and clean, they have one and two bedrooms, screened porches and air conditioning; seven have full kitchens. Scallop beds lie off their small beach. Rates are $49-$70 per night, $315-$495 by the week.

Information: Gulf County Chamber of Commerce, P.O. Box 337, Gulf Breeze, FL 32562, (904) 932-7888.

No-Name Beach, Alabama

Undiscovered even by many Alabamians, an estimated four miles of white sand and clear turquoise water lie within the Bon Secour National Wildlife Refuge on Pleasure Island, west of Gulf Shores. Aside from what nature provides and some designated parking areas, literally nothing is there, and therein lies its charm.

Backed by tall dunes, this is what the Gulf Coast looked like before the French delivered the first thrusts of civilization in 1699. Bring a picnic, water, some portable shade and sunscreen, and enjoy.

If you're lucky, you may see small red foxes, raccoons, coyotes and sea turtles; the latter laid 50 nests in 1994, a record. The forests, swamps and beach of this refuge also provide the largest migratory bird rest on Pleasure Island.

Nearby Gulf Shores and Orange Beach have many concessions, four championship golf courses and outstanding fishing.

Accommodations: House, cottage and condo rentals are numerous. An example: Fully equipped units at Seaside Beach and Racquet Club, P.O. Box 278, Gulf Shores, AL 36547, (800) 662-4438, are $93-$178 daily in summer, $52-$128 in winter.

Information: Bon Secour National Wildlife Refuge, P.O. Box 1650, Gulf Shores, AL 36547, (334) 540-7720.

WEEKEND GETAWAYS

W eekend getaways were invented long before anyone had heard of fax machines, networking or even car pools. And now they are more popular than ever — especially among travelers who need a break from tight schedules, traffic and tension.

Where you go will depend partly on where you live. Many choose to drive, but more Americans are hopping a plane for three-day or longer getaways farther from home.

Each of our weekend jaunts offers an opportunity to rejuvenate your body and soul, perhaps even help you rekindle a romance or adjust your attitude. All are accompanied by lodging suggestions; rates are per night for two people, but don't forget to ask about weekend specials.

New York City, New York

For an intimate experience in the Big Apple, move out of the core and consider a romantic interlude in New York's colorful neighborhoods.

There now are several good hotels in the heart of Chinatown, including the Holiday Inn Downtown on Lafayette Street. By day, you might as well be in bustling Hong Kong. After dark, the neighborhood is shuttered tight, a quiet, calm and peaceful place.

Adjoining Chinatown is Little Italy. Within walking distance are trendy SoHo, NoHo, TriBeCa, Greenwich Village and the East Village, all noted for loft galleries and al fresco cafes, unusual shopping and lively clubs. The Lower East Side, World Trade Center, Wall Street, South Street Seaport and ferries to the Statue of Liberty and Ellis Island are nearby.

A twilight cruise on the Staten Island Ferry (50 cents) should not be missed, and it's only a couple of subway stops to the other side of the Brooklyn Bridge for one of the most romantic views of the city skyline.

If you have not visited the Statue of Liberty in many years, you'll find the grand old lady as inspiring as ever — and certainly in much better shape since the repair and face lift she underwent for her 100th birthday in 1986.

Seeing the statue up close still evokes a sense of awe and, yes, even a surge of pride and patriotism. You can spend an hour or two simply walking around, looking at this remarkable structure from different perspectives and liking all of them.

In the pedestal, a fascinating museum explains how the statue was built and what it symbolizes. A copper replica of Lady Liberty's left foot gives visitors an idea of the scale of the statue. In the lobby stands the old porch, replaced by a new one in 1986.

Millions visit the statue; be prepared for long lines (two hours or more in summer to climb the steps to the crown). Visitors arrive on ferries from Battery Park in lower Manhattan. The boats continue to Ellis Island, the restored immigration entry port.

Accommodations: Holiday Inn Downtown, from $155, 138 Lafayette St., New York, NY 10013, (800) HOLIDAY or (212) 966-8898.

Information: New York Convention and Visitors Bureau, Two Columbus Circle, New York, NY 10019, (800) 692-8474 or (212) 397-8222. Statue of Liberty National Monument, Ellis Island, New York, NY 10004, (212) 363-3200.

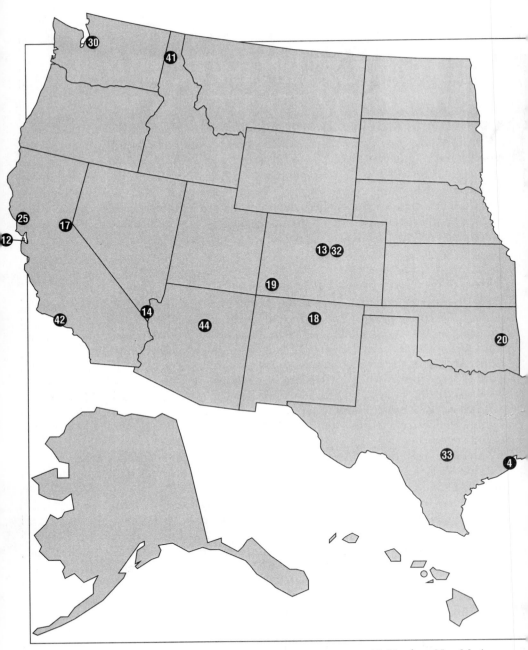

1 New York City, New York
2 Calumet, Michigan
3 Green Bay, Wisconsin
4 Galveston, Texas
5 Key Largo, Florida
6 Traverse City, Michigan
7 Newport, Rhode Island
8 Kansas City, Missouri
9 Bloomington, Minnesota

10 Reading, Pennsylvania
11 Indiana Dunes, Indiana
12 San Francisco's Chinatown, California
13 Central City, Colorado
14 Laughlin, Nevada
15 Ledyard, Connecticut
16 Vicksburg, Mississippi
17 Lake Tahoe, California

18 Northern New Mexico
19 Durango, Colorado
20 Lake Eufaula, Oklahoma
21 Islamorada, Florida
22 Dahlonega, Georgia
23 Camden, Maine
24 Lake Geneva, Wisconsin
25 California's North Coast
26 Essex, Connecticut

WEEKEND GETAWAYS

Calumet, Michigan

Copper doesn't have the cachet of silver or gold, but it made many people rich in Upper Michigan's Keewanaw Peninsula. Though the most productive veins petered out years ago, there's still plenty of copper in the ground, and the region remains known as copper country.

A half-dozen years before the California Gold Rush of 1849, the discovery of copper here set off a mineral boom. For decades, most of the country's copper was mined here from veins so rich that the metal often was found in its native state as huge chunks of pure copper.

A new national historical park in Calumet is preserving that heritage. The Coppertown USA museum tells the story well, and copper goods of all kinds (as well as chunks of native copper) are for sale.

Accommodations: Bostrom-Johnson Inn, $50, 1109 Calumet Ave., Calumet, MI 49913, (906) 337-4651.

Information: Keewanaw Tourism Council, 1197 Calumet Ave., Calumet, MI 49913, (800) 338-7982.

Green Bay, Wisconsin

Paris is known as the City of Light, New York as the Big Apple, New Orleans as the Big Easy.

Then there's Green Bay — the Toilet Paper Capital of the World.

That may not have much cachet, but don't sell Green Bay short. This city has a lot going for it. It's the home of football's Green Bay Packers, and even if you aren't a Packers fan, you'll enjoy visiting the Packers Hall of Fame, the only such hall in the league.

Rail America, the official national railroad museum, has about 50 locomotives and cars on display. Astor Park's Victorian Days recall when John Jacob Astor ran the fur trade here, and Heritage Hill State Park displays 16 historic buildings.

That's not shabby for a city of 90,000.

Accommodations: Regency Suites, $89-$120, 333 Main St., Green Bay, WI 54301, (800) 236-3330 or (414) 432-4555.

Information: Green Bay Area Visitor and Convention Bureau, P.O. Box 10596, Green Bay, WI 54307, (800) 236-3976.

Galveston, Texas

It's hard to think of a city as large as Galveston as a getaway destination, but that's exactly what it is for Houstonians and others near the Gulf Coast of Texas.

With its miles of sandy beach, a restored historic area and plentiful accommodations, Galveston teems with weekenders. A major gathering spot is the renovated Strand historic district, where restored 19th-century buildings now house shops, bars, restaurants and apartments.

Other attractions include Moody Gardens' Rainforest Pavilion, housed in a giant glass pyramid, and Pier 21, a tourist complex with a marina, restaurant and audiovisual show that tells the story of a hurricane that ravaged Galveston in 1900. A half-hour away is NASA's $70 million Space Center Houston.

Accommodations: The Victorian Condo-Hotel, $59-$199, 6300 Seawall Blvd., Galveston, TX 77551, (800) 231-6363 or (409) 740-ͻ

Information: Galveston Convention and Visitors Bu   ., 2106 Seawall Blvd.,

Galveston, TX 77550, (800) 582-4673.

Key Largo, Florida

The largest of the Florida Keys also is the closest to Miami, an hour's drive away.

Many Miamians own second homes at Key Largo, but for those who don't there are plenty of small motels and a couple of large ones. Some Keys lovers go there to unwind in languid lassitude, but for those who are more active, diving, fishing and boating are big lures.

Glass-bottom boats cruise over the coral formations in John Pennekamp Coral Reef State Park, and a gambling boat goes out daily. Restaurants and bars are plentiful and busy.

Accommodations: Marriott Key Largo Bay Beach Resort, $99-$160, 103800 Overseas Highway, Key Largo, FL 33037, (800) 932-9332 or (305) 453-0000.

Information: Key Largo Chamber of Commerce, 105950 Overseas Highway, Key Largo, FL 33037, (800) 822-1088.

Traverse City, Michigan

Summertime on the northwest coast of lower Michigan from Traverse to Mackinac is busy indeed, and if you don't make reservations ahead of time, you may be unable to find space within 100 miles.

The lake beaches are the main attraction, but golf is a major magnet as well. Good restaurants and accommodations are available in many locales, particularly Petoskey and Harbor Springs. At Sleeping Bear Dunes, you can climb on sand hills more than 400 feet high, and the little town of Leland will charm you.

A big summer event in this major cherry-growing area is the annual Cherry Festival in July.

Accommodations: Grand Traverse Resort, $89-$225, 6300 N. U.S. 31, Acme, MI 49610, (800) 748-0303 or (616) 938-2100.

Information: Michigan Travel Bureau, P.O. Box 30226, Lansing, MI 48909, (800) 543-2937.

Newport, Rhode Island

At the turn of the century, the rich and famous spent summers in Newport in their "cottages," as they called the magnificent mansions they built here.

That era and lifestyle are gone, but visitors still flock to Newport in summertime. They stroll along the seaside Cliff Walk, where they can see many of the millionaire mansions. They watch or take part in summer regattas and enjoy the ambience of a historic port city and its dock-side restaurants and boutiques. Later they can relax in a pleasant B&B or take in one of the many clubs in the evening.

Accommodations: Cliffside Inn, $165-$325, 2 Seaview Ave., Newport, RI 02840, (800) 845-1811.

Information: Newport County Convention and Visitors Bureau, 23 America's Cup, Newport, RI 02840.

Kansas City, Missouri

Enter the 55-acre complex of Country Club Plaza and you might think you've suddenly been transported to Spain. Indeed, its landmark structure is a replica of the Giralda Tower in Seville, and the tree-lined walks, fountains and murals complement its Moorish and Spanish architecture.

All manner of shops and restaurants reside within the area, selling everything from Kansas City's popular cinnamon rolls to haute couture. And if that's not enough, Kansas City has another grand mall, the Crown Center, with a popular central square that is the site of many summer festivals.

Accommodations: Holiday Inn Crowne Plaza, $109-$149, 4445 Main St., Kansas City, MO 64111, (800) 347-5292 or (816) 531-3000.

Information: Convention and Visitors Bureau of Greater Kansas City, 1100 Main St., Kansas City, MO 64105, (800) 767-7700.

Bloomington, Minnesota

People do shop at the Mall of America, the biggest mall in the United States, but many come just to enjoy the fun and games at the Camp Snoopy amusement park in the center of this huge rectangular structure.

There's a roller coaster that loops around the park, a log flume ride, Legoland (with everything from airplanes to a triceratops made of plastic blocks) and dozens of other attractions. Shoppers can roam for days in the four-level mall, which has branches of just about every brand name you've ever heard of, plus restaurants and bars, among them Planet Hollywood.

Accommodations: Mall of America Grand Hotel, from $89, 7901 24th Ave. S., Bloomington, MN 55425, (800) 222-8733 or (612) 854-2244.

Information: Mall of America, 60 E. Broadway, Bloomington, MN 55425, (612) 883-8800.

Reading, Pennsylvania

This is the self-proclaimed outlet capital of the world, a place where you can buy everything from cough drops and tropical fish to Bass shoes and London Fog coats at a discount.

More than 6 million visitors flock to Reading and surrounding Berks County every year. Most of them make a beeline for one of the seven main outlet complexes in and around Reading, a pioneer in the outlet mall business. Several of the complexes are in old factories.

Accommodations: Hampton Inn, $72-$76, 1800 Papermill Road, Reading, PA 19610, (800) HAMPTON or (610) 374-8100.

Information: Reading and Berks County Visitors Bureau, 801 Hill Road, P.O. Box 6677, Reading, PA 19610.

Indiana Dunes, Indiana

For anyone who knows America's ocean beaches, the lake beaches of the Midwest seem tame. But they're easily accessible to millions, and some are especially attractive.

Many residents of Chicago and students from Notre Dame in South Bend take their sun at Indiana Dunes, a stretch of dunes and beach on the southern shore of Lake Michigan. On pleasant summer days, hundreds of sun-seekers settle on the beach or up on the dunes, venturing now and then into modest waves that lap at the sand.

Few notice the skyscrapers of Chicago, barely visible on the northwest horizon.

Accommodations: Indian Oak Resort & Spa, $60-$150, 558 Indian Boundary Road, Chesterton, IN 46304, (800) 552-4232 or (219) 926-2200.

Information: Porter County Convention, Recreation and Visitors Commission, 800

Indian Boundary Road, Chesterton, IN 46304, (800) 283-TOUR.

San Francisco's Chinatown, California

Exotic is the word for San Francisco's Chinatown, the largest Chinese settlement in the country.

Enter through the great Oriental gate over Grant Avenue, with its carved dragons and dogs, and you quickly are immersed in a different culture. Grocers offer shark fins and glazed ducks; shop windows display jade and silks. Signs are in Chinese and so is the spoken word.

You can choose from more than 60 teas at China Herbs and Native Produce Co., snack on pot stickers, taro root turnovers and other dim sum dishes at Asia Garden restaurant, smell incense at the Tien Hou Temple, watch fortune cookies being made at the Golden Gate Fortune Cookies Co., buy Oriental cooking utensils at the Wok Shop and Chinese dolls at China Plus, and load up on ginseng at Ten Ren Tea Co.

It's an experience not to be forgotten.

Accommodations: Cornell Hotel, $85-$100, 715 Bush St., San Francisco, CA 94108, (800) 232-9698 or (415) 421-3154.

Information: San Francisco Convention and Visitors Bureau, 201 Third St., Suite 900, San Francisco, CA 94103, (415) 974-6900.

Central City, Colorado

Central City is a one-time gold rush mining town that in its 19th-century heyday attracted such visitors as Horace Greeley, Mark Twain, Walt Whitman, Oscar Wilde and President Ulysses S. Grant.

When the ore veins petered out, Central City went into decline, its only attractions being a superb opera house and the face of a beautiful woman painted on a barroom floor by a newspaper artist in the 1930s. So it remained until 1991, when Colorado passed a law permitting gambling in three depressed mountain cities. One was Central City.

Within a year, Central City was transformed into a roaring casino-crazy complex. Today, virtually every building in its small downtown is filled with slot machines. Women dressed in 1890s outfits pass out discount coupons at casino entrances. The dinging of the slots is incessant, and you can't even buy gasoline in town because the only two gas stations were turned into casinos. The Opera House, however, is still slot-free.

Accommodations: Harveys Wagon Wheel Hotel, $65-$100, P.O. Box 519, Central City, CO 80427, (800) HARVEYS.

Information: Central City Information, P.O. Box 249, Central City, CO 80427, (800) 542-2999.

Laughlin, Nevada

Everybody has heard about the high-rollers who bet more on one roll of the dice in Las Vegas or Reno than some people earn in a year. Laughlin is for low-rollers.

There are no $75 floor shows here, no parades of limousines. Names on nightclub marquees are more likely to be Mickey Gilley and Charley Pride than Frank Sinatra or Wayne Newton. Laughlin targets middle America, its recreational vehicles and modest wallets.

Some things, though, are just like Vegas — the bargain lunches and dinners, for instance. And, as always, the house has the best odds.

Accommodations: Don Laughlin's Riverside Resort, $14-$75, 1650 Casino Drive, Laughlin, NV 89029, (800) 227-3849 or (702) 298-2535.

Information: Laughlin Visitors Bureau, P.O. Box 502, Laughlin, NV 89029, (800) 452-8445 or (702) 298-3321.

Ledyard, Connecticut

Foxwoods, New England's first gambling casino, deviates from normal casino operations in a way you're likely to notice immediately: One wall is glass; you can see the woods outside. Most casinos don't want their customers distracted by looking out windows.

In addition to blackjack, craps, roulette and poker, Foxwoods has almost 4,000 slot machines.

Like many other casinos in America, this one is run by American Indians, the Mashantucket Pequots. Overnight packages are available from the Days Inn, Comfort Inn and Mystic Hilton, all of which operate shuttle buses to the casino.

Accommodations: Foxwoods, from $100, P.O. Box 609, Route 2, Ledyard, CT 06339, (800) 442-1000.

Information: (800) PLAY-BIG.

Vicksburg, Mississippi

Raft-borne Huckleberry Finn tested his luck on the Mississippi River, and so did a riverboat pilot named Mark Twain. Now thousands of less-celebrated folks are doing the same — at gaming tables on modern riverboats. Gambling has returned to America's greatest river bigger than it ever was in its 19th-century heyday.

More than twenty gaming boats are operating on the river within Mississippi and along the state's Gulf coast. None of the riverboats actually move, however; they're affixed to docks.

In Vicksburg, known for its Civil War battlefield, gambling has become a prime attraction. Tunica, a small town in northwestern Mississippi, also offers several gaming boats. Others are in Natchez, Philadelphia, Greenville and Lula.

Accommodations: The Corners, $85-$120, 601 Klein, Vicksburg, MS 39180, (800) 444-7421 or (601) 636-7421.

Information: Mississippi Division of Tourism, P.O. Box 1705, Ocean Springs, MS 39566-1705, (800) WARMEST.

Lake Tahoe, California

This gleaming gem of a lake in the mountains shared by Nevada and California is loved for extra-clean air and tree-filled horizons swooping down into the clearest liquid this side of the Caribbean. And while it's easily accessible from Reno and Sacramento, Lake Tahoe feels as though it's on some utopian continent.

Casinos — found on the Nevada side of the lake, of course — are almost vacant during the day while visitors pursue outdoor endeavors. Summer is an especially good season for visitors who revel in mountain biking, parasailing, rafting, kayaking, scuba diving, fishing, golfing, horseback riding, roller blading, hot-air ballooning and tennis.

The casinos come alive at night, but nocturnal options also include showroom productions and fine dining. Harrah's Summit Restaurant on the lake's South Shore, for example, has a sensational view of the lake and an exotic menu laden with such dishes as a black and red caviar mosaic with blue corn blinis.

Tahoe's North Shore is more placid. Head for the Cal-Neva Lodge, a '50s-style place that has a colorful past, thanks to former owner Frank Sinatra.

Accommodations: Cal-Neva Lodge, $89 and up, P.O. Box 368, Crystal Bay, NV 89402, (800) 225-6382 or (702) 832-4000.

Information: Incline Village/Crystal Bay Visitors & Convention Bureau, 969 Tahoe Blvd., Incline Village, NV 89451, (702) 832-1606. Lake Tahoe Visitors Authority, 1156 Ski Run Blvd., South Lake Tahoe, CA 96150, (916) 544-5050.

Northern New Mexico

The region surrounding Santa Fe is rich in the legacy of American Indians, whose eight major pueblos have survived marauding Spaniards as well as commercializing Anglos. While these villages of rock, straw and mud were ignored by early Spanish adventurers, modern visitors find much to revere about pueblo lifestyle and history.

At each pueblo, nature is honored in celebrations of song, dance and art. Most pueblos offer shopping, bingo and recreational opportunities that include fishing and horseback expeditions.

The multistoried dwellings at Taos Pueblo have an unforgettable mountain back-drop, and fine art and handicrafts — including paintings, beadwork, silver jewelry and pottery — are sold in shops.

Nambe Pueblo, about 20 miles northeast of Santa Fe, has a scenic waterfall and fishing lake. The 700-year-old pueblo houses 400 residents who continue to make pottery, beadwork and weavings. Santa Clara Pueblo, 22 miles from Santa Fe, boasts cliff dwellings dating to the 14th century. Artisans are especially renowned for their pottery.

San Juan Pueblo is the headquarters for the Eight Northern Indian Pueblos Council. Residents live in ancient and modern facilities on a 12,200-acre reservation about 20 miles northeast of Santa Fe. The restaurant here serves a feverish green chile stew and excellent Indian fry bread.

Accommodations: Garrett's Desert Inn in Santa Fe, $84-$109, 311 Old Santa Fe Trail, Santa Fe, NM 87501, (800) 888-2145 or (505) 982-1851. Sagebrush Inn in Taos, $95-$140, P.O. Box 557, Taos, NM 87571, (800) 428-3626 or (505) 758-2254.

Information: San Juan Pueblo Council, P.O. Box 1099, San Juan Pueblo, NM 87566, (505) 852-4400.

Durango, Colorado

Durango has been discovered as one of America's most livable ski towns — so don't be surprised to find that the population in this Four Corners dandy has begun to swell.

The charming hamlet in southwest Colorado has clung to its romantic heritage, rooted in the gold-and-silver boom of a century ago. Victorian buildings lining the historic downtown streets are occupied by appealing bistros and shops, and at the end of Main Avenue you can board the Durango-Silverton Narrow Gauge Railroad. The vintage train takes a breathtaking mountain route you can trace by car along U.S. 550.

For an intriguing look into a mysterious past, head 36 miles west to Mesa Verde National Park to explore the preserved cliff dwellings of the ancient Anasazi civilization.

Thrill-seekers can take on the challenge of white-water rafting or half-day horseback tours into the San Juan National Forest. Jeep tours into the mountains also are fun.

Accommodations: The historic Strater Hotel downtown, $105-$165, 699 Main

Ave., Durango, CO 81301, (800) 247-4431.

Information: Durango Chamber of Commerce, P.O. Box 2587, Durango, CO 81302, (800) 525-8855.

Lake Eufaula, Oklahoma

Lake Eufaula, about 80 miles south of Tulsa and 120 miles east of Oklahoma City, stretches its arms across green, hilly eastern Oklahoma. The lake offers 102,000 acres of sparkling water — perfect for water-skiing, jet-skiing, fishing and even houseboating.

Oklahoma is known for its state park system. Fountainhead, on the lake's northwestern side, is ideal for vacationers who want their golf, tennis, horseback riding, water-skiing, fishing and children's programs all at one place, close to their lodge. Arrowhead Park, on the lake's southeastern shore, also has a lodge (owned by the Choctaw Nation), hiking trails, boat rentals, camping, fishing and swimming.

Labor Day brings an American Indian powwow. Belle Starr, infamous "queen of the bandits" who hailed from nearby Porum, is honored at an ongoing country music jamboree and Wild West show staged at the lake-side Belle Starr Entertainment Center and Outlaw Village.

Downtown Eufaula is undergoing a renovation. Behind those spiffed-up historic facades are great little antique shops.

Accommodations: Fountainhead Resort, $75-$95, HC 60, Box 1355, Checotah, OK 74426, (800) 345-6343. Arrowhead Resort, from $55, HC 67, Box 5, Canadian, OK 74425, (800) 422-2711 or, in Oklahoma only, (918) 339-2711.

Information: Lake Eufaula Association, P.O. Box 792, Eufaula, OK 74432, (918) 689-7751. Eufaula Chamber of Commerce, P.O. Box 738, Eufaula, OK 74432, (918) 689-2791.

Islamorada, Florida

Islamorada, a town midway between Key West and Miami on Upper Matecumbe Key, is the perfect remedy for anyone who hasn't seen the sun in a while. Pronounced *eye-la-more-ah-da*, it's a pleasant, sophisticated beach town with fish markets, shell shops, motels and fishing charter outfits mixed with expensive homes and condos.

Fishing here is unsurpassed. Don't be surprised if 20 red snapper are yours within a few hours. But if you're up for real sport, take on the challenge of bonefishing in the surf. It will be a long time before you forget the thrill of this chase.

Long Key State Park at Mile Marker 67.5 is a peaceful place for swimming and picnicking. Fossil-imprinted rocks and horseshoe crabs are found among the shells.

Accommodations: Chesapeake Resort, from $130, P.O. Box 909, Islamorada, FL 33036, (800) 338-3395.

Information: Monroe County Tourist Development Council, P.O. Box 1147, Key West, FL 33041, (800) FLA-KEYS.

Dahlonega, Georgia

The mountain town of Dahlonega, GA, is about 90 miles north of Atlanta. Tucked into the Blue Ridge foothills, it's a gentle country place in the woods close to the start of the Appalachian Trail.

Today, Dahlonega is experiencing its second boom in 165 years, a long wait by most standards. The site of the first gold rush in the United States, Dahlonega was big news when gold was discovered in the hills in 1828. A couple of mines still offer gold panning, and the story is told in full at Dahlonega Gold Museum State Historic Site, which crowns the tidy brick square.

Visitors can stop at the old-fashioned general store and the cozy Nature's Cellar Cafe & Wine Bar, a new-age hangout with black bean burritos and spinach-mushroom lasagna. Two miles from the square, Crisson Gold Mine offers a first-hand try at gold panning.

The place to eat is the family-style Smith House. Feast on light fried chicken, beef tips, baked ham, rice and gravy, cream corn, collard greens, green beans, squash, sweet potatoes, stewed apples, coleslaw, biscuits and strawberry shortcake with ice cream, coffee, tea and lemonade. It's all fresh, all good — sticky, messy and fattening — and well worth $11.50.

Accommodations: Worley Homestead Inn, an 1845 home off the square, from $65 including a hearty breakfast, 410 W. Main St., Dahlonega, GA 30533, (706) 864-7002.

Information: Dahlonega Chamber of Commerce, 101 S. Park St., Dahlonega, GA 30533, (706) 864-3711 or (800) 231-5543.

Camden, Maine

Few images are more romantic than a jagged coastline punctuated by lighthouses and the masts of tall ships. The Maine coast, with its seafaring heritage, sunny lobster shacks, quiet beaches, misty coves and pretty farms, is the place to find that romance.

You can take a shoreline cruise from Camden's postcard-perfect harbor overlooking Penobscot Bay. Landlubbers can stick to Camden Hills State Park north of town, where hiking opportunities abound. Trails cover the reserve from the rocky shore to the top of Mount Battie.

While Camden, halfway between Portland and Bar Harbor, is growing in reputation at a rate that alarms longtime fans, one constant is the Camden Harbour Inn, established in 1874. There's no better view of the harbor than from the inn's front porch, and the popularity of its restaurant is well-deserved.

Accommodations: Camden Harbour Inn, $125-$225, 83 Bayview, Camden, ME 04843, (207) 236-4200.

Information: Rockport-Camden-Lincolnville Chamber of Commerce, P.O. Box 919, Camden, ME 04843, (207) 236-4404 or (800) 223-5459.

Lake Geneva, Wisconsin

The resort town of Lake Geneva rests beside the 5,000-acre Geneva Lake in southeastern Wisconsin, not far from Milwaukee and Chicago. The lake's beauty is likened to the scenic waters of Europe. It was a summer White House location during Calvin Coolidge's presidency.

Vacationers have a long list of pastimes to pursue, starting on verdant golf courses where you'll play beside the water. Evening concerts in Flatiron Park are scheduled on Thursdays in July and August.

Geneva Lake is blessed with Big Foot Beach State Park, named for Chief Big Foot of the Potawatomi people who lived in the area. Picnicking, swimming, sailing, fishing and water-skiing are a few of the splashy options. Geneva Lake Cruise Line offers a variety of narrated boat tours.

Accommodations: Interlaken Resort and Country Spa, $105-$160, W4240 State

Road 50, Lake Geneva, WI 53147, (800) 225-5558. T.C. Smith Inn Bed and Breakfast, $115-$395, 865 Main St., Lake Geneva, WI 53147, (800) 423-0233.

Information: Lake Geneva Convention & Visitors Bureau, 201 Wrigley Drive, Lake Geneva, WI 53147, (800) 345-1020.

California's North Coast

This is a land where trees grow more than 300 feet high, where herds of elk roam the beach, where rocky headlands jut into a restless sea.

Though much of California has succumbed to malls and expressways, the North Coast remains largely pristine. The world's tallest trees — the coastal redwoods — are found here in great stands. Some are so big you literally can drive a car through tunnels in their trunks.

Trails through the redwoods are accessible on the 31-mile Avenue of the Giants. Coastal towns are full of character. Mendocino, a trendy town that has been the scene of many movies ("East of Eden," "The Summer of '42," "Same Time Next Year"), is the premier destination. It has good restaurants and a busy cultural calendar.

Albion is a good whale-watching spot. A nice inland base is Ferndale, which boasts a number of Victorian homes.

Accommodations: In Ferndale, the Gingerbread Mansion Inn, P.O. Box 40, Ferndale, CA 95536, (800) 952-4136 or (707) 786-4000, has ten rooms full of Victorian ambience. Rates are $140-$350 a night, including hot breakfast and afternoon tea. Less expensive accommodations are available in Arcata and Eureka.

Information: Eureka/Humboldt County Convention and Visitors Bureau, 1034 Second St., Eureka, CA 95501, (800) 346-3482.

Essex, Connecticut

Near the mouth of the Connecticut River, this charming town is a favored getaway for New Yorkers. Once known for its shipbuilding, this riverfront settlement now counts tourism as its raison d'etre.

Tony boutiques, antique galleries and ice cream emporiums line its tree-shaded main street. Yachts from New York and Long Island Sound pack the marinas in summertime.

That's also when visitors take in legitimate theater at the historic Goodspeed Opera House or at the Ivoryton Playhouse, embark on a sightseeing ride on the Valley Railroad or a Connecticut River boat, and crowd the lively bar at the Griswold Inn.

Summer's the time for jazz, too, both at the Griswold and during the annual Great Connecticut Traditional Jazz Festival.

Accommodations: Rooms at the Griswold Inn, 36 Main St., Essex, CT 06426, (203) 767-1776, run $90-$175 year-round. Other historic accommodations in the area include the Bee and Thistle, Old Lyme Inn and the Inn at Chester.

Information: Old Saybrook Chamber of Commerce, P. O. Box 625, Old Saybrook, CT 06475, (203) 388-3266.

Annapolis, Maryland

Most people think of Annapolis as the home of the U.S. Naval Academy — a major presence, to be sure. But Maryland's capital also offers history and culture in large doses.

Visitors invariably tramp through the wooden-domed Maryland State House to see where George Washington resigned his commission as commander in chief in 1783 and where Congress in 1784 ratified the Treaty of Paris, ending the Revolutionary War.

America's last Liberty Tree — the rallying point for the Sons of Liberty in pre-Revolutionary Days — stands on the campus of St. John's College, the third-oldest in the country after Harvard and William and Mary. But Annapolis also ranks high in culture.

"What other city our size (population 33,187) has its own opera, ballet and symphony?" asks Herman Schieke of the city's visitors bureau. It also has theater-in-the-round, a dinner theater and a variety of festivals. And if you're drawn to the sea, there's no better place for sailing than Chesapeake Bay.

Accommodations: Historic Inns of Annapolis, 58 State Circle, Annapolis, MD 21401, (800) 847-8882, has rooms for $125-$260.

Information: Annapolis Anne Arundel County Convention and Visitors Bureau, 26 West St., Annapolis, MD 21401, (410) 280-0445.

Pocono Mountains, Pennsylvania

Welcome to the Poconos, land of heart-shaped tubs and giant round beds with mirrored headboards. You can even find a room with a 7-foot Jacuzzi shaped like a champagne glass!

Cove Haven, near Lakeville, PA, once was open only to bona fide honeymooners, but now it's a fun getaway for couples of all ages and at any stage of courtship.

When you're not in your room, you can take advantage of free water-skiing (including lessons) on the resort's lake, speedboating, indoor and outdoor swimming pools, indoor roller skating and archery. There are nightly floor shows in the giant theater, where the entertainment tends toward the bawdy.

Be sure to allow time for long, lovely drives through the Pocono Mountains, about two hours from either New York or Philadelphia.

Accommodations: A two-night all-inclusive package starts at $390 per couple at Cove Haven, Route 590, Lakeville, PA 18438, (800) 233-4141.

Information: Pocono Mountains Vacation Bureau, 1004 Main St., Stroudsburg, PA 18360, (800) POCONOS.

Galena, Illinois

Lead and shipping were the big businesses in this old mining town, and those who struck it rich in its 1850s heyday built well.

But when the lead ore petered out and the river dried up, the town began to die. Along came tourism, and those historic old brick homes and offices got a second lease on life.

Today, boutiques, antique shops, restaurants and bed-and-breakfast inns occupy yesteryear's buildings, making Galena a delightful romantic getaway for couples. More than 400,000 visitors each year spend a night in Galena, most of them young professional twosomes or older couples whose children are grown.

With 85 percent of its structures on the National Register of Historic Places, Galena's mostly Federal and Italianate buildings are a stroller's delight. Especially interesting are the post-Civil War home of Ulysses S. Grant and the refurbished Desoto House Hotel, where such illustrious figures as Abraham Lincoln and Susan B. Anthony once stayed.

More than 50 B&B inns await visitors, many with antique furnishings, fireplaces and whirlpools. Galena boasts a variety of restaurants. Benjamin's has live music on weekends for stay-up-late folks.

Accommodations: De Zoya House B&B, 1203 Third St., Galena, IL 61036, (815) 777-1203, has rooms with private bath and full breakfast for $85. Rooms at the Desoto

House Hotel are $95-$175, 230 S. Main St., Galena, IL 61036, (815) 777-0090.

Information: Galena Jo Daviess County Chamber of Commerce, 101 Bouthillier St., Galena, IL 61036, (800) 747-9377 or (815) 777-0203.

Seattle, Washington

If your idea of a romantic trip is going somewhere you can remain sleepless, well, this probably is not the place for you.

Seattle is not exactly a hotbed of 24-hour activity (try Vegas for that). But it's a terrific place for wandering arm-in-arm down tree-lined streets and sharing long conversations while sipping cafe latte at one of this city's trademark coffee bars. Wander down by the docks for a fresh seafood meal, or float through the nearby San Juan Islands on a day-sailer.

If you stay at Pioneer Square, you can walk to the Washington State Ferry, Kingdome, cruise ships, Seattle Art Museum, Pike Place Market and more. And maybe you'll even get some sleep.

Accommodations: The boutique Pioneer Square Hotel, $89 per well-appointed room, is the only lodging in historic Pioneer Square near the waterfront, 77 Yesler Way, Seattle, WA 98104, (206) 340-1234.

Information: Seattle-King County Convention and Visitors Bureau, 520 Pike St., Suite 1300, Seattle, WA 98101, (206) 461-5840.

Lake of the Ozarks, Missouri

In central Missouri lies a "dragon lake" stretching out its limbs to create hidden shores and coves. An action-packed summer getaway, Lake of the Ozarks offers 17,087 acres of natural beauty, water sports, horseback riding, golf, water parks and five commercial underground caves.

Everything from luxury resorts to Mom-and-Pop motels dot the shores, and houseboating is popular, too. Osage Beach, Camdenton and Sunrise Beach are among several colorful lakeside towns to pick as a home base. Entertainment includes live country-music shows, outdoor theater and picturesque lakefront boardwalks.

Accommodations: At Osage Beach, Marriott's luxury Tan-Tar-A Resort, from $59 per person, Box 188TT, Osage Beach, Mo 65065, (800) 826-8272 and Inn at Grand Glaize, from $137 per couple for two nights, P.O. Box 969, Osage Beach, MO 65065, (800) 348-4731. At Sunrise Beach, Rock Harbor Lakeside Resort & Motel, $40-$68, Route 3, Box 350, Sunrise Beach, MO 65079, (573) 374-5586.

Information: Lake of the Ozarks Chamber of Commerce, P.O. Box 1570, Osage Beach, MO 65065, (314) 365-2645 or (800) 451-4117.

Denver, Colorado

What could be more manly than going out with the guys for a beer? Denver's revitalized lower downtown area (LoDo), once a decrepit warehouse district, now is home to 11 microbreweries and brew pubs within walking distance of each other.

You can sample Wilderness Wheat Amber or Railyard Ale at the Wynkoop Brewery, the biggest brew pub, or try Bitches Brew Black Bitter Stout at the Mercury Cafe, which claims to be America's smallest brewery. Even at Coors Field, you can get microbrewery beer (Slugger's Stout, Squeeze Play Wheat) and watch the National League's Rockies play baseball.

There's a big, modern amusement park (Elitches) downtown, too, though the tilta-whirl is probably contraindicated after a brewery tour. Another plus: There are more than 4,000 hotel rooms in Denver to fall into.

Accommodations: Hyatt Regency Denver Downtown, $79-$195, 1750 Welton St., Denver, CO 80202, (800) 233-1234 or (303) 295-1234.

Information: Denver Metro Convention and Visitors Bureau, 225 W. Colfax, Denver, CO 80202, (800) 645-3446 or (303) 892-1112.

Texas Hill Country

Revered by many Texans as a sort of heartland, the Texas Hill Country is an imprecisely defined crescent of deep-carved layered limestone covering almost 25,000 square miles west and north of Austin and San Antonio. The scenic area makes a relaxing weekend jaunt from Dallas, Fort Worth and Houston as well as from San Antonio and Austin.

Much different than the stereotypical image of flat Texas countryside, terrain along the Balcones Escarpment is characterized by rolling hills, craggy canyons and cliffs, an abundance of lakes and streams, lots of oak, cedar and cypress trees and flower-carpeted prairies.

The dominating presence of nature and the paucity of major tourism developments induce in visitors a quest for simple, personal pleasures: wine tasting, photographing wildflowers, tubing on the Guadalupe River, sailing or fishing at Lake Travis, and attending small-town festivals and rodeos.

German immigrants settled much of this area in the 1840s, and even today such towns as Fredericksburg and New Braunfels retain distinctively German-style architecture, traditions, culture and language. For a special Hill Country experience, overnight at the historic YO Ranch near Kerrville.

Accommodations: The Y.O. Ranch, $85 per person, including three meals, Highway 41 W., Mountain Home, TX 78058, (800) YO-RANCH.

Information: Texas Tourism Division, Texas Department of Commerce, P.O. Box 12728, Austin, TX 78711-2728, (800) 888-8839.

The Berkshires, Massachusetts

Enjoy the hospitality of a historic inn or bed-and-breakfast farmhouse in western Massachusetts. Spend the day driving or hiking over rolling hills, poke through art galleries, go fishing or hunting for antiques.

Listen to glorious music at Tanglewood, in Lenox, summer home of the Boston Symphony Orchestra while you picnic under the stars. Concert goers fill the 6,000 seats, but as many as 10,000 people spread blankets and sit on the lawn. Spend another evening watching ballet at Jacob's Pillow Dance Festival, in Becket, or at one of the area's many summer theaters.

You can stroll around Stockbridge, immortalized by resident Norman Rockwell, and Lenox, home of many literary giants of the 19th century. Also worth a visit is Hancock Shaker Village, home of an unusual sect.

Accommodations: Red Lion Inn, dating from colonial times, $87-$159 a night, Main St., Stockbridge, MA 01262, (413) 298-5545. For lodging as low as $40 a night, Berkshire B&B Homes, P.O. Box 211, Williamsburg, MA 01096, (413) 268-7244.

Information: Berkshire Visitors Bureau, Berkshire Common, Box PR, Pittsfield, MA 01201, (800) 237-5747 or (413) 443-9186.

Shenandoah Valley, Virginia

Only a few hours' drive from major cities of the East is a peaceful, scenic valley with historic landmarks around every bend. For an introduction to Virginia's Shenandoah Valley, take the Skyline Drive along the Blue Ridge Mountains. Meadows and woods, farms and historic towns are spread out below 75 lookout points.

Staunton, birthplace of President Woodrow Wilson, was settled in 1736 as colonists began to push westward. The Museum of American Frontier Culture, a unique outdoor history museum, illustrates this period.

Staunton is a good base for exploration. Thomas Jefferson's Monticello is outside Charlottesville, and a Civil War battlefield is at New Market.

Accommodations: Frederick House, a B&B near Wilson's birthplace, $65-$115, 28 N. New St., Staunton, VA 24401, (800) 334-5575 or (703) 885-4220.

Information: Shenandoah Valley Travel Association, P.O. Box 1040, New Market, VA 22844, (703) 740-3132.

Pleasant Hill, Kentucky

City dwellers who want to reduce the stress can relax and unwind in peaceful Shaker Village. It's in Pleasant Hill, a hamlet between historic Lexington and Harrodsburg.

Guests sleep in bedrooms furnished with reproductions of Shaker antiques and hand-woven rugs and curtains and stroll among 30 original buildings constructed in the 1830's by the now-vanished Shaker religious community. Artisans demonstrate traditional crafts, and a riverboat glides along the Kentucky River at the bottom of the hill. The dining is excellent, and the atmosphere is guaranteed to slow you down.

Both Harrodsburg and Lexington are worth exploring. At Harrodsburg, "The Legend of Daniel Boone" and "Shadows in the Forest," two outdoor dramas, are presented nightly, Tuesday through Sunday, in alternate weeks, June through August.

Accommodations: $56-$100 a night, in original Shaker buildings. Admission to all buildings and the riverboat ride is $9.

Information: Shaker Village of Pleasant Hill, 3501 Lexington Road, Harrodsburg, KY 40330, (606) 734-5411.

Asheville, North Carolina

Asheville's setting, high in the mountains of western North Carolina, is without compare. Want a complete escape into unspoiled wilderness? Go hiking or fishing in Great Smoky Mountains National Park, only a little over an hour away. Prefer to fantasize about a life of luxury? Visit Biltmore, a mansion and lavish estate established in the 1890s by George W. Vanderbilt.

Asheville is a center of Southern crafts and traditions. Visit the Folk Art Center at Milepost 382 of the Blue Ridge Parkway and enjoy old-time fiddling and dancing on Saturday nights at Shindig-on-the-Green, in front of City Hall.

Accommodations: The Grove Park Inn and Country Club, a national historic landmark dating to 1913, from $125 per day, 290 Macon Ave., Asheville, NC 28804, (800) 438-5800.

Information: Asheville Area Convention and Visitors Bureau, P.O. Box 1010, Asheville, NC 28802, (800) 257-1300 or (704) 258-6111.

Door County, Wisconsin

Door County, a thumb of land jutting into Lake Michigan in northeastern Wisconsin, is a favorite escape for Chicago and Milwaukee residents. Boating, swimming, fishing, biking and hiking are popular. Visitors are attracted to several small resort towns, two state parks, beaches, maritime museums, a historic lighthouse and restaurants serving fresh local fish and produce.

B&B inns and small-scale resorts are scattered throughout the peninsula. Many require a two-night minimum stay on summer weekends.

Accommodations: White Gull Inn in Fish Creek, nearly a century old, $90-$178, P.O. Box 160, Fish Creek, WI 54212, (414) 868-3517.

Information: Door County Chamber of Commerce, Box 406, Sturgeon Bay, WI 54235, (800) 52-RELAX or (414) 743-4456.

Cape May, New Jersey

Located on the southernmost tip of New Jersey far from the madding crowds, Cape May is a national historic landmark in toto — the perfect beach resort for those who want to soak up more than rays.

The town's Victorian inns and mansions transport you to another place in time, when luminaries like presidents Buchanan and Grant strolled through town and Captain Kidd floated in from the high seas to refill his water casks at the Cape May Lily Pond.

Browse through art galleries and boutiques and enjoy walking, trolley or carriage tours of the historic district. Or comb beaches for tide-worn quartz pebbles known as "Cape May diamonds."

Come summer, crashing waves compete with the sounds of music during the Cape May Music Festival. There's also a Summer Theater Festival and a 10-day Victorian Week Festival.

The spirit of Cape May lives on at the historic Mainstay Inn & Cottage. The inn, built in 1870 as a gambling club by wealthy Southern planters, is authentic down to the brass chamber pots under the beds.

Breakfast and afternoon tea are served on the veranda, and the inn's co-owner just happens to be the man who restored the town's historic Cape May Point Lighthouse. Follow him up the spiral staircase for a grand tour.

Should you get homesick for the 20th century, the seaside resort of Wildwood, just 10 minutes away, offers miles of carnival-like boardwalk. And 45 minutes down the Garden State Parkway is Atlantic City, with an equally large, boisterous boardwalk lined with gambling casinos.

Accommodations: Mainstay Inn & Cottage, from $135 including full breakfast and tea, 635 Columbia Ave., Cape May, NJ 08204, (609) 884-8690. No smoking is permitted, and children must be 6 or older. Alternate option: Sand Castle, a guest house with rooms from $85, 829 Stockton Ave., Cape May, NJ 08204, (609) 884-5451 or(800) 346-5451.

Information: Chamber of Commerce of Greater Cape May, P.O. Box 556, Cape May, NJ 08204, (609) 884-5508; or Cape May County Chamber of Commerce, P.O. Box 74, Cape May Courthouse, NJ 08210, (609) 465-7181.

Washington, DC

The nation's capital celebrates July 4th with panache to make you proud, and free events cater to a variety of interests.

You can hear the Declaration of Independence recited at the National Archives and watch Colonial military maneuvers and a parade of marching bands along Constitution Avenue. Top jazz artists add some brass and sass to the nation's party, playing at Freedom Plaza on Pennsylvania Avenue. At dusk, you can settle on the Capitol lawn and listen to the National Symphony Orchestra perform patriotic and classical tunes.

Festivities end with a bang: A spectacular fireworks display over the Mall and the Washington Monument provides a blaze of red, white and blue rocket bursts.

Washington belongs to all Americans — especially on July 4th. While you're here, be sure to take the family to the museums and exhibits in the District of Columbia.

The National Postal Museum includes interactive displays about the history of the U.S. mail and stamps. The U.S. Holocaust Museum offers thoughtful, informative and heart-wrenching information about this World War II tragedy. A special exhibit from a child's perspective tells what it was like to suffer and survive.

Admission to July 4th celebrations, the U.S. Holocaust Museum and all Smithsonian museums is free.

Accommodations: Capitol Reservations, a reservation service, offers discounts on hotels in the city and suburbs, at (800) VISIT-DC or (202) 452-1270. For example, at press time, Capitol Reservations was quoting rooms at the L'enfant Plaza Hotel, three blocks from the Smithsonian museums, at $99 a night (including parking) compared to the usual rate of $230, 480 L'enfant Plaza S.W., Washington, DC 20024, (800) 243-1166 or (202) 484-1000. Other lower-priced hotels are available.

Information: For brochures about attractions, accommodations and restaurants, write the Washington, DC, Convention & Visitors Association, 1212 New York Ave. N.W., Washington, DC 20005, (202) 789-7000.

Coeur d'Alene, Idaho

Think of a nostalgic country town with resort ambience cozying up to the shores of one of America's most beautiful lakes. That's Coeur d'Alene, in northern Idaho, a rising star in the Pacific Northwest. It's only 30 miles from Spokane, WA.

As an aquatic playground, Coeur d'Alene has few rivals. Its slender 26-mile Lake Coeur d'Alene is famous for dinner cruises, fishing, boating, jet skiing, canoeing, windsurfing and parasailing. Beautiful mountains and lush forests surround the area.

Take a gondola ride to Silver Mountain ski resort for summertime picnicking, hiking and mountain biking. Visit the Silverwood Theme Park and ride a narrow-gauge steam train. Tee off at the lakeside Coeur d'Alene Resort Golf Course, where you have to take a boat to reach a floating island green.

Accommodations: Coeur d'Alene Resort, luxurious lakefront hotel, $89-$199, P.O. Box 7200, Coeur d'Alene, ID 83816, (800) 688-5253. In town, the Blackwell House bed and breakfast, $75-$125, 820 Sherman Ave., Coeur d' Alene, ID 83814, (800) 899-0656 or (208) 664-0656.

Information: Coeur d'Alene Chamber of Commerce, P.O. Box 850, Coeur d'Alene, ID 83816-0850, (208) 664-3194.

Santa Barbara, California

Santa Barbara is idyllic Southern California, a red-tiled Spanish colonial town nestled between the mountains and the sea, about 90 miles north of Los Angeles.

Ocean breezes entice visitors to enjoy the beach and water sports or explore missions, Moorish-style buildings, courtyards, gardens and museums.

Drive through Mission Canyon to the historic Santa Barbara Mission and natural history museum. Go sailing or windsurfing, head to the white sand beaches or rent roller skates, bikes or pedal carriages to navigate the seaside boardwalk. Follow State Street's red tile walking tour to historical landmarks, unique boutiques, surf shops and sidewalk cafes.

Linger over brunch and live music at the elegant Four Seasons Biltmore Hotel and enjoy its beautiful grounds.

Accommodations: Bath Street Inn, $90-$115, 1720 Bath St., Santa Barbara, CA 93101, (805) 682-9680. Both are B&Bs. The Orange Tree Inn, $60, 1920 State St., Santa Barbara, CA 93101, (805) 569-1521.

Information: Santa Barbara Convention & Visitors Bureau, 510-A State St., Santa Barbara, CA 93101, (805) 966-9222 or (800) 676-1266. Call (800) 927-4688 for a visitor's guide.

Charleston, South Carolina

Preservation is a way of life in Charleston, with its stately antebellum homes, cobblestone lanes, horse-drawn carriages, glorious palmettos and the gracious ambience of the Old South.

It's a city that easily can be explored by foot on your own, but there are organized options as well, including tours by carriage, trolley or mini-van.

Visitors can stroll through Waterfront Park and watch the ships come in at Charleston Harbor, trace 300 years of history at the Charleston Museum or take a water tour to Fort Sumter, where the Civil War began.

Accommodations: Capers-Motte House, a bed-and-breakfast inn (circa 1735) in the historic district, $95-$100, 629 Church St., Charleston, SC 29401, (803) 722-2263.

Information: Charleston Trident Convention and Visitors Bureau, P.O. Box 975, Charleston, SC 29402, (800) 868-8118.

Sedona, Arizona

Against a dramatic backdrop of red rocks, Sedona glows in a breathtaking setting, about two hours' drive north of Phoenix and about the same distance south of the Grand Canyon.

The town itself has a south-of-the-border flavor, colorfully exemplified by the Tlaquepaque, a Mexican-style village of artisans, shops and restaurants. Art aficionados will enjoy the town's many galleries.

The area's crimson landscape and wooded canyonlands are a major attraction. A drive on scenic roads shows off buttes and monoliths dubbed Coffee Pot Rock, Courthouse Butte and Bell Rock. Spend an afternoon picnicking in Oak Creek Canyon. Explore the back country with expert guides who conduct Jeep tours, hikes to Indian ruins and exotic llama treks. Get a bird's-eye view of the country from the basket of a hot-air balloon, or fly by helicopter to a secluded mesa for a candlelight dinner.

Accommodations: L'Auberge de Sedona, from $130, P.O. Box B, Sedona, AZ 86339, (800) 272-6777. Bell Rock Inn, from $79, 6246 Highway 179, Sedona, AZ 86351, (800) 881-7625.

Information: Sedona/Oak Creek Chamber of Commerce, P.O. Box 478, Sedona, AZ 86339, (520) 282-7722 or (800) 288-7336.

Nashville, Tennessee

Spend a weekend in Nashville, TN, and you may become a country-music convert.

You also will learn about another side to this city, known as "The Athens of the South."

There are seemingly countless country music stops here, but the most popular is the Grand Ole Opry House, known for its appearances by top singers. Next door is Opryland USA, a theme park with thrill rides and a paddlewheeler that includes musical revues on its river cruises. Among Nashville's other musical attractions worth a visit is the Country Music Hall of Fame and Museum.

Nashville, the state capital, has more than a dozen colleges and universities, partially contributing to its tag as "Athens of the South." In Centennial Park, you also will see the Parthenon, the only full-size replica of the Athens landmark. A drive around the city shows off numerous 19th-century mansions, many adorned with Greek columns and classical statuary. Nearby is President Andrew Jackson's home, the Hermitage.

Accommodations: Opryland Hotel, from $179, 2800 Opryland Drive, Nashville, TN 37214, (615) 889-1000. Doubletree Inn, from $89, 315 Fourth Ave. N., Nashville, TN 37219, (800) 528-0444. B&B inns also are popular and start at $55; call (800) 458-2421 for central reservations.

Information: Nashville Convention & Visitors Bureau, 161 Fourth Ave. N., Nashville, TN 37219, (615) 259-4760.

Lancaster County, Pennsylvania

As you enter Lancaster County, you might drive past a black horse-drawn carriage driven by a man wearing dark clothes and a wide-brimmed hat seated next to a woman in a plain gown and white prayer cap. These people aren't part of a movie set. They're devout members of the Amish religious sect.

The Amish live only about 60 miles west of Philadelphia yet a world away from 20th-century society, in communities around the city of Lancaster. Towns such as Bird in Hand, Intercourse, Eden and Strasburg offer an inside look into their simple life. The Amish Homestead is a 71-acre working farm utilizing no modern machinery, electricity or telephones. In touring, remember to respect the privacy of residents.

This also is Pennsylvania Dutch country, with a strong heritage of Germans who settled on rich farmlands. The Landis Valley Museum showcases the German history. In the town of Lancaster, a guided walking tour goes to historic landmarks, including sites dating to Colonial times. The nearby Ephrata Cloister explains life in an early communal society. And for chocolate lovers, Hershey is a short drive away.

Accommodations: Strasburg Inn, from $59 with breakfast, 1 Historic Drive, Strasburg, PA 17579, (717) 687-7691. Limestone Inn, $65-$80 with breakfast, 33 E. Main St., Strasburg, PA 17579, (717) 687-8392.

Information: Pennsylvania Dutch Convention & Visitors Bureau, 501 Greenfield Road, Lancaster, PA 17601, (800) 735-2629 or (717) 299-8901.

Finger Lakes, New York

With an abundance of water sports, museums, wineries and genteel towns, New York state's Finger Lakes area can satisfy a diversity of interests in one getaway.

Each lake is worthy of a weekend visit, so take your pick. Seneca and Cayuga are the two longest. Sightseeing cruises operate daily on Seneca Lake from the town of Watkins Glen, also famous for its international race course and Watkins Glenn State Park. The Ivy League town of Ithaca, home of Cornell University, is at the fingertip of Cayuga Lake and offers waterskiing, sailing and bicycling. Canandaigua Lake is another favorite; its town of the same name has the historic Granger Homestead and Sonnenberg Gardens nearby.

The Pleasant Valley Wine Company Visitors Center is in Hammondsport at the tip of Keuka Lake. And in Naples, the Swiss-styled Widmer Wine Cellar offers wine appreciation courses, tastings and tours.

Accommodations: In Ithaca, the Divi Ramada Inn, from $76, 222 S. Cayuga St., Ithaca, NY 14850, (800) 753-8485 or (607) 272-1000. In Canandaigua, The Inn on the Lake, from $83, 770 S. Main, Canandaigua, NY 14424, (800) 228-2801 or (716) 394-7800. In Geneva, Belhurst Castle, circa 1890, from $65, Route 14 S., P.O. Box 609, Geneva, NY 14456, (315) 781-0201.

Information: Finger Lakes Association, 309 Lake St., Penn Yan, NY 14527, (315) 536-7488 or (800) KIT 4 FUN.

Philadelphia, Pennsylvania

The City of Brotherly Love always sizzles in the summer, with free concerts most weekends at Penn's Landing on the Delaware River waterfront, the annual International Theater Festival for Children and a host of special musical events. The best include the Jam on the River.

Whatever your reason for visiting Philadelphia, be sure to take a walk down funky South Street, salivate over the great cheeses and salamis at the Italian Market in South Philly, visit the Liberty Bell and explore the magnificent Art Museum. Keep in shape by jogging along the Schuylkill River.

Accommodations: Wyndham Franklin Plaza in midtown, from $160, #2 Franklin Plaza, Philadelphia, PA 19103, (215) 448-2000, or Holiday Inn Independence Mall, from $89, Fourth & Arch St., Philadelphia, PA 19106, (800) 843-2355.

Information: Philadelphia Visitor's Center, 16th and JFK Ave., Philadelphia, PA 19102, (800) 537-7676.

Thousand Islands, New York

Alexandria Bay, NY, about two hours north of Syracuse, is the perfect base for exploring the lovely Thousand Islands, which float verdantly along 50 miles of the St. Lawrence River between Canada and New York State.

Some are hardly big enough to support the two trees necessary to qualify as an island. Others accommodate farms, golf courses, high-spired churches and elegant estates with Victorian gingerbread houses, landscaped gardens, dainty gazebos and floating boat garages the size of small homes.

The best way to see the Thousand Islands is by boat. Empire Boat Tours and Uncle Sam's Boat Tours offer two-hour scenic tours from Alexandria Bay on 400-passenger boats. The tours include a stop at the Rhinelandlike Boldt Castle, built on a heart-shaped island by turn-of-the-century millionaire developer George Boldt for his beloved wife Louise.

You'll glide by Irving Berlin's house, "Always," where he wrote the famous song of the same name, and pass under the Thousand Islands Bridge, which links the United States with Canada. Two-hour boat tours cost $12 for adults and $6.50 for children 4-12 on Uncle Sam's Boat Tours, (800) 532-2628.

Accommodations: Capt. Thomson's Resort, on the waterfront at Alexandria Bay, starts at $70 a night, P.O. Box 68, Alexandria Bay, NY 13607, (800) 253-9229.

Information: Thousand Islands International Council, Box 400, Alexandria Bay, NY 13607, (800) 847-5263.

NATURAL
WONDERS

There are few vacations as popular as a trip to one of America's spectacular national parks. Yet as anyone who has navigated the crowded roads of Yellowstone or Yosemite knows, summertime visits often can be an unpleasant encounter with hordes of fellow vacationers.

We choose instead to turn to America's lesser-known national parks, as well as often-overlooked state parks, national forests, national wildlife reservations and national monuments. Each provides a variety of outdoor experiences minus the madding crowds.

Here's a selection of the best natural wonderlands across the country. Rates for accommodations are per night for two people.

Devils Tower, Wyoming

Rising starkly from the plains of northeastern Wyoming, this soaring monolith may look familiar — it was the alien base in the movie "Close Encounters of the Third Kind." Up close, the majesty of this 867-foot rock is overpowering.

Huge vertical columns striate its sides. Gathered in mammoth disarray around its base are large chunks of rock that have broken off the tower. Aloof and forbidding, this lonely stone sentinel always has been a site sacred to American Indians, who make an annual pilgrimage here.

Once regarded as unclimbable, the tower now is scaled by more than 1,000 people every year. Less ambitious visitors walk trails that encircle the base and clamber on the jumbled rocks.

Accommodations: R-Place Bed & Breakfast, $60, Box 8, Devils Tower, WY 82714, (307) 467-5938.

Information: Devils Tower National Monument, P.O. Box 10, Devils Tower, WY 82714, (307) 467-5283.

Bryce Canyon, Utah

Queen Victoria looks down from her rocky throne in the Queen's Garden. Thor's Hammer, next to the Temple of Osiris, resembles a giant mallet. Alley Oop and Dinny add a touch of comic relief.

All are hoodoos — odd-shaped pinnacles left standing by erosion. Bryce Canyon has an army of hoodoos marching down the face of an eroded plateau.

You can look down on those strange rock formations from the rim trail or hike or ride horseback into them on any of eight trails.

Accommodations: Motel rooms, cabins and suites in the park are available from $80-$115. TW Services, P.O. Box 400, Cedar City, UT 84721, (801) 586-7686.

Information: Bryce Canyon National Park, Hwy. 63, Bryce Canyon, UT 84717, (801) 834-5322.

Niagara Falls, New York

Yes, the place reeks with commercialism, but the falls themselves are magnificent.

They aren't the highest falls in America, but because of the volume of water that spills over three separate cataracts — more than a half-million gallons every second — they are the most impressive.

On the American side are the American and Bridal Veil falls, best viewed from Prospect Point. Horseshoe Falls, the broadest and most beautiful, is seen best from a bluff-top walk on the Canadian side.

You also can ride to the top of several towers to see the falls, get close to their base in the Maid of the Mist boat or descend by elevator to the Cave of the Winds close to the rushing water. As for the cities of Niagara Falls (U.S. and Canadian), both are unabashedly touristy, boasting every kind of attraction imaginable.

Accommodations: Comfort Inn The Pointe, from $73, One Prospect Pointe, Niagara Falls, NY 14303, (800) 284-6835 or (716) 284-6835.

Information: Niagara Falls Visitor Center, 310 Fourth St., Niagara Falls, NY 14303, (800) 338-7890.

Okeefenokee National Wildlife Reservation, Georgia

Called the "land of trembling earth" by the Creek Indians, this is one of the largest freshwater wetlands in the country. Extensive marshes, called prairies, are found in the swamp along with large stands of cypress trees and lakes stained brown by the tannin in decaying vegetation. Beds of peat cover many areas; since the peat does not touch solid bottom, the ground there can be made to "tremble" by stomping on it.

Alligators, bears, deer and bobcats live in the swamp. A variety of aquatic birds makes the park one of the nation's finest bird-watching sites.

There are three entrances to the refuge. Guided boat tours, nature trails, boardwalks, interpretive centers, canoeing and other activities are offered.

Accommodations: Days Inn, from $40, 1201 S. Second St., Folkston, GA 31537, (800) DAYS INN or (912) 496-2514.

Information: Okeefenokee National Wildlife Reservation, Rte. 2, Box 3330, Folkston, GA 31537, (912) 496-3331.

Crater Lake, Oregon

Several qualities make this volcanic lake remarkable, but the most surprising is its color: Crater Lake is a deep, vibrant blue.

So startling is its color that one early visitor wondered aloud if he actually had been looking at the sky. American Indians in the region refused to gaze upon the lake, believing disaster would befall anyone who did.

Today, the sight of this lake still bewitches visitors, who spend hours moving among overlooks on the rim drive. Hardy types can hike to the lake surface 2,000 feet below for a ride on the park boat.

Accommodations: The Crater Lake Lodge, $99-$185, P.O. Box 2704, White City, OR 97503, (541) 830-8700.

Information: Crater Lake National Park, P.O. Box 158, Crater Lake, OR 97604, (503) 594-2211.

Craters of the Moon, Idaho

One of the strangest landscapes in America covers much of the southern quarter of Idaho. Miles and miles of lava fields, deposited in the not-so-distant past, extend as far

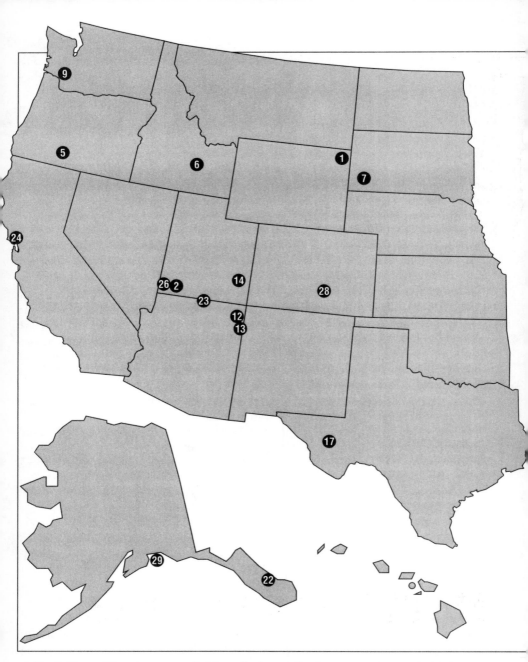

1 Devils Tower, Wyoming
2 Bryce Canyon, Utah
3 Niagara Falls, New York
4 Okeefenokee National Wildlife
  Reservation, Georgia
5 Crater Lake, Oregon
6 Craters of the Moon, Idaho

7 Mount Rushmore, South
  Dakota
8 Hobe Sound/Jensen Beach/
  Juno Beach, Florida
9 Mount St. Helens, Washington
10 The Outer Banks, North Carolina
11 Grayton Beach, Florida

12 Canyon de Chelly, Arizona
13 Window Rock, Arizona
14 Arches National Park, Utah
15 Gulf State Park, Alabama
16 Cape Henlopen State Park,
   Delaware
17 Fort Davis State Park, Texas

NATURAL WONDERS

as the eye can see.

It may not look exactly like the surface of the moon, but it certainly resembles nothing else on Earth. At Craters of the Moon National Monument, paved trails make it easy to explore both the ropy pahoehoe flows and the jagged aa-type lava. You can hike to the rim of a big crater or to the mouths of several small spatter cones and enter large lava tubes.

Lava flows from various ages created the Snake River plain, which is 45 to 60 miles wide and 400 miles long. While large parts are stark, cities and potato farms rest on other sectors.

Accommodations: Arco Inn, $40-$50, including a continental breakfast, P.O. Box 154, Arco, ID 83213, (208) 527-3100

Information: Craters of the Moon National Monument, P.O. Box 29, Arco, ID 83213,(208) 527-3257.

Mount Rushmore, South Dakota

Chiseled into the granite of the Black Hills of South Dakota, the stone likenesses of four American presidents attract more than 2 million visitors a year to this remote locale.

The figures are massive — George Washington's nose is 20 feet long and his eyes are 11 feet wide. His was the first face completed by sculptor Gutzon Borglum in 1930. Then came Thomas Jefferson, Abraham Lincoln and Theodore Roosevelt, each representing a different facet of American civilization.

A few miles away, a much larger sculpture of Sioux Chief Crazy Horse is taking shape. Visitors can make out the outline of Crazy Horse's head (87 feet high), his extended arm (263 feet) and his horse's head (219 feet high). Korczak Ziolkowski, who worked on Mount Rushmore, started this enormous project in the 1950s. Though he died some years ago, the work is continuing.

Other tourist targets in the area include Jewel Cave National Monument, Wind Cave National Park, Badlands National Park and Custer State Park, home to 1,500 bison. You can hobnob with the Flintstones in Bedrock City, ride a narrow-gauge steam railroad or hike and ride horses to your heart's content. Be sure to wander the restored streets of downtown Deadwood, where Wild Bill Hickok drew his "dead man's hand." Deadwood is now filled with casinos.

Accommodations: Rushmore View Inn, $75-$92, P.O. Box 197, Keystone, SD 57751, (605) 666-4466.

Information: Mount Rushmore Visitors Center, P.O. Box 268, Keystone, SD 57751, (605) 574-2523, or South Dakota Tourism, 711 E. Wells Ave., Pierre, SD 57501, (800) SDAKOTA.

Hobe Sound/Jensen Beach/Juno Beach, Florida

OK, so the hour is inconvenient, to say the least. The goal is worth it, though.

Few sights are as stirring as watching a giant sea turtle heave herself out of the surf, waddle laboriously through the sand to high ground, dig a deep hole and sit over it to lay a hundred or so golf ball-size eggs.

The catch is that the turtles only do this on deserted beaches in the dead of night. From May to August on Florida's east coast, rangers at several locales lead midnight beach walks to watch the spectacle. If you prefer, you can go on your own.

Remember that turtles and their eggs are protected. Don't approach a turtle until she has begun laying; otherwise, you'll scare her off.

Accommodations: In Hobe Sound, Comfort Inn, from $69, 18903 SE Federal Highway, Jupiter, FL 33469, (407) 747-9085; in Jensen Beach, Courtyard by Marriott, from $95, 10978 SE Ocean Drive, Jensen Beach, FL 34957, (407) 229-1000; in Juno Beach, Holiday Inn, from $49, 13950 U.S. Highway 1, Juno Beach, FL 33408, (407) 622-4366.

Information: Guided walks at Hobe Sound, P.O. Box 214, Hobe Sound, FL 33475, (407) 546-2067; Jensen Beach, 1910 NE Jensen Beach Blvd., Jensen Beach, FL 34957, (407) 334-3444; Juno Beach, 14200 U.S. 1, Loggerhead Park, Juno Beach, FL 33408, (407) 627-8280.

Mount St. Helens, Washington

You know the story and you've seen the pictures. Mount St. Helens in southwest Washington blew her top during a massive eruption in 1980, burying people, animals and trees in a huge outpouring of volcanic material.

But the enormity of the event doesn't hit home until you actually visit the place. Now the new Coldwater Visitor Center and the road to it provide the best views yet of the shattered summit, the millions of flattened trees and the mud that roared down the Toutle River Valley and turned vast tracts into wastelands.

Watch for the miracle of nature, too, including new plant growth, the softening of harsh landmarks and the return of animal life.

Accommodations: Timberland Motor Inn, $50-$110, 1271 Mount St. Helens Way, Castle Rock, WA 98611, (360) 274-6002.

Information: Mount St. Helens Visitor Center, 3029 Spirit Lake Highway, Castle Rock, WA 98611, (360) 274-2100.

The Outer Banks, North Carolina

The Outer Banks, a series of barrier islands stretching 130 miles along the coast of North Carolina, boast some of the most spectacular beaches on the East Coast.

The area has something to delight everyone. Jockey's Ridge State Park manages to bring out the kid in every visitor. That's because it's home to the tallest sand dune on the East Coast, making it a great place for kite flying, hang gliding, hiking, picnicking and picture-taking.

You'll find a 1.5-mile self-guided nature trail here, with 14 stations and a natural history museum. Guided tours can be arranged on request.

With such prime conditions for kite flying, it's no surprise that a couple of miles up the road, between Kill Devil Hills and Kitty Hawk, is the Wright Brothers National Memorial. It commemorates the first flight accomplished Dec. 17, 1903, by the Ohio bicycle mechanics.

Some beaches, like those at Kitty Hawk, are lined with hotels and cottages. Many others are unpopulated strands backed by dunes and sea oats. A landmark is the black-and-white striped Cape Hatteras lighthouse.

Accommodations: Days Inn in Kill Devil Hills, $95, 1801 N. Virginia Dare Trail, Kill Devil Hills, NC 27948, (800) 325-2525. The Nags Head Inn, $39-$99, P.O. Box 1599, Nags Head, NC 27959, (800) 327-8881.

Information: Outer Banks Chamber of Commerce, P.O. Box 1757, Kill Devil Hills, NC 27948, (919) 441-8144.

Grayton Beach, Florida

The panhandle of Florida has such extraordinary beaches that this region was given the nickname of Miracle Strip many years ago.

Grayton Beach, near Destin, was named the best beach in the United States by Stephen Leatherman, director of the Laboratory for Coastal Research and professor of geography at the University of Maryland. Leatherman, who has been choosing the top 20 U.S. beaches for several years, says Grayton "is kind of the perfect beach, if there is one."

Stretching into Alabama and Mississippi, these white sand beaches are made of powdery quartz, which makes a distinctive squeak when you walk on it. The sand slopes gently into the sea, and gulf waters here are translucent green.

There are pockets of tourist excess here and there on this coast, but much of its pristine beauty remains.

Accommodations: Rivard of South Walton, from $50, 15 Pine St., Santa Rosa Beach, FL 32459, (800) 423-3215.

Information: South Walton Tourist Development Council, P.O. Box 1248, Santa Rosa Beach, FL 32459, (800) 822-6877.

Canyon de Chelly, Arizona

Red rock monoliths, sandstone buttes and mesas dotting the landscape make Canyon de Chelly (pronounced *deh-shay*) special.

Located in the northeast corner of Arizona, it's a 130-acre parcel of Navajo land, which at 25,000 square miles is the largest American Indian reservation in North America. The reservation draws many visitors, but most head to better-known sites, such as Monument Valley.

Yet Canyon de Chelly National Monument, which encompasses Canyon de Chelly, Canyon del Muerto and Monument Canyon, is probably the most impressive site within the reservation. This land was the home of the Anasazi, the "ancient ones," early ancestors of the Pueblo people.

The area has more than 100 village sites, from pit houses to multistory pueblos, that date back as far as the fourth century. Among them is the White House (the ruins include a white plaster wall), which can be reached by hiking a 2.5-mile trail. This structure had 175 rooms and four kivas, or ceremonial rooms, and could house 100 people.

Two rim drives offer spectacular views. The 36-mile South Rim Drive leads to eight overlooks, including Face Rock Overlook with a view of canyon dwellings in an opposite wall. The 34-mile North Rim Drive leads to four overlooks.

Accommodations: Thunderbird Lodge in Chinle, $61, P.O. Box 548, Chinle, AZ 86503, (520) 674-5841, is a National Park Service-authorized hotel and restaurant, with buildings of adobe and stone and American Indian decor.

Information: Canyon de Chelly National Monument, P.O. Box 588, Chinle, AZ 86503, (520) 674-5500.

Window Rock, Arizona

From Window Rock, their capital, the Navajo Indians rule a starkly beautiful land. Covering an area as large as the state of West Virginia, it encompasses such major tourist destinations as Monument Valley and Canyon de Chelly.

Recognized by the United States as a sovereign nation in an 1868 treaty, the Navajos have their own elected officials, police force, language, religion and a spirit that enabled them to survive in a difficult land.

For visitors, a trip to Navajo Country means an opportunity to buy their wonderful crafts — rugs, pottery, jewelry — and see one of the most scenic regions of America.

Dozens of movies and commercials have been set among Monument Valley's red sandstone towers. Canyon de Chelly winds for 30 miles between 1,000-foot-high cliffs; Spider Rock, an amazing 800-foot pinnacle, stands near one end. Ancient Anasazi cliff dwellings in Navajo land are among the best-preserved in Arizona.

Accommodations: Navajo Nation Inn, $67-$83, P.O. Box 2340, Window Rock, AZ 86515, (800) 662-6189.

Information: Navajo Nation Tourism Office, P.O. Box 9000, Window Rock, AZ 86515, (520) 871-7370.

Arches National Park, Utah

A landscape of narrow sandstone canyons, balanced rocks and the world's greatest concentration of naturally carved sandstone arches await the visitor to this eastern edge of Utah.

Arches, made a national monument in 1929 and a national park in 1971, is an untamed wilderness, the product of wind, water and time. More than 1,500 arches are found mainly in narrow walls called "fins" formed in prehistory by water that froze and broke up the sandstone.

It's ideal for short hikes of one to five miles through landscape dotted with pygmy forests of piñon and juniper trees. One of the best walks is to 45-foot-high Delicate Arch, perhaps the park's most spectacular. Or you can drive out to see where parts of "Indiana Jones and the Last Crusade" were filmed.

Accommodations: Best Western Greenwell in Moab, from $99, 1055 Main, Moab, UT 84532, (801) 259-6151 or (800) 528-1234. For campers: Devils Garden Campground has a spectacular location, but arrive early. It has only 54 sites ($8 per night plus $4 entrance fee), and while RVs are welcome, there are no hookups.

Information: Arches National Park, P.O. Box 907, Moab, UT 84532, (801) 259-8161.

Gulf State Park, Alabama

In Gulf Shores, you'll find everything that America has ever placed beside the ocean for amusement, from a wave pool to miniature golf courses, fast-food outlets to video arcades.

But if you head to the eastern end of Gulf Shores, you'll find out why people came here in the first place. Gulf State Park is a 2.5-mile stretch of white beach along the Gulf of Mexico that also includes 6,000 acres of marshlands, forests and freshwater lakes. It's a place to remind the kids that nature is the primary attraction of the ocean.

The park's naturalist offers guided canoe trips on Little Lake, and canoes and johnboats can be rented. Bicycling, pier fishing, swimming in a beach-side pool, the ocean or Lake Shelby, an 18-hole golf course and tennis should keep everyone happy. To get farther off the beaten path, head to nearby Bon Secour National Wildlife Refuge, a protected 4,000-acre coastal barrier habitat.

Accommodations: The resort hotel at the park has 144 motel units, and there are 21 cabins on stilts next to Fort Shelby. Hotel lodging starts at $99, and cabins are $327 a week, P.O. Box 437, Gulf Shores, AL 36547, (800) 544-GULF. For campers: There are 468 sites, some with RV hookups. Many are located by Middle Lake. Camping fees are $10-$20.

Information: Gulf State Park, 20115 State Highway 135, Gulf Shores, AL 36542, (334) 948-PARK, or (800) ALA-PARK.

Cape Henlopen State Park, Delaware

On the southern Delaware shore, near where ferries cross the bay to New Jersey, lies Cape Henlopen State Park, a great reminder of the way the Atlantic Coast used to look before it was heavily developed.

It boasts hiking trails, tennis and basketball courts, a softball field and a nine-hole Frisbee golf course.

You can climb a nearby tower for a spectacular view of the coast. The Great Dune, at 80 feet high, is thought to be one of the largest sand dunes on the East Coast.

But the 3,400 acres of protected shoreline at this park contain smaller treasures that are just as spectacular, from piping plover nests to cranberry bogs. Be sure to visit the Seaside Nature Center.

Accommodations: New Devon Inn in Lewes, $85, P.O. Box 516, Lewes, DE 19958, (302) 645-6466. For campers: There are 158 campsites in the park ($15).

Information: Cape Henlopen State Park, 42 Henlopen Drive, Lewes, DE 19958, (302) 645-8983.

Fort Davis State Park, Texas

A trip to the Fort Davis area means history, science and the great Texas outdoors. Fort Davis sits at an altitude of 5,050 feet. It's named for a frontier fort constructed by the U.S. Army near the intersection of the Chihuahua Trail and the San Antonio-El Paso Trail.

The fort was built to keep travelers and freight safe from attack by Apaches. Named for then-Secretary of War Jefferson Davis, it was garrisoned almost continually from 1854 to 1891. Fort Davis also was headquarters of the 9th U.S. Cavalry, a regiment of black troops much respected by the Indians.

In addition to a museum and visitors center, there are restored officers quarters, barracks and a commissary. There's also a sound reproduction of the 1875 retreat parade and living history programs with volunteers in period costume throughout the summer.

Outside town, the Davis Mountains State Park offers lodging, picnicking and hiking on its 1,800 acres, a longhorn herd and a scenic drive with vast views of the West Texas landscape.

Not to be missed is the McDonald Observatory atop 6,800-foot Mount Locke, considered to be among the top observatories in the world. It boasts a 107-inch reflecting telescope; guided tours of the dome and immediate grounds are conducted year-round. Once a month (on Wednesdays nearest the full moon) the observatory allows visitors to view the sky through the big telescope, the only facility in the United States that does so. Reservations are required; be sure to book three to six months in advance. "Star parties" are held on Tuesdays, Fridays and Saturdays, giving visitors a visual tour of the constellations through 14- and 16-inch telescopes.

Accommodations: Indian Lodge, $55, P.O. Box 1458, Fort Davis, TX 79734, (915) 426-3254, is pueblo-style with rustic decor in Davis Mountains State Park. For campers: The state park, P.O. Box 1458, Fort Davis, TX 79734, (915) 426-3337, allows camping and has RV hookups ($8-$13, $4 entrance fee).

Information: Fort Davis National Historic Site, P.O. Box 1456, Fort Davis, TX 79734, (915) 426-3224.

Watoga State Park, West Virginia

This park derives its name from Watauga, the Cherokee word for "river of many islands." In fact, the Greenbrier River runs along several miles of its boundary. There are more than 10,000 acres of lakes, trails, woodlands and camping areas here.

Options for outdoor fun are bountiful. There are organized bird-watching walks around 11-acre Killbuck Lake. You may also see black bear, deer, beaver and raccoon. You can cast for trout and bass or go tubing in the Greenbrier River. You also can opt for swimming in an Olympic-sized pool, mountain biking or hiking along 30 miles of trails, or horseback riding at Jadlee Stables. There's also a junior naturalist program for kids.

Accommodations: There are 33 cabins at Watoga (from $332 a week); nine are deluxe and the rest are standards. For campers: There are 88 campsites ($12-$14) in wooded areas along the Greenbrier River or Beaver Creek.

Information: Watoga State Park, HC 82, Box 252, Marlinton, WV 24954, (800) CALL-WVA.

Adirondack State Park, New York

The sheer size of Adirondack State Park is daunting. The state of New York set aside 5.7 million acres as parkland in 1892, making it the largest park in the contiguous United States. Nearly half of the park is wilderness.

The park has some of our country's most beautiful forested mountains and pristine lakes. It once was so inaccessible that it was among the last places in the East to be explored.

Its size ensures plenty of space to escape. Water-skiing, boating, biking, swimming, horseback riding and hiking are a few of the options here. Industrious visitors can climb Mount Marcy, highest peak in New York state and one of the richest bird habitats in the East, attracting species that range from peregrine falcons to snow geese.

Accommodations: Stagecoach Inn in Lake Placid, $70, 370 Old Military Road, Lake Placid, NY 12946, (518) 523-9474. For campers: Numerous campground options are available, from rustic to modern.

Information: Lake Placid/Essex County Visitors Bureau, Olympic Center, 216 Main St., Lake Placid, NY 12946, (518) 523-2445.

Mount Greylock, Massachusetts

While many tourists think of Massachusetts in terms of beautiful — but crowded — Cape Cod, those in the know head west to the Berkshires. One of the state's least-known gems is Mount Greylock, at 3,491 feet the highest peak in the state. From its summit on a clear day, you can see five states and a distance of about 100 miles.

Greylock has inspired many writers who summered in the Berkshires, among them Herman Melville, who reportedly admired the mountain's whalelike shape while writing "Moby Dick" at his nearby farm.

The 10,000-acre preservation that surrounds Mount Greylock is a popular place for picnicking, camping and hiking on 45 miles of trails. A stand of 200-year-old red spruce trees form one of the last old-growth forests in the Northeast.

You needn't be a hiker or mountaineer to enjoy Mount Greylock. You can drive up the south side of the mountain through Lanesboro and down the north side through North Adams. The mountain is open from mid-May until October, when brilliant fall foliage is at its peak.

Accommodations: Bascom Lodge, $60, P.O. Box 1800, Lanesboro, MA 01237, (413) 743-1591, at the summit, was built in the 1930s. The rustic lodge is run by the Appalachian Mountain Club.

Information: Mount Greylock, P.O. Box 1800, Lanesboro, MA 01237, (413) 499-4262.

Grafton Notch State Park, Maine

While the White Mountains of New Hampshire are renowned for their beauty, they've also got the crowds that popularity provokes. The solution is to cross the state line to Bethel, ME, and drive 25 miles north to visit Grafton Notch State Park.

This small but dramatic cul-de-sac in the Mahoosic Range is a great choice for families looking for short hikes to scenic waterfalls, like Mother Walker Falls, and caves, like Moose Cave. Those with more energy can hike up Old Speck, the third-highest mountain in the state. The restless can pick up the Appalachian Trail, which runs through the park.

Throughout the park, you'll enjoy picnic areas, swimming holes and spectacular views of the White Mountains. On the way here, you'll pass through the town of Newry and its Artists' Bridge, the most famous of Maine's eight covered bridges.

Accommodations: Sudbury Inn in Bethel, $75, P.O. Box 369, Bethel, ME 04217, (207) 824-2174.

Information: Grafton Notch State Park, HCR, Box 330, Newry, ME 04261, (207) 824-2912.

Cruising Southeast Alaska

Where else on Earth can you wake to the cry of an eagle, watch the powerful antics of humpback whales and thrill to the sight and sound of tons of ice thundering from the face of a glacier? Only in Southeast Alaska — an awesome land that teems with wildlife and natural beauty.

Aboard the 70-passenger ships Sea Lion or Sea Bird of Special Expeditions, you'll cruise beyond the well-known and often-visited sites between Sitka and Juneau. Rather than gazing from afar at this stunning coastal wilderness, you'll explore it up close in the company of experienced naturalists.

Cost: Rates range from $2,990 to $4,190 per person, double occupancy.

Information: Special Expeditions, 720 Fifth Ave., New York, NY 10019, (800) 762-0003.

Houseboating Lake Powell, Arizona

Nestled in Glen Canyon National Park and straddling the border of Utah and Arizona, Lake Powell boasts more shoreline than California. Ringed by dramatic red rock cliffs and canyons, these sparkling waters provide a picture-perfect setting for a houseboating expedition.

Wahweap Marina, six miles north of Page, AZ, is the southern gateway to Lake Powell and the most convenient place to rent a houseboat. Wahweap offers fully equipped, reasonably priced vessels that sleep six to 12 adults. Following a familiarization session, you'll cast off aboard your floating motel, free to roam this watery wonderland.

Anchor in your own private cove, fire up the grill, pour a drink and sit back to watch the sunset reflect gloriously off reddened cliffs and ravines.

Cost: Three-, four- and seven-day rental plans are available at rates that range from $690 for three days aboard a 36-foot boat to $2,038 for a week at the helm of a 50-footer.

Information: Lake Powell Resorts and Marina, P.O. Box 56909, Phoenix, AZ 85079, (800) 528-6154.

Cruising Wine Country, California

The hidden deltas of the Sacramento and San Joaquin rivers offer timeless rural landscapes and winding waterways where migratory waterfowl abound. Thanks to Alaska Sightseeing/Cruise West and its nimble, 82-passenger Spirit of Alaska, you can cruise Northern California's placid inland waterways all the way to Sacramento and the vineyards and wineries of the Napa and Sonoma valleys.

Four- and five-day "California Wine Country Cruises" begin and end at San Francisco's Pier 40. After cruising San Francisco and San Pablo bays, you'll journey up the Napa River to explore America's premier wine country, stopping for tours and tastings at top wineries.

Cost: Rates range from $499 to $1,299 per person, double occupancy.

Information: Alaska Sightseeing/Cruise West, 2401 Fourth Ave., Suite 700, Seattle, WA 98121, (800) 426-7702.

Cumberland Island, Georgia

There are several ways to experience Cumberland Island National Seashore, a wildlife sanctuary off the southern coast of Georgia.

You can take the 45-minute, reservations-only National Park Service ferry from St. Mary's (no cars or bicycles permitted) and set up camp on the beach. You can ferry in for the day and return to the mainland at night. Or you can take a private ferry owned by the Greyfield Inn, the only one on the island, and settle into the lap of luxury.

Whether you choose rugged or ritzy, the best things on Cumberland are free. This includes miles of deserted beaches and dunes and wooded nature trails into the ruins of the old Carnegie estate. There are lakes, secret ponds and estuaries housing gators, otters and 300 species of birds. The views are priceless.

Camping is permitted only at designated sites, and reservations are required both for the ferry and campsites. The earlier you make them, the better — space is limited. Only 300 people are permitted on the island at any one time.

Nothing can be purchased on the island, so bring in everything you need, but pack light. You'll have to tote your gear one-half to three miles to the campsites. All have water; beach camps closest to the ferry also have cold showers.

The luxe way to visit the island is with reservations at the three-story Greyfield Inn, built in 1901 for a daughter of the Carnegie family. With antiques, fine art, inlaid fireplaces, a spacious library and gourmet cuisine (dinner is by candlelight), it's the island's sole concession to elegance.

Activities include beachcombing, swimming, fishing and clam digging, birdwatching, cycling and guided walking, driving and natural history tours.

Accommodations: Camping is free but reservations are necessary, (912) 882-4335. The ferry is approximately $10 per adult, $6 per child and $8 per senior citizen, round trip. At the Greyfield Inn, rates start at $245, including meals and activities, P.O. Box 900, Fernandina Beach, FL 32035, (904) 261-6408. The inn, which is closed in August, offers private ferry service, bicycles and private Jeep tours. Mainland lodging: Riverview Hotel in St. Mary's, from $50 including full breakfast, 105 Osborne St., St. Mary's, GA 31558, (912) 882-3242.

Information: Cumberland Island National Seashore, P.O. Box 806, St. Mary's, GA 31558, (912) 882-4336.

Cedar Breaks, Utah

There's definitely a family resemblance. A baby first cousin to larger and better-known Bryce Canyon National Park, this huge natural amphitheater's 2,000-foot-high walls glow with ribbons of lavender, terra cotta, gold, rose, purple and pink sandstone.

Early morning or evening light is particularly stunning. As at many national monuments near national parks, this one near Cedar City in southwest Utah offers similar ambience without the summer crowds.

Accommodations: Brian Head Resort, from $95, 223 Hunter Ridge Road, Brian Head, UT 84719-0008, (800) 27 BRIAN or (801) 677-2035.

Information: Cedar Breaks National Monument, 82 N. 100 E., Cedar City, UT 84720, (801) 586-9451.

St. Croix, U.S. Virgin Islands

Popular snorkeling destinations sometimes disappoint, but not this U.S. national monument on the island of St. Croix. Even if you just want to sit on the beach or roll in the waves, this tiny island delivers a memorable day.

Nowhere is the Caribbean greener or more pristine than in this 700-acre natural aquarium 1.5 miles off St. Croix's northeastern coast. Underwater visibility is in the 100-foot range, and two easy-to-follow underwater trails show off the colorful coral reef and tropical fish. Most day charters out of Christiansted include a picnic lunch.

Accommodations: Hotel Caravelle, from $99, 44A Queen Cross St., Christiansted, St. Croix, U.S.V.I. 00820, (800) 524-0410 or (809) 773-0687.

Information: Christiansted National Historic Site, P.O. Box 160 C'sted, St. Croix, U.S.V.I. 00821-0160, (809) 773-1460; St. Croix Hotel & Tourism Association, P.O. Box 24238, Gallows Bay, St. Croix, U.S.V.I. 00824, (800) 524-2026 or (809) 773-7117.

Florissant, Colorado

So, what did the world look like 35 million years ago? Perfect imprints of fragile insects and plants that thrived during the Oligocene Epoch, along with huge petrified sequoia stumps, fascinate visitors to Florissant Fossil Beds, a geological wonderland 30 miles west of Colorado Springs.

The monument's freshly restored 1878 Hornbek homestead illustrates female frontier pluck, and the gaslights and gaming of very Victorian Cripple Creek are a short drive away.

Accommodations: Country Inn, from $59, P.O. Box 5108, Woodland Park, CO 80866, (800) 456-4000 or (719) 687-6277.

Information: Florissant Fossil Beds National Monument, P.O. Box 185, Florissant, CO 80816, (719) 748-3253.

Growler Island, Alaska

A romantic night on your own private island awaits adventurers in Alaska's Prince William Sound.

From Valdez, take the day-excursion boat run by Stan Stephens Charters. During the trip, you'll cruise the waters around Columbia Glacier and stop for a salmon dinner at Growler Island. When the other participants leave after dinner, you remain to savor the night on the island in your own tent.

A staff on the island sees to your needs, and you're free to make your own tranquil discoveries in canoes and paddleboats. At night, all is quiet in the long twilight.

Cost: All-inclusive cost for a couple for lodging, meals, boat transport and sightseeing is $377 for the first night, $200 for extra nights.

Information: Stan Stephens Cruises, P.O. Box 1297, Valdez, AK 99686, (800) 992-1297.

Sapelo Island, Georgia

Just 35 miles north of Georgia's touristy Golden Isles — Sea Island, St. Simons and Jekyll — lies another barrier island that's more on the wild side.

On Sapelo Island, wild turkeys and blackbeard deer run through the woods. Bald eagles soar over the trees, and shrimp and young fish thrive in the salt marshes. The beaches are broad and totally undeveloped.

The island will stay a wild beauty because Sapelo is a state park and accessible only by boat. The Department of Natural Resources gives tours of the island on Wednesdays, Saturdays and special extended tours on the fourth Tuesday of each month. Additional tours on Friday are offered during the summer only. Tickets can be purchased at the Sapelo Island Visitors Center in Meridian, $10 for adults, $6 for children, P.O. Box 15, Sapelo Island, GA 31327, (912) 437-3224.

Signs of civilization are scant: There are a few buildings and homes, part of a scientific institute, and an arrow-straight, unpaved roadway cut through the woods by German engineers in the 1930s. Rangers call it the Autobahn.

Accommodations: Open Gate B&B, $48-$53, Vernon Square, Darien, GA 31305, (912) 437-6985.

Information: Sapelo Island State Park, P.O. Box 15, Sapelo Island, GA 31327, (912) 485-2251.

IDYLLIC
SMALL TOWNS

D o you have a favorite little getaway not far from your home, popular locally, but not well-known to the rest of the world? Hundreds of these gems are tucked away around the country, offering a bounty of vacation activities at low cost.

A small town can showcase the personality of its state. It can serve up a terrific regional museum, flaunt fine period homes or simply invite you, the visitor, to stop and smell the roses.

We scanned the country looking at rural towns and small cities that are good finds for affordable trips. Places where lower-cost lodging is available, and where eateries serve hearty, home-style cooking at prices that city slickers can't believe - such as $3 for a rib-sticking breakfast.

We focused on small towns where quality and uniqueness still are treasured. Even those of us who grew up in cities like to think that small towns are where the best of America lies, untouched and full of innocent promise.

Here's our list of the best small-town vacations; all lodging prices are for a double room for two.

Lake Havasu City, Arizona

Imagine coming upon London Bridge — the real thing, not a replica — spanning a river in the Arizona desert. And surrounding it, an ersatz Tudor city.

It's not a mirage. It's a promoter's dream, and you have to admire the gall of Robert McCullough, who bought London Bridge from the city of London, took it apart and rebuilt it in Lake Havasu City, AZ.

The wonder of it is that this totally incongruous, wonderfully preposterous idea succeeded. Vacationers flock to Lake Havasu City, even when the temperature hits 115 degrees, and they browse in stores called "shoppes." Beats me. Maybe there's something in the water.

Accommodations: Best Western Lake Place Inn, $59-$89, 31 Wings Loop, Lake Havasu City, AZ 86403, (800) 258-8558.

Information: Lake Havasu City Visitors and Convention Bureau, 1930 Mesquite Ave., Suite 3, Lake Havasu City, AZ 86403, (800) 242-8278.

Eufaula, Alabama

Golf you may know, but have you ever played an 18-hole fishing course?

You can test your casting and catching skills at Tom Mann's Fish World in Eufaula. At each of 18 designated positions on a private lake, each requiring different angling skills, you see how many fish you can catch within a specified time.

Bass fishing's also good on 45,200-acre Lake Eufaula, site of a state park with resort facilities. Adjacent is the Eufaula National Wildlife Refuge, which attracts 400,000 visitors a year.

Eufaula is much more than a glorified fishing hole, though. It has dozens of well-preserved homes, a mix of Greek Revival, Italianate and Victorian styles dating to the 1830s. Particularly fine is the Kendall Manor, now a B&B. More than 700 buildings are in the historic district.

Accommodations: Holiday Inn, $49, P.O. Box 725, Barbour and Riverside Drive, Eufaula, AL 36027, (334) 687-2021.

Information: Eufaula/Barbour County Tourist Council, P.O. Box 1055, Eufaula, AL 36072, (800) 524-7529.

Eureka Springs, Arkansas

By now, everyone has heard of Branson, MO, the Cinderella of the country music world. An hour's drive south and just across the Arkansas border is Eureka Springs, a star of a different sort — and far more enchanting.

With narrow, twisting streets, hillsides peppered with Victorian homes and a downtown full of old stone buildings, Eureka Springs is one of the prettiest towns in America.

Founded when mineral water was regarded as a cure for practically every ill, Eureka Springs today is known for its art galleries, collectibles shops and boutiques. Two Victorian homes are open to the public, and the Thorncrown Chapel is an architectural masterpiece.

Best way to get around town is by trolley — there are six routes, each color-coded. A major summer attraction is the Great Passion Play, an outdoor drama with a cast of 200.

Accommodations: Best Western Inn of the Ozarks, from $44, P.O. Box 431, Eureka Springs, AR 72632, (800) 528-1234.

Information: Eureka Springs Chamber of Commerce, P.O. Box 551, Eureka Springs, AR 72632, (501) 253-8737.

Gruene, Texas

Deep in the heart of Texas — San Antonio, Austin, LBJ country and the like — you will find a tiny, historic community called Gruene (pronounced "Green") on the scenic Guadalupe River. This old German settlement came upon hard times during the Depression but was rescued by a group of businessmen who restored many of its buildings.

Now on the National Register of Historic Places, Gruene makes a pleasant stop, day or night. The old gristmill has become a picturesque restaurant with excellent catfish, the Victorian mansion of founder Henry D. Gruene has been transformed into a lovely B&B, and two wineries have tasting shops here.

The restored dance hall, the oldest in Texas, is a popular site for country music events on most days during summer, on weekends only in winter. You also can poke around antique shops, pottery shops and a general store.

Accommodations: Gruene Mansion Inn, from $95, 1275 Gruene Road, Gruene, TX 78130, (210) 629-2641.

Information: Town of Gruene, 1601 Hunter Road, New Braunfels, TX 78130, (210) 629-5077.

San Juan Bautista, California

Want to visit a place that's always jumping?

Go to San Juan Bautista, which lies on the most famous earthquake-producing feature in the United States, the San Andreas Fault. Tremors of 2.0 or more on the Richter scale occur an average of seven to 10 times a week. (In three visits, however, the

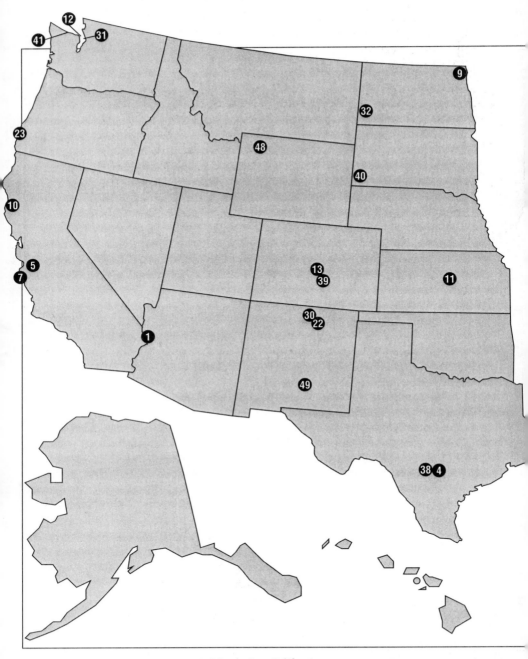

1 Lake Havasu City, Arizona
2 Eufaula, Alabama
3 Eureka Springs, Arkansas
4 Gruene, Texas
5 San Juan Bautista, California
6 Freeport, Maine
7 Carmel-by-the-Sea, California
8 Amana, Iowa
9 Cavalier, North Dakota
10 Mendocino, California
11 Lindsborg, Kansas
12 Port Townsend, Washington
13 Breckenridge, Colorado
14 Mountain View, Arkansas
15 Hilton Head Island,
   South Carolina
16 Berea, Kentucky
17 Millwood, Virginia
18 Adamstown, Pennsylvania
19 Mystic, Connecticut
20 Woodstock, Vermont
21 Berkeley Springs, West Virginia
22 Las Vegas, New Mexico
23 Bandon, Oregon
24 Hot Springs, Arkansas
25 Manchester, Vermont
26 Lumberville, Pennsylvania

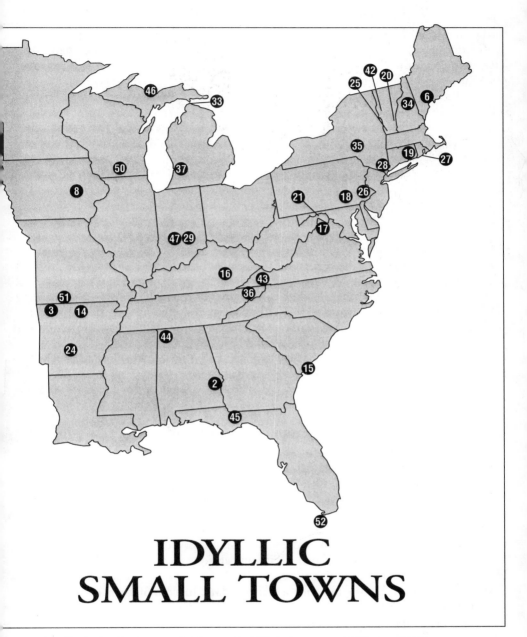

IDYLLIC
SMALL TOWNS

author never felt even a jiggle.)

Visiting an earthquake-prone region isn't the main reason to come to this charming city, though. One of Father Junipero Serra's biggest California missions stands here on the Camino Real; the large church (with a handy seismograph mounted just outside the entrance) is a beauty. The city also boasts many antique shops, and an old hotel, livery and jail have been restored in the central plaza.

If quakes worry you, though, down a quick one at the gazebo at the Fault Line restaurant, which sits directly atop the San Andreas fault. If a quake hits while you're there, the d-d-drink's on the h-h-house.

Accommodations: Posada de San Juan, $78-$130, P.O. Box 2130, San Juan Bautista, CA 95045, (408) 623-4030.

Information: San Juan Bautista Chamber, P.O. Box 1037, San Juan Bautista, CA 95045, (408) 623-2454.

Freeport, Maine

For more than 80 years, the venerable L.L. Bean has had a store on Main Street. It's still the top dog (and open 24 hours a day), but Ralph Lauren, Calvin Klein, Brooks Bros. and more than 100 other retailers now vie for customers in this shopping town.

On good summer days, the streets are crowded with shoppers moving from outlet to outlet. But despite its emergence as an outlet center, Freeport retains much of its New England village ambience — a plus for visitors.

Accommodations: Freeport Inn, $50-$110, 335 U.S. Route 1, Freeport, ME 04032, (800) 242-8838 or (207) 865-3106.

Information: Maine Publicity Bureau, P.O. Box 2300, Hallowell, ME 04347, (800) 533-9595.

Carmel-by-the-Sea, California

Tucked into a seaside forest in the southern bend of the Monterey Peninsula, 128 miles south of San Francisco, Carmel is as picturesque a square mile as you'll ever see.

This area's meeting of ocean, cliffs and forests make for incredible scenery — along Pebble Beach's famed Seventeen Mile Drive, Highway 1 through Big Sur and in the lesser-known but strikingly beautiful Point Lobos State Reserve.

There's golfing at Pebble Beach, horseback rides through the Del Monte Forest, tennis at the municipal courts and early California history at the Carmel Mission.

There are more than 70 art studios, galleries and antique shops in Carmel. All manner of intriguing shops line Ocean Avenue and fill the secluded courtyards on side streets. Saks Fifth Avenue and I. Magnin anchor Carmel Plaza. Just out of town, the Barnyard and the Crossroads Shopping Center have shops in garden settings.

Accommodations: Carmel Garden Court Inn, P.O. Box 6226, Carmel, CA 93921,(408) 624-6926, from $125, is a charming spot. All rooms have wood-burning fireplaces, wet bars and VCRs, and rates include a continental breakfast served on your private patio.

Information: Carmel Business Association, P.O. Box 4444, Carmel-by-the-Sea, CA 93921, (408) 624-2522 or (800) 550-4333.

Amana, Iowa

When a German religious group settled in Amana a century ago, life was strictly ordered — mostly hard work and little play.

The women fixed meals in community kitchens while the men worked on the farms. There was a prayer service every evening. Self-sufficiency was the byword; the sect even made refrigerators under the Amana name.

The old ways are mostly gone today. There's only one communal kitchen left, and it's just for show. Tourism is now the mainstay of Amana's seven villages, which attract more than a million visitors a year.

Visitors can see bread baked on heated stones. Craftspeople sell brooms and baskets made the old way. Old-time goods and foods are marketed, and Amana restaurants do a huge business serving hearty, family-style meals.

Accommodations: Amana Holiday Inn, $82-$88, P.O. Box 187, Amana, IA 52203, (319) 668-1175.

Information: Amana Colonies Convention Bureau, 39 38th Ave., Suite 100, Amana, IA 52203, (800) 245-5465 or (319) 622-3828.

Cavalier, North Dakota

It's odd that an island people, immigrants from Iceland, chose a place in America that was as far as they could get from the sea.

But more people of Icelandic descent live in North Dakota and neighboring Manitoba, Canada, than in any other place on Earth save Iceland itself. The story of those hardy immigrants — and of 20 other ethnic groups that settled in the region — is told at the Pioneer Heritage Center at Icelandic State Park.

In addition to exhibits, the park has moved pioneer farmhouses and other structures onto parkland. Every August, Winnipeg, Manitoba, an hour's drive north of the park, stages one of North America's biggest festivals to salute all the ethnic groups.

Accommodations: Cedar Inn, $36, 502 Division Ave. S. #1, Cavalier, ND 58220, (701) 265-8341.

Information: Icelandic State Park, 13571 State Highway 5, Cavalier, ND 58220, (701) 265-4561.

Mendocino, California

There's nothing undiscovered about Mendocino, but that doesn't diminish its charm. Situated on California's rocky North Coast, Mendocino looks like a New England village transplanted to the Pacific.

The town, founded in the logging days, struggled through the 1930s and was resuscitated by artists and writers. Today its Victorian ambiance attracts many weekenders who love the combination of rugged coast, attractive B&Bs, tony shops, art galleries and good restaurants. The Anderson wine valley, offering tastings, is only a few miles away.

Accommodations: The John Dougherty House, $95-$185, P.O. Box 817, Mendocino, CA 95460, (800) 486-2104 or (707) 937-5266.

Information: Mendocino Coast Chamber of Commerce, P.O. Box 1141, Fort Bragg, CA 95437, (800) 726-2780.

Lindsborg, Kansas

Red wooden Dala horses, hand-carved and hand-decorated, are seen everywhere, the symbol of this charming town of Swedish descendants.

Adapted from Old World toys, the horses reflect Lindsborg's rich heritage. Swedish immigrants arrived in the Smoky Valley of central Kansas in 1869, and Swedish themes dominate life in Lindsborg today. Scandinavian imports fill the shops. Red hearts and bright flowers adorn windows.

Hungry? Try a Swedish smorgasbord in one of the cafes. Festivals also bear the Swedish imprint. The Midsummer's Day Festival is held on the third Saturday of June, the three-day Svensk Byllningfest in October of odd-numbered years, the Lucia Fest on the second Saturday of December.

McPherson County Old Mill Museum displays the Swedish Pavilion from the 1904 World's Fair as well as exhibits relating to early settlers.

Accommodations: Swedish Country Inn, $50-$61, including breakfast, 112 W. Lincoln, Lindsborg, KS 67456, (800) 231-0266.

Information: Lindsborg Chamber of Commerce, Box 191, Lindsborg, KS 67456, (913) 227-3706.

Port Townsend, Washington

Set on the tip of the Olympic Peninsula at the entrance to Puget Sound, Port Townsend is full of colorful gingerbread Victorian homes, several of which are bed-and-breakfast inns. Along the waterfront, restored Victorian buildings house shops, restaurants and art galleries.

Wooden boats are a hallmark of Port Townsend. They're built on the waterfront and celebrated in an annual early September festival.

You can walk or bike past historic buildings or take a home tour or gallery walk. Coastal areas can be explored by sea kayak or tugboat tours. Fort Worden State Park and Old Fort Townsend State Park have well-marked hiking trails, and miles of shoreline beckon beachcombers.

Shops are in Downtown and Uptown, areas separated by steps. Northwest arts and crafts are a specialty in many shops. You'll also find antique stores, jewelers, gift and clothing stores — and more than a half-dozen independent bookshops.

Accommodations: Manresa Castle, P.O. Box 564, Port Townsend, WA 98368, (360) 385-5750, from $70 including continental breakfast. It has sweeping views of the city, water and mountains — and a terrific restaurant serving fresh local seafood.

Information: Port Townsend Chamber of Commerce, 2437 E. Sims Way, Port Townsend, WA 98368, (360) 385-2722.

Breckenridge, Colorado

This 134-year-old authentic Victorian mining town, 85 miles west of Denver, is loaded with Old West and 19th-century charm — including gas lamps, colorful frontier architecture and gingerbread-trimmed homes.

A ski resort in winter, Breckenridge offers plenty of activity (and lower lodging prices) for summer's visitors. You can play a round at the Jack Nicklaus-designed municipal golf course, ride the 40-mile paved bike path to Vail, pan for gold or go fly-fishing, horseback riding, river rafting or mountain biking. There are jeep tours to ghost towns, gallery walks, historical walking and mining tours and a summer concert series.

Sports gear is prominent on the shopping scene — stuff for everything from skiing to fly-fishing. You also will find gold nugget jewelry, crystal and mineral specimens, Southwestern art and Western clothing and accessories. Silverthorne, a half-hour drive, has more than 50 outlet stores.

Accommodations: River Mountain Lodge, P.O. Drawer 1190, Breckenridge, CO 80424, (800) 325-2342, from $49, offers accommodations ranging from studios to two-bedroom units. Beaver Run Resort, P.O. Box 2115, Breckenridge, CO 80424, (800) 525-2253, from $110.

Information: Breckenridge Resort Chamber, P.O. Box 1909, Breckenridge, CO 80424, (303) 453-6018 or (800) 221-1091 (reservations).

Mountain View, Arkansas

Nestled in the Ozarks, Mountain View is a nationally recognized center of folkways.

The Ozark Folk Center, a state park, re-creates the life and crafts of the pre-1920 Ozarks. Talented craftspeople fashion baskets, quilts, brooms and dulcimers. There also are blacksmiths, potters and woodcarvers. If you're interested in learning a particular craft, hands-on study programs can be arranged.

In the evening, the center's auditorium vibrates with the sounds and dances of traditional mountain music. Members of the audience are quick to jump on the stage for jig dancing and clogging. The show often moves from the stage to Mountain View's Courthouse Square.

The Ozark Folk Center's shop sells handmade items such as baskets, chairs, quilts, dolls, clothing, toys and preserves. There also are crafts and antique shops around Courthouse Square and along nearby byways.

You'll find excellent trout fishing and float trips on the White River, creek swimming and nature trails in the Ozark National Forest and underground explorations in Blanchard Springs Caverns.

Accommodations: The Lodge at the Ozark Folk Center, P.O. Box 500, Mountain View, AR 72560, (501) 269-3871 or (800) 264-3655, from $45.

Information: Mountain View Chamber of Commerce, P.O. Box 133, Mountain View, AR 72560, (501) 269-8068.

Hilton Head Island, South Carolina

With 21 golf courses, 300 tennis courts and 12 miles of beaches, Hilton Head Island excels in outdoor options.

Stables provide trail rides, and eight public marinas offer boat-rental facilities and sailing. Saltwater fishing is terrific, and there are inlets for canoeing and rowing. Kids love crabbing, flying kites, riding bikes on the hard sand beaches and watching bottle-nosed dolphins frolic offshore.

Nestled on the Intracoastal Waterway, the 42-square-mile island is a mix of 11 major planned resort and residential communities and semitropical, low-country geography — sea marshes, creeks, lagoons and heavily wooded forests.

Shoppers can browse The Mall at Shelter Cove and 35 other shopping areas. Finds include antiques, galleries, locally made jewelry, hammocks, hobby and sporting goods, handicrafts, clothing, gifts and specialty shops. There are two outlet centers on the island and another is nearby.

Accommodations: Although there are several budget-priced chain motels in Hilton Head, villa rentals, starting at $450 per week, can be a fine value — especially for families. Shoreline Rental Co., P.O. Box 6275, Hilton Head, SC 29938, (800) 334-5012, is one of many villa rental agencies on the island.

Information: Hilton Head Island Chamber of Commerce, P.O. Box 5647, Hilton Head Island, SC 29938, (803) 785-3673.

Berea, Kentucky

Berea, at the edge of the bluegrass region and the foot of the Cumberland Mountains, is widely known for its preservation of Appalachia's culture and crafts.

The heart of the town is Berea College, whose 1,500 students are chosen on the basis of academic ability and financial need. None pays tuition; all work at least 10 hours a week.

Local shops and studios feature high-quality work from quilters, basket weavers, woodworkers, jewelers and candle and furniture makers. Most of the shops are concentrated on College Square, including the Log House Sales Room, where student-made items are sold, and Old Town Berea, where shops occupy restored buildings.

The Appalachian Museum focuses on the culture of the Southern mountains in the 19th and 20th centuries. There's a replica of Daniel Boone's fort at Fort Boonesborough State Park. Shaker Village at Pleasant Hill is a restored 19th-century community settled by the Shakers, a religious group. Renfro Valley, a historic country music center, offers live entertainment.

Accommodations: Boone Tavern Hotel, C.P.O. 2345, Berea, Ky 40404, (800) 366-9358, from $63, is operated by Berea College students. Furniture in the 59 guest rooms is made in the college workshop.

Information: Berea Tourism Commission, P.O. Box 556, Berea, KY 40403, (606) 986-2540 or (800) 598-5263.

Millwood, Virginia

This hamlet is set in the heart of Northern Virginia's beautiful, rolling hunt country.

Fine antiquing is the draw here — five shops plus a 40-year-old general store in Millwood, and more in nearby villages such as Delaplane and Aldie. You'll find more antique shops, galleries and everything for the horse and hunt not far away in Middleburg.

Local wineries give tours and tastings, and several ranches offer horseback riding. Sky Meadows State Park is great for picnicking and hiking. Be sure to visit Long Branch, an elegant restored 18th-century manor house with exquisite antiques.

The Burwell-Morgan Mill in Millwood, built in 1782, still grinds wheat and corn for sale. A bike trail begins there.

Accommodations: The River House, Route 1, Box 135, Boyce, VA 22620, (540) 837-1476. Built in 1780, this B&B offers five guest rooms, each with private bath and fireplace, starting at $80. Price includes a four-course brunch.

Information: Clarke County Chamber of Commerce, P.O. Box 365, Berryville, VA 22611, (703) 955-4200.

Adamstown, Pennsylvania

Known as the "Antiques Capital of the United States," Adamstown has one of the largest concentrations of antiques in the nation. More than 3,000 dealers congregate here, and in nearby Denver, on Sundays. An increasing number of dealers — now up to about half on any given day — also are open at other times of the week.

If antiques haven't gobbled up your shopping budget, it's an easy drive to the dozens of outlets at Lancaster and Reading. Adamstown is in the heart of Pennsylvania Dutch Country, where Amish and Mennonite communities offer distinctive crafts.

There are several golf courses in the area, and Stoudt Brewing Co., a micro-brewery, is worth a visit.

Accommodations: Adamstown Inn, 62 W. Main St., Adamstown, PA 19501-0938, (800) 594-4808, from $65, is a Victorian B&B inn.

Information: Pennsylvania Dutch Convention & Visitors Bureau, 501 Greenfield Road, Lancaster, PA 17601, (800) 735-2629, extension 2405.

Mystic, Connecticut

Located in southeastern Connecticut, Mystic was a major shipbuilding center for the whaling and fishing industries in the 18th century.

The Mystic Seaport Museum preserves that heritage. At this indoor and outdoor museum you can board 19th-century sailing vessels and see the historic homes and trades of a maritime village.

Highlights at the Mystic Maritime Aquarium are beluga whales, Atlantic bottle-nosed dolphins, seals and sea lions. You also can sail on a windjammer, board a fishing charter or tour the town's historic homes.

Mystic has everything that draws shoppers to New England — antiques, crafts and outlet stores. The Mystic River Antiques Center draws 30 dealers, and 25 shops can be found at Mystic Factory Outlets.

At Olde Mistick Village, shops cluster around a village green in a re-created 18th-century community. The Mystic Seaport Museum has several shops: a bookstore, a gift shop, a bakery and a gallery and print shop.

Accommodations: Whaler's Inn and Motor Court, 20 E. Main, Mystic, CT 06355 (800) 243-2588, from $95, has been sheltering travelers since the Civil War.

Information: Mystic Chamber of Commerce, P.O. Box 143, Mystic, CT 06355, (203) 572-9578.

Woodstock, Vermont

Woodstock, VT, is the epitome of the small New England town. Federal-style buildings frame the neat-as-a-pin town green, where daily walking tours and events are posted on the Town Crier Chalk Board.

There are wonderful shops to explore, all within a few blocks. Reading enthusiasts will enjoy the Yankee Bookshop. North Wind Artisans' Gallery has a delightful cache of pottery, glassware, weavings and handmade jewelry. Gallery on the Green features watercolor prints, photographs and acrylic paintings.

At Billings Farm and Museum, you can taste farm life circa 1890, sampling hand-churned butter, watching hand-milking and chair-caning or riding a hay wagon towed by enormous Belgian draft horses.

The concentration of historic inns in Woodstock is unmatched. On the square is Woodstock Inn & Resort, irresistible after an $8 million renovation. It was once owned by Laurance Rockefeller, the primary force behind the town's restoration.

Accommodations: Woodstock Inn & Resort, $145-$279, 14 The Green, Woodstock, VT 05091, (800) 448-7900. Canterbury House, $85-$145, 43 Pleasant St., Woodstock, VT 05091, (802) 457-3077.

Information: Woodstock Chamber of Commerce, P.O. Box 486, Woodstock, VT 05091, (802) 457-3555.

Berkeley Springs, West Virginia

A fountainhead of warm mineral waters that evolved as the nation's first health spa is at the heart of the charming mountain village of Berkeley Springs in West Virginia's eastern panhandle.

Just 100 miles northwest of the Washington/Baltimore metroplex, it has been an ideal weekend retreat since 1776 when Lord Fairfax and the Colony of Virginia conveyed the springs and some acres around it to George Washington and a prominent group of investors.

Berkeley Springs became something of a summer White House, regularly visited by presidents Madison, Van Buren, Fillmore and Polk. Today you still can enjoy a variety of treatments for a nominal fee. The town also is chock-a-block with antique stores, boutiques, restaurants and inns.

Accommodations: Coolfront Resort, $77-$124 per person, including breakfast and dinner, 1777 Cold Run Valley Road, Berkeley Springs, WV 25411, (304) 258-4500.

Information: Travel Berkeley Springs, 304 Fairfax St., Berkeley Springs, WV 25411, (800) 447-8797.

Las Vegas, New Mexico

No, this is not the neon-happy Las Vegas whose every room is filled with chattering slot machines. This Las Vegas is in New Mexico, 67 miles east of Santa Fe and light years from Nevada's gambling mecca.

It's a place where you still can get a fountain soda in the drugstore, but make no mistake: Las Vegas may be quiet but it has a lot going for it.

Few cities have seen as much history as this town of 15,000 that stands where the Rockies end and the Great Plains begin. No other U.S. city has as many buildings on the National Register of Historic Places (more than 900).

Every fortune-seeker, settler and wagon that came west on the Santa Fe Trail passed through Las Vegas. Now, tourists enjoy the town's Old West ambiance, and movie-makers have used the unspoiled town as a backdrop for many films, including "Easy Rider" and "Red Dawn."

You can stroll around the plaza and think you're back in the bad old days when miscreants were hanged there regularly. A few steps away is the old Santa Fe Trail.

Accommodations: The beautifully restored Plaza Hotel, 230 Old Town Plaza, Las Vegas, NM 87701, (505) 425-3591, has rooms for $65 plus tax.

Information: Las Vegas Chamber of Commerce, P.O. Box 128, Las Vegas, NM 87701, (505) 425-8631 or (800) 832-5947.

Bandon, Oregon

This is a place for contemplation. Often hooded by fog, this scenic, rugged coast has a brooding mien. Dark, jagged rocks called stacks poke out of the beach and gulls flutter over the froth of chilly water. Bundled-up walkers make footprints in the glistening sand as they search for shells and stones, watch for sea birds and sea life, and explore the inner self.

Yet isolation here is by choice. The coastal towns, accustomed to millions of visitors each year, offer warm companionship and wonderful seafood. During the busy summer, festivals, theater and other events brighten the days.

Quite special is the $24 million Oregon Coast Aquarium, with four indoor galleries and 2.5 acres of outside pools, caves, cliffs and bluffs that shelter coastal sea and bird life.

Accommodations: In summer, expect to pay $65-$95 for a room at the Gorman Motel, 1110 SW 11th St., Bandon, OR 97411, (503) 347-4430, or from $40 at the

Sunset Motel, P.O. Box 373, Bandon, OR 97411, (503) 347-2453.

Information: Oregon Tourism Commission, 775 Summer St., Salem, OR 97310, (800) 547-7842 or (503) 986-0000.

Hot Springs, Arkansas

Historians say that in 1541, Hernando DeSoto and his conquistadors were the first Europeans to dip their toes in a thermal spring nestled in the Ouachita Mountains of what today is west-central Arkansas.

Since that time, the city of Hot Springs has become renowned as a healing spa and a graceful resort. It remains a popular and convenient weekend getaway destination for residents of mid-America's major cities.

The city's foremost attraction is Bathhouse Row with its eight beautifully preserved turn-of-the-century spas — now the centerpiece of Hot Springs National Park, the nation's only urban national park. Only the historic Buckstaff remains open as a working bathhouse, but you'll find complete spa facilities at several leading hotels, including the venerable Arlington Resort Hotel, the Park Hilton and the Majestic Resort.

Art has come to rival the city's famed water as a drawing card; more than 25 galleries line the Central Avenue Historic District. As the boyhood home of President Bill Clinton, Hot Springs offers a tour map pointing out young Clinton's residences, schools and favorite hangouts.

Accommodations: Best Western Sands Motel, $39-$69, 1525 Central Ave., Hot Springs National Park, AR 71901, (501) 624-1258.

Information: Hot Springs Convention and Visitors Bureau, 134 Convention Blvd., Hot Springs, AR 71901, (800) 772-2489.

Manchester, Vermont

Oh, give me a home where the beefalo roam. In Wyoming? No, try Manchester, VT, a quintessential New England town that offers (in addition to beefalo) performing arts festivals, antiques and crafts shops galore and a string of designer outlets.

To visit the beefalo — cattle bred with bison to yield low-fat beef — head three miles out of town to Birch Hill Inn. The inn is tucked in meadows that are surrounded by the Green Mountains. Antique-furnished rooms overlook mountains, a trout-stocked fishing pond (they'll cook what you catch) and grassy pastures where the beefalo roam and the deer (sorry, no antelope) play.

Whether you follow trails to the mountains or take a snooze on the back porch, you'll seldom hear a discouraging word around this place. Unless it's from the beefalo, whom you'll undoubtedly meet for dinner.

Accommodations: Barnstead Innstead, a restored 1830s New England barn with heated pool in Manchester Village, from $65, Box 988, Manchester Center, VT 05255, (802) 362-1619 or (800) 331-1619.

Information: Manchester Chamber of Commerce, P.O. Box 928, Manchester Center, VT 05255, (802) 362-2100.

Lumberville, Pennsylvania

This historic village in Bucks County on the banks of the Delaware River may sound like the sticks, but it's a sophisticated spot. City slickers come to while away their weekends on walks along country roads where antiques shops and country inns peek from the trees.

There's nothing "hicksville" about the 1740 House, either. A restored complex of frame barns and outbuildings, its elegant rooms with period furnishings have terraces overlooking the river.

From the inn, guests can hike, fish, swim or tube down the tranquil river, or cross on a nearby footbridge to the New Jersey side, where there's a historic mill to tour.

Other attractions include the historic town of New Hope, a former art colony where tourists ply canals on mule-drawn barges, browse for antiques or local crafts, and enjoy fine dining and top theater productions at the Bucks County Playhouse, a restored riverfront mill.

Down River Road a stretch is Washington's Crossing State Park (you'll have to return in winter for the live re-enactment) and Peddlers Village, an antiquer's heaven.

You can have a wonderful time going nowhere on pretty back roads that wander aimlessly over hill and dale and cross the river on picturesque toll bridges that still cost a quarter.

Last one out of Lumberville: Turn out the lights.

Accommodations: 1740 House, from $75 including full breakfast, River Road, Lumberville, PA 18933, (215) 297-5661. No children under 12 on weekends. Alternate option: Wedgewood Inn, an 1870 Victorian home in New Hope that's on the National Register of Historic Places, from $95, 111 W. Bridge St., New Hope, PA 18938, (215) 862-2570.

Information: New Hope Chamber of Commerce, P.O. Box 633, New Hope, PA 18938, (215) 862-5880 for recorded information or (215) 862-5030.

Watch Hill, Rhode Island

Watch Hill is an enclave of turn-of-the-century Victorian homes on a hilly peninsula that overlooks peaceful Little Narragansett Bay on one side and the Atlantic Ocean on the other. It's the summer home of wealthy city folk, who often can be observed in tennis whites on their manicured lawns.

But this is old Yankee money. In other words, it's not a showy place. The town has the quiet charm of a 19th-century resort. In fact, the most exciting thing to do is to order an ice cream soda in the Olympia Tea Room on Main Street or maybe browse for some beach reading at the Book and Tackle Shop.

On the other side of Main Street, the harbor is always busy with sailboats, and watching the sun set is a major pastime. Take the kids down to the end of the block, where they can ride the oldest carrousel in the country. Watch Hill has a fine beach, and the glitzy mansions at Newport are less than an hour away.

On second thought, it might be more relaxing to have another ice cream cone and watch the sun set.

Accommodations: Shelter Harbor Inn is a converted farmhouse with rates of $92 and up, including full breakfast, 10 Wagner Road, Westerly, RI 02891, (401) 322-8883 or (800) 468-8883.

Information: Greater Westerly Area Chamber of Commerce, 74 Post Road, Westerly, RI 02891, (401) 596-7761 or (800) 732-7636.

Nyack, New York

It's hard to believe that one of the great little Victorian towns of America is just 25 miles from New York City. But Nyack has all the charm of a small town.

Perched on the bank of the Hudson River, antiques and crafts shops abound. The town's best-known native son, the painter Edward Hopper, lived at 82 N. Broadway, now an art gallery. Nyack is an inviting town, ideally made for strolling tree-lined streets past Victorian homes with porches and gables.

Nyack also is well-positioned for excursions to area historic homes like the Van Cortlandt manor in Croton-on-Hudson and to Sunnyside in Tarrytown, the home of Washington Irving.

Accommodations: Best Western Nyack, from $69, 26 Route 59, Nyack, NY 10960, (914) 358-8100 or (800) 528-1234.

Information: Nyack Chamber of Commerce, P.O. Box 677, Nyack, NY 10960, (914) 353-2221.

Columbus, Indiana

Back in the 1930s, this little town on the prairie launched an ambitious plan to commission private and public buildings from world-renowned architects. The results have the town fathers proclaiming Columbus as "the architectural showplace of America."

There are buildings by such masters as Eliel and Eero Saarinen, Kevin Roche, John Dinkaloo, Harry Weese, I.M. Pei and Richard Meier. In fact, there are more than 50 outstanding works of architecture in the town, and a guided tour is a must.

Columbus is just 40 miles south of Indianapolis, and it's also a reasonable drive to Cincinnati.

Accommodations: The Columbus Inn, from $80, including full breakfast, is a carefully restored Romanesque Revival building, 445 Fifth St., Columbus, IN 47202, (812) 378-4289.

Information: Columbus Visitors Center, 506 Fifth St., Columbus, IN 47201, (812) 372-1954.

Taos, New Mexico

Nestled in the foothills of the Sangre de Cristo mountains, this picturesque town has been an art colony for well over a century. There are loads of art galleries for browsers and a range of fascinating museums that are astonishing for such a small town.

Visit the Kit Carson Home, where Carson lived for 24 years. The famous gunslinger is buried nearby. The D.H. Lawrence Ranch is where the famed British novelist lived and was later buried. And be sure to visit the Taos Pueblo, the cultural capital of the Pueblo Nation, with its 13th-century adobe terraces.

If you're heading to Santa Fe, some 70 miles southwest of Taos, take the "High Road to Taos" along Routes 3 and 76, which winds through scenic villages like Chimayo.

Accommodations: Sagebrush Inn, from $70, includes rooms where Georgia O'Keeffe once painted, P.O. Box 557, Taos, NM 87571, (800) 428-3626 or, in New Mexico, (505) 758-2254.

Information: Taos County Chamber of Commerce, P.O. Drawer I, Taos, NM 87571, (800) 732-TAOS.

Langley, Washington

Langley is just two blocks long, a true small town on the southeastern shore of Whidbey Island, just 30 miles north of Seattle in Puget Sound. There are spectacular mountain and water views, and if you're lucky, you might see pods of Orcas, the legendary killer whales.

The second-longest island in the continental United States at 60 miles, Whidbey is readily accessible by bridge or ferry. The island boasts public beaches and state parks, 250 campsites and, as the saying goes, more cows than residents.

Many residents in Langley make and sell their arts and crafts, from hand-blown glass to textiles, jewelry and pottery.

Accommodations: Country Cottage of Langley is a charming 1927 cottage with rates from $80, including full breakfast, 215 Sixth St., Langley, WA 98260, (360) 221-8709.

Information: Langley Chamber of Commerce, P.O. Box 403, Langley, WA 98260, (360) 321-6765.

Medora, North Dakota

For such a tiny town, Medora packs an impressive past. It's best-known for two of the biggest characters of the Badlands: the Marquis de Mores and Teddy Roosevelt.

The marquis was a wealthy Frenchman who established the town, naming it for his New York-born wife. He had ambitious plans to slaughter cattle and ship them in refrigerated railroad cars — which then was a revolutionary idea. The ambitious marquis didn't succeed with his plans but his mansion, a 26-room structure filled with French furnishings, can be visited today.

Teddy Roosevelt came to the Badlands in 1883 to hunt buffalo and other big game and eventually established a ranch here. It was in Medora that he came across the Rough Riders Hotel, which provided him with the name of his famed regiment in the Spanish-American War. The town is now the gateway to the 70,000-acre Theodore Roosevelt National Park.

Accommodations: Rough Riders Hotel, from $70, is a restored historic hotel, Box 198, Medora, ND 58645, (701) 623-4433 or (800) MEDORA1.

Information: Theodore Roosevelt National Park, P.O. Box 7, Medora, ND 58645, (701) 623-4466.

Mackinac Island, Michigan

Historic Mackinac Island is a speck of land, 2 miles by 3 miles, afloat on Lake Huron off Michigan's northern wooded coastline. To get there, take the ferry, and don't worry about renting a car. None is allowed on the island, making it a delightful time warp. Savor the slower pace as you walk, bicycle or take a horse-drawn "taxi" around idyllic Mackinac Island.

Colorful shops and famous fudge kitchens line the town's main street. Local history is rich with the imprint of American Indians, French fur trappers and British troops. Fort Mackinac was established on the island to protect against Indian raiders. Don't miss the historic Grand Hotel, on a hill outside the town. It's known for its long front porch lined with rocking chairs facing a great view of the straits.

Pack a picnic lunch and bike around the island. The road is level most of the way and provides good views.

Accommodations: Grand Hotel, $170-$275 per person, including breakfast and a five-course dinner, 2177 Commons Parkway, Okemos, MI 48864, (800) 334-7263 or (906) 847-3331. Inn on Mackinac, from $74, including breakfast, P.O. Box 7706, Ann Arbor, MI 48107, (800) 462-2546.

Information: Michigan Travel Bureau, Department of Commerce, P.O. Box 30226, Lansing, MI 48909, (517) 373-0670 or (800) 543-2937.

North Conway, New Hampshire

Glorious mountain scenery, outdoor recreation, uniq[ue]
summer theater are only some of the assets that bring v[isitors to]
Mount Washington Valley.

Bargain-hunters flock to North Conway to browse thr[ough]
factory outlet stores, where designer sportswear, jewelr[y and]
crystal are discounted deeply. In addition, the League of Ne[w]
has a shop in North Conway, and on Saturdays during summer [a]
market in Conway. Shoppers get an added bonus in New Hampshire — they [don't have]
to pay any sales tax.

Kids enjoy visiting Storyland, Six Gun City and Santa's Village in nearby towns;
families can go hiking, canoeing, boating or fishing in the White Mountains.

Accommodations: Junge's Motel, from $36, 1858 White Mountain Highway,
North Conway, NH 03860, (603) 356-2886.

Information: Mount Washington Valley Visitors Bureau, P.O. Box 2300, North
Conway, NH 03860, (603) 356-3171 or (800) 367-3364.

Cooperstown, New York

Most famous for its National Baseball Hall of Fame, Cooperstown is also called the
Village of Museums. Well worth a stop in this central New York state town are the
Farmers Museum and Village Crossroads, Fenimore House (with one of the nation's
best folk art collections as well as memorabilia of novelist James Fenimore Cooper), Old
Middlefield Schoolhouse Museum, Petrified Creatures Museum and the Cooperstown
Art Association Gallery.

Sports fans will want to include the National Soccer Hall of Fame in nearby Oneonta.
Enjoy a performance of the Glimmerglass Opera (in English) in Cooperstown, tour
Lake Otsego by boat and round out your vacation with a visit to the wilderness areas
of nearby Catskill State Park.

Accommodations: Knott's Motel, about 15 miles south on Route 28, near Oneonta,
from $59, Route 28, Box 190, RD1, Oneonta, NY 13820, (607) 432-5948.

Information: Otsego County Tourism Bureau, 12 Carbon St., Oneonta, NY 13820,
(800) 843-3394.

Johnson City, Tennessee

Johnson City is in the heart of northeast Tennessee, the oldest part of the state and
an area brimming with early American history.

A long list of historic sites — including homes of Davy Crockett and the 17th U.S.
president, Andrew Johnson — can be visited in Johnson City and the nearby towns of
Kingsport, Elizabethton, Greeneville and Jonesboro.

Summers are lively with fairs, music, festivals and historic re-enactments.

Johnson City's also a scenic beauty, close to the Appalachian Trail. In late June the
top of nearby Roan Mountain is ablaze with 600 acres of rhododendron. Camping,
hiking, fishing and white-water rafting are favorite activities.

Accommodations: Days Inn, in Johnson City, from $40, 2312 Browns Mill Road,
Johnson City, TN 37601, (615) 282-2211.

Information: Convention & Visitors Bureau, P.O. Box 180, Johnson City, TN
37605, (615) 926-2141 or (800) 852-3392.

Michigan

...ct a town named Holland to be Dutch and this one certainly is — and proud
...located in the lower part of the state, near dune-rimmed Lake Michigan, and
...enter of Dutch culture in the United States.
...tch Village, Windmill Island and the Netherlands Museum all celebrate the ethnic
...kground of many of the town's residents. Restaurants also entice visitors to sample
...utch delicacies. Hundreds of thousands of tulips appear on every street and lawn each
spring for Holland's Tulip Festival, one of the largest annual celebrations in the nation.

The Gerald Ford Museum in nearby Grand Rapids, the arts colony of Saugatuck and
the great water playground of Lake Michigan add to the area vacation possibilities. At
Grand Haven in summer, nightly musical concerts are presented on the waterfront.
The music is electronically synchronized with lights and water at what is called the
"world's largest musical fountain."

Accommodations: Blue Mill Inn, in Holland, from $40, 409 U.S. 31, Holland, MI
49423, (616) 392-7073.

Information: Holland Area Chamber of Commerce, 272 E. Eighth St., Holland, MI
49423, (616) 392-2389.

New Braunfels, Texas

German immigrants settled this town in 1845, and the influence of the "old country"
is still strong — in foods, traditions and culture.

Tubing on a spring-fed river in the city's outstanding Landa Park, fishing and boating
in nearby Canyon Lake and rafting on the Guadalupe River are major summertime
attractions. Families enjoy Schlitterbahn Water Park's chutes from a German castle
and Landa Park's miniature train. Tour a winery and visit museums that chronicle early
Texas pioneer days and showcase handmade furniture. Shop for bargains at a large mall
of factory outlet stores.

Several scenic drives lead from town into the Texas Hill Country. Attractions nearby
include Natural Bridge Caverns, a 200-acre drive-through wildlife ranch and the city
life of nearby San Antonio.

Accommodations: Hotel Faust, New Braunfels, from $39, 240 S. Seguin, New
Braunfels, TX 78130, (210) 625-7791.

Information: Chamber of Commerce, P.O. Box 311417, New Braunfels, TX 78131,
(210) 625-2385 or (800) 572-2626.

Cripple Creek, Colorado

Not much more than a ghost town today, Cripple Creek was once a glittering gold
mining center, with five opera houses providing entertainment for its 25,000 residents.

Despite its small size, Cripple Creek provides summer visitors an excellent getaway,
high in the mountains just west of Colorado Springs.

During the summer, you can enjoy watching the nation's oldest melodrama
productions, on the stage of the historic Imperial Hotel. Relive the mining era at the
exceptionally interesting Cripple Creek District Museum, and ride a steam train on a
narrow-gauge railroad through an area of abandoned mines. Visit the Old Homestead,
formerly a notorious brothel.

For a change of pace, drive to nearby Colorado Springs to tour the U.S. Air Force
Academy, the U.S. Olympic Training Center, the Garden of the Gods and other
attractions.

Accommodations: Imperial Hotel, built in 1896, $40, P.O. Box 869, Cripple Creek, CO 80813, (719) 689-2713.

Information: Chamber of Commerce, P.O. Box 650, Cripple Creek, CO 80813, (719) 689-2169 or (800) 526-8777.

Custer, South Dakota

Few small towns in the nation can boast so many natural and scenic attractions in the immediate vicinity as Custer.

Black Hills National Forest has more than a million acres of woods, mountains, lakes and streams. Wind Cave National Park, the national monuments of Mount Rushmore and Jewel Cave, and the ambitious mountain-carving work in progress called Crazy Horse Memorial, are all larger-than-life wonders.

Choose from a wide variety of summer entertainment: country music performances in Custer, fife and drum concerts in Hill City, summer theater in Custer State Park, gambling in Deadwood, the Black Hills Passion Play in Spearfish, rodeo in Rapid City. For a special thrill, book a helicopter ride over Mount Rushmore and the Black Hills, out of Keystone.

Accommodations: Bavarian Inn, on U.S. 16, near Custer, from $38, P.O. Box 152, Custer, SD 57730, (605) 673-2802 or (800) 657-4312.

Information: Black Hills, Badlands & Lakes Association, 900 Jackson Blvd., Rapid City, SD 57702, (605) 341-1462.

Port Angeles, Washington

Port Angeles, at the top of Washington's Olympic peninsula, is headquarters of the Olympic National Park, a ruggedly beautiful region that's on UNESCO's list of World Heritage Sites.

The park's 1,400 square miles, home to countless birds and animals, contain 60 glaciers, three rain forests and 57 miles of wild coastline. Waterfalls rush down from snowcapped mountains and alpine meadows to join the waters of the Pacific, where rocky monoliths stand guard offshore.

Summer visitors hike, fish and take part in naturalist programs and guided walks. U.S. 101 offers a scenic drive of the entire peninsula, and a ferry across the Juan de Fuca Strait goes to the Canadian city of Victoria, British Columbia.

Accommodations: Lake Crescent Lodge, west of Port Angeles, from $72, 416 Lake Crescent Road, Port Angeles, WA 98363, (360) 928-3211.

Information: Olympic National Park Headquarters, 600 E. Park Ave., Port Angeles, WA 98362, (360) 452-4501.

Middlebury, Vermont

A charming college town, Middlebury is within a day's drive of everything the small and beautiful Green Mountain State has to offer. It's a perfect spot for blending historic and scenic excursions.

The town was settled in 1761 and has a traditional New England village green, once the center of activities. Don't miss the classic Middlebury Inn, dating to 1827, on the green, and the nearby Sheldon Museum with its extensive collection of Vermont memorabilia.

A short drive and ferryboat ride away in New York is Fort Ticonderoga, scene of a victorious raid against the British by the Green Mountain Boys during the Revolutionary War. The Shelburne Museum, to the north in Shelburne, is a 42-acre outdoor museum with collections of historic objects and folk art housed in 37 buildings. Nearby Lake Champlain and the Green Mountain National Forest provide ample outdoors fun.

Accommodations: Blue Spruce Motel, $50-$65, R.D. 3, Box 376, Middlebury, VT 05753, (802) 388-4091. Swift House Inn, a historic home, $90 and up, including continental breakfast, 25 Stewart Lane, Middlebury, VT 05753, (802) 388-9925.

Information: Information Center, 2 Court St., Middlebury, VT 05753, (802) 388-7951 or (800) 733-8376.

Abingdon, Virginia

Cobblestone streets, good restaurants, shopping for local handicrafts and the nation's longest-running professional repertory theater are among the attractions of this small town in the highlands of southwestern Virginia. The Barter Theater got its start during the Depression, an era when some members of the audience traded produce for admission tickets.

Camping, mountain climbing, horseback riding and pack trips with llamas (they carry all the gear!) are popular activities. Live bluegrass and traditional mountain music are presented every Saturday night at the Carter Family Memorial Music Center in nearby Hiltons.

Accommodations: Comfort Inn, $51, including continental breakfast, Interstate 81, Exit 7, Abingdon, VA 24210, (540) 676-2222. The historic Martha Washington Inn, $135 and up, 150 W. Main St., Abingdon, VA 24210, (540) 628-3161.

Information: Abingdon Visitor Center, 335 Cummings St., Abingdon, VA 24210, (540) 676-2282 or (800) 435-3440.

Florence, Alabama

Florence, on the Tennessee River in northwestern Alabama, is the largest town in a region known as "The Shoals." Joe Wheeler State Park and lakes created by dams on the Tennessee River offer superb outdoor recreation.

The largest American Indian mound in the Tennessee Valley is in Florence. An annual music festival, featuring jazz, blues and gospel, honors W.C. Handy, "father of the blues," who was born here. His birthplace can be visited.

Ivy Green, birthplace and childhood home of Helen Keller, is nearby in Tuscumbia and is open to the public year-round. The play about her childhood, "The Miracle Worker," is performed here each summer. The Alabama Music Hall of Fame, also in Tuscumbia, has a fully equipped state-of-the-art recording studio and exhibits relating to the achievements of the state's musicians.

Accommodations: Best Western Executive Inn in Florence, $54, 504 S. Court St., Florence, AL 35630, (800) 248-5336 or (205) 766-2331. Joe Wheeler State Resort Lodge, from $66, P.O. Drawer K, Rogersville, AL 35652, (800) 544-5639.

Information: Chamber of Commerce of the Shoals, 104 S. Pine St., Florence, AL 35630, (205) 764-4661.

Havana, Florida

Whether you seek antiques or "junque," this piece of the past provides. A railroad town in the Florida Panhandle that chugged into life shortly after the turn of the century, Havana rode the ups and downs of tobacco economics for more than 50 years before finally fading into back-road obscurity.

Today Havana bustles anew as a major center for antiques and arts in America's Southeast. Best of all, this is a "park your car and walk everywhere" kind of place, with more than two dozen vintage stores and warehouses restored to fresh life. Most shops are open Wednesday through Sunday.

Accommodations: Gavers Bed & Breakfast, $65-$75, 301 E. 6th Ave., Havana, FL 32333, (904) 539-5611.

Information: Gadsden County Chamber of Commerce, P.O. Box 389, Quincy, FL 32353, (800) 627-9231 or (904) 627-9231.

Marquette, Michigan

Michigan's wild and beautiful Upper Peninsula beckons those seeking a nature-oriented escape, and Marquette is a good base for exploring this scenic area of the Great Lakes.

Buy meat-filled turnovers at a local bakery and have a picnic on the beach, where you can watch huge freighters carrying loads of iron ore across Lake Superior. Cruise on the lake and hike in the 328-acre Presque Isle Park or nearby countryside. Follow State Route 28 east for a scenic drive to the Hiawatha National Forest and Pictured Rocks National Lakeshore, which you can visit by boat from Munising. In the evenings, sample local restaurants, where the specialty is fresh Lake Superior whitefish.

The Marquette County Historical Society Museum and the Maritime Museum offer insights into the area's heritage. The Michigan Iron Industry Museum in nearby Negaunee and the National Ski Hall of Fame and Museum in Ishpeming also are worth a visit.

Accommodations: Tiroler Hof in Marquette, $50, 150 Carp River Hill, Marquette, MI 49855, (906) 226-7516.

Information: Upper Peninsula Travel & Recreation Association, P.O. Box 400, Iron Mountain, MI 49801, (906) 774-5480 or (800) 562-7134.

Nashville, Indiana

An arts center in the heart of scenic Brown County, Nashville boasts galleries, antiques shops and several good restaurants featuring country-style cooking. Log cabins around the village and covered bridges in the countryside add to the charm and photographic appeal of the area, south of Indianapolis.

Brown County State Park, the largest of Indiana's state parks, includes two lakes, many miles of hiking trails and drives through wooded hills, an observation tower and lots of native wildlife. In addition to this 16,000-acre park, nearby Yellowwood State Forest and Hoosier National Forest offer a variety of opportunities for outdoor recreation.

Country music jamborees and plays at the Brown County Playhouse are presented on summer evenings.

Accommodations: Salt Creek Inn, $55-$71, 551 E. State Road 46, Nashville, IN 47448, (812) 988-1149.

Information: Brown County Convention and Visitors Bureau, Box 840, Nashville, IN 47448, (800) 753-3255 or (812) 988-7303.

Cody, Wyoming

Summers are action-packed in Cody, in northwest Wyoming near Yellowstone

National Park. You can tour Western museums, see a rodeo with real cowboys, ride the range, fish, hike, raft rivers and explore Yellowstone.

The town, founded by Buffalo Bill Cody, celebrates its Western heritage with a Frontier Festival and an American Indian powwow in June and rodeo performances every night from early June to late August.

The Buffalo Bill Historical Center is a complex of four first-class museums: Whitney Gallery of Western Art, Plains Indian Museum, Buffalo Bill Museum (housing personal memorabilia of Cody) and Cody Firearms Museum. Also, many artists live in the area, and some have studios open to the public. Old Trail Town and Museum of the Old West is a collection of pioneer cabins from the area.

Accommodations: Big Bear Motel, from $49, P.O. Box 2015, Cody, WY 82414, (800) 325- 7163 or (307) 587-3117.

Information: Cody Visitors and Convention Council, P.O. Box 2777, Cody, WY 82414, (307) 587-2297.

Ruidoso, New Mexico

Each summer visitors flock to the Sierra Blanca Mountains of southern New Mexico to fish in clear lakes and streams, enjoy cool breezes and explore the historic area and crafts shops. Mon Jeau Lookout in Lincoln National Forest gives a magnificent view of the surrounding woods and mountains.

Western history is evident in all directions — in the 19th-century Fort Stanton, the ghost town of White Oaks, Billy the Kid's old hangout in Lincoln and more. Summer also brings horse racing at Ruidoso Downs.

The small town is a popular regional resort, particularly in summer; so reservations are advised.

Accommodations: Cree Manor Inn, from $65 ($420 per week), P.O. Box 3559, Ruidoso, NM 88345, (505) 257-4058.

Information: Ruidoso Chamber of Commerce, P.O. Box 698, Ruidoso, NM 88345, (505) 257-7395 or (800) 253-2255.

New Glarus, Wisconsin

It's easy to think you're in Europe when you arrive in New Glarus, in southern Wisconsin. It's Swiss, and neighboring towns celebrate English and Norwegian heritage.

Immigrants from Switzerland settled New Glarus in 1845 and established a dairy and cheesemaking industry. Early public buildings and furnishings have been preserved in the Swiss Historical Village, and the town hosts two Swiss celebrations each summer.

In Mineral Point, the Pendarvis Cornish Restoration provides a look at the log and limestone homes built by miners from Cornwall, England. And at Mount Horeb, Little Norway has a museum of Norse antiques and a pioneer farmstead from 1856.

Also in the area are the Cave of the Mounds, a registered National Natural Landmark in Blue Mounds, and Frank Lloyd Wright's home and school, Taliesin, near Spring Green.

Each summer Platteville has a Shakespeare Festival.

Accommodations: Chalet Land-haus in New Glarus, $64, P.O. Box 878, New Glarus, WI 53574, (608) 527-5234.

Information: Wisconsin Department of Tourism Development, P.O. Box 7606, Madison, WI 53707, (608) 266-2161 or (800) 372-2737.

Branson, Missouri

If your idea of a good small-town vacation is a quiet rural hideaway, Branson is not your best option. Although this town in the Missouri Ozarks has fewer than 4,000 residents, it's rapidly becoming a music center to rival Nashville and Las Vegas. Some 30 theaters feature live entertainment — country music, for the most part.

But there is plenty of variety away from the main strip. There are caves to explore, three large lakes surrounded by wooded hills, two theme parks, lots of reasonably priced family restaurants and individually owned craft shops.

A popular outdoor pageant, "Shepherd of the Hills," depicts life in the Ozarks at the turn of the century. It is performed nightly from late April to mid-December.

Accommodations: Gages Long Creek Lodge (also campground and marina), from $37.50, 915 Long Creek Road, Ridgedale, MO 65739, (417) 334-1413.

Information: Branson/Lakes Area Chamber of Commerce, Box 1897, Branson, MO 65615, (417) 334-4138.

Key West, Florida

Forever flamboyant, Key West is unlike any other city in America, and no wonder. Situated more than 100 miles down a chain of sandy keys, it's closer to Havana than to Miami.

To all appearances, it's a tropical island. Palm trees rustle like dry paper in the warm breeze. Narrow streets lined with picket fences and lovely old frame houses boast back yards lush with hibiscus, frangipani and oleander. Its gin-clear harbors hum with battered fishing boats, handsome yachts and an increasing number of cruise ships.

Key West natives are a patchwork mix of English, Bahamian, Cuban, African and myriad others who came to seek their fortunes or just loaf in the sun. Modern times have seen a migration of writers, artists, musicians and folks of virtually every sexual, political and religious persuasion.

For all its funkiness, Key West is a traveler's haven with many classy hotels, inns, shops, restaurants and nightclubs. Visitors stay busy fishing, diving, boating and shopping. Don't miss Key West's signature ritual: the nightly sunset celebration at Mallory Square.

Accommodations: Hampton Inn, from $99, 2801 N. Roosevelt Blvd., Key West, FL 33040, (800) HAMPTON or (305) 294-2917.

Information: Key West Chamber of Commerce, 402 Wall St., Key West, FL 33040, (800) FLA-KEYS.

ACTIVE ADVENTURES

A re you stressed out? Have you spent the past year meeting everyone's needs but your own? Do you avoid a closeup mirror for fear of finding extra chins?

Make your next vacation an active holiday. A week of outdoor adventure or exercise and proper diet can trim you, tone you and establish new habits for a healthier lifestyle.

The choices are numerous - a rigorous or relaxing schedule, tennis or golf, mountain hiking or canyon biking.

Consult your physician before doing any strenuous or new exercises. Beware of diets that promote rapid weight loss through extended fasting or other radical practices.

Here are best bets, from shapeups with time for pampering to rugged outdoor fun.

Riding the Range in Colorado

Think of this place as Mayberry with boots. There are many Western dude ranches that cater to families, but you can count on Lake Mancos Ranch in Mancos, CO, to deliver the quintessential Western experience: horseback riding, hayrides and cookouts, and clean air and clean living in private, modern cabins, all run by the same family, the Sehnerts, since 1956. The log lodge here feels like 1956, down to a photo on the wall of a very young Johnny Carson, circa 1962, on vacation here with two of his sons.

"We don't believe in bells and whistles," says Kathy Sehnert. So forget the video games this week and enjoy the pool, Jeep tours, wildflower hikes and fishing as well as the special programs for young children and teens. Trail rides take you over terrain that ranges from easy to challenging, depending on the riding ability of participants. Visits to nearby Mesa Verde National Park also are popular with families.

Cost: All-inclusive rates: $958-$1,050 weekly for adults, $783-$856 for children under 18.

Information: Lake Mancos Ranch, 42688 County Road N., Mancos, CO 81328 (800) 325-WHOA or (970) 533-7900.

Rafting in Luxury in Utah

The concepts of rafting and luxury don't usually cross paths, but they do in grand style on a four-day, three-night river trip through Cataract Canyon on the Colorado River in Utah's Canyonlands National Park.

Yes, it's still rafting, and it's still camping, but along the way you are served gourmet meals (five-course dinners featuring the cuisine of a different country each night, with appropriate wines and spirits) by wait-persons in black tie at tables on the riverbank.

Guides get you down the river, set up camp and serve meals. You don't have to do a thing but savor the rarity of the experience under starry skies.

Cost: $941 a person.

Information: Sheri Griffith Expeditions, P.O. Box 1324, Moab, UT 84532, (800) 332-2439 or (801) 259-8229.

Llama Trekking in New Mexico

A great trip for adventurers is a five-day high-country trek with llamas to carry all your gear. The trip starts in Santa Fe and moves from camp to camp — at altitudes of 9,000 to 12,000 feet — in the Sangre de Cristo range of the southern Rockies.

The Pecos Wilderness is filled with mountain lakes, trout streams, wildflower meadows, glacial cirques, high peaks and lush forested valleys.

Cost: Southwestern meals, sleeping bag, pads, tent, solar shower, guides and llamas are included for $655.

Information: American Wilderness Experience, P.O. Box 1486, Boulder, CO 80306, (800) 444-0099 or (303) 444-2622.

Kayaking in Alaska

"A lot of long-lasting relationships have started on our trips," says Sue Warner, whose company leads kayakers on trips through Glacier Bay National Park's tranquil East Arm, including several days exploring famous Muir Inlet.

"All of our trips have a high preponderance of single sign-ups," says Warner. "If you are a single person, our trips are a perfect way to see Alaska and experience true wilderness without the danger or loneliness of doing it yourself. It's a great way to meet people, too."

Eight-day, seven-night trips require no prior kayaking experience and include all gear and equipment.

Cost: Rates of $1,890 include floatplane charters, and there is no single supplement.

Information: Alaska Discovery, 5449 Shaune Drive, Suite 4, Juneau, AK 99801, (800) 586-1911.

Hiking and Biking in Colorado

Special singles-only departures are offered on six-day back-country adventures near Vail, CO. The trips start in Vail Village, combining days of hiking, biking or rafting the Arkansas River with nights spent at country lodges featuring four-poster beds, quilts and hot tubs.

The trip is designed to accommodate beginners in hiking and mountain biking, but you should be in shape to do six to 10 miles of hiking or 20 to 30 miles of biking in one day. Don't worry — the routes aren't straight uphill.

Cost: $1,055, including rafting, meals, accommodations, support vehicle and guides. Bike rental is an extra $99.

Information: Roads Less Traveled, P.O. Box 8187, Longmont, CO 80501, (303) 678-8750.

Stress Management in Arizona

Miraval-Life in Balance, an all-inclusive luxury resort in Tucson, AZ, aspires to balance the lives of its guests — body, mind and spirit — through personally tailored programs of stress management, self-discovery and recreation.

The ambitious package includes luxury accommodations, three gourmet meals daily and use of the 130-acre property, including a trilevel pool with cascading waterfalls, an acupressure stonewalk and whirlpool, a Zen rock garden and desert botanical garden, saunas, horseback riding, tennis, hiking and mountain biking.

Also included are personalized workshops in such offerings as meditation, yoga, tai chi, dance and massage, as well as confidence-building courses such as rock climbing. You also get one personal-service treatment daily (massage, facial, etc.). You do as much or as little as you want; there is no set curriculum.

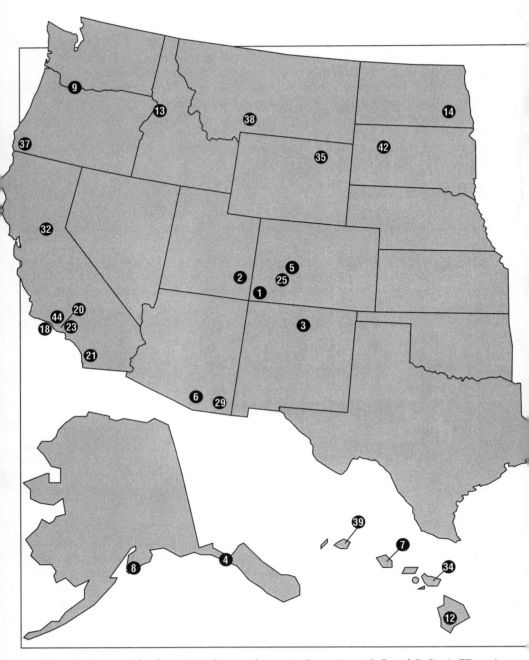

1 Riding the Range in Colorado
2 Rafting in luxury in Utah
3 Llama Trekking in New Mexico
4 Kayaking in Alaska
5 Hiking and Biking in Colorado
6 Stress Management in Arizona
7 Beach Scenes in Hawaii
8 Halibut Fishing in Alaska

9 Multisport Adventure in Oregon/ Washington
10 Canoe Capers in Minnesota
11 Sailing Classes for Women, Maryland
12 Scenic Sailing in Hawaii
13 Rafting the Rapids in Idaho
14 Play Pioneer in North Dakota
15 Canoe and Kayak in North Carolina

16 Coastal Cycling in Wisconsin
17 Safari in Alaska*
18 Island Hopping in California
19 Spa Touches in Florida
20 Fitness Challenge in California
21 Cut the Stress in California
22 Ship Out to Shape Up*
23 Change your Lifestyle in California
24 Focus on Tennis in Florida

ACTIVE ADVENTURES

Cost: This one isn't for the budget-conscious: Rates for singles start at $1,245 for three nights.
Information: Miraval-Life in Balance, 16500 N. Lago del Oro Parkway, Tucson, AZ 85739, (800) 825-4000.

Beach Scenes in Hawaii

Oahu is arguably the most beautiful of the Hawaiian islands, and a good bet for those who want to do things outdoors. Little-visited areas outside Waikiki include uninhabited islands, waterfalls and jungles. The summertime breakers along Waikiki's beachfront are just big enough to learn to surf, but not too big for beginners. Numerous operators in booths behind beachfront hotels offer surfing lessons for around $20 hourly, with guarantees that you'll be standing on a board during the first hour.

Twenty minutes from Waikiki is the famed Hanauma Bay snorkeling area, where colorful corals and sea life are easily accessible from shore. Hiking on the Maunawili Trail starts on Honolulu's outskirts, a 10-minute drive from Waikiki, and climbs past waterfalls to cloud-fringed mountain peaks.

You can ride horses at 4,000-acre Kualoa Ranch, where parts of the movie "Jurassic Park" were filmed, or travel by kayak, 21-speed mountain bike or four-wheel all-terrain vehicle at Waimea Valley, a sort of botanical/cultural theme park on Oahu's North Shore.

Information: Waikiki/Oahu Visitors Association, 1001 Bishop St., Pauahi Tower, Suite 477, Honolulu, HI 96813, (808) 524-0722.

Halibut Fishing in Alaska

Salmon anyone? Well, no, not if you're really looking for big fish. Alaskans' favorite fish is often the hallowed halibut. A decent-sized one here has to be at least a few hundred pounds.

Alaska's prime halibut fishing grounds are near Homer. Possible sales to local canneries potentially can moderate costs.

Cost: Daily fishing trips start at around $125. Full-blown charters, with a captain and gear, start at around $200 daily.

Information: Central Charter Bookings, 4241 Homer Spit Road, Homer, AK 99603, (800) 478-7847 or (907) 235-7847.

Multisport Adventure in Oregon/Washington

For those who can't decide what sort of adventure they want, this operation at the dramatic Columbia River Gorge on the Oregon/Washington border might be the ticket.

In the course of a single week you can mountain bike in the shadows of Mount Rainier, ski or snowboard on Mount Hood's Palmer Glacier (the only place in North America open through the summer for winter sports), raft the Deschutes River, climb Smith Rock or try your hand at windsurfing.

There may be no other place in the United States where you can do so many different things on one trip, and no experience is required.

Cost: Accommodations, meals, transportation, instruction, guides and equipment are included in rates of $1,295-$1,395 for a seven-night trip.

Information: Odyssey Multisport Adventures, 110 W. Burlington Ave., La Grange, IL 60525, (800) 789-2770.

Canoe Capers in Minnesota

This northeastern corner of Minnesota may well be the best area in the
for canoeing. It's a 2.2 million-acre wilderness (if you include Cana
Quetico Provincial Park) containing 5,000 lakes and 3,000 islands. You
days or weeks, fish along the way, camp every night and beat your chest like an ape if
you like; no one is likely to be bothered by your shenanigans out here.

But do remember to sling your foodstuffs high into a tree while you sleep. Your
likeliest neighbors, local bears, might otherwise help themselves. Permits are required
and limited, so plan early.

Cost: Canoe rentals run $15-$35 daily. An outfitted trip with a guide (there are
numerous outfitting services) costs $60-$75 daily. Air charters for remote drop-offs and
pick-ups run $100-$150 a person.

Information: Minnesota Office of Tourism, 100 Metro Square, 121 Seventh Place
East, St. Paul, MN 55101, (800) 657-3700.

Sailing Classes for Women, Maryland

Sailing is one of the last frontiers of personal freedom, presenting exhilarating
experiences meeting nature's challenges. Learning seafaring skills is fun in these hands-
on, live-aboard sailing instruction programs for women. There's no pressure and no
hassles but plenty of encouragement and support.

Coastal and offshore courses are offered in Annapolis, where picturesque towns and
historic ports of call dot the landscape as you sail through the waters of Chesapeake Bay.
Programs also are available in Key West and San Diego.

Cost: Rates are $395 for three days to $995 for seven days.

Information: Women for Sail, 900 16th Terrace, Key West, FL 33040, (800) 346-
6404.

Scenic Sailing in Hawaii

There is a wilder side to Hawaii — one of coral reefs, windy passages, jagged sea cliffs
and deserted beaches, all far beyond the familiar tourist haunts.

A sailing vacation is the perfect way to explore this other Hawaii. All you have to do
is assemble a group of four to six mates and sign up for a custom charter on the Maile.
This fully crewed Gulfstar 50, offered by Sausalito's Ocean Voyages, is based on the Big
Island's Kona Coast. Days are filled with wilderness hikes, snorkeling and diving on
coral reefs, seasonal whale-watching and spirited ocean sailing.

Accommodations include two spacious private cabins, each with a private head and
shower. The main salon converts into another double, making this an ideal boat for two
or three couples or a family of up to six.

Cost: Rates are all-inclusive except for alcoholic beverages. At $6,000 per week for
six people or $5,000 for four people, the cost figures to be less, per person, than at many
island resorts.

Information: Ocean Voyages, 1709 Bridgeway, Sausalito, CA 94965, (415) 332-
4681.

Rafting the Rapids in Idaho

Idaho's Snake River threads a seemingly bottomless gorge called Hells Canyon. This
7,000-foot abyss is one of nature's grandest achievements — and the setting for
exhilarating white-water rafting.

, five-day guided descent in large, oar-powered rubber rafts supplied by an experi-
-nced local outfitter, such as Coeur d'Alene's River Odysseys West, will leave all 80
miles of fabled Hells Canyon forever etched in your mind.

The Snake is a full-bodied river, and its upper portions provide huge roller-coaster
rapids. In other sections, swimming is great and fishing can be good, depending upon
water flow and season.

Stops allow time for hikes to view Indian rock art and pioneer homesites and to spot
wildlife. Camp is set up nightly on grassy sites above pristine sandy beaches. Rafting
season runs from mid-May to September.

Cost: $960 per person or $860 for youngsters up to age 16.

Information: River Odysseys West, P.O. Box 579, Coeur d'Alene, ID 83816, (800)
451-6034.

Play Pioneer in North Dakota

Each year, a string of covered wagons sets out single-file across the prairie near
Jamestown, ND. Modern-day pioneers in bonnets and overalls stride beside their
teams. Later, with wagons circling a roaring campfire, the settlers cook dinner and
spend the evening singing trail songs.

The Fort Seward Wagon Train is as real as it gets. Come June, some 150 promising
pioneers will assemble at Jamestown's Fort Seward Park to register for a weeklong ride
that simulates as closely as possible America's great 19th-century westward migration.

Organized and conducted for 26 years by a local non-profit group bent on preserving
North Dakota's pioneer heritage, the train of 12 to 15 wagons, each tended by an
experienced teamster, covers 15 to 30 miles a day across unspoiled prairie. Everybody
is assigned cooking and camp duties. Period attire is required and, please, no Styrofoam
coolers, radios or other modern conveniences.

Cost: $265 adults, $190 youths 13-18, $140 kids under 12 including wagons, horses,
teamster guides and food.

Information: Fort Seward Inc., Box 244, Jamestown, ND 58401, (800) 222-4766.

Canoe and Kayak in North Carolina

For those whose work is tedious or sedentary, an active, hands-on vacation dedicated
to learning an outdoor skill might be just the answer. If this sounds right for you,
consider Nantahala Outdoor Center.

White-water canoeing and kayaking are specialties at this unique training center in
North Carolina's Great Smoky Mountains, where U.S. canoe and kayak teams
prepared for the 1996 Olympic Games based in Atlanta.

Canoeing and kayaking courses range from three days to a week, with training
programs offered at five skill levels from novice to expert.

Cost: Packages that include meals, lodging and equipment are $330 for a weekend
course to $1,025 for a full week of training. Nights are spent at rustic cabins or campsites
at Nantahala Outdoor Center, 13 miles southwest of Bryson City.

Information: Nantahala Outdoor Center, 13077 Highway 19 W., Bryson City, NC
28713, (800) 232-7238 or (704) 488-2175.

Coastal Cycling in Wisconsin

This easy-to-moderate cycle tour samples Door County, a thumb-shaped peninsula
on Lake Michigan. It's an area long popular with travelers seeking an unspoiled haven

and some of the best scenery in the upper Midwest.

On the five-day trip, cyclists pedal the entire length of the peninsula, pausing at waterfront villages, orchards and turn-of-the-century lighthouses. One day is spent exploring Washington Island, the country's largest Icelandic settlement. You'll have plenty of time, too, for swimming and sunning on some of the prettiest beaches on Lake Michigan.

Guides lead daily rides of 25 to 50 miles.

Cost: Lodging in country inns and resorts is included in the rate of $995 per person, double occupancy.

Information: Vermont Bicycle Touring, P.O. Box 711, Bristol, VT 05443, (800) 245-3868.

Safari in Alaska

Here's a perfect itinerary for adventure travelers looking for a gentle, comfortable experience in Alaska. This seven-day trip from American Wilderness Experience includes exciting but not-too-strenuous activities that are especially attractive to seniors on safari.

You'll enjoy a tasty salmon bake and scenic float down the Kenai River, a wildflower hike in the Kenai Mountains, a full-day yacht cruise along glacier-choked fiords, a visit to the Alaska bush town of Talkeetna, a wildlife tour of Denali National Park and a ride on the famed Alaska Railroad. Pack plenty of film for exceptional photo opportunities.

Cost: Prices starting at $2,295 include lodging in a variety of fine hotels, mountain lodges and rustic cabins, all meals and full escort service. A nine-day tour starting at $2,995 adds two extra days at Denali National Park. Tours begin and end in Anchorage.

Information: American Wilderness Experience, P.O. Box 1486, Boulder, CO 80306, (800) 444-0099.

Island Hopping in California

When Southern Californians look to escape life in the fast lane, the really savvy ones motor north on U.S. 101. And for those with a nautical getaway in mind, Ventura is a great place to start.

A fast-growing coastal community just beyond the heat and smog of San Fernando Valley, Ventura is headquarters for Channel Islands National Park. This island chain is an important breeding ground for seals and sea lions and boasts an amazing array of plant, bird and sea life.

Hop the park concessioner's boat to Anacapa Island or Santa Barbara Island and spend the weekend camping, with plenty of opportunities for hiking, diving and photography. Or catch one of the commercial tour vessels and go island-hopping for the day.

Early summer, while the islands still are green and flowery, is one of the best times to go. Make boat and camping reservations at least a week or two in advance.

Cost: Boat rides start at $37 per adult and $20 per child. Camping is free, but you must first obtain a permit through the park service.

Information: Channel Islands National Park, 1901 Spinnaker Drive, Ventura, CA 93001, (805) 658-5700. Camping permit information, (805) 658-5711.

Spa Touches in Florida

Florida's Safety Harbor Spa and Fitness Center, across the bay from Tampa, has gyms, weight training and cardiovascular machines, indoor and outdoor pools, nine tennis courts, nearby golf courses and men's and women's bath-massage areas. Bike rides, race walks and 25 coed exercise classes are offered daily.

The menu is low-fat, low-cholesterol and delicious. Gourmet cuisine — spa or full fare — is served for breakfast, lunch and dinner. Nondieters order larger portions, hamburgers and other standards.

The upbeat, casual ambience is a refuge from high-pressure, overly structured lives.

Cost: From $99 per day, includes spa services, meals and lifestyle options.

Information: Safety Harbor Spa and Fitness Center, P.O. Box 248, Safety Harbor, FL 34695, (813) 726-1161 or (800) 237-0155.

Fitness Challenge in California

The Ashram, sometimes called boot camp, challenges takers to a gung-ho fitness program. Before daybreak, hike four to eight miles through the mountains. After fresh orange juice with bran for breakfast, the drill continues with weight training, calisthenics, swimming pool, volleyball and an afternoon hike.

There's no pampering here, but daily massages relieve aching muscles. Relaxing meditations are held in a hilltop geodesic dome at dusk.

The Ashram fits 10 guests into a charming five-bedroom, three-bathroom house. Uniformed in Ashram red sweatsuits, corporate captains, prime-time personalities and ordinary folk all share accommodations. Guests are co-ed; room assignments normally are not. Meals are family style. Lunch may be tossed tofu salad or tomato stuffed with rice and herbs. Dinner brings steamed veggies or a baked potato. Total intake: about 600 calories. Weight drops off.

Guests receive "I survived the Ashram" T-shirts so they won't forget having met this physical and mental challenge.

Cost: $1,900 per person per week.

Information: The Ashram, P.O. Box 8009, Calabasas, CA 91302, (818) 888-0232.

Cut the Stress in California

The Golden Door, a sublimely serene Japanese-style Garden of Eden near San Diego, emphasizes calm, quiet and fitness.

Normally, sessions are for women only, limited to 39 each week; but special men-only and couples-only weeks are designated. Even during couples' weeks, guests normally occupy separate rooms.

Individualized exercise schedules, alternating workouts and pampering, begin at 6 a.m. with the morning stretch and hike. Schedules are rigorous, but relaxation is also emphasized.

An "Inner Door" program is designed to reduce stress and increase left-brain creativity. Two-hour sessions are as rigorous as physical workouts, but participants lift thoughts instead of weights.

"Inner Door" exercises in drawing, writing and color-coding thoughts are designed to release tension and re-energize participants.

The Golden Door provides workout clothes. Maids do personal laundry. Delicious, exquisitely prepared meals total 1,000-1,600 calories daily.

Cost: $4,425 per person per week.

Information: The Golden Door, P.O. Box 463077, Escondido, CA 90246-3077, (800) 424-0777.

Ship out to Shape up

The fitness craze has come to cruises, where the latest indulgence is shaping up at sea. Some ships simply have exercise rooms, while others have full fitness programs.

Among the choices are Golden Door's mini-spa aboard Cunard's QE2 and Royal Caribbean Cruise Line's ShipShape program.

ShipShape offers aqua exercises in the pool, aerobics, line dance classes and specially designed senior fitness classes. Add to all that your own exercise nightly in the disco.

ShipShape participation is optional and geared to any level of fitness. There's no extra charge. Participating passengers are awarded "ShipShape dollars" to buy T-shirts and other ShipShape souvenirs.

Cost: From $699 per person, double occupancy for seven-night cruises(price does not include airfare or taxes).

Information: A travel agent or Royal Caribbean Cruise Line, 1080 Caribbean Way, Miami, FL 33132, (800) 526-7225; Cunard Line, 555 Fifth Ave., New York, NY 10017-2453, (800) 223-0764.

Change Your Lifestyle in California

Pritikin Longevity Centers in California and Florida combat heart disease, hypertension, diabetes and obesity through medically supervised eating and exercise. Even those not battling these conditions embrace the healthful Pritikin lifestyle.

The diet emphasizes complex carbohydrate foods, especially whole grains and fresh fruits and vegetables, with limited non-fat dairy foods, poultry, fish and lean meat.

Seminars teach how eating too much fat, sugar and refined flour affects the body and how stress and smoking contribute to health problems.

Food preparation, shopping and dining-out workshops initiate lifestyle change. Exercise programs based on walking, jogging and stretching can be followed at home. Pritikin physicians monitor each participant's program and progress.

Pritikin offers one-, two- or three-week programs.

Cost: $3,480 for a basic one-week program for primary participants, $1,511 for companions.

Information: Pritikin Longevity Centers, 1910 Ocean Front Walk, Santa Monica, CA 90405, (800) 421-9911.

Focus on Tennis in Florida

Tennis and fitness packages are tops at Florida's exclusive Saddlebrook Resort, the U.S. Professional Tennis Association's headquarters and regional training center.

Saddlebrook has 37 tennis courts (five lit at night) separated by awning-covered islands with ice-water fountains and spectator chairs, plus three swimming pools and a fully equipped fitness center.

Packages are run by Harry Hopman International Tennis, a program used by many tennis stars. It features daily five-hour clinics with four players maximum per instructor/court, matched play with instructors after drill, audio-visual analysis, tennis-oriented fitness and agility exercises and motivational lectures. You also can go to aerobics classes and use the resort amenities.

Cost: From $690, per person, double occupancy, for six-night package.

Information: Saddlebrook Resort, 5700 Saddlebrook Way, Wesley Chapel, FL 33543, (800) 729-8383.

Hike to Fitness in Colorado

The Aspen Club Spa, an all-around fitness and sports resort, offers personalized packages that can be centered around daily three- to five-hour guided hikes on Colorado's splendid mountain trails. Begin with the Ute Trail and advance to Cathedral Lake, American Lake, Conundrum Hot Springs and other nearby scenic areas.

The program is supervised by the Club's Fitness & Sports Medicine Institute's expert staff that has trained Martina Navratilova, Danny Sullivan, Billy Jean King and other elite athletes. It includes: EKG; tests for maximum stress, strength and flexibility; body fat analysis; stretch and fitness classes; nutritional consultation and relaxing massages; plus use of swimming pool, tennis and squash courts.

A personal fitness guidebook is prepared for you to take home.

The Club offers special classes in the Pilates Method, a series of progressive exercises to strengthen and tone every muscle in your body.

Cost: About $1,800 for a personalized seven-day package, excluding meals.

Information: Aspen Club, 1450 Crystal Lake Road, Aspen, CO 81611, (303) 925-8900.

Cycling Canyonlands of National Parks

Cycling excursions organized by Backroads Bicycle Touring are geared for vacationers of all ages and all levels of fitness.

Backroads has tours worldwide, but trips through majestic Bryce, Zion and Grand Canyon national parks are U.S. favorites. These offer guests the option of inn accommodations or camping out, as well as alternate routes for beginners, intermediate and advanced cyclists.

You have all day to cover a distance that should take three to five hours of constant cycling, but a support van is nearby in case you get winded. The van also carries luggage, spare parts, food and refreshments.

Scheduled stops allow you to hike or horseback ride through red rock country or just smell the fresh air and flowers.

Cost: $1,498 inn, $978 camping for nine-day canyonlands tour; $129 bike rental, $25 sleeping bag rental. Groups limited to 18-26.

Information: Backroads Bicycle Touring, 801 Cedar St., Berkeley, CA 94710-1800, (800) 462-2848.

Summer Camp in Connecticut

For years, this 300-acre facility in Kent, CT, was a summer camp for children. But for the last 20 seasons, adults have had all the fun at Club Getaway— from talent shows to hula-hoop contests, three-legged races, campfire sing-alongs and sports instruction.

Activities are posted daily and include rock climbing and windsurfing lessons and guided hiking and biking tours to nearby antique centers. Tennis courts are not lit, but the volleyball court is, and games often go past midnight, as does dancing in the casual lakeside disco.

Cabins sleep four, similar ages are matched. Club Getaway operates daily during the summer, weekends only through autumn.

Cost: $179 per person for two-night weekends, $49 per day mid-week, including all meals.

Information: Club Getaway, Box 606, Lenox Hill Station, New York, NY 10021,

(212) 935-0222.

Learn to Sail in Rhode Island or Florida

For those who've yearned to sail, here's your chance. Offshore Sailing School has week-long sessions for all levels, from beginners to advanced and racing. After learning the ropes here, many sign up for the school's chartered yacht cruises in the Caribbean and Mediterranean.

The summer "Learn to Sail" program at the historic Admiral Farragut Inn near Newport, RI, includes three days of morning classroom instruction and afternoon sailing, accommodations and breakfast at the inn, and a graduation party.

A Florida school, at the South Seas Plantation, Captiva Island, operates year-round.

Cost: From $850 per person, double occupancy, or $895 single occupancy, three nights, excluding airfare.

Information: Offshore Sailing School, 16731-110 McGregor Blvd., Fort Myers, FL 33908, (800) 221-4326.

Singles Ride the Range in Arizona

Most ranches in the West are family oriented, but Grapevine Canyon Ranch, 85 miles from Tucson, is different. It's for adults only and attracts many singles.

The accent is on comfort, hospitality and responsive horses, with a heated pool and private cabins with sundecks to soothe muscles and psyches after a day on horseback. Host/owner Gerry Searle is an expert on Western lore and a cowboy artist. The kitchen serves such items as barbecue, cornish hens, and steaks broiled over mesquite.

Experienced riders can go on overnight pack trips (extra cost), and there is hiking and fishing in the canyon. Mexico is one hour away.

Cost: From $130 per day, per person, excluding airfare.

Information: Grapevine Canyon Ranch, P.O. Box 302, Pearce, AZ 85625, (800) 826-3185.

Summer Tennis Camps in Vermont

Sugarbush, VT, is one of a growing number of ski resorts no longer closing doors in the summer. Sugarbush has a summer tennis camp attracting several dozen participants a session.

The program offers either 2 1/2 or five hours daily instruction and play, video playbacks, tournaments, full access to the resort's nearby sports center, with four pools and golf facilities, and breakfast daily.

Stowe, VT, 34 miles east of Burlington, is just as spectacular in the summer. That's when the hills turn green and flowers abound, cafes move outdoors and the Topnotch resort tennis program gets into full swing.

Participants can sign up for private instruction and unlimited court time, subject to availability.

The resort offers daily morning walks in the adjoining woods, afternoon cookies and tea, and discounts on nearby golf courses. There's also a golf program, and couples can split instruction, one partner taking golf lessons while the other concentrates on tennis.

When not on the court, guests can explore the region. Be sure to ride the Jay Peak Aerial Tram, a 60-passenger sky-train that affords wonderful views of Vermont's Green Mountains.

Cost: At Sugarbush $238-$298 per person, two-day weekend package. At Stowe, tennis packages begin at $93 daily per person, double occupancy, including accommodations and spa facilities.

Information: Sugarbush Tennis Camp, RR1, Box 350, Warren, VT 05674, (802) 583-2391. Topnotch at Stowe Resort and Spa, 4000 Mountain Road, Box 1458, Stowe, VT 05672, (800) 451-8686.

Volunteer Research Project

If you ever considered joining the Peace Corps, fantasized about going on an archaeological dig or just want to help save wildlife, an Earthwatch project is a vacation for you.

Earthwatch is a non-profit institution that helps scientific research projects by finding volunteers to assist with field work. These are not fancy resort vacations; depending on the project, accommodations range from tents to nearby barracks or a rented house.

Earthwatch will match volunteers with their areas of interest. Among numerous opportunities are excavating a graveyard of Ice Age mammoths in Hot Springs, SD, or documenting birds in the Virginia National Wildlife Refuge near Norfolk.

Each project is an average of 14 days and directed by a university professor or a conservation or environmental group.

Cost: $495-$2800 per person, excluding transportation to the site. Because you are a volunteer, all expedition-related expenses may be tax-deductible.

Information: Earthwatch, 680 Mount Auburn St., P.O. Box 403-BO, Watertown, MA 02172, (800) 776-0188 or (617) 926-8200.

Run the Rapids in Gold Rush Land

The American River runs through California's Gold Rush country, offering great waters and canyon scenery.

Abandoned mines dot the route through the river's North Fork. Two-day trips include the option of bed-and-breakfast lodging instead of riverside camping, and a choice of paddling or just going along for the ride. You also may opt for a day hot-air ballooning over the rapids.

This trip is good for beginners at running rapids because the first stretch is gentle enough for guides to give instruction on reading the river, local history and wildlife.

Cost: $402 per person, two-day trip, including four meals.

Information: OARS, Box 67, Angels Camp, CA 95222, (800) 346-6277.

Relieve the Stress in Illinois

With young Americans into fitness, spas increasingly are vacation destinations. The Heartland combines West Coast-style fitness-wellness programs with Midwestern warmth and attention.

The lakeside country estate is outside Chicago. The focus is on relieving stress and tension, and even social activities have a relaxed air, without any fancy pretenses.

It offers all kinds of activities— from aerobics to yoga and weight training, with tennis and massages in between. The resort supplies sweats, slippers, rain gear and evening lounging PJs. There are three vegetarian meals a day, plus several snacks; second helpings are encouraged. Facials and massages are part of the package.

Cost: $560 per person, double occupancy, $720 single, two-night weekends; $1,400 and $1,800 respectively, for five nights; $1,960 and $2,520 for seven nights, including transportation from downtown Chicago.

Information: Spa-finders, 91 Fifth Ave., Suite 301, New York, NY 10003, (800) ALL-SPAS.

Learn to Surf in Hawaii

The long, slow breakers off Maui are a windsurfer's paradise, attracting hundreds of surfers. Beginners usually hang 10 over boards on the leeward north side of the island, while the more experienced surfers head for the windward side.

Maui Windsurfari is the oldest and still one of the largest surfing packagers on the island. Even if you just want to watch the fun, perhaps with a camera, you can participate in the daytime camaraderie and join in group outings in the evenings.

Cost: A seven-day Windsurfari package, starting at $506, includes accommodations, equipment and a rental car. Non-sailors can deduct $225.

Information: Maui Windsurfari, Box 330254, Kahului, HI 96733, (800) 736-6284 or (808) 871-7766.

Ride the Range in Wyoming

Intense horsing around, for horsemen of all skill levels, is the focus of Paradise Guest Ranch, one of the oldest in the West, in Buffalo, WY.

The dude ranch, by the Bighorn Mountains in the northern part of the state, matches you with a horse that's yours for the week. Choose one-hour, half-day or all-day riding trips through the surrounding lodgepole and aspen forests.

Highlights of the week include a talent show, the Saturday ranch rodeo with events for both children and adults, Saturday night square dancing, a Friday night chuckwagon dinner and campfire guitar singalongs every week.

The facilities include a recreation hall and main lodge, an enclosed whirlpool spa, a heated outdoor pool and 18 comfortable log cabins — ranging from one to four bedrooms each — with housekeeping service.

Cost: $950-$1,175 for adults for a week, $850-$1,075 for children ages 6-12, $650-$855 for ages 3-5 and $425-$600 for ages 2 and under, including all meals and activities.

Information: Paradise Guest Ranch, P.O. Box 790, Buffalo, WY 82834, (307) 684-7876.

Mountaineering in North Carolina

Outward Bound, developed to toughen British sailors during World War II, teaches survival skills, tests physical and mental mettle and develops muscles and self-esteem.

Nationwide, Outward Bound's five schools offer 500 different wilderness courses concentrating on backpacking, rock and mountain climbing, sailing and kayaking, dog sledding and other conditioning and stamina-building skills.

The multiskill backpacking courses in North Carolina's Blue Ridge Mountains can be for general vacationers or special focus groups such as teens, senior citizens or women. Participants backpack, cook out, participate in service projects, learn rock climbing, rappelling, mountain biking, aerial ropes and canoeing. They also run mini-marathons.

The toughest challenge is 'soloing,' enduring the wilderness alone, for a specified period of time, with scheduled safety checks by group leaders.

Cost: $495-$6,995 per person for five-83 days of Blue Ridge Mountains courses, including meals and equipment. Financial aid is available.

Information: North Carolina Outward Bound, 2582 Riceville Road, Asheville, NC 28805, (704) 299-3366 or (800) 841-0186. Outward Bound National, Route 9D, R2 Box 280, Garrison, NY 10524-9757, (800) 243-8520.

River Rafting in Oregon

The Rogue River winds you through the Siskiyou National Forest, a treat of classic Oregon greenery where the woods harbor black bear and mule deer. This OARS (Outdoor Adventure River Specialists) raft trip keeps all members of the family happy.

Rapids add excitement, but for participants who would rather hike and forego the white water, rough spots can be avoided while the rest of the gang paddles through. If you want, try your skill in a kayak or simply let the guide and the currents carry you through this lush landscape.

You float on the water about four hours each day, stopping for lunch, fishing and scenic outlooks. There's also time to explore fern grottoes and swim in natural pools. At night, star gaze in a cavernous sky.

Cost: Four-day trips are offered May through September at a cost of $595 for adults, $540 for children under 17. Minimum age is 5. Five-day trips are offered June through September. Cost is $690 per adult, $630 for children under 17.

Information: OARS offers a variety of family raft and float trips in Utah, Wyoming, Idaho, California and Oregon. OARS, P.O. Box 67, Angels Camp, CA 95222, (209) 736-4677.

Fly-Fishing for Women, Montana

Women are taking up fly-fishing in record numbers, and it's little wonder. They're discovering that fly-fishing takes you to beautiful places so you can connect with nature, learn something new and get away from it all.

But most importantly, it's big-time fun. Women take naturally to the sport, which requires balance, grace and brains. With Montana's famous blue-ribbon trout streams, female guides and a comfy base at a Big Sky hotel, this could be the perfect place to begin.

Cost: $1,375 for five days in early September.

Information: Rainbow Adventures, 15033 Kelly Canyon Road, Bozeman, MT 59715, (800) 804-8686 or (406) 587-3883.

Sea Kayaking in Hawaii

If you want to expand your personal (and physical) horizons, this nine-day tour for 10 people includes sea kayaking along Kauai's Na Pali Cliffs from Haena to Polihale. That's one of the most spectacular stretches of coast in the Hawaiian islands — sort of a "just you and the waves" experience.

You'll also paddle your way to the Nu'alolo reefs for snorkeling and up a few rivers for ecological explorations. Day hikes from base camps into Kauai's rugged interior fill out the program.

Except for a few included meals, this is a BYOF trip — you'll be buying food in local markets and cooking in camp.

Cost: $1,095 from Honolulu including interisland airfare, ground transportation, six nights of camping, two nights of lodging, three breakfasts, equipment, permits and fees.

Information: Remarkable Journeys, P.O. Box 31855, Houston, TX 77231-1855, (800) 856-1993 or (713) 721-2517.

Alaska Wilderness Exploration

How can a *cheechako* (tenderfoot) explore the remote wilderness of Alaska without toting all the basic necessities of life on his or her back? Sign up for a new trip offered by Earthquest that features day hikes from a base camp.

It's a geological and environmental tour de force in the Twin Lakes area of Lake Clark National Park, so beautiful it's called Little Denali by those in the know. There are no crowds or tour buses here, however. You'll have all that beauty almost to yourself.

Three week-long trips are scheduled from June to August; the first and last nights are spent in a hotel, the remaining nights at the base camp.

Cost: $1,600 per person, double occupancy including all equipment, food, accommodations and dinner at the hotel, transportation from Anchorage and guides. Personal gear, such as sleeping bags and special clothing, is not included.

Information: North Star, P.O. Box 1724, Flagstaff, AZ 86002, (800) 258-8434 or (520) 773-9917.

Go Native in American Indian Country

If you've always wanted to sleep in a tepee or hogan and eat traditional native food, here's your chance. Guided people-to-people discovery vacations in America's Southwest provide enriching and interactive encounters with members of the Navajo, Hopi, Apache, Yaqui, Lakota Sioux and other American Indian tribes.

Anthropologists and native guides add insider perspectives, and optional activities include rafting, hiking, horseback riding, camping and ceremonies.

Trips run from three to 12 days; sites range from the high mesas above Arizona's Painted Desert to the Black Hills of the Dakotas.

Cost: From $250, including basic activities, land transportation, most meals, equipment, guides and camping and/or hotel.

Information: Discovery Passages, 1161 Elk Trail, Box 630, Prescott, AZ 86303, (520) 717-0519.

Tending the Farm in South Dakota

Four sheep and cattle ranches near the tiny town of Faith, SD, (population 548) invite guests to participate in ranch life on the great American plains.

You'll help with the daily chores, chow down on country-style meals at the family dinner table, have fishing and hunting privileges, explore dinosaur digs, watch wildlife and attend area rodeos and powwows.

Cost: A day trip costs $80 per person, including the noon meal; overnight stays are $110 per person, including three meals and accommodations.

Information: Faith Chamber of Commerce, Box 246, Faith, SD 57626, (605) 967-2001.

Skip Barber Racing School

Do you dream of driving in the Indy 500? Or do you just want better odds on surviving in today's traffic?

Either way, professional instruction in advanced car-control skills is yours at the world's largest racing school. Classes generally range from one to three days and are available at 21 racetracks across the country. The three-day competition course guarantees to qualify you for a racing license — if you graduate.

Tracks where the schools are available include Laguna Seca on California's Monterey Peninsula, Las Vegas Speedway Park and Indiana's famed Indianapolis Raceway Park.

The Skip Barber Racing School can recommend local accommodations at each of their 21 locations. Many offer special discounts for the school's students.

Cost: $495-$2,250.

Information: Skip Barber Racing School, 29 Brook St., P.O. Box 1629, Lakeville, CT 06039, (800) 221-1131 or (203) 824-0771.

Get Fit for Less in California

One of the best bargains in fitness spas is in gorgeous Ojai, the real-life mountain setting for the mythical Shangri-La in the Ronald Coleman classic, "Lost Horizons."

Just 1 1/2 hours northwest of Los Angeles by car, the Oaks at Ojai offers a full roster of aerobics classes, machine workouts, pool classes, massages and wonderful hikes into the mountains. Meals are tasty but low in calories.

When not working out, guests can walk or bike Ojai, Southern California's most artsy town. Visitors can browse through studios, explore the town's Mission Revival architecture and catch a summer concert in oak-studded Libbey Park.

Other options include a dip in the mineral waters at Wheeler Hot Springs, six miles west of town, or a day trip by boat from Ventura, 14 miles southwest of Ojai, to the Channel Islands, where offshore waters abound with sea lions, harbor seals and birds.

Cost: Rates are from $129 per day per person, double occupancy, including all tips and taxes, three meals, 16 exercise classes, pool, sauna, machines, hikes, health and fitness lectures.

Information: The Oaks at Ojai, 122 E. Ojai Ave., Ojai, CA 93023, (805) 646-5573 or (800) 753-6257.

FAMILY VACATIONS

Family vacations have long been considered the ideal opportunity to spend quality time together. But the secret to making a family trip successful is not trying to be an inseparable unit from dawn to dusk. Instead, pick a vacation packed with lots of options for all ages so that everyone has opportunities to break away from the group.

The best family vacations are planned together. Young children need to visualize where they are going and what they will be doing. Sharing travel brochures and pinpointing the destination on a map gives them security.

Teens are less likely to grouch about the family vacation if they've been included in the decision-making process. Discuss options and let them know the kinds of activities that each offers.

We make the following suggestions with the goal of having everyone in your entourage find something intriguing, whether you end up participating en masse or individually.

Diamonds in Arkansas

Diamonds aren't just a girl's best friend; they're everybody's. At least it seems that way at Crater of Diamonds State Park in Murfreesboro, AR, where more than 80,000 visitors a year dig for the precious baubles.

For a modest fee, visitors can dig to their heart's content, hoping to unearth a multicarat gem. A goodly number of these novice prospectors stop on the way to or from Hot Springs, a spa resort that has taken a new lease on life since the election of native son Bill Clinton to the presidency. Chief tourist destinations are the historic old bathhouses.

Accommodations: Queen of Diamonds Inn, $50, P.O. Box 668, Murfreesboro, AR 71958, (501) 285-3105.

Information: Crater of Diamonds, Rte. 1, Box 364, Murfreesboro, AR 71958, (501) 285-3113, and Hot Springs National Park, P.O. Box 1860, Hot Springs, AR 71906, (501) 624-3383.

Touring by RV

For a truly memorable family trip, fly or drive to a good jumping-off spot like Denver, rent a recreational vehicle and take off on a tour of the West. In a month you can hit most of the major sights, including Mount Rushmore, Yellowstone, the Grand Canyon, Jackson Hole, Las Vegas and Vail.

Traveling by RV is not cheap, but the advantages offset the cost. You can cook most of your meals in the vehicle, and the kids can play games in the back room. On travel days, you can get in 100 miles or more before they even wake up.

Cost: A 7-day RV rental from Cruise America starts at $723 per week.

Information: Go Camping America Committee, P.O. Box 2669, Reston, VA 22090, (800) 47-SUNNY; Cruise America, 11 W. Hampton, Mesa, AZ 85210, (800) 327-7799.

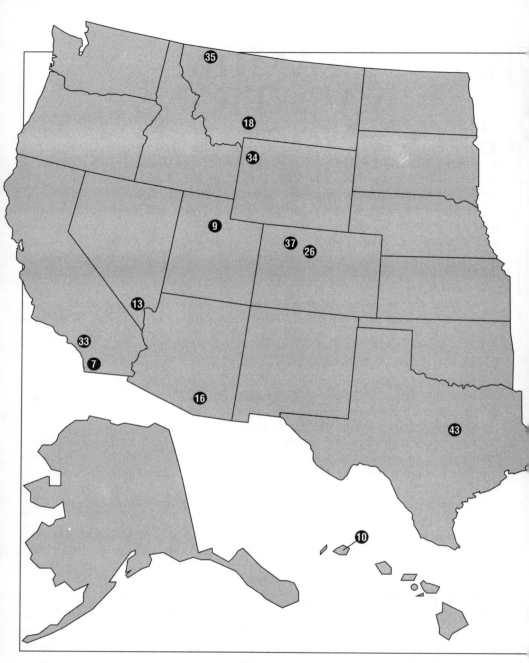

1 Diamonds in Arkansas
2 Touring by RV*
3 Behind the Scenes at Theme Parks*
4 Western North Carolina
5 Washington for Kids
6 Wisconsin Dells
7 San Diego, California
8 Maine Windjammers
9 Sundance, Utah
10 Hawaii, Family-style
11 Fontana Dam Village, North Carolina
12 Mickey and a Cruise*
13 Vegas, Family-style
14 Club Med Sandpiper, Florida
15 Sarasota, Florida
16 Tanque Verde Guest Ranch, Arizona
17 Georgia's Golden Isles
18 Riding the Range in Montana
19 A Finnish Farm in Wisconsin
20 Float the Buffalo in Arkansas
21 Myrtle Beach, South Carolina
22 Boston and Cape Cod, Massachusetts*

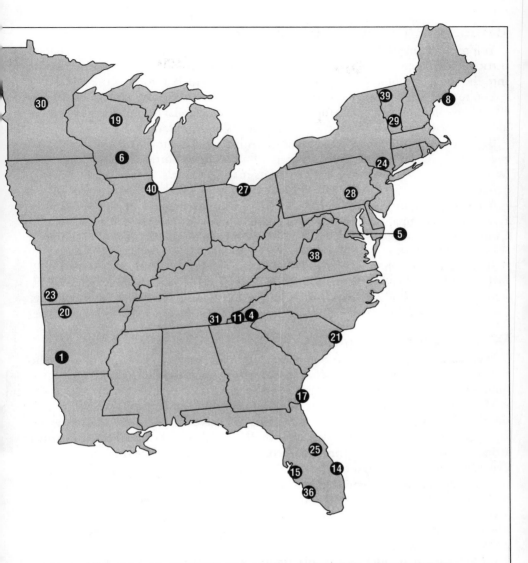

FAMILY VACATIONS

Behind the Scenes at Theme Parks

You're riding in the back of a flatbed truck, looking at the gazelles, cape buffaloes, ostriches and zebras on the veldt. Suddenly a large head, attached to a long neck, reaches into the truck to nibble at an apple; the giraffe knows there is food in the vehicle.

You're on a photo safari, a special backstage excursion at Busch Gardens in Tampa, FL. It is one of a number of such tours offered by Busch. Similar behind-the-scenes tours also are offered by Walt Disney World and Sea World in Florida.

Busch's behind-the-scenes programs are mostly related to the care of its thousands of zoo animals. Disney tours cover a variety of areas, from horticulture to magic. Sea World tours show how the park cares for its marine animals. All are popular family activities.

Accommodations: In Tampa, Holiday Inn – Tampa Busch Gardens, $86, 2701 E. Fowler Ave., Tampa, FL 33612, (800) 99 BUSCH or (813) 971-4710. In Orlando, Courtyard Marriott, $89-$169, P.O. Box 22204, 1805 Hotel Plaza Blvd., Lake Buena Vista, FL 32830, (800) 223-9930 or (407) 828-8888.

Information: Busch Gardens, P.O. Box 9158, Tampa, FL 33674, (813) 987-5082 or (813) 987-5283; Walt Disney World, P.O. Box 10000, Lake Buena Vista, FL 32830, (407) 824-4321 or (407) 824-2222; Sea World, 7007 Sea World Drive, Orlando, FL 32821, (800) 327-2424 outside Florida, (800) 432-1178 within the state.

Western North Carolina

Every summer, families in the Southeast pack up the station wagon and head for the hills — the mountains of western North Carolina. The highest in eastern America, these mountains are cool and inviting territory in the hot summer months.

Many rent cabins for a week, in scenic spots like the Highlands/Franklin area, and simply do whatever the moment suggests. Kids carve hiking staffs from downed saplings and search for mica rocks. The whole family can schedule day trips to area attractions or visits to local tennis courts or swimming pools. The ruby mines in the Cowee Valley make a pleasant half-day outing. People uncover all kinds of precious and semiprecious stones at these digs, including star sapphires, garnets and rubies. At nightfall, the temperatures drop enough to build a campfire under starry skies, the perfect site for storytelling and marshmallow roasting.

Accommodations: Bloom Cottage, $300 per week, 40 Jim Berry Road, Franklin, NC 28734, (305) 782-6294.

Information: Franklin Chamber of Commerce, 180 Porter St., Franklin, NC 28734, (800) 336-7829; Highlands Chamber of Commerce, P.O. Box 404, Highlands, NC 28741, (704) 526-2112.

Washington for Kids

Unlike theme parks, everything is real in Washington, DC — and kids love the place. Washington is full of activities for families with children of all ages. They can watch an FBI agent fire a machine gun on an FBI tour, see millions of dollars being printed at the Bureau of Printing and Engraving, look at live creepy-crawly things at the National Museum of Natural History's Insect Zoo, touch a moon rock, see movies made in space, or gaze upon Dorothy's ruby slippers from the Wizard of Oz. And that's just a sampling.

Accommodations: Capitol Reservations, a reservation service at (800) VISIT-DC, offers discounts on area hotels such as the Capitol Hills Suites, $79-$99, 200 C St.,

Washington, DC 20003, and the Henley Park Hotel, $99-$109, 10th and Massachusetts Ave., Washington, DC 20001.

Information: Smithsonian Museums Visitors Information and Reception Center, 1000 Jefferson Drive, Washington, DC 20560, (202) 357-2700; Washington, DC, Visitor Information Center, 1212 New York Ave. NW, Washington, DC 20005, (202) 789-7000.

Wisconsin Dells

The Dells are unusually shaped sandstone formations along the Wisconsin River, and they form the core of a glitzy tourist strip that goes for miles.

Miniature golf, go-cart tracks, three water theme parks, zillions of motels and fast-food stops — the Dells is a tourist gulch. But kids and families love it, just as they swarm to Orlando's similar International Drive.

Highlights include cruising the river on Wisconsin "ducks," retired World War II amphibious vehicles; exploring Tommy Bartlett's Robot World, a commercial hands-on science attraction; and visiting Circus World in nearby Baraboo, where the circus began in 1884.

Accommodations: Days Inn, $55-$175, P.O. Box 381, Wisconsin Dells, WI 53965, (608) 254-6444.

Information: Wisconsin Dells Visitor and Convention Bureau, P.O. Box 390, Wisconsin Dells, WI 53965, (800) 22-DELLS.

San Diego, California

A beautiful harbor, two world-class zoos, a park full of museums, a marine theme park and a climate that's pleasant year-round: This city's a winner with families.

Seven museums make their home in Balboa Park, offering such kid-friendly doings as 3-D laser light shows, a walk-through mine tunnel, an Omnimax theater, classic automobiles, spacecraft and giant model railroad exhibits. The San Diego Zoo and the San Diego Wild Animal Park are wonderful habitats for animals.

Around the harbor are other family magnets: places to go rollerblading or fly a kite, tours by ships and of ships, biking paths. At the Sea World theme park, kids can walk through a submerged plastic tunnel as sharks circle around them.

Accommodations: Holiday Inn – Hotel Circle, $84-$104, 595 Hotel Circle S., San Diego, CA 92108, (800) 433-0469 or (619) 291-5720.

Information: San Diego Convention and Visitors Bureau, 401 B St., Suite 1400, San Diego, CA 92101, (619) 236-1212.

Maine Windjammers

No matter what the age of your children, vacations offer quality time away from work and worries — especially for parents with adult children. A coastal cruise on a tall ship off the coast of Maine is a good way to spend time with your big kids.

Thirteen Maine windjammers sail three- and six-day cruises from May through October. These schooners follow the wind, docking in small coves not accessible to larger vessels. Participants can learn the ropes, find out how to read charts, help hoist the sails or simply savor the scenery and salt air. Cabins are simple, most with shared baths.

Shore treats often include a lobster bake, strolls on isolated beaches and views from wind-swept summits. On-board menus feature — what else — fresh New England seafood.

Cost: Depending on the ship, three-day cruises range from $295 to $429 per person. Six-day cruises range from $495 to $675.

Information: Maine Windjammer Association, P.O. Box 317, Rockport, ME 04856, (800) MAINE-80.

Sundance, Utah

Politically correct, environmentally conscious and just plain beautiful, Sundance shines on 5,000 acres of protected wilderness at the base of Utah's mighty 12,000-foot Mount Timpanogos.

About an hour from Salt Lake City's airport, this retreat in the shadow of the Wasatch Range of Utah's Rocky Mountains was created by Robert Redford in 1969.

A vacation here is as big as all outdoors, and just as exciting. Although high season comes with the snow, summer's bonuses include hillsides of wildflowers, horseback trail rides and day trips, guided hikes, hot-air balloon flights, fly-fishing forays, hayride dinners, water-skiing clinics, outdoor theater and free movies.

At the Sundance Kids Day Camp, complimentary from 9 a.m. to 4 p.m. Monday through Saturday for ages 6 to 12, your children will learn about American Indian myths and crafts, go hiking and horseback riding, and participate in a theater workshop.

Cost: Standard rooms start at $115. Junior suites with a mini-kitchen start at $175. Rates include breakfast and the Kids Day Camp, which operates with a minimum of four children. Register your kids when you make reservations.

Information: Sundance, Rural Route 3, Box A-1, Sundance, UT 84604, (800) 892-1600 or (801) 225-4107.

Hawaii, Family-Style

Even a Hawaiian getaway fantasy can blossom at an affordable price. At little cost, you can explore canyons, swim along reefs abundant with rainbow-colored fish and coral, and drive scenic roads. The bougainvillea, hibiscus and sugar cane on Kauai have recovered from the 1992 hurricane, and ferns once again feather the roadsides.

Rates are low at the 12 rustic cabins at Kokee Lodge amid the woods, plum groves and trails at 4,345-acre Kokee State Park. You can hike through forests to overlooks of adjacent Waimea Canyon. You'll be dazzled by the pink-and-gray striated rock formations and fluted ridges touched by cascading waterfalls.

At Kokee Lodge, a basic housekeeping cabin comes with a refrigerator, wood stove, utensils, linens, towels, blankets, toilets and showers. A nearby restaurant serves breakfast and lunch daily. Be sure to try the Portuguese bean soup.

Cost: Cabins accommodate three to seven people. Depending on size, rates are $35 or $45 per cabin. Maximum length of stay is five days. Book early; favorite cabins often are reserved a year in advance.

Information: Kokee Lodge, P.O. Box 819, Waimea, Kauai, Hawaii 96796, (808) 335-6061.

Fontana Dam Village, North Carolina

Fontana Dam Village was created 50 years ago for workers who built the highest dam in the Tennessee Valley Authority system (more than 700 feet). Today, the same cottages they occupied are used by families vacationing in western North Carolina's mountain country.

While the kids play softball, go swimming or hammer out copper designs in a crafts class, Mom and Dad can take art lessons, work out in the new fitness center, go country dancing or simply relax in one of America's most scenic regions.

Hiking trails wind through the forests and hills. One leads to an observation tower atop the summit of Shuck's Stack, more than a mile high. Rafting is available on the nearby Nantahala River.

Cost: Cottages rent for $69-$189 per night. Inn rooms are $79.

Information: Fontana Dam Resort, P.O. Box 68, Fontana Dam, NC 28733, (800) 849-2258 or (704) 498-2211.

Mickey and a Cruise

Premier Cruise Lines combines two family fantasies: pampered relaxation at sea for parents and the excitement of Florida's Walt Disney World for kids. This may be the best way to "do Disney."

Premier combines a three- or four-day Bahamas cruise with a four- or three-day tour of Disney. The weeklong package also includes a rental car and a guided tour of NASA's Spaceport USA.

Our suggestion: Visit the theme parks first. Let the kids run wild through the Magic Kingdom, Epcot and MGM Studios. Then board the Big Red Boat and relax. Your children and teens will be happily occupied from 9 a.m. to 10 p.m. with kite flying, scavenger hunts, Nintendo games and dances. You can lounge on deck and catch the sunsets.

Cost: One-week packages that include cruise and Disney World start at $1,239 per person, double occupancy, and $679-$779 for third and fourth passengers, including round-trip airfare from most gateway cities. Premier also has five-passenger cabins and cost-cutting rates for single parents with children.

Information: Premier Cruise Lines, 400 Challenger Road, Cape Canaveral, FL 32920, (800) 327-7113.

Vegas, Family-Style

Be prepared: Vegas can be an exhausting family experience — though there's no doubt your kids will love the MGM Grand Theme Park and the Wet 'n' Wild Water Theme Park. There's a bombastic profusion of video game arcades, including fantastically realistic motion simulator movie rides that are now a big part of almost every casino.

Circus Circus has Grand Slam Canyon, a theme park under dome with a number of rides, including a roller coaster. Luxor has an enormous VirtuaLand, a three-part Egyptian adventure that includes a flight simulator trip.

Alas, the fun can run into big bucks without ever hitting the gaming tables. That's not a problem, though, in a town that caters to all budgets.

Many hotel rooms are moderately priced, and meals can range from an inexpensive buffet to a feast. There are plenty of free things to see, including a dazzling pirate show at Treasure Island every few hours, Siegfried and Roy's white tigers on display behind thick glass at the Mirage, and the moving statues inside Caesar's Palace.

Splurge one night. Take the kids to see Cirque du Soleil at Treasure Island. It costs a bundle ($57.20 for adults, $28.60 for kids under 12), but it's by far the best stage show in Vegas.

Accommodations: MGM Grand, $45-$169, 3799 Las Vegas Blvd. S., Las Vegas, NV

89109, (800) 929-1111 or (702) 891-7777.

Information: Las Vegas Convention and Visitors Authority, 3150 Paradise Road, Las Vegas, NV 89109-9096, (702) 892-0711.

Club Med Sandpiper, Florida

Club Med keeps things in the family at Sandpiper, a country club-style facility on the St. Lucie River in Florida. There's time for activities together and apart, giving every member of the family a chance to indulge personal interests.

Supervised activities for children include circus workshops, sailing, water skiing, swimming and diving. Babes as young as 4 months can be cared for by a trained staff while parents play tennis or golf, sail, water ski or learn other sports. Programs are flexible. You can do it all or just drop in for a favorite activity.

You know what it will cost upfront because one price pays for almost everything (golf, billiards and deep sea fishing are extra).

Cost: Rates start at $980 weekly for adults, $637 for children under 12. Some weeks, children under 5 are free.

Information: Club Med, 7975 N. Hayden Road, Scottsdale, AZ 85258, (800) CLUB-MED.

Sarasota, Florida

If you have both young children and teens, Sarasota has the variety you need to keep them all entertained— beaches, fun museums, wildlife sanctuaries, fishing and sailing.

For many years this was the winter home of Ringling Bros. Circus. John Ringling's estate is now a museum complex open to the public. It includes his lavish Venetian-style home, a renowned collection of Baroque art and a huge display of circus posters, costumes and wagons. Across from the estate, Ringling's 1921 Rolls Royce and hundreds of other vintage vehicles, wind-up music boxes and arcade games intrigue all ages visiting Bellm's Cars & Music of Yesterday.

Myakka State Park, a wildlife sanctuary, has airboat rides. Midway Groves offers guided tours through its juice processing plant, and popular Broadway plays are performed at the Asolo Theater.

In the evening, families migrate to the beaches of Longboat Key, over the causeway, to watch the sun set.

Accommodations: Holiday Inn on Longboat Key, from $136 a day per room, children under 18 free, 4949 Gulf of Mexico, Longboat Key, FL 34228, (800) 465-4329.

Information: Sarasota Convention & Visitors Bureau, 655 N. Tamiami Trail, Sarasota, FL 34236, (800) 522-9799 or (813) 957-1877.

Tanque Verde Guest Ranch, Arizona

Tanque Verde Guest Ranch situates you next to Tucson's Saguaro National Monument, which beckons with miles of trails for horseback riding in a dramatic desert landscape of tall cactuses.

Younger kids 4-11 can participate in a children's program with their own riding and dining schedule or swim in the pool while mom and dad choose their own trail ride. The whole family will savor ample ranch-style meals, especially the barbecues.

May is a good time to vacation here; lower summer prices are in effect but the desert hasn't yet heated up. Also, by late August the temperatures are down slightly and prices still are low.

Cost: All-inclusive rates, including lodging, dining and up to three trail rides daily per person, start at $385 per day in May for a family of four.

Information: Tanque Verde Guest Ranch, 14301 E. Speedway Blvd., Tucson, AZ 85748, (800) 234-3833 or (520) 296-6275.

Georgia's Golden Isles

Back in the 1500s, Spanish explorers named Georgia's coastal island group the Golden Isles — possibly because they were thinking of little else but gold. Locals, however, will tell you that the islands earned the name for their radiant beauty, lustrous sand beaches and glorious weather.

To most present-day visitors who cross causeways from Brunswick to explore or stay on St. Simons, Sea, Little St. Simons and Jekyll islands, they still are golden. And, with the exception of Jekyll, which bustles with tourism development, these islands offer a low-key, highly refined atmosphere for anyone seeking a quiet getaway.

Buffered from the mainland by lovely marshes — which in 1870 inspired poet Sidney Lanier to pen "Marshes of Glynn" — St. Simons, Sea and Little St. Simons provide a perfect mix of historic attractions (including old plantations and a pre-Colonial fort), miles of beaches and bike trails, fishing, boating and birding.

Accommodations: The Cloister, Sea Island's distinguished five-star resort, $147-$290 per person, double occupancy, 100 First St., Sea Island, GA 31561, (800) SEA-ISLAND or (912) 638-3611; Lodge at Little St. Simons, accessible only by boat and sans phone and TV, $290-$515, all-inclusive, P.O. Box 21078, Little St. Simon's, GA 31522.

Information: Brunswick and the Golden Isles Visitors Bureau, 2000 Glynn Ave., Brunswick, GA 31520, (800) 933-2627.

Riding the Range in Montana

Families interested in riding, fishing, hiking, nature photography and homestyle meals will find it all, and more, at The 63 Ranch, near Bozeman, MT.

The ranch has hayrides, square dances, bird-watching, cave exploring, campfire sing-alongs and even a steam bath in a traditional Indian "sweat lodge."

Children as young as 4 can learn to ride at this working ranch, established in 1863. Even younger children are led on horses at the corral. More experienced riders can join ranch cowboys moving cattle and can learn to lasso.

Rustic log cabins with modern bathrooms are tucked among aspen and pine at Mission Creek Canyon, framed by snowcapped peaks. The ranch will arrange pack trips to nearby Yellowstone National Park. Mission Creek, which runs through the ranch, is full of wild trout.

Cost: Cabin rates are $710-$820 per week per person; children 4 to 11 are $25 less.

Information: Adventure Guides, 7550 E. McDonald Drive, Suite M, Scottsdale, AZ 85250, (800) 252-7899.

A Finnish Farm in Wisconsin

Three generations of Palmquists take care of the dairy cows, the 800 acres of timber and crops and the vacationers who have been filling the spare rooms and logger's cabins since 1949. This is a working farm, in the heart of Wisconsin's lake-dotted northwoods.

"Palmquist's The Farm," as it's known, features family-style meals cooked on a wood-burning range and served in the rustic, beamed farmhouse. Finnish specialties vie with homemade ice cream and maple syrup from the farm's own sugar house as kid-pleasing favorites.

Guests can help with farm chores, bicycle along country roads, hunt for fossils along an Ice Age trail or go fishing or canoeing. A traditional Finnish sauna, horse-drawn hayrides and campfire sing-alongs add to the camaraderie.

Cost: Rates are $46 a day per adult, $23 for children 5-12, $18.40 under 5; includes two meals. Infants are free.

Information: "Palmquist's The Farm," N5136 River Road, Brantwood, WI 54513, (715) 564-2558 or (800) 519-2558.

Float the Buffalo in Arkansas

The most famous float stream in Arkansas is the Buffalo National River, flowing out of the Ozarks through towering limestone bluffs and unspoiled wilderness. There are guided day-trips and longer floats for all ages and experience levels, as well as guided fishing trips for native smallmouth bass.

Camping is available at Buffalo National River campgrounds. There are also fully equipped, air-conditioned log cabins at Buffalo Point and other locations.

Off-river, the Buffalo Outdoor Center holds photography workshops, arts and crafts seminars, hiking trips and cave explorations. Local musicians perform regularly in the area.

Accommodations: Buffalo National River Campgrounds, $8 per night for drive-in and walk-in sites with full hook-ups, group sites are $1 per person with a $10 minimum. Buffalo Point cabins, $80 a night for two, $15 each person over 12, $5 under 12. Rafts, $20 per person, per day, plus shuttle to/from river.

Information: Buffalo Outdoor Center, P.O. Box 1, Ponca, AR 72670 (501) 861-5514 or (800) 221-5514.

Myrtle Beach, South Carolina

Myrtle Beach, SC, has 60 miles of beaches, 65 golf courses, 150 tennis courts, 50,000 hotel and condo rooms and nine family campgrounds— more than enough options to satisfy a vacationing family.

The beaches are especially good for young children because waves, tides and the dropoff are gentle. Fishermen have choices, from surf casting to deep-sea fishing, shrimping or crabbing from a lakeside dock.

The boardwalk on the Grand Strand boasts numerous video arcades, miniature golf courses and an amusement park. Bike riding is popular, as is touring Brookgreen Gardens, which contains more than 500 pieces of sculpture amid native trees and flowers. The grounds include an avenue of massive 200 year-old oak trees, dripping with Spanish moss.

Accommodations: Northampton Tower at Kingston Plantation, starting from $109 (winter) or $269 (summer) per night, 9800 Lake Drive, Myrtle Beach, SC 29572, (803) 449-0006 or (800) 333-3333; Beach Colony, starting from $36 (winter) or $123 (summer) per night, 5308 N. Ocean Blvd., Myrtle Beach, SC 29577, (800) 222-2141.

Information: Myrtle Beach Area Chamber of Commerce, P.O. Box 2115, Myrtle Beach, SC 29578, (800) 356-3016.

Boston and Cape Cod, Massachusetts

Boston and nearby Cape Cod make a kid-pleasing combination, mixing historic sights and beaches.

The city is a manageable size, with a concentration of sights connected to famous names and events familiar to school-age children from their studies. Much of the touring is outdoors. The Freedom Trail, a walk through the city, stops at historic spots such as the Old North Church, where Paul Revere hung his famous lantern, and the USS Constitution, better known as "Old Ironsides." Even adults can enjoy tossing simulated crates of tea overboard at the Tea Party Ship and Museum. The Boston Children's Museum is filled with hands-on activities and in the same complex as the Computer Museum. John F. Kennedy's birthplace, the JFK Library and Harvard are easy trips via public transportation.

The restored downtown is anchored by Faneuil Hall Marketplace, built originally in 1826, and now housing gourmet and snack food areas plus souvenir and fine arts shops.

Cape Cod beckons with many beaches along the ocean, bays and lakes. The quiet offshore islands of Martha's Vineyard and Nantucket are a fun ferry ride away. For activities, take your choice of deep-sea fishing, whale-watching, whaling museums, bike riding along special roadways, tours of cranberry bogs and processing plants, lazing at the beach or flying a kite in the stiff breezes.

Accommodations: In Boston, Doubletree Guest Quarters, an all-suite hotel, $89 up per night, two locations, (800) 424-2904. On Cape Cod, Dan'l Webster Inn at Sandwich, dating to 1692, $129-$199, children 12 and older, $10 extra, 149 Main St., Sandwich Village, MA 02563, (800) 444-3566 or (508) 888-3622. Also, Bed & Breakfast Cape Cod, P.O. Box 341, West Hyannisport, MA 02672, (800) 686-5252 or (508) 775-2772. Martha's Vineyard Reservations, Box 1322C, Vineyard Haven, MA 02568, (508) 693-7200.

Information: Greater Boston Convention and Visitors Bureau, Prudential Tower, Suite 400, Box 990468, Boston, MA 02199, (800) 888-5515 or (617) 536-4100. Cape Cod Chamber of Commerce, Routes 6 and 132, Hyannis, MA 02601, (508) 362-3225. Nantucket Chamber of Commerce, 48 Main St., Nantucket, MA 02554, (508) 228-1700.

Table Rock Lake, Missouri

You're so stressed that a slow boat to China sounds promising? How about a slow houseboat on Table Rock Lake, an hour south of Springfield, MO.

With plenty of uncrowded shoreline, you're not likely to bump sterns with anyone. And the fish are jumping in a lake so clear it's a Midwest mecca for divers.

If you develop cabin fever, you can hike or bike along the lake, enjoy tennis, golf or shopping in Kimberling or head for Branson, the town that stole Nashville's thunder as the center for country music.

In addition to summerlong performances by country stars, Branson is home to Silver Dollar City, an Ozark theme park with local artisans who demonstrate mountain crafts, and Marvel Cave, where you can explore underground passageways by cable car.

Summer festivals include the American Folk Music Festival in mid-June, the National Quilt Festival in late August and the National Crafts Festival in mid-September. Call the Branson Chamber of Commerce for dates and rates.

Cost: Tri-Lakes Houseboat Sales and Rental in Kimberling City, from $200 a night for a houseboat that sleeps four, 49 Lake Road, Kimberling City, MO 65686, (417)

739-2370. The houseboats have bathrooms with showers, dining and sleeping areas and fully equipped kitchens.

Information: Branson Chamber of Commerce, P.O. Box 1897, Branson, MO 65616, (417) 334-4136.

Mountain Magic in New York

Your kids' eyes will widen when you pull up to this castlelike Victorian hotel complete with towers and turrets. Situated cliffside on Lake Mohonk and surrounded by a 7,500-acre nature preserve, Mohonk Mountain House gives your family a kingdom of outdoor opportunities.

Besides tennis and golf, you can hike in the woods, ride horseback along forest trails, swim in the lake — or just relax under a pine tree with a good book.

This hotel lends itself to family reunions — and you don't have to cook or make beds. From Memorial Day through Labor Day, a daily program for children keeps kids ages 2-12 busy with hayrides, beach parties, sing-alongs and campfires from 9:30 a.m. to 12:30 p.m. and 2 to 5 p.m. An evening session from 7:30 to 9 p.m. keeps your kids entertained while you and your spouse enjoy a romantic dinner.

Special themes on summer weekends include arts, music and a Garden Holiday complete with a croquet tournament, garden party and ball.

Cost: Approximately $289-$391 per night, double occupancy, includes three meals a day and afternoon tea. When children ages 4-12 share a room with adults, the additional cost per child is $60 ($90 for children older than 12). Each session of the children's program is free.

Information: Mohonk Mountain House, Lake Mohonk, New Paltz, NY 12561, (914) 255-4500 or (800) 772-6646.

Walt Disney World, Florida

Take the plunge with Walt Disney World's Splash Mountain, a log flume ride at the Magic Kingdom's Frontierland. This action attraction starts peacefully, a float trip backed by the music of "Zip-A-Dee-Doo-Dah," when zap — your boat drops five stories into the spray (the world's longest flume drop) at 40 miles an hour.

That's just some of the fun at Epcot, Disney-MGM and the Magic Kingdom, where the possibilities are endless — even if your wallet isn't. To keep costs down, dine on burgers, salads and sandwiches at the inexpensive eateries and put the kids on a strict souvenir diet. Let memories make up most of the take-home magic.

You and your family can have fun within a budget by booking accommodations at the All-Star Sports or All-Star Music resorts, moderate on-site accommodations that don't skimp on the Disney extras. If tents are more your family's style, Fort Wilderness Resort offers campsites as well as trailer homes for rent.

Overnighting near the park saves time and energy — not to mention parking fees. It's easy to slip back to your resort for an afternoon of poolside napping, and you can return to the park in time for the night's laser shows and fireworks. Other bonuses: Disney resort guests can enter the Magic Kingdom one hour earlier and book dinner reservations before arriving in town.

Cost: Rooms at the the All-Star Sports and All-Star Music resorts start at $69. Campsites at Fort Wilderness start at $35, and trailer homes rent from $185 per night. Individual one-park admission to Magic Kingdom, Epcot Center or Disney-MGM costs $37 for ages 10 and older, $30 for ages 3-9. Kids under 3 are free. A four-day Park-

Hopper Pass costs $137 for ages 10 and older, $109 for kids 3-9, and allows unlimited admission to all three areas. A five-day World-Hopper Pass adds another day of admission, plus unlimited entrance to River Country, Typhoon Lagoon, Discovery Island and Pleasure Island.

Information: Walt Disney World Central Reservations, P.O. Box 10000, Lake Buena Vista, FL 32830, (407) W-DISNEY.

Snow Mountain Ranch, Colorado

Wildflowers dot the hillsides in summer, and hiking trails take you through aspen groves where ridgetops offer sweeping views of snow-covered peaks. Snow Mountain Ranch, operated by YMCA of the Rockies, provides 4,950 acres of meadows, mountains and trails for outdoor enthusiasts — plus hotel amenities at budget prices.

Wide-open spaces and a wide range of activities make Snow Mountain a favorite place for multigenerational vacations. You can hike hand-in-hand with your kids or grandkids to a waterfall, fish in a nearby lake or sign up for a breakfast horseback ride that provides flapjacks and cowboy coffee along with panoramic views.

While your kids ages 3 and older enjoy nature-oriented programs Monday through Friday, you can learn batik and basketmaking at the adult craft shops.

Individual cabins and motel-style rooms are available. Each of the 45 cabins has a kitchen and is equipped with dishes, bedding and towels. A restaurant offers an alternative when you're not in the mood to cook.

Cost: Prices range from $98 per night for a two-bedroom cabin that sleeps five to $242 for a five-bedroom vacation home that sleeps 12. Lodge rooms that sleep six are $59-$86 with a half-bath and showers down the hall. Registration priority goes to members of YMCA of the Rockies ($125 to join). Reservations are taken as early as mid-January for members and mid-April for non-members for the following summer, and the place fills quickly.

Information: YMCA of the Rockies, Snow Mountain Ranch, P.O. Box 169, Winter Park, CO 80482, (303) 887-2152. (There is a similar facility at Estes Park, CO.)

On Track in Ohio

Life's little ups and downs are lots of fun at Cedar Point Amusement Park at Sandusky, a good place to base a Lake Erie family vacation. The park, situated on a 364-acre peninsula, is famous for its 12 roller coasters and bills itself as the largest ride park in the country.

Thrill-seeker favorites include the Magnum XL200, one of the tallest and fastest coasters in the world, reaching heights of 205 feet and speeds of up to 72 miles an hour. The Mean Streak, a 161-foot-tall wooden wonder, has dips and drops calculated to make you shriek with delight.

For more sedate fun, try the steam train or a carousel, or climb the treehouse in the Berenstain Bears outdoor play area. The adjacent Challenge Park has go-carts and miniature golf, and Soak City offers water slides for cooling off.

Leave the man-made fun behind for some natural wonders by boarding a Lake Erie island-hopping cruise. Boats depart from Sandusky for day-trips to Kelleys Island, where hiking and biking trails lead you to archaeological sites and grooves left by ice-age glaciers. Plus, the fishing's fine.

Cedar Point admission fees are $28.95 if you are 4 feet or taller, $6.95 if you are under 4 feet tall.

Accommodations: Hotel Breakers, $90-$210, P.O. Box 5006, Sandusky, OH 44871-5006, (419) 627-2106.

Information: Cedar Point Amusement Park, P.O. Box 5006, Sandusky, OH 44871, (419) 627-2350.

Hershey, Pennsylvania

What child could resist visiting Chocolatetown USA, where the smell of chocolate lingers in the air and the street lights look like foil-wrapped candy kisses?

Hershey is a dream come true. Start with the Chocolate World Visitors Center, with its free simulated chocolate factory tours that explain how chocolate bars are made. Move on to the Hershey Museum, an 11-acre zoo, botanical gardens and the more than 45 rides at Hersheypark, including water rides, roller coasters, a monorail, ferris wheels and several arcades.

This is also Pennsylvania Dutch country, with Amish villages, family-style smorgasbord restaurants serving local fare (save room for a slice of wet-bottomed shoo-fly pie), farmer's markets and crafts shops.

Accommodations: Hershey Lodge, $176 per person, double occupancy, for one-night package, including lodging and passes to museum and amusement park.

Information: Hershey Information and Reservations, 300 Park Blvd., Hershey, PA 17033, (800) HERSHEY.

Retreat to Plymouth, Vermont

For outdoor activities of the less-rugged, heart-in-your-throat variety, check out this mountain retreat. Hawk Inn and Mountain Resort, in central Vermont's Green Mountains, is a AAA four-diamond, Mobil four-star resort that has more activities than you could ever hope to take advantage of.

Enjoy the spa, nature trails (with guided hikes and bird-watching walks), boating, canoeing, a swimming pond with sandy beach, horseback riding, tennis and bicycling (on either mountain or touring bikes). Go to the Orvis fly-fishing school, or try gold panning.

One-day camps for ages 5-12 allow parents some private time. In the evenings, enjoy lawn performances of music, magic and mime.

Hawk Inn, at Plymouth, is close to the antique-shop heaven of Woodstock, also the home of Ben & Jerry's, where whimsical ice cream factory tours (with tastings) are $1 for adults; free for children under 12.

Cost: $139-$209 per room, double occupancy, $9 a night for children 3-17, $25 a night for ages 18 and older, all prices including breakfast.

Information: Hawk Inn and Mountain Resort, Route 100, HCR 70, P.O. Box 64, Plymouth, VT 05056, (802) 672-3811 or (800) 685-4295.

Paul Bunyan Country, Minnesota

If you're longing for a relaxing lake cottage that has enough options to keep the kids busy and out of your hair all week, Gull Four Seasons Resort is it.

The informal getaway is in the heart of Minnesota's cool, beautiful Paul Bunyan country, on Gull Lake. It's one of the largest of 464 freshwater lakes in the Brainerd resort area in central Minnesota.

The resort offers indoor and outdoor pools, a sandy beach, fishing, tennis, sauna, whirlpool, a playground, a recreation room, walking trails and boating.

At Brainerd's Paul Bunyan Amusement Center, a giant statue of the legendary logger welcomes you by name.

Other attractions are a re-created 1870s logging village called Lumbertown USA with train and riverboat rides, the Croft Mine Historical Park, where you can see iron ore mining, and the Brainerd International Raceway.

Cost: $67 per night for chalets or cabins with one to three bedrooms. Deluxe condos are higher.

Information: Gull Four Seasons Resort, 1336 St. Columbo Road, Brainerd, MN 56401, (218) 963-7969 or (800) 964-4855.

Choo Choo in Chattanooga, Tennessee

The small, southern city of Chattanooga, TN, can't be beat for family attractions, historic sights and natural wonders. It's at its best in summer, especially during the Riverbend sports and music festival in late June.

The Chattanooga Choo Choo station is now a shopping center-hotel complex that includes a model railroad museum and some accommodations in train cars.

Don't miss riding up Lookout Mountain on the incline railway - its 73 percent grade is the world's steepest. Rock City Gardens offers a view of seven states among its unusual rock formations and children's fairyland-type exhibits.

Ruby Falls cave features a lighted 145-foot underground waterfall, and nearby Raccoon Mountain Adventure Park has an alpine slide and a hang gliding simulator.

History fans can view dioramas of Civil War scenes at Battles for Chattanooga and enjoy nearby Chickamauga-Chattanooga National Military Park, the largest and oldest military park in the country.

Accommodations: Radisson Read House, historic property, $79 per room, $89 per suite, 827 Broad St., Chattanooga, TN 37402, (615) 266-4121 or (800) 333-3333. (Children stay free).

Information: Chattanooga Convention & Visitors Bureau, 1001 Market St., Chattanooga, TN 37402, (800) 322-3344.

Cruising in Hawaii

A cruise lets your family sample the Hawaiian Islands the easy way. You can walk through lava fields and watch sulphur steaming from the ground at Volcanoes National Park. You can get a bird's-eye view via helicopter of the fluted Na Pali Cliffs and cascading waterfalls on Kauai. You can snorkel through schools of rainbow-colored fish on Molikini and learn about military history at Pearl Harbor on Oahu.

And on an American Hawaii cruise, you can do all this without moving from hotel to hotel or rushing to catch inter-island flights. Summer programs for kids on the SS Independence keep children ages 5 and over busy with hula lessons, arts and crafts and scavenger hunts.

Cost: A four-person cabin for a seven-day cruise starts at $1,545 per person for the first two people, plus air supplements. Children 18 and younger sail free with two full-fare adults in many cabin categories. Exceptions are Christmas and New Year's cruises, when children cruise for $195.

Information: American Hawaii Cruises, 2 N. Riverside Plaza, Chicago, IL 60606, (800) 765-7000.

California Theme Parks

A trip to Disneyland brings out the little kid in even the most work-weary adult. Favorite rides such as Big Thunder Mountain Railroad and Space Mountain and such attractions as Submarine Voyage and Michael Jackson's Captain EO still bring smiles.

Nearby, Knott's Berry Farm offers a different kind of theme park fun, more down-home than razzmatazz. Kids can ride the high-speed roller coaster Boomerang, ogle the dinosaurs and get wet at the Big Foot Rapids.

A one-day passport at Disneyland is $33 for adults, $25 for children ages 3-11 and free to younger kids. At Knott's Berry Farm, admission is $29 for ages 12 and older, $19 for ages 3-11 and seniors, and free for younger ones.

Accommodations: $230 family package per night at Hilton Suites Orange, including a two-room suite, breakfast for everyone, one free meal for children under age 12 and two Disneyland passes good for five consecutive days, 400 N. State College Blvd., Orange, CA 92668, (800) HILTONS or (714) 938-1111.

Information: Disneyland Guest Relations, 1313 Harbor Blvd., P.O. Box 3232, Anaheim, CA 92803, (714) 999-4565. Knott's Berry Farm, 8039 Beach Blvd., Buena Park, CA 90620, (714) 220-5200.

Wagon Trains in Wyoming

Pioneer history comes to life against the backdrop of the snow-covered peaks of the Grand Tetons. Listen to the creak of the wheels as you head in to the Bridger-Teton National Forest as part of a wagon train team. The landscape - streams, lakes and mountain ranges - is pure West.

But the pioneers never had it so cushy. Your wagons feature padded seats and rubber tires, accompanied by a chuck wagon chef who grills steak, chicken and ribs. This trip lets the whole family enjoy some history, even preschoolers who can sprawl comfortably in the wagons. Participants age 6 and older can sit tall in the saddle atop their own horse.

At night your guide leads cowboy sing-alongs under the starry skies. Then you'll bed down in the wagon or put your sleeping bag out in the moonlight - just as those first settlers did.

Cost: Four-day trips are $545 for adults, $450 for children under 16. Six-day trips are $700 for adults, $600 for children under 16. Participants can spend half of each day on horseback. If you want to ride all day, there's an extra fee.

Information: American Wilderness Experience, P.O. Box 1486, Boulder, CO 80306, (800) 444-0099.

Flathead, Montana

Families will never get bored in Flathead. This relatively undiscovered bit of Big Sky Country smiles with the openness of the West and offers some of its best scenery. Tucked in northwest Montana next to Glacier National Park, this piece of cowboy country lures golf enthusiasts with seven courses where the "birdies" are eagles and tundra swans.

Kids love Flathead Lake, ringed by mountains, with 186 miles of shoreline, 32 islands and enough fishing to last all summer. Take a boat ride to Painted Rocks to see the petroglyphs left by the Blackfoot Indians, and picnic on Wildhorse Island, a state park where deer and sheep graze.

Glacier Raft Co. provides more adventure with float trips along the boundaries of scenic Glacier National Park. But for the best views, cross the Continental Divide on the Going-to-the-Sun Highway, one of America's most scenic routes.

Accommodations: Grouse Mountain Lodge, $125, kids under 12 stay free, 1205 Highway 93 W., Whitefish, MT 59937, (800) 321-8822. This resort is near golf facilities and arranges raft trips, lake cruises and other activities.

Information: Glacier Raft Co., P.O. Box 218, W. Glacier, MT 59936, (800) 332-9995. Flathead Convention and Visitors Bureau, 15 Depot Park, Kalispell, MT 59901, (800) 543-3105.

Beach and Spa in Florida

Just looking at the still stretch of San Carlos Bay on Florida's Gulf Coast can calm even the most burned-out city dweller. A favorite activity at Sanibel Harbour Resort & Spa is simply enjoying the view from your condominium balcony.

But there's lots to do for families, both together and apart, at this waterfront resort. Practice volleying with your kids on the tennis courts or follow a canoe trail through the mangrove forest on this 80-acre property. Treat yourself to a picnic and a beach stroll along the broad white sands of Sanibel Island's public beach.

The comprehensive Kids Klub program ($15 per child, per day) keeps children ages 5-12 busy 10 a.m.-4 p.m. daily and 6-8:30 p.m. Fridays and Saturdays. With your kids happily occupied, head for the spa, where soothing treatments include aromatherapy massage, herbal wraps and loofa salt glow treatments.

Cost: From $246 per person for 3 days and 2 nights for two adults, including breakfast daily, one Champagne Sunset Cruise, one hour tennis court time, unlimited use of all spa facilities and exercise classes. Four children under 12 can stay free (room only) if they share the condominium with their parents.

Information: Sanibel Harbour Resort & Spa, 17260 Harbour Pointe Drive, Fort Myers, FL 33908, (941) 466-4000 or, for reservations, (800) 767-7777.

Steamboat Springs, Colorado

Colorado summers are as spectacular as its winters and a lot less pricey. Wildflowers dot the mountains, and warm weather brings a host of fun outdoor activities.

At Steamboat Springs, a ski resort high in the Rockies, summer means hot-air ballooning, mountain biking, fishing, hiking, llama trekking, white-water rafting and horseback riding. Festivals, concerts, art workshops and special programs for parents and kids add to the excitement.

At the Steamboat Kids Adventure Club, children ages 3-5 and 6-12 enjoy hiking, kayaking, arts and crafts and miniature golf. Lodging options include motels, hotels and condominiums, and flexible packages add to the convenience.

Cost: Starting at $122 per adult, double occupancy, for a three-night Family Getaway package at a downtown motel, including admission to the downtown Hot Mineral Springs Pool, a gondola ride up Mount Werner, admission to a Friday or Saturday night rodeo, and one day at the Kids Adventure Club. A child under 12 shares the room for $46. For reservations, call Steamboat Reservation Services, (800) 922-2722.

Information: Steamboat Springs Chamber Resort Association, P.O. Box 774408, Steamboat Springs, CO 80477, (303) 879-0880.

Wintergreen Resort, Virginia

Wintergreen, an upscale 10,800-acre family resort in Virginia's Blue Ridge Mountains, offers country living for city slickers. Naturalists lead family hikes, and kids take to the outdoors with a comprehensive day camp that teaches them about the environment through play. After a day of golfing, tennis, boating on Lake Monocan, swimming in the oversize pool and horseback riding, families reconvene in their rental condominiums or homes, all of which are decked out with modern conveniences. Many sport splendid views.

At Kids in Action, children ages 2 1/2-5 go on butterfly hunts, look for critters in streams and learn arts and crafts. Kids ages 5-12 hike, canoe, fish and swim. Because of the popularity of the children's programs, book them when you reserve your lodging.

Kids Night Out, available weekends during the summer, continues the fun. Parents can take advantage and savor a romantic dinner for two.

Cost: A Family Package begins at $256 per night for a four-night stay in a two-bedroom condominium. Package includes Fun Passes, unlimited use of The Wintergarden Spa, and free breakfast and dinner for children.

Information: Wintergreen Resort, P.O. Box 706, Wintergreen, VA 22958, (800) 325-2200.

Mountain of Fun In Vermont

Splash into summer on the Giant River Ride, a 300-foot-long water flume, or race laps with your preteen in the mountainside pool. At Smugglers' Notch, an unpretentious ski resort nestled in Vermont's Green Mountains, water games comprise just part of an action-packed summer program.

A tennis package allows you and your kids ages 7-17 to practice at daily clinics, volley with free court time and come away with a videotaped analysis of your game.

At Alice's Wonderland, a state-certified child-care center, tots ages 6 weeks-3 years find loving arms. At Discovery Dynamos, kids ages 3-6 explore woods and water, play games and enjoy arts and crafts. At Adventure Rangers, preteens 6-12 compete in mini-Olympics, take swimming lessons and gather around evening bonfires. The Mountain Explorer program challenges teens 13-17 with a rope obstacle course, mountain bike treks and orienteering.

Cost: Starting at $725 for FamilyFest packages for four spending five nights in studio accommodations. Prices increase in July and August.

Information: Village at Smugglers' Notch , Route 108, Smugglers' Notch, VT 05464, (800) 451-8752.

City Safari in Chicago, Illinois

You can go on safari, city-style, in Chicago by visiting the museums near the lake front. At the Shedd Aquarium and the Oceanarium, billed as the world's largest indoor marine mammal exhibit, you can watch belugas and dolphins breach and dive, and you'll discover the underwater worlds of seals, penguins and tropical fish.

With the Field Museum of Natural History's "Into the Wild: Animals, Trails & Tails," listen and learn about birds and critters. This hands-on exhibit walks you through habitats as diverse as wetlands, prairies, lakes and cliffs. On Wednesdays, admission is free. Stop by the Lincoln Park Zoo petting area from 10 a.m. to 2 p.m.

Save time to saunter along the lake and watch the sailboats, window shop along Michigan Avenue and eat pizza, Chicago-style.

Accommodations: From $119 a night (kids under age 18 free) at the Hyatt Regency Chicago, 151 E. Wacker Drive, Chicago, IL 60601, (312) 565-1234 or Hyatt Worldwide Reservations, (800) 233-1234. The hotel is well-located and offers the family-friendly Camp Hyatt program. Ask about the 50 percent discount for adjoining rooms.

Information: Chicago Tourism Office, 78 E. Washington St., Chicago, IL 60602, (800) ITS-CHGO.

Digging for Dinosaurs

If dinosaurs are high on your family's interest list, how about five days at Dino Camp in far western Colorado?

While the kids work in a simulated quarry salted with authentic casts of bones just ripe for discovery, their parents dig for the real thing in the nearby Mygatt-Moore Quarry, an ancient Jurassic watering hole.

Professional paleontologists direct all; solving a dinosaur murder mystery is one of the fun challenges.

Farther north, Paleo Field School of Montana State University welcomes amateurs at its digs 90 miles south of Glacier National Park. You'll explore with ice picks and paint brushes, just as the paleontologists do. Fees begin at $95 for adults, $75 for children 10-14, for a one-day session, including food and tools. Children must be at least 10 years old, and sessions are limited.

Accommodations: For Colorado dig, package includes meals plus comfortable lodgings for $800 for adults, $550 for kids age 6 and older.

Information: Dinamation International Society, 550 Crossroads Court, Fruita, CO 81521, (800) DIG-DINO. Paleo Field School, Montana State University, Bozeman, MT 59717, (406) 994-6618.

Amtrak Adventures

Amtrak trains can do more than transport you to your destination. They can make the trip itself an adventure and provide your lodging and meals along the way.

For example, Amtrak's Empire Builder, between Chicago and Seattle, offers an exciting way to see the Great Plains and the Rockies. The trip takes about 43 hours, including two nights on the train. Lounge cars offer games, videos, cartoons for the kids and first-run movies in the evenings. With wraparound windows, the upper level of the lounge car provides panoramic views.

A family of four can get its own family bedroom, stretching the width of the car on the lower level. The private compartment has a sofa and chairs for daytime and sleeping accommodations at night; showers and restrooms are a few steps away.

All meals are included with the price of the bedroom.

Cost: At press time, the lowest summer fare for two adults and two children in the family bedroom — covering transportation, accommodations, food and entertainment aboard — was $1,524.

Information: Amtrak, (800) USA-RAIL.

Safari in Texas

It's a jungle down there in the Lone Star State, where Fossil Rim Wildlife Center offers adventures that are so near, yet safari. The private refuge for rare and endangered species is located 60 miles southwest of Dallas and Fort Worth.

Piling aboard open jeeps, you'll run with the wildebeests, get within shooting range (by camera, of course) of endangered white rhinos, cheetahs, gazelles and 34 other species, and fall asleep to the serenade of howling wolves.

Nature trails lead through range and forest, or you can hunt for fossils or tour facilities where endangered species are bred.

Accommodations: $55 per person per night in bunkhouses at Fossil Rim. Includes breakfast, dinner, educational programs and a tour of the facility.

Information: Fossil Rim Wildlife Center, P.O. Box 2189, Glen Rose, TX 76043, (817) 897-2960.

SCENIC DRIVES

When was the last time you saw the real America? We don't mean the homogenized version that thrives off freeway exits, where the motel names are the same from Anchorage to Atlanta. We mean the real McCoy — the behind-the-scenes America where long johns flap on clotheslines and little girls skip rope on tree-shaded sidewalks.

The following scenic drives will take you into the heart of a slower country where people and scenery are more than passing blurs. Several of the drives are designated National Forest Scenic Byways that offer beauty on an official scale. Others are nobody-knows-me roads that wander nowhere in particular, certainly nowhere you've ever heard of. Some are short enough to be a day-trip, while others can be the focal point of a week's vacation.

Should you find your "hurry-up habits" playing backseat driver, remember that the destination is incidental to the journey — and may not even be on the map. It's the getting-there part that matters, so slow down. You may find a lost part of yourself in the process.

Lodging rates are per night for two persons. Mileages are approximate and exclude side trips.

Queen Kaahumanu Highway in Hawaii

The route: From Kamuela, in the Kohala Mountains, take Route 19 west and south along the west coast of the Big Island of Hawaii to Kailua Kona.

Distance: About 30 miles.

Skirting the dry west coast of the Big Island of Hawaii, Queen Kaahumanu Highway, Route 19, cuts through stark volcanic formations, alternately giving views of black rock and blue ocean.

The beds of old and recent lava provide unusual roadside scenery — acres of naked black rock with an occasional, and startling, flower springing from a fissure. Even roadside graffiti here takes unusual forms: white rocks laid in patterns on the black lava.

Several of Hawaii's finest resorts are situated on the coast, surrounded by lush vegetation that springs up from the volcanic soil when it is watered.

A side trip on the Hawaii Belt Road provides marvelous views of the coast as it ascends toward the interior. At about 3,000 feet you will come upon the sprawling Parker Ranch, largest in the United States after the King Ranch in Texas. The ranch welcomes visitors.

Accommodations: The Royal Waikoloan, $120-$275, 69-275 Waikoloa Beach Drive, Kamuela, HI 96738, (800) 822-4282 or (808) 885-6789.

Information: Kohala Coast Resort Association, 69-275 Waikoloa, Kaahumanu, HI 96743, (808) 885-4915.

Vermont's Green Mountains

The route: From Newport in northernmost Vermont, take Route 100 south to West Dover.

Distance: About 195 miles.

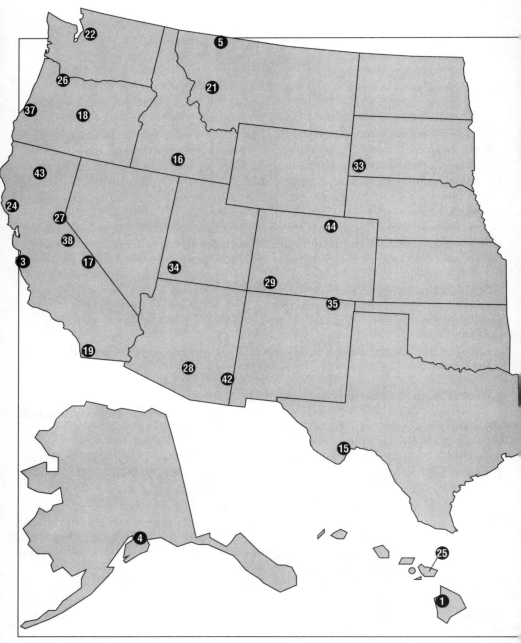

1 Queen Kaahumana Highway in Hawaii
2 Vermont's Green Mountains
3 Big Sur in California
4 Seward Highway in Alaska
5 Going-to-the-Sun Highway in Montana
6 Great River Road in Minnesota
7 White Mountains, New Hampshire
8 Ocean Highway, Florida Keys
9 Crossing Vermont
10 Rhode Island Coast
11 Virginia Highlands
12 Covered Bridges in Ohio
13 Door County, Wisconsin
14 Arkansas Ozarks
15 Big Bend in Texas
16 Sawtooth Scenic Byway, Idaho
17 Highs and Lows in California
18 Cascade Lakes, Oregon
19 California: Sea, Mountains, Desert
20 Florida: Pines to Captivating Isles
21 Montana's Big Sky and Ghost Towns
22 Washington's Olympic Peninsula
23 Maine's Rugged Coast
24 California's Mendocino County
25 Hana Highway, Maui, Hawaii
26 Columbia River Gorge and Mount Hood, Oregon

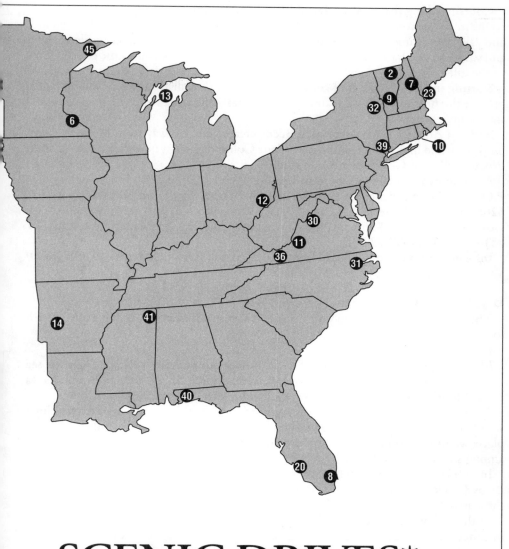

SCENIC DRIVES*

Coursing along the eastern edge of the Green Mountains, Vermont's Route 100 is scenic in any season. In summer, the two-lane road takes motorists through green hills and valleys, pausing at picturesque villages and romantic inns, meandering along rivers and wood-fenced farms. Take time to fish in clear streams, bike on scenic paths or hike in the hills.

Starting in late summer and continuing through the fall, autumn's brilliant colors speckle the hills, pumpkin pyramids decorate farm entrances and the scent of wood smoke tinges the air.

Some of America's most charming B&Bs create a home away from home in towns on or near the highway, including the Four Columns Inn in Newfane, Castle Inn in Proctorsville and Governor's Inn in Ludlow.

Accommodations: Four Columns Inn, $110-$175 ($210-$275 including dinner), P.O. Box 278, Newfane, VT 05345, (800) 787-6633; Castle Inn, $135-$185 ($185-$208 including dinner), P.O. Box 207, Proctorsville, VT 05153, (800) 697-7222; Governor's Inn, $95-$259 ($190-$299 including dinner), 86 Main St., Ludlow, VT 05149, (800) GOVERNOR.

Information: Vermont Travel Division, 134 State St., Montpelier, VT 05602, (800) VERMONT.

Big Sur in California

The route: From Carmel on California's coast near Monterey, take Highway 1 south to San Simeon.

Distance: About 93 miles.

Many people believe this highway is the most scenic in America. Like a gigantic sea snake, Big Sur highway undulates over the sea-gripping fingers of California's Santa Lucia Mountains, soaring high above the crashing rollers of the Pacific Ocean.

At turnouts and overlooks, motorists pause to admire this rugged coast from as high as 800 feet above the sea. Restaurants and inns cling to cliffs and headlands, and in the places where the road swings down close to sea level you can find secluded campgrounds among stately redwood trees.

In its 93 miles from Carmel to San Simeon, Highway 1 crosses 20 bridges, including Bixby Creek Bridge, a soaring, graceful span that is the most photographed bridge in the state.

At the end of the road, in San Simeon, stands one of the most remarkable structures in America, the 100-room, hilltop Hearst Castle, where publisher William Randolph Hearst hosted Hollywood stars. It's open for tours.

Accommodations: In San Simeon, Best Western Cavalier Inn, $66-$110, 9415 Hearst Drive, San Simeon, CA 93452, (805) 927-4688 or (800) 528-1234. In Seaside, near Monterey, Days Inn, $99-$119, 1400 Del Monte Blvd., Seaside, CA 93955, (800) DAYS INN or (408) 394-5335. In Carmel, La Playa Hotel, $116-$215, P.O. Box 900, Carmel, CA 93921, (800) 582-8900.

Information: Monterey Peninsula Chamber of Commerce, P.O. Box 1770, Monterey, CA 93942, (408) 649-1770.

Seward Highway in Alaska

The route: This National Forest Scenic Byway follows Seward Highway (Route 1) south from Anchorage to Seward through parts of Chugach National Forest.

Distance: 127 miles.

Be sure to brake for moose, elk, deer, Dall sheep, bald eagles, maybe even a lumbering bear on this scenic drive past Alaska's most spectacular peaks, glaciers, looking-glass lakes and meadows.

Begin near Anchorage at Potter Point State Game Reserve, a marsh refuge with a boardwalk trail that harbors nesting waterfowl. The road heads south for Turnagain Arm. Use the telescope at the vista point to spot whales. Around the bend, waterfalls crash down mountains brightened by bluebells, and Dall sheep nibble on high, grassy cliffs.

Entering Portage, spruce skeletons in a sunken forest bear silent witness to the 1964 earthquake that leveled the town and trees.

A side route leads to Portage Glacier, Alaska's most popular tourist attraction, where you can gawk at glaciers and icebergs floating on a vast lake. There's also an informative visitor center.

Entering the Kenai Mountains, where waterfalls tumble past dense thickets of cranberry and blueberry bushes, the road parallels Kenai Lake, a 24-mile aquamarine jewel. Ssshhhhhhh! If you're very quiet, you could catch a glimpse of a moose loose in the meadow.

Accommodations: The Voyageur in Anchorage, from $149, 501 K St., Anchorage, AK 99501, (800) 247-9070 or (907) 277-9501.

Information: Chugach National Forest, 3301 C St., Suite 300, Anchorage, AK 99503, (907) 271-2500; Alaska Division of Tourism, P.O. Box 110801, Juneau, AK 99811-0801, (907) 465-2010; Anchorage Visitor Information Center, 546 W. Fourth Ave., Anchorage, AK 99501, (907) 274-3531.

Going-to-the-Sun Highway in Montana

The route: From West Glacier follow Going-to-the-Sun Highway north to Apgar and Lake McDonald, over Logan's Pass to St. Mary.

Distance: About 50 miles.

As you rise higher and higher on the Going-to-the-Sun Highway in Montana's Glacier National Park, you'll see vista after vista of serrated peaks, their flanks bearing the telltale gouges and streaks of past glacial movement.

The great body of ice that once overlaid the region also left behind deep valleys, waterfalls and lakes, all of which add to the beauty of the drive. Wildlife is abundant.

Not all the glaciers are gone, of course. There are still 50 of them in the park, many visible from the highway, and some can be approached via side roads. Even in summertime, snowdrifts remain on the road at higher elevations, notably at Logan's Pass Visitor Center at 6,680 feet.

Accommodations: Lodging reservations for inns and cabins along the Going-to-the-Sun Highway can be made through Glacier Park, Inc., $27-$282, Dial Corp Center, Phoenix, AZ 85077-0928, (602) 207-6000.

Information: Glacier National Park, West Glacier, MT 59936, (406) 888-5441.

Great River Road in Minnesota

The route: Take U.S. 61 south from Red Wing, MN, to La Crosse, WI.

Distance: About 100 miles.

"This stretch of river is one of the loveliest places in America," author Garrison Keillor once said.

Indeed it is. From Red Wing, MN, to LaCrosse, WI, the Mississippi River cuts a wide swath, with limestone bluffs rising as high as 600 feet on each side. In one place, it widens into a natural lake, Pepin, where water-skiing was invented in the 1920s.

Scenic U.S. 61 takes you along the river and through pretty turn-of-the-century towns with restored main streets and ambient inns. One of them, Wabasha, was the setting for the movie "Grumpy Old Men." Another, Red Wing, has become a trendy weekend destination favored by Twin Cities residents.

Accommodations: St. James Hotel, $75-$155, 406 Main St., Red Wing, MN 55066, (800) 252-1857 or (612) 388-2846.

Information: Minnesota Office of Tourism, 121 Seventh Place E., Metro Square Building, Suite 100, St. Paul, MN 55101, (800) 657-3700.

White Mountains, New Hampshire

The route: A loop through the White Mountains from North Conway. Go north on Route 16 to Glen, west on U.S. 302 to Twin Mountain, south on U.S. 3 (or I-93) to North Woodstock, east on Route 112 (Kancamagus Highway) to Conway and north on Route 16 back to North Conway.

Distance: About 95 miles.

Views of the Presidential Range, highest peaks in the Northeast, are accentuated by glimpses of clear streams and rivers, lakes and ponds. A wide variety of trees makes a variegated forest — and spectacular fall colors — against the rugged granite peaks of New Hampshire's White Mountains.

Along the western side of this loop, several natural wonders have been attracting visitors for generations: The Old Man of the Mountain, a Lincolnesque rock formation; the Flume, a towering waterfall; Profile Lake; and Lost River Gorge.

A ride on the steep cog railway to the top of Mount Washington — where winds are strong enough to whip out hairpins — is an adventure to remember.

Some of New England's most brilliant foliage decorates the mountainsides in Franconia Notch each fall.

Accommodations: In Jackson, Christmas Farm Inn, from $68 per person with two meals, Box CC, Jackson, NH 03846, (800) HI ELVES, (603) 383-4313. In Franconia, Franconia Inn, $65-$100, Route 116, Eastern Road, Franconia, NH 03580, (603) 823-5542.

Information: White Mountains Attractions Association, Box 10, N. Woodstock, NH 03262, (603) 745-8720 or (800) FIND MTS.

Ocean Highway, Florida Keys

The route: Round trip from Miami to Key West. Follow U.S. Highway 1 south, which ends at Key West.

Distance: About 330 miles round trip.

No highway matches this ocean-going one for a unique trip. It spans two bodies of water and connects the Florida Keys, dollops of land that stretch southwest toward Cuba.

The 42 bridges between Florida's mainland and Key West give views of the Atlantic Ocean, a strong, deep, sapphire blue on the left side, and the Gulf of Mexico, a softer aquamarine on the right. Their colors sparkle in the sun and constantly change to darker or lighter as clouds and breezes shift.

Near Key Largo, visit John Pennekamp Coral Reef State Park, the first underwater park in the country, and the dolphins at Dolphins Plus. Drop in to see the tiny, rare deer protected at the Key Deer National Wildlife Station. All along the route, watch for pelicans, herons and roseate spoonbills.

Accommodations: In Key West, Quality Inn, from $65, 3850 N. Roosevelt Blvd., Key West, FL 33040, (305) 294-6681 or (800) 221-2222. Key West Reservation Service, (954) 340-4786.

Information: Florida Keys Visitors Bureau, 402 Wall St., Key West, FL 33040, (800) FLA-KEYS or (800) 648-6269.

Crossing Vermont

The route: From Woodstock, in central Vermont, take U.S. 4 west to Rutland, then U.S. 7 south to Manchester Depot. Take Routes 30/11 east to Route 100 and go north to U.S. 4, then back east to Woodstock.

Distance: A 120-mile loop.

Cross Vermont in any direction and you'll enjoy a visual feast of rolling pastures and pretty villages, steepled churches and general stores, red barns and covered bridges. This loop through the Green Mountains is a succession of Currier & Ives paintings come to life.

In Killington, New England's quintessential ski town, you can enjoy summer theater and equestrian festivals or head to Killington Ski and Summer Resort and ride the 3.5-mile gondola tramway for panoramic views of five states and Canada.

Rutland is famous for the Norman Rockwell Museum. Manchester, a study in quiet grace with its elm-bordered streets and marble sidewalks, is home to the Southern Vermont Art Center, with a beautiful botany trail and sculpture garden. Just outside town is Mount Equinox, the highest mountain in the Taconic Range. A five-mile road winds to the top.

Don't pass through little Ludlow without stopping at the historic Crowley Cheese Factory, reputed to be the oldest one in the country.

Accommodations: Pinnacle Sun & Ski Lodge in Manchester, $49-$59, P.O. Box 2424, Manchester Center, VT 05255, (802) 824-6608.

Information: Vermont Department of Travel and Tourism, 134 State St., Montpelier, VT 05602, (802) 828-3236 or (800) VERMONT.

Rhode Island Coast

The route: From Watch Hill, at the southwestern tip of the state, take Route 1A east to coastal U.S. 1, then northward to Route 138. Go east over the Newport Bridge (toll) to Newport.

Distance: About 50 miles.

Rhode Island may be tiny enough to fit into Alaska's pocket. But mile-for-mile it packs a wealth of attractions, from windswept beaches and American Indian settlements to 19th-century towns frozen in time.

In Watch Hill, a Victorian-era seaside resort, you can watch spectacular sunsets over the ocean from the huge front porch at Ocean House, one of several grand Victorian hotels gracing the town.

For a bird's-eye view of the Rhode Island coastline, climb the 100-foot Observation Tower atop McSparren Hill. From nearby Galilee, a historic fishing port with several wonderful seafood restaurants, ferry to Block Island, famous for its Victorian waterfront, or take a whale-watching cruise.

Bring sensible shoes for exploring Newport's colonial district or for strolling three-mile Cliff Walk, a National Recreation Trail lined with ornate mansions, including The Breakers, a four-story, 70-room limestone villa built for Cornelius Vanderbilt II.

Then follow Ocean Drive along the coast past extravagant estates to Hammersmith Farm, the childhood summer home of Jacqueline Kennedy Onassis. A summer White House during the Kennedy administration, it is Newport's only working farm.

Accommodations: The Inn at Newport Beach, a mile from downtown Newport, from $110, Memorial Blvd., Newport, RI 02840, (800) 786-0310.

Information: Rhode Island Department of Economic Development and Tourism, 7 Jackson Walkway, Providence, RI 02903. For a free tourism vacation kit, call (401) 277-2601 or (800) 556-2484.

Virginia Highlands

The route: From Longdale Furnace, off Interstate 64 in west-central Virginia, take Route 850 north to Route 770. Go south on Route 770 to graveled Forest Road 447 and back to Longdale Furnace. For overnight lodging, take Interstate 64 to Lexington.

Distance: 20 miles for scenic loop only, 40 miles including side trip to Lexington for overnight lodging.

For an Appalachian summer minus the crowds of the Skyline Drive and Blue Ridge Parkway, drive the Highlands Scenic Tour in George Washington National Forest. It's an unhurried and private peek at this neck of the woods.

The 20-mile byway winds along hairpin curves from 1,300 to 3,100 feet, delivering spectacular views as it passes the rusted ruins of 19th-century pig iron operations. Ramshackle mining buildings, furnaces and two towering chimneys are all that remain of the once-thriving mining venture at Longdale Furnace.

Lining charming Route 770 are stone walls built 150 years ago by slaves and prisoners. In the spring, you'll find the mountains and valleys carpeted with wildflowers and rhododendrons. And the byway also is awesome in fall, when the mixed hardwood forests erupt in a blaze of color.

Accommodations: Comfort Inn-Virginia Horse Center in Lexington, from $75, P.O. Box 905, Lexington, VA 24450, (703) 463-7311.

Information: George Washington National Forest, Harrison Plaza, 101 N. Main St., P.O. Box 233, Harrisonburg, VA 22801, (540) 564-8300.

Covered Bridges in Ohio

The route: Covered Bridge Scenic Byway in Wayne National Forest, in southeastern Ohio. Take Route 26 northeast from Marietta to Woodsfield and return.

Distance: 88 miles round-trip.

This scenic byway meanders through slumbering farmlands, historic towns and a quartet of covered bridges more than a century old. In Marietta, a one-time riverboat town, you can take a trolley car tour of the picturesque waterfront. You also can visit Mound Cemetery, built around two large Indian burial mounds, or browse the Middleton Doll Factory in nearby Belpre. The factory resembles a giant doll house.

Just past the Knowlton Covered Bridge near Cline, follow the back road (brake for cows and chickens) to historic Ring Mill and Walter Ring House, which was home to four generations of milling families from 1846 to 1921. At Lamping Homestead, stop for a picnic or fish at a stocked five-acre pond before heading to Woodsfield, a quiet rural charmer with a few antique shops.

Accommodations: Holiday Inn in Marietta, from about $49, 701 Pike St., Marietta,

OH 45750, (614) 374-9660 or (800) 465-4329.

Information: Wayne-Hoosier National Forest, 811 Constitution Ave., Bedford, IN 47421, (812) 275-5987.

Door County, Wisconsin

The route: From Sturgeon Bay, in northeastern Wisconsin, take Route 57 north to Route 42 and Gills Rock. Return south on Route 42 to Sturgeon Bay.

Distance: A loop of about 120 miles.

With New England-style villages, farms and a rugged coastline dotted with historic lighthouses, it's easy to see why Door County is nicknamed the "Cape Cod of the Midwest." Talk about a movable feast — loosen your seat belts for non-stop country fairs, cheese festivals, farm stands, cherry orchards and seafood eateries serving Door County's famous fish boil.

Favorite attractions along the moody Lake Michigan coast include Cave Point Park, where waves thunder through peek-a-boo limestone sea caves. Nearby is the observation tower at Potawatomi State Park and historic Cana Island Lighthouse, located a quarter mile offshore and accessible during low tide via a stone causeway.

Tucked in Sister Bay along the milder Green Bay coastline are picturesque villages such as Ephraim (1853), a Moravian village that hosts a lively ethnic festival each June. And at the top of the peninsula is Gills Rock, a tiny seaport overlooking the infamous Porte des Morts (Door of Death), a strait where many sailing vessels in the 1800s and early 1900s met their demise.

Accommodations: White Lace Inn in Sturgeon Bay, $75-$175, 16 N. Fifth Ave., Sturgeon Bay, WI 54235, (414) 743-1105.

Information: Door County Chamber of Commerce, P.O. Box 406, Sturgeon Bay, WI 54235, (414) 743-4456 or (800) 52-RELAX.

Arkansas Ozarks

The route: Follow Route 7 north from Hot Springs to Harrison.

Distance: About 160 miles.

The Arkansas Ozarks may be remote, but they're no cultural backwater. The forested hills are alive with the sound of folk music, theater and mountain crafts. And with the most extensive network of bed-and-breakfast establishments in the country, you're never far from "home" in the Ozarks.

In the resort town of Hot Springs, cruise Lake Hamilton aboard the Belle of Hot Springs or visit Hot Springs National Park, where water from 47 springs is piped into public bathhouses where you can take "the cure."

Farther north is Harrison, the "Crossroads of the Ozarks" with museums, galleries and antique shops. Try a guided canoe trip on the nearby Buffalo National River. Or, head east to Blanchard Springs Caverns, where elevators carry you down to stream-carved caves that gleam with minerals and stalactites.

And don't miss nearby Mountain View, where the renowned Ozark Folk Center offers folk music, arts and crafts year-round.

Accommodations: Williams House B&B Inn in Hot Springs, 420 Quapaw Ave., Hot Springs National Park, AR 71901-5201, (501) 624-4275.

Information: Arkansas Department of Parks & Tourism, 1 Capitol Mall, Little Rock, AR 72201, (501) 682-7777. For a free vacation planning kit, call (800) NATURAL.

Big Bend in Texas

The route: In Big Bend National Park, in West Texas, take Route 170 east from Panther Junction Visitor/Park Headquarters to Rio Grande Village Visitor Center. Go back past headquarters and follow the Ross Maxwell Scenic Drive to Santa Elena Canyon. Return to Route 170 and take the Chisos Basin Drive, then backtrack to park headquarters.

Distance: About 120 miles.

Named for the U-shaped bend of the Rio Grande that runs along the southern border of the park, Big Bend National Park is the Lone Star State's last great wilderness area. You can still feel the frontier spirit of the Indians, cavalry troops and cowboys who once called it home.

Rugged and remote (the nearest town of any size is nearly 100 miles away), this national park is amazingly diverse. In one day, you can drive past harsh desert plains, (watch for roadrunners), high valleys and deep canyons to forested mountains and towering pinnacles.

The best drive in the park is Ross Maxwell Scenic Drive, which threads up 30 miles between the Chisos Mountains and Burro Mesa to a spectacular overlook. Then it descends to the banks of the Rio Grande at the mouth of Santa Elena Canyon, where only a sliver of daylight penetrates the narrow passage between tall sheer walls. The shorter but equally spectacular road up Chisos Basin (seven miles) winds steeply through canyon country and red rock cliffs to Chisos Mountains Lodge, which overlooks the basin.

Accommodations: Chisos Mountains Lodge, from $65, Big Bend National Park, TX 79834, (915) 477-2291.

Information: Park Superintendent, Big Bend National Park, P.O. Box 129, Big Bend, TX 79834, (915) 477-2251.

Sawtooth Scenic Byway, Idaho

The route: In south-central Idaho, take Route 75 north from Shoshone to Stanley.

Distance: 61 miles.

Idaho is more than potatoes, and this byway — from volcanic flats to jagged, snowcapped peaks — proves it.

Before heading into the mountains, visit the Shoshone Indian Ice Caves, volcanic lava tubes with year-round ice used by prehistoric Indians. In Ketchum, a quaint resort town and former Ernest Hemingway haunt, visit Ore Wagon Museum to see mining wagons that hauled ore in the 1800s, or go ice-skating at the year-round rink.

Next door to Ketchum is Sun Valley, a storybook ski town that offers every imaginable outdoor activity. You can hike or mountain bike the Centennial Trail to the top of the mountain or browse chic boutiques and spend the afternoon sipping and sunning at a sidewalk cafe.

From town, the byway spirals into Sawtooth National Forest and up to Galena, a near-ghost town with a historic lodge and trails winding into wildflower meadows and dense forests.

At Galena Summit, the byway corkscrews down to ranch lands and sagebrush country, where Stanley, a charming historic mining town, huddles beneath towering peaks.

Accommodations: Best Western Christiania Lodge in Ketchum, from $82, P.O. Box 2196, Ketchum, ID 83340, (800) 535-3241 or (208) 726-3351.

Information: Sawtooth National Forest, 2647 Kimberly Road E., Twin Falls, ID 83301, (208) 737-3200.

Highs and Lows in California

The route: From Badwater Basin in Death Valley National Monument, go north to Route 190 and westward to Route 136 and on to Lone Pine. Then take Whitney Portal Road 13 miles to Whitney Portal and the Mount Whitney Trail.

Distance: About 102 miles.

Here's a study in scenic contrasts. This drive climbs from the lowest point in the Western Hemisphere (282 feet below sea level near Badwater) to the base of Mount Whitney, which at 14,494 feet is the highest peak in the contiguous United States.

On the way you pass blistered salt flats and undulating sand dunes, barren mountains housing the tumble-down remains of old mining camps and a rugged pass where the jagged peaks of the Sierra Nevada suddenly loom into view.

The pretty town of Lone Pine, nestled at the base of the Sierra Nevada range, is the last outpost for those bound for Mount Whitney.

Accommodations: Best Western Frontier Motel in Lone Pine, from $50, 1008 S. Main, Lone Pine, CA 93545, (619) 876-5571.

Information: Superintendent, Death Valley National Monument, P.O. Box 579, Death Valley, CA 92328, (619) 786-2331. Lone Pine Chamber of Commerce, P.O. Box 749, Lone Pine, CA 93545, (619) 876-4444.

Cascade Lakes, Oregon

The route: From Bend, take Route 46 west through the Cascade Range to Route 58 and to Eugene.

Distance: About 153 miles.

If you thought Oregon was all wet, the Cascade Lakes Highway will correct that misunderstanding. This scenic byway begins on the eastern edge, the dry side, of the mountains.

From Bend, a booming year-round recreation town, the scenic byway winds up through rolling sagebrush, skirting the popular ski resort of Mount Bachelor and then Todd Lake, the first of many mirror lakes on the byway. The byway continues to twist and curve to Crane Prairie and Crane Prairie Reservoir, which boasts abundant wildlife.

Farther along, a spur of the byway (Route 42) climbs past glacier-sculpted lakes to the resort town of Sunriver. Or continue on Route 46 down the mountain and over to Eugene, a picture-postcard college town in lush western Oregon that's chockablock with bookstores, cafes, galleries, museums and sports shops.

Accommodations: Red Lion Inn in Eugene, $80, 205 Coburg Road, Eugene, OR 97401, (800) RED LION or (503) 342-5201.

Information: Deschutes National Forest, 1645 Highway 20 E., Bend, OR 97701, (503) 388-2715.

California: Sea, Mountains and Desert

The route: From San Diego, take Interstate 5 north past Carlsbad, then take Highway 78 east past Escondido to 53, take 53 to 522 in Borrego Springs, follow 522 east to Highway 86 north to the Coachella Valley.

Distance: About 160 miles.

Sandy beaches, snowcapped mountains and sun-soaked deserts — all in the same

160-mile scenic drive? Sounds like tourist bureau hype, but thanks to its unique geography and near-perfect California climate, San Diego County can make such a promise.

From any beach in the San Diego area, head north on Interstate 5 past Oceanside, then go east on Highway 78 toward Escondido. You'll wind up San Pasqual Valley through boulder-strewn hills into the Laguna Mountains and the historic mining town of Julian, now popular to the point of being chic. Highway 78 climbs eastward over the 8,000-foot Santa Rosa Mountains where vantage points reveal the half-million-acre Anza-Borrego Desert State Park below. The largest state park in the lower 48 is best reached via Route S3 through Borrego Springs.

Continuing east on Route S22, then north on Highway 86, you'll encounter Salton Sea, a salty lake 234 feet below sea level. A few miles beyond, you'll traverse the irrigated farmlands of the Coachella Valley. Dozens of vineyards and date groves line highways leading from Indio toward Palm Springs.

Accommodations: Carlsbad Inn Beach Resort, $140-$198, 3075 Carlsbad Blvd., Carlsbad, CA 92008, (800) 235-3939 or (619) 434-7020.

Information: San Diego Convention and Visitors Bureau, 401 B St., Suite 1400, San Diego, CA 92101, (619) 236-1212.

Florida: From Pines to Captivating Isles

The route: From Fort Myers, take Six Mile Cypress Parkway to Sanibel Causeway.
Distance: About 20 miles.

One of the most compelling scenic drives in the Sunshine State leads from Fort Myers through forests of pine and palmetto, cypress sloughs and delicate marshes, and on to the beautiful white-sand beaches of Sanibel and Captiva islands.

Begin this rewarding ride with a tour of the Edison/Ford winter homes in Fort Myers. Sprawled beside the Caloosahatchee River, the neighboring estates of inventor Thomas Edison and automaker Henry Ford have been restored so authentically as to make visitors imagine the old pioneers of science and industry had just stepped out for a walk.

As you leave Fort Myers, visit Six Mile Cypress Slough Reserve, a splendid wetland ecosystem that's home to a diversity of plants, birds and animals. Continue southwest on Six Mile Cypress Parkway to Sanibel Causeway, which links the mainland to the islands.

Sanibel-Captiva Road extends some 12 miles, connecting the two slender barrier islands by a short bridge at Blind Pass. It comes to a halt at South Seas Plantation on Captiva's northern tip — a good resort choice should you choose to stay awhile.

Accommodations: Sheraton Harbor Place, $79-$129, 2500 Edwards Drive, Fort Myers, Fl 33901, (800) 325-3535 or (813) 337-0300.

Information: Lee County Visitor Bureau, P.O. Box 2445, 2180 W. First, Fort Myers, FL 33902, (800) 533-4753.

Montana's Big Sky and Ghost Towns

The route: From Drummond, in the Garnet Range of Western Montana, take Highway 1 south to Anaconda and on to Interstate 90.
Distance: About 63 miles.

Montana isn't the sort of place to visit from an interstate highway, so if you find yourself cruising I-90 from Missoula to Butte, say farewell to the four-lane at Drummond and treat yourself to non-stop vistas along the Pintler Scenic Route. You can rejoin I-90 near Anaconda, 63 miles to the southeast.

The Pintler (Highway 1) opens with pastoral punch, threading a grand wheat-grass valley. Flanked by snowcapped mountains and, yes, with a river running through it, Flint Creek Valley is Big Sky Country in spades.

Although grazing looks to be good here, it was gold and silver, not ranching, that brought settlers. The region's history comes to life at the 1867 gold-rush town of Philipsburg, where the leading attraction is the Ghost Town Hall of Fame. Drive a few miles up a dusty mining road behind Philipsburg to Granite, a ghost town that once produced $45 million worth of high-grade silver.

In Anaconda you can explore a classic company town. "Copperopolis," as some wags called it, once boasted the world's largest copper smelting complex. Nowadays Anaconda is pouring Superfund dollars into an 18-hole Jack Nicklaus-designed golf course — covering much of the unsightly slag left behind in memory of King Copper.

Accommodations: Best Western Executive Motor Inn, $62-$67, 201 E. Main St., Missoula, MT 59802, (406) 543-7221.

Information: Travel Montana/Gold West Country, 1155 Main, Deer Lodge, MT 59722, (800) 879-1159 or (406) 846-1943.

Washington's Olympic Peninsula

The route: From Seattle, take the Washington State Ferry to Bainbridge Island, then Highway 305 to Highway 3 to Highway 104 to U.S. 101 north to Highway 20 to Port Townsend. Backtrack on Highway 20 to U.S. 101 and go west to Port Angeles. Continue west and then south to Aberdeen. Take U.S. 12 east to pick up U.S. 101 north and return to Bainbridge Island for ferry to Seattle.

Distance: About 275 miles.

With the beauty of beach, mountain and rain forest to behold, a motor tour of Washington's Olympic Peninsula ranks among America's finest scenic drives.

From Seattle, set out early for Olympic grandeur via the Washington State Ferry to Bainbridge Island. Continuing to the peninsula, you'll have time to peruse historic Port Townsend, said to be the country's best-preserved Victorian seaport, and to make an afternoon drive 6,450 feet up into Olympic National Park for sunset atop Hurricane Ridge. Overnight in nearby Port Angeles after tackling a dinner of Dungeness crab, one of the region's culinary delights.

The next day, travel U.S. 101 through the tall timbers of Olympic National Forest and along the wave-lashed western shore of the peninsula, overnighting in Aberdeen. Complete the circle trip by turning inland and taking U.S. 101 along Hood Canal on the peninsula's eastern flank. Head back to Seattle via the ferry from Bainbridge.

Accommodations: Inn at Queen Anne, $65-$80, 505 First Ave. N., Seattle, WA 98109, (800) 952-5043 or (206) 282-7357.

Information: North Olympic Peninsula Visitor and Convention Bureau, P.O. Box 670, Port Angeles, WA 97365, (800) 942-4042.

Maine's Rugged Coast

The route: From Portland, take U.S. 1 north past Freeport and Rockport. Near Ellsworth, take Route 3 south to Bar Harbor.

Distance: About 164 miles.

For clearing cobwebs and relieving tension, there's nothing like a getaway drive along the brisk and beautiful Maine coast. Portland is a popular place to begin a spin up the coast, following U.S. 1, which rims the rugged, cove-indented shoreline and passes through a colorful collection of small towns.

About 20 miles north of Portland is the town of Freeport, home of the legendary L.L. Bean and famous among shoppers the world over for its wall-to-wall factory outlet stores. Farther up the coast, the neighboring villages of Rockport and Camden present a tasty mix of B&Bs, antique shops and stately old sea captains' homes.

After crossing the Penobscot River, you'll head south on Route 3 toward Mount Desert Island and Bar Harbor. Once Maine's poshest resort, "Bah Habbah" has suffered the inevitable incursion of T-shirt and souvenir shops, but the view over the harbor is still a fine one.

Accommodations: Best Western Merry Manor Inn, $54-$89, 700 Main St., Portland, ME 04106, (800) 528-1234 or (207) 774-6151.

Information: Maine Publicity Bureau, P.O. Box 1057, Route 1, Yarmouth, ME 04096, (800) 533-9595 or (207) 846-0833.

California's Mendocino County

The route: From Gualala, on the California coast north of San Francisco, take Highway 1 north to Rockport.

Distance: About 100 miles.

For nearly 100 miles, Highway 1 twists along the rugged coastline of Northern California's Mendocino County. It passes through countryside as quiet and peaceful as the fog and mist that often pervade its capes and coves.

From Gualala in the south to Mendocino about midway up the county coastline, there is a scattering of suitably isolated inns, including Gualala's Old Milano, the elegant redwood Harbor House in Elk, and historic 1853 Little River Inn at Little River, each a unique sanctuary for privacy and relaxation.

Should you muster the energy to go to town, Mendocino can perk you up without inducing the kind of culture shock you get in Carmel, with its frenetic fluffiness. Mendocino's eclectic mix of weathered sheds and saltbox houses, Victorian B&Bs and Gothic mansions clutches a bluff above sea and surf.

Accommodations: Harbor House, $175-$265, including breakfast and dinner, P.O. Box 369, Elk, CA 95432, (707) 877-3203.

Information: Mendocino Coast Chamber of Commerce, 332 N. Main St., Fort Bragg, CA 95437, (800) 726-2780 or (707) 961-6300.

Hana Highway, Maui, Hawaii

The route: Round trip from Kahului Airport to Hana, on the north coast of Maui. Route 360, called the Hana Highway, is often one lane and has more than 600 twists and turns and 56 small bridges.

Distance: About 100 miles round trip, but allow at least three hours each way. No gas or food most of the way.

It's as thrilling and seemingly unreal as a Disneyland ride. Every turn and switchback on the road is flanked by the wonders of the Maui coastline, from serene green fields of taro plants to steep, black lava cliffs dropping down to the ocean.

Around a bend you may come face to face with waterfalls, shimmering pools or vegetation unimaginable on the mainland. Neon eucalyptus trees are striped in psychedelic green and orange — one would swear they'd been painted. Vines as thick as tree branches form a tunnel upward to a lookout point. Ginger plants, spider plants and philodendra grow as big as Volkswagens.

Near the end of the road lies legendary Hana, a misty outpost beneath Mount Haleakala. Once home to Hawaiian royalty and the site of battles between chiefs, Hana now is so quiet and peaceful that "heavenly" has become a common part of its name. Ranching is big here, and the main attraction in town is the cluttered Hasegawa General Store.

Many vacationers on Maui make Hana a day trip — a full day. Lodging is limited to one luxury hotel and a few small places.

P.S. If you think the road is bad before Hana, follow it beyond the town to the Pools at Kipahulu.

Accommodations: Hotel Hana Maui, a Sheraton, from $319, P.O. Box 8, Hana Maui, HI 96713, (808) 248-8211 or (800) 325-3535. Hana Bay Vacation Rentals, 14 cabins, cottages and other sites, $85-$170, (800) 657-7970. Heavenly Hana Inn, from $175, P.O. Box 790, Hana, HI 96713, (808) 248-8442.

Information: Hawaii Visitors Bureau, 2270 Kalakaua Ave., Suite 801, Honolulu, HI 96815, (808) 923-1811 or (800) GO HAWAII.

Columbia River Gorge and Mount Hood, Oregon

The route: A loop from Portland, OR, east along the Columbia River and back through Mount Hood National Forest. Take Columbia River Scenic Highway (old U.S. 30) and Interstate 84 to the town of Hood River, then go south on Route 35 into Mount Hood National Forest and east on U.S. 26 back to Portland.

Distance: About 160 miles.

Views of the Columbia River Gorge on one side of the highway compete with waterfalls tumbling down the forested mountainside on the other.

Fishing streams and nature trails invite side trips into a half-dozen state parks along the way. Exhibits at the Bonneville Dam visitor center explain the history and nature of the region. In spring and late summer, vacationers can watch salmon make their way over the dam on fish ladders.

Mount Hood National Forest, part of the Cascade Range, is a year-round playground for mountain-lovers. This drive takes you by snowcapped Mount Hood, 11,235 feet, which frequently can be seen from Portland.

Accommodations: In Portland, Red Lion Inn-Columbia River, $120, 1401 N. Hayden Island Drive, Portland, OR 97217, (800) RED LION or (503) 283-2111. In Government Camp, Timberline Lodge, 60-year-old historic landmark on the side of Mount Hood, from $62, Timberline Lodge, Timberline, OR 97028, (800) 547-1406 (reservations) or (503) 272-3311.

Information: Oregon Economic Development Department, Tourism Division, 775 Summer St. N.E., Salem, OR 97310, (800) 547-7842.

Lake Tahoe Circle, California/Nevada

The route: A loop around Lake Tahoe from South Lake Tahoe, CA. Follow Route 89 west and north to Tahoe City, then Route 28 east and south to U.S. 50 back to South Lake Tahoe.

Distance: About 75 miles.

A vacation in this area can combine lively nights of gambling and star-studded entertainment with restful days wandering in some of the nation's most glorious wilderness scenery.

Lake Tahoe, more than a mile above sea level, is the largest alpine lake in North America. Huge canyons formed by glaciers mark the western (California) shore, and boulders and thick forests line the eastern (Nevada) shore. A tram ride from South Lake Tahoe offers great views of the area, as does a four-mile side trip up the mountain from Incline Village, on the north end of the lake.

Back-country camping is available in Lake Tahoe Nevada State Park.

Accommodations: In South Lake Tahoe, Travelodge South, from $49, 3489 Lake Tahoe Blvd., South Lake Tahoe, CA 95156, (800) 982-1466 or (916) 544-5266. In Crystal Bay, NV, Cal-Neva Resort, from $59, P.O. Box 368, Crystal Bay, NV 89402, (800) CAL-NEVA or (702) 832-4000.

Information: Lake Tahoe Visitors Authority, 1156 Ski Run Blvd, South Lake Tahoe, CA 96150, (916) 544-5050 or (800) AT TAHOE.

Phoenix-Flagstaff, Arizona

The route: A loop from Phoenix north to Flagstaff and return via Prescott and Wickenburg. Head north to Flagstaff via I-17, then southwest to Prescott on U.S. 89A, then U.S. 89 back to Phoenix.

Distance: About 330 miles.

This trip includes the dry, hot, low desert of the Phoenix area and the high, cool forests and mountains of Flagstaff and Prescott.

Take the fast road north and enjoy the transition, stopping at three contrasting stops along the way. A two-mile side trip from Cordes Junction leads to the futuristic town of Arcosanti, where the architecture blends with the ecology. Fort Verde State Historical Park commemorates an early U.S. cavalry outpost, and Montezuma Castle National Monument is one of the best-preserved cliff dwellings of ancient American Indians in the Southwest.

From Flagstaff, you can make a circle trip northward to the Grand Canyon. U.S. 89A leads south through the woods and rippling streams of Oak Creek Canyon to Sedona, a popular arts colony nestled in the shadow of spectacular red rocks. Jerome, once a thriving mining city, is now a picturesque ghost town perched on a mountainside, and Wickenburg is the center of dude ranch country.

Accommodations: In Flagstaff, Best Western Pony Soldier, from $51, 3030 E. Route 66, Flagstaff, AZ 86004, (520) 526-2388 or (800) 356-4143. In Sedona, Bell Rock Inn, from $79, 6246 Highway 179, Sedona, AZ 86351, (520) 282-4161. In Prescott, Prescott Country Inn, from $79, 503 S. Montezuma, Prescott, AZ 86303, (520) 445-7991.

Information: Arizona Office of Tourism, 2702 N. Third St., Suite 4015, Phoenix, AZ 85004, (602) 542-TOUR.

San Juan Skyway, Colorado

The route: A loop through rugged mountains from Durango. Take U.S. 550 north through Silverton and Ouray to Ridgway, Route 62 west to Placerville, Route 145 through Telluride to Cortez and U.S. 160 back to Durango.

Distance: About 235 miles.

The skyway winds through the San Juan Mountains in southwestern Colorado, crossing four mountain passes at elevations above 10,000 feet and past 13 summits of more than 14,000 feet.

Abrupt dropoffs and sharp switchbacks demand careful driving, but the highway is well maintained. Frequent rainbows—sometimes double—arch over the valleys. Old mining towns sit on the the sides of jagged mountains. Wildflowers carpet the high meadows in summer, and high waterfalls tumble over rocks. Fog in the Silverton caldera occasionally gives the impression that a long-dead volcano is coming to life.

In autumn, groves of aspen turn from green to bright gold.

Accommodations: In Durango, Silver Spur, from $34, 3416 Main Ave., Durango, CO 81301, (970) 247-5552. In Telluride, Victorian Inn, from $55, P.O. Box 217, Telluride, CO 81435, (970) 728-6601.

Information: Chamber Resort Association, P.O. Box 2587, Durango, CO 81302, (970) 247-0312 or (800) GO DURANGO.

Scenic Parkways, Virginia/North Carolina

The route: From Shenandoah National Park in Virginia to the Great Smoky Mountains National Park on the border of North Carolina and Tennessee. Take Skyline Drive ($5-per-car fee), which starts at Front Royal and ends at Rockfish Gap, near Waynesboro, VA. There, pick up the Blue Ridge Parkway (no fee) to the Great Smokies.

Distance: About 575 miles (105 on Skyline Drive, 470 on Blue Ridge Parkway).

These two connecting scenic parkways, maintained by the National Park Service, are intended for meandering, not for rapid transportation. They're a delight to drive because no commercial traffic or billboards are allowed on the route, and there are no traffic signals.

The route ambles along hillsides and hazy mountaintops of Appalachia, with frequent lookouts over verdant river valleys, villages and pasturelands. Hiking trails, picnic grounds and campsites are plentiful, and special programs are presented by park naturalists at several locations.

Many access points make it easy to explore adjacent areas, such as Jefferson's home near Charlottesville, VA. Brochures available at visitor centers give mile-by-mile information about points of interest on the route.

Accommodations: In Shenandoah National Park, VA, Skyland Lodge, $46-$81, 1 N. Broad St., Luray, VA 32835, (800) 999-4714 or (540) 999-2211. In Boone, NC, Quality Inn, $82-$165, 949 Blowing Rock Road, Boone, NC 28607, (704) 262-0020.

Information: Shenandoah National Park, Route 4, Box 348, Luray, VA 22835, (540) 999-2243. Blue Ridge Parkway, P.O. Box 341, Arden, NC 28704, (704) 687-8722 or (800) 228-7275.

Outer Banks, North Carolina

The route: Along North Carolina's barrier islands and Cape Hatteras National Seashore. Enter via U.S. 158 from Elizabeth City or U.S. 64 through Manteo. Go south on Business U.S. 158 to the Cape Hatteras National Seashore and pick up Route 12 to Ocracoke. Return to the mainland at Cedar Island by toll ferry (advance reservations a must) and follow Route 12 and U.S. 70 to Morehead City.

Distance: About 200 miles, from Elizabeth City to Morehead City.

Miles and miles of unspoiled, uninhabited beaches, deep-sea fishing without equal and lots of history are highlights of this drive.

The Wright Brothers National Memorial in Kitty Hawk commemorates the birth of air travel. At Manteo explore a replica of a 17th-century ship, sniff the herbs and flowers in the Elizabethan Gardens and enjoy "The Lost Colony," an outdoor historical drama.

Then amble along the Cape Hatteras National Seashore, a long, narrow sand spit covered with dunes, grasses and wildflowers. Stop to fish, comb the beach for shells or watch migratory waterfowl. Tour some of the country's oldest lighthouses — located at Bodie, Hatteras and Ocracoke.

Accommodations: In Kill Devil Hills, Best Western Ocean Reef, from $56, P.O. Box 1440, Kill Devil Hills, NC 27948, (800) 528-1234 or (919) 441-1611. In Nags Head, Nags Head Inn, $39-$169, P.O. Box 1599, Nags Head, NC 27959, (800) 327-8881 or (919) 441-0454.

Information: Cape Hatteras National Seashore, Route 1, Box 675, Manteo, NC 27954, (919) 928-4531.

The Northway, New York

The route: Interstate 87 north from Glens Falls to Plattsburgh, NY.

Distance: 120 miles.

The Northway is a fast but beautiful superhighway. Within an hour's detour are Colonial and Revolutionary landmarks, wilderness trails and campgrounds in the Adirondacks and cruises on Lake Champlain.

The Museum of the Adirondacks, 43 miles northwest of Chestertown in a superb setting, tells the story of the land and people in this region. Nature trails lead to dramatic views at Natural Stone Bridge and at Ausable Chasm.

Accommodations: Briar Dell, from $50, Rural Route 2, Box 2372, Lake George, NY 12845, (518) 668-4819.

Information: Beekmantown Welcome-Information Center, P.O. Box 51, West Shazy, NY 12992, (800) 487-6867.

Norbeck Scenic Highway, South Dakota

The route: In the Black Hills area of South Dakota, the Norbeck Memorial National Scenic Highway is the back road to Mount Rushmore. From Custer, follow U.S. 16A east and northwest to Route 244. Go west to U.S. 16, then southeast on Route 87, the Needles Highway, back to U.S. 16A.

Distance: About 65 miles.

Iron Mountain Road, as the northerly leg of U.S. 16A is called, twists and turns on its way to Mount Rushmore. Glimpses of the giant mountainside sculpture of four presidents appear from many viewpoints, sometimes framed by tunnels through the mountains.

The road goes through Custer State Park, where one of the largest herds of bison in the world makes its home. A band of burros lives here, also, and the animals delight in begging for food from tourists.

Route 244 goes past the entrance to Mount Rushmore National Memorial and Horse Thief Lake. Switchbacks and corkscrew turns on Needles Highway reveal vistas of magnificent rock formations and slender spires. Nearby are Jewel Cave National Monument and two national parks — Wind Cave and Badlands.

Accommodations: Bavarian Inn, $68-$78, P.O. Box 152, Custer, SD 57730, (605) 673-2802 or (800) 657-4312.

Information: Black Hills, Badlands and Lakes Association, 900 Jackson Blvd., Rapid City, SD 57702, (605) 341-1462.

Technicolor Canyons, Southern Utah

The route: South from Cedar City on Interstate 15 to Route 17, east to Route 9, east to U.S. 89, north to Long Valley Junction and Route 14 west to Cedar City.

Distance: 148 miles.

Southern Utah is a wonderland of brilliantly colored canyons, cliffs, arches and spires. This loop drive passes through a corner of Zion National Park and connects with turnoff roads to Bryce Canyon National Park and Cedar Breaks National Monument.

The steep, red cliffs of Zion National Park are covered with "hanging gardens" of wildflowers during spring and summer. The red rocks in Bryce Canyon resemble cathedrals, castles and skyscrapers. A huge natural amphitheater in Cedar Breaks has walls stretching upward 2,000 feet, their hues subtly changing all day as the sun's rays shift.

Vacationers with plenty of time will want to explore Glen Canyon National Recreation Area and Lake Powell, to the east, and Capitol Reef and Canyonlands national parks to the north.

Accommodations: Lodges in Zion and Bryce Canyon national parks are operated by TW Recreational Services, P.O. Box 400, Cedar City, UT 84721, (801) 586-7686. Rates at Zion are $70 for motel rooms, $74 for cabins and $115 for suites. At Bryce Canyon, respective rates are $70.60, $82.10 and $113.88.

Information: Color Country Travel Region, 906 North/1400 West, St. George, UT 84770, (801) 628-4171 or (800) 628-4980.

Art Colonies and Pueblos, Northern New Mexico

The route: Raton to Santa Fe via U.S. 64 to Taos, Route 68 and U.S. 84 to Santa Fe.

Distance: 170 miles.

Early pioneers made their way into what now is New Mexico over 7,834-foot-high Raton Pass. U.S. 64 closely parallels the trail; in places, ruts made by stagecoach wheels can still be seen from the highway.

Tree-covered mountain slopes give way to deep canyons, rippling mountain streams and fertile valleys. The terrain constantly changes, with the Sangre de Cristo mountains forming a dramatic backdrop and the Rio Grande carving its way southward.

Three cultures flourish in the region — Anglo-American, Spanish-American and American Indian. Taos Pueblo, which is open to the public for a nominal admission fee, has been inhabited by American Indians for more than 1,000 years. Visitors can browse the craft shops and sample bread cooked in kivas.

Santa Fe, founded in 1610 by Spanish settlers, is the oldest capital city in the United States. Art galleries and historic buildings line its narrow, crooked streets and border a lovely central plaza.

For a scenic day trip, follow what the locals call the High Road between Santa Fe and Taos: Routes 76, 75 and 518 via Chimayo, known for its blankets and historic sanctuary.

Accommodations: House guests of Mabel Dodge Luhan, a Taos arts patron, included Georgia O'Keeffe and D.H. Lawrence. Her home now is a bed-and-breakfast inn. The Mabel Dodge Luhan House, $75 with shared bath, $75-$150 with private bath, P.O. Box 3400, Taos, NM 87571, (505) 758-9456 or (800) 846-2235. In Santa Fe, La Fonda Hotel, dating back to the Santa Fe Trail days, $169-$200, 100 E. San Francisco St., Santa Fe, NM 87501, (800) 523-5002.

Information: New Mexico Tourism and Travel Division, Joseph Montoya Building,

Room 105, 1100 St. Francis Drive, Santa Fe, NM 87503, (800) 545-2040.

Appalachian Scenic Byway, Virginia

The route: Virginia Route 603 from Trout Dale to Mount Rogers, U.S. 58 to Volney.

Distance: 56 miles.

In southwestern Virginia, rolling hills and hazy horizons yield soft summer visions on this gentle drive to Mount Rogers, at 5,729 feet the highest point in Virginia.

Wildflowers bloom and horses graze in open pastures near Trout Dale, where the Mount Rogers Scenic Byway flows like a lazy river past gentlefolk's farms and snoozing villages lost in time. At Fairwood Valley, the Virginia Highlands Horse Trail offers 67 miles of riding paths and a horse camp. From there, the road climbs through hardwood forests to the evergreen summit of Whitetop Mountain, often crowned with snow.

The fishing's great up here; so is the hiking and horseback riding. Enjoy both on the local segment of the Appalachian Trail, which runs from Maine to Georgia, or take a bike ride on the more level Virginia Creeper Railroad bed, now a national recreation trail.

Schedule your trip for early August and you'll also enjoy the Virginia Highlands Festival. Held in nearby Abingdon, it features Appalachian arts, crafts and music.

Accommodations: The Martha Washington Inn, a historic hotel in Abingdon, from $130, P.O. Box 1037, Abingdon, VA 24210, (800) 555-8000 or (703) 628-3161.

Information: Jefferson National Forest, 5162 Valley Pointe Parkway, Roanoke, VA 24019; Washington County Chamber of Commerce, 179 E. Main St., Abingdon, VA 24210, (703) 628-8141.

Coastal Highway, Oregon

The route: U.S. 101 along Oregon's north coast from Florence to Astoria.

Distance: 185 miles.

More than 40 public parks line this route. Sandy beaches and dunes mark the shoreline, and picturesque lighthouses guard bluffs and peninsulas along the way. Local residents sometimes gather to watch storms sweep in from the ocean at Depoe Bay and other viewpoints.

Just north of Florence is Sea Lion Caves. An elevator carries visitors down to sea level, close to thousands of sea lions playing on the rocks.

Dozens of monolithic rocks rise from the ocean floor along the north coast. One of the most famous and most photographed is Haystack Rock, off Cannon Beach.

Accommodations: Sylvia Beach Hotel, overlooking the ocean, $63-$134 including breakfast, 267 N.W. Cliff, Newport, OR 97365, (503) 265-5428. (Guest rooms are named for famous authors.)

Information: Oregon Tourism Division, 775 Summer St. N.E., Salem, OR 97310, (800) 547-7842.

Yosemite National Park, California

The route: From Fish Camp north on Route 41 to Tioga Pass Road, open only from June 1 to mid-October, east to Lee Vining.

Distance: 70 miles.

Noted naturalist John Muir believed that "the noblest forest, the loftiest granite domes, the deepest ice-sculpted canyons" were in Yosemite. Crowds come every summer to see for themselves.

This tour crosses Yosemite's high country, avoiding the overcrowded 'Yosemite Valley. Many visitors overlook this magnificent region, which includes groves of giant sequoia trees, mountain meadows and lakes, and more than a dozen peaks that rise above 10,000 feet. Even on the hottest days of July and August there's apt to be enough snow here and there for a friendly snowball fight.

Accommodations: Best Western Lake View Lodge, from $82, P.O. Box 345, Lee Vining, CA 93541, (619) 647-6543.

Information: Yosemite National Park, P.O. Box 577, Yosemite National Park, CA 95389, (209) 372-0200 or (209) 372-0265.

Hudson River Valley, New York

The route: U.S. 9 from Yonkers to Hudson.

Distance: About 100 miles.

If Rip were still kicking today, he wouldn't sleep a wink for fear of missing a minute of this drive through the storybook hollow immortalized by Washington Irving.

The scenery is breathtaking — and the region's towering palisades and pine forests inspired the Hudson River School art movement. But the route passes so many historic sites that you'll need a month of Sunday drives to see them all.

Brake for Washington Irving's romantic Sunnyside estate, perched on the Hudson banks near Tarrytown, and the Old Dutch Church of Sleepy Hollow fame. In quaint Nyack, an antiques/arts center bustling with summer fairs and street festivals, The Tappen Zee Theater puts on lively performances.

At Bear Mountain, you'll find hiking trails and ponds for paddling, plus a Trailside Museum with zoo, beaver lodge and reptile house the kids will love. The nearby Culinary Institute of New York, Franklin Delano Roosevelt National Historic Site and Vanderbilt Mansion also are worth visits.

It's hard to believe this quiet hollow is only two hours from the Big Apple.

Accommodations: Rhinebeck Village Inn, 6 Route 9 S., Rhinebeck, NY 12572, $54-$67, (914) 876-7000.

Information: Hudson River Valley Tourism, P.O. Box 355, Salt Point, NY 12578, (800) 232-4782.

Florida's Emerald Coast

The route: U.S. 98 from Pensacola to Panama City Beach.

Distance: About 100 miles.

Locals call this scenic and affordable corner of Florida "The Redneck Riviera" and pray that Miami vices — and prices — never creep up here.

Most others call it "The Emerald Coast," and it's not hard to see why. Beginning in Pensacola, a gracious town with antebellum homes and historic landmarks, the highway passes miles of aqua sea fringed by sugar-white beaches rising to dunes.

Farther east, Destin, a sophisticated resort town, has many gourmet restaurants as well as the Sandestin Spa. We're not sure what came first, the restaurants or the spa.

The road passes more deserted beaches and pine forests — where is everybody? Then suddenly there's Seaside, a cluster of pastel Victorian houses with picket fences that look as though they were drop-shipped from Disneyland.

In Panama City Beach, a historic port turned resort, shoulder-to-shoulder condos and motels line scenic beaches. Pineapple Willie's, a combination disco-saloon, is rumored to be the best watering hole in the West — West Florida, that is.

Accommodations: In Destin, Surfside Resort, from $129, 1096 Old Highway 98, Destin, FL 32541, (800) 336-4853 or (904) 837-4700; and Sandpiper Cove, from $95 a night or $570 a week, 775 Gulfshore Drive, Destin, FL 32541, (800) 874-0448.

Information: Pensacola Convention and Visitors Bureau, 1401 E. Gregory St., Pensacola, FL 32501, (800) 874-1234 or, in Florida, (800) 343-4321.

The Natchez Trace Parkway, Mississippi

The route: The northern end of the Natchez Trace Parkway from J.P. Coleman State Park south to Tupelo.

Distance: About 60 miles.

This Southern belle comes to you courtesy of the National Park Service, which has taken great pains to preserve and display her unique beauty. Pine and spooky cypress alternate with peaceful stands of reeds swaying in still waters.

This drive begins in pretty J.P. Coleman State Park, where rustic cabins and a balconied lodge overlook serene Pickwick Lake. A few miles south in Tishomingo State Park, a canyon hike leads over a swinging bridge past granite outcrops and waterfalls.

West of the parkway on U.S. 72, the historic town of Corinth beckons Civil War enthusiasts with a self-guided walking tour of several war sites. Meanwhile, restoration efforts are bringing the nearby ghost town of Jacinto back from the dead.

The Natchez Trace Parkway Visitor Center at Tupelo on the trace offers a film and informative exhibits; official maps and guides also are for sale.

Brake for Tupelo, where Elvis lives (at least in memory) at the tiny, two-room shotgun house built by his father. Nearby are two attractions no self-respecting Elvis fans dare miss: The official Elvis Presley Memorial chapel, and the official Elvis Presley Lake and Campground. Funny, we never figured Elvis for an outdoor kind of guy.

Accommodations: Trace Inn, a historic inn in Tupelo, from $39, 3400 W. Main St., Tupelo, MS 38801, (601) 842-5555.

Information: Natchez Trace Parkway Visitor Center (Milepost 266), Rural Route 1, NT-143, Tupelo, MS 38801, (800) 305-7417 or (601) 842-1572.

Cactus to Spruce, Arizona's Scenic Byway

The route: U.S. 666 from Morenci to Eagar, AZ.

Distance: 123 miles.

You'll get your kicks on Route 666, a historic road that spirals from 4,000 to 9,000 feet through steep, sheer-walled canyons and high, rolling mountains. Pray your brakes work, and if you're a road warrior, be forewarned that there are no guardrails in some sections — and it's a looooooong way down.

The Coronado Trail Scenic Byway begins in Morenci, where an open-pit copper mine gleams blue and turquoise. You'll pass wildflower meadows, steep gorges and rivers as you head for Apache Forest. Stands of immense ponderosa pines thin near timberline, and you sometimes can see dramatic thunderstorm displays on the distant horizon.

At the top is Hannagan Meadows, a rustic lodge that serves lunch and is a good place for a breather. At 9,100 feet, you couldn't ask for cleaner air.

Accommodations: Hannagan Meadows Lodge in Alpine, AZ, from $55 ($67 for cabins), HC 61, Box 30, P.O. Box 335, Alpine, AZ 85920, (602) 339-4370.

Information: Apache-Sitgreaves National Forest, P.O. Box 640, Springerville, AZ

85938, (602) 333-4301; Arizona Office of Tourism, 1100 W. Washington, Phoenix, AZ 85007, (602) 542-8687.

Trinity Heritage Scenic Byway, California
The route: Route 3 north from Weaverville, County Road 204 to Lewiston, County Road 105 to Route 3 to Forest Road 17 to Interstate 5.
Distance: 111 miles.

The Trinity Alps are California's last scenic secret, probably because you can't rush them.

Not on a road like this, anyway. It roller coasters through topsy-turvy mountains and valleys that collide at unlikely angles in the northern part of the state.

The route begins in Weaverville, a historic gold rush town where you can take a walking tour past a restored blacksmith's shop, miner's cabin, museum and many 100-year-old homes on the National Register of Historic Places.

As it climbs through evergreen forests to Lewiston, another well-preserved boom-or-bust town, the road passes many fishing lakes, then switches back in earnest to Trinity Vista. The view delivers a peek at Mount Shasta, the 14,162-foot active volcano to the north.

Passing Coffee Creek, another gold rush town, the road follows the old Portland-Sacramento Stagecoach Route. It takes motorists past wildflower meadows before a last-gasp ascent to 6,800 feet, where the Pacific Crest Trail crosses the road on its 2,600-mile journey from Mexico to Canada.

Watch out for hikers crossing the road. It could be months since they've last seen a car.

Accommodations: Weaverville Victorian Inn, from $58, P.O. Box 2400, Weaverville, CA 96093-2400, (916) 623-4432.

Information: Shasta-Trinity National Forest, 2400 Washington Ave., Redding, CA 96001, (916) 246-5222; California Office of Tourism, 801 K St., Suite 1600, Sacramento, CA 95814, (800) 862-2543.

Peak-to-Peak Scenic Byway, Colorado
The route: Route 7 in Colorado from Estes Park to Route 72, then Route 119 to Central City.
Distance: 55 miles.

Considering the altitude, you almost need oxygen for this one. The Colorado scenery, as well as the hairpin turns, are likely to leave you breathless.

The drive begins in historic Estes Park, home of the old Stanley Hotel of "The Shining" fame.

The road takes a deep breath (and so should you) before ascending through pristine forests past waterfalls and lakes to Indian Peaks Wilderness, where the jagged 14,000-foot peaks of the Continental Divide march to the horizon. Keep your zoom lens handy for shots of eagles, bighorn sheep, deer, elk, mountain lions, moose and coyotes.

After more dizzying twists and curves, the road rolls into Central City, a restored mining town with vertical Victorian neighborhoods and a world-famous opera house once frequented by Oscar Wilde and Charles Dickens. Save your change for the new casinos.

Accommodations: Inn at Estes Park, from $82, P.O. Box 1408, Estes Park, CO 80517, (800) 458-1182 or (303) 586-5363.

Information: Arapaho and Roosevelt National Forests, 240 W. Prospect Road, Fort Collins, CO 80526, (303) 498-1100; Estes Park Chamber of Commerce, 500 Big Thompson Ave., Estes Park, CO 80517, (800) 443-7837; Colorado Travel and Tourism Authority, P.O. Box 22005, Denver, CO 80222, (800) COLORADO.

North Shore Scenic Byway, Minnesota

The route: Route 61 from Schroeder to Red Cliff.

Distance: 58 miles.

This scenic slice of Minnesota lakeshore drive offers ever-changing moods and vistas, from pounding storms to peaceful sunsets over rocky hillsides rising 1,500 feet above Lake Superior.

A few miles from the beginning of the drive near Schroeder, sheets of river water glisten down granite cliffs and waterfalls cascade off mountains into the lake. The tiny town of Tofte offers some great arts and crafts shops. Head on to Moose Mountain, where an aerobic scramble up rocky bluffs will reward you with a 360-degree panoramic view.

At Black Point, the jagged Sawtooth Mountains loom into view across the water. On a clear day, you can see Grand Marais, a bustling arts and crafts center whose resident lighthouse keeps a constant vigil over the lake.

Accommodations: Superior Inn in Grand Marais, from $79, P.O. Box 456, Grand Marais, MN 55604, (218) 387-2240.

Information: Superior National Forest, P.O. Box 338, Duluth, MN 55801, (218) 720-5324; Minnesota Office of Tourism, 121 E. Seventh Place, 100 Metro Square Building, St. Paul, MN 55101-2112, (800) 657-3700.

SKI TOWNS
FOR NON-SKIERS

Every winter, when the first snowflakes fall on mountains across North America, many are reminded that theirs is a mixed marriage of sorts: a relationship between a skier and a non-skier.

Ski-school dropouts have discovered that they have two choices when resorts open for the season: Go along or stay at home. If you opt for the latter, you miss a lot of fun.

Non-skiers usually end up having the best time of all. They never have to stand in lift lines, they never get their togs wet and they can use the facilities off-hours when the queues are shorter. They also can stake out the sunny corner table at the best outdoor restaurant at midmorning, earning the gratitude of all their skiing friends at lunchtime.

Here are several excellent ski resorts that appeal to non-skiers, along with ideas on things to do, places to stay and where to get more information in advance of your trip.

Aspen, Colorado

Non-skiers are idolized in chic little Aspen, where it's a point of pride among truly fashionable visitors to avoid skiing entirely. Really, dahling, there's hardly enough time to cover those 200 or so boutiques without having to ride the lifts, too.

The town is filled with high-ticket, one-of-a-kind discoveries you can't live without, plus dog-sled rides, hot-air ballooning, country line dancing, parasailing, snowshoeing, ice skating, sleigh rides, museums and live performances at the landmark Wheeler Opera House.

Accommodations: The 92-room Little Nell, c/o Aspen Skiing company, P.O. Box 1248, Aspen, CO 81612, (800) 525-6200, is the top hotel for a special splurge. Rates start at $400 for two people in high season. However, more modest Aspen accommodations are available.

Information: Aspen Central Reservations, (800) 290-1325. Aspen Chamber Resort Association, 425 Rio Grande Place, Aspen, CO 81611, (970) 925-1940.

Park City, Utah

Besides the great skiing, Park City boasts 64 buildings on the National Register of Historic Places. However, this is one old silver mining town that has not become too gentrified or expensive to enjoy.

A free trolley travels hilly Main Street, where you can hop off to buy a Mrs. Fields chocolate-chip cookie (world headquarters are here), see what's playing at the 69-year-old Egyptian Theater or take in a club to hear Chicago-style blues. For a treat, ride the free shuttle to nearby Deer Valley to dine at the famous Mariposa restaurant (reserve ahead).

When the snow melts, it's time for hot fun in the summertime, from tram-assisted hiking in mountains ablaze with wildflowers to horseback riding, mountain biking, golf, tennis and ballooning.

There's also an outdoor festival for every interest, including jazz, pop, country music and Shakespeare. Plan to kick around downtown to explore museums and historic buildings.

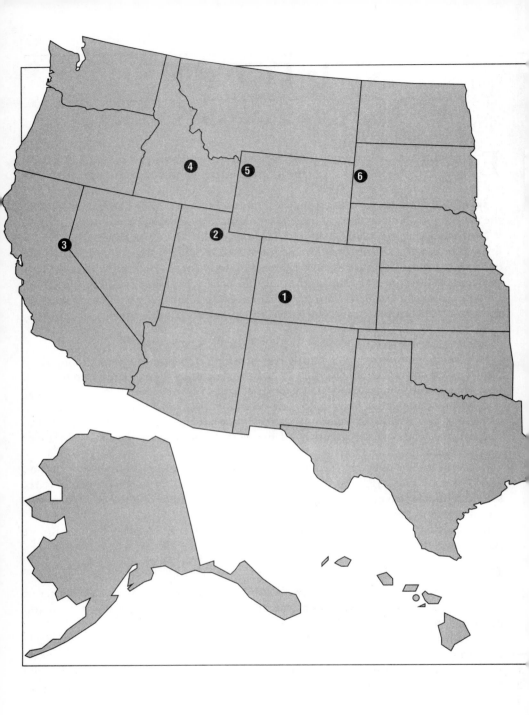

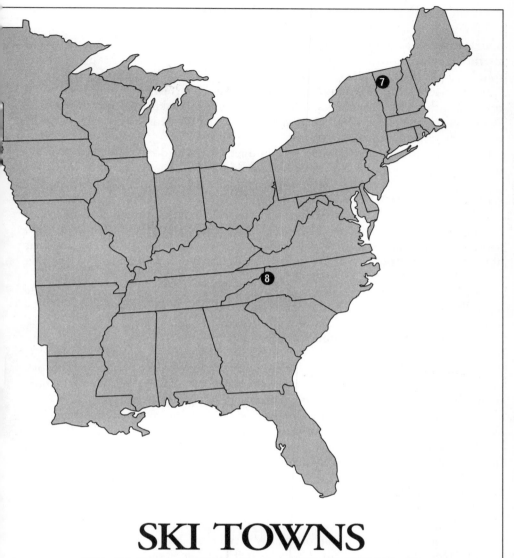

SKI TOWNS
FOR NON-SKIERS

1 Aspen, Colorado
2 Park City, Utah
3 Heavenly, Nevada/California

4 Sun Valley, Idaho
5 Jackson Hole, Wyoming
6 Terry Peak, South Dakota

7 Stowe, Vermont
8 Beech Mountain, North Carolina

Accommodations: Washington School Inn, P.O. Box 536, Park City, UT 84060, (800) 824-1672. It's a bed-and-breakfast establishment that once served as a schoolhouse, within walking distance of most restaurants and shops. A full breakfast and afternoon tea are included in rates that start at $200 a night for two people. Or hang your hat at the Prospector Square Hotel, P.O. Box 1698, 2200 Sidewinder Road, Park City, UT 84060, (800) 453-3812 or (801) 649-7100. It's a modern, comfortable hotel complex with health club and restaurant located on the outskirts of town. It's no Ritz West, but at these prices, you'd spend more for lunch in Aspen. Priced from $67 ($77 for a studio that accommodates four).

Information: Park City Chamber of Commerce/Convention and Visitors Bureau, P.O. Box 1630, Park City, UT 84060, (800) 453-1360.

Heavenly, Nevada/California

Heavenly, one of the largest ski resorts in the United States, straddles the border of Nevada and California on the south shore of Lake Tahoe. The area is conveniently close to the casinos on the Nevada side, giving you at least a slim chance of recouping the costs of your winter vacation. You'll find plenty of big-name entertainment as well as low-cost buffets in the casino hotels.

Browse among the movie artifacts at Planet Hollywood cafe in Caesars Tahoe or try a paddle-wheel cruise aboard the Tahoe Queen across the lake to access North Lake Tahoe ski areas like Squaw Valley and Northstar.

Accommodations: Try the quiet Embassy Suites on the California side, 4130 Lake Tahoe Blvd., South Lake Tahoe, CA 96150, (916) 544-5400 or (800) EMBASSY. There are no jangling slot machines in the lobby. Rates start at $146 for two people; a ski package including lift tickets starts at $99 per person. If you want something more romantic, check out the intimate Christiania Inn, P.O. Box 18298, South Lake Tahoe, CA 96151, (916) 544-7337. It's close to the ski lifts but away from the crowds. Weekend rates start at $85 for two people; suites are $175.

Information: Lake Tahoe Visitors Authority in South Lake Tahoe, 1156 Ski Run Blvd., South Lake Tahoe, CA 96150, (800) AT-TAHOE.

Sun Valley, Idaho

While skiers test their skills on one of the 78 challenging runs on Mount Baldy, you can spin like Nancy Kerrigan on the outdoor ice rink or soak away your cares in the steaming outdoor pool at the famous Sun Valley Lodge.

Ernest Hemingway wrote "For Whom the Bell Tolls" here, and celebrities from Gary Cooper and Clark Gable to Paul Newman and Clint Eastwood have stayed at one time or another.

The manicured village of Sun Valley is not at the slopes of this granddaddy of American ski resorts; skiers will have a small commute through the authentically Western town of Ketchum. But it's worth driving to the ski area and back to have walking access to the posh shops and restaurants of Sun Valley, as well as a charming little movie theater that plays the classic "Sun Valley Serenade" every day at 5 o'clock.

Accommodations: Sun Valley Lodge, with its elegant dining room and music for dancing, is top choice here. Rates start at $129 a night for two people. Pretty little Sun Valley Inn, from $99, is a good alternative. Contact both c/o Sun Valley Resort, below.

Information: Sun Valley Resort, 1 Sun Valley Road, Sun Valley, ID 83353-0010, (800) 786-8259.

Jackson Hole, Wyoming

Skiers like the fact that Jackson Hole's Teton Village has classy skiing on uncrowded slopes, and you'll love the Old West flavor of the town of Jackson with its colorful saloons and trendy restaurants.

In town, after knocking back some red-eye whiskey at the Cowboy Bar, with its Reno-bright lights and saddles for seats, you can mosey next door to the art deco Cadillac Grille for some ahi tuna with pink peppercorns. Slopeside, you can grab a beer at the Mangy Moose, then hit the Alpenhof for medallion of caribou chasseur.

Don't miss the daylong snow coach tour to nearby Yellowstone National Park, where you can watch the buffalo and elk through clouds of steam from the hot springs. Another great game-viewing spot is the National Elk Refuge on the edge of Jackson.

Accommodations: Top lodging choice in town is the classic old Wort Hotel, Box 69, Jackson, WY 83001. Its Silver Dollar Bar has 2,000 silver dollars embedded in its 46-foot bar. Nightly rates start at $110 for two people. At the slopes, try the cozy European ambience of the Alpenhof, from $105 for two people, Box 288, Teton Village, WY 83025.

Information: Jackson Hole Central Reservations and lodging information, P.O. Box 2618, Jackson, WY 83001, (800) 443-6931.

Terry Peak, South Dakota

The Black Hills of South Dakota is where Kevin Costner danced with wolves. It's also where the buffalo roam, and where Wild Bill Hickok and Calamity Jane became an item and were later buried in Deadwood's Mount Moriah Cemetery side by side with matching rock mounds and white granite tombstones.

Skiers can view five states from the top of Terry Peak, and later gaze at the heads of four presidents at Mount Rushmore and the huge carving-in-progress of Chief Crazy Horse near Custer.

Or you can check out some of the 80 bustling casinos in nearby Deadwood, a national historic landmark. The long-dormant town got into the gaming business in 1989 on the premise that gambling would generate funds to restore the deteriorating buildings.

At peak season, visitors bring in as much as $1 million a day, which means they should be able to gold-plate those buildings soon. Cowboys and dance hall girls are as plentiful now as in 1876, when 25,000 miners were looking for gold.

A couple of miles away, Lead (pronounced "leed") is home of the Homestake Gold Mine, the largest underground gold mine still operating in the Western Hemisphere. Gold from the mine helped establish the Hearst family fortune.

Accommodations: There's rustic, moderately priced lodging at the slopes: Best Western Hickok House in Deadwood, from $40, 137 Charles St., Deadwood, SD 57732, (800) 837-8174 or (605) 578-1611; Best Western Golden Hills Resort in Lead, from $69, 900 Miners Ave., Lead, SD 57754, (605) 584-1800 or (800) 528-1234.

Information: Terry Peak Ski Area, P.O. Box 774, Lead, SD 57754, (800) 456-0524 or (605) 584-2165. South Dakota Department of Tourism, 711 E. Wells Ave., Pierre, SD 57501-3369, (800) SDAKOTA.

Stowe, Vermont

Stowe Ski Resort is named for the famous New England village where it's located, but you won't be able to say you skied Stowe Mountain — the two interconnected mountains at the slopes are Mount Mansfield and Spruce Peak.

With its historic Green Mountain Inn and the slender white spire of Christ Community Church rising above the village shops and houses, Stowe is a picture postcard of a New England town. When you take a closer look, though, you'll find nearly as much Alpine and Tyrolean architecture as New England clapboard. And you may have a chance to study local building styles in detail if you get stuck in the sometimes-paralyzed town traffic.

Don't be surprised to find yourself warbling "The Sound of Music" when you see the rustic Tyrolean-style Trapp Family Lodge, the poshest place to stay. After their famous escape from wartime Europe, the singing family settled here and opened their first ski lodge in the late 1940s.

Johannes von Trapp, the youngest son of Georg and Maria von Trapp, operates the present lodge, opened in 1983 after fire destroyed the original one. You can set out on 150 miles of cross-country ski trails right from the lodge.

Accommodations: Trapp Family Lodge rates start around $138 per person, double occupancy, 42 Trapp Hill Road, Stowe, VT 05672, (800) 826-7000.

Information: Stowe Mountain Resort, 5781 Mountain Road, Stowe, VT 05672, (800) 253-4SKI.

Beech Mountain, North Carolina

Most skiers don't think about the southern mountains, but Virginia, West Virginia and North Carolina have a dozen good ski resorts, all of which have snow-making capabilities when Mother Nature doesn't cooperate.

Beech Mountain is a low-key, friendly and inexpensive ski resort five miles from Banner Elk up a winding, scenic road lined with pubs, restaurants and bed-and-breakfast inns.

While the skiers are on the slopes, non-skiers should hit the road on the world-famous Blue Ridge Parkway, especially the area between Grandfather Mountain and Blowing Rock. The dramatic Linn Cove Viaduct there was the last section to be completed more than 42 years after construction began in 1935. Craft shops sell quilts, baskets, handmade chairs and pottery of museum-shop quality.

Accommodations: A few miles away in Blowing Rock, relax at the rustic Hound Ears Lodge and Club, P.O. Box 536, Blowing Rock, NC 84060, (704) 963-4321. Rates are around $250 for two people in winter, including breakfast and dinner.

Information: For Beech Mountain lodging at the slopes, 1007 Beech Mountain Parkway, Beech Mountain, NC 28604, (800) 438-2093.

HAUNTED HIDEAWAYS

Would ghostly goings-on add to the charm of your lodging? Hotels, inns and guest rooms with claims of unexplained occurrences are more common across the United States than most people imagine. While some, like the Myrtles in St. Francisville, LA, have made a name for themselves because of their reputed specters, others, like The Lodge on Lake Lure, keep their apparitions relatively quiet.

The inns profiled here promise not to disappoint in any category of ambience — ghostly or otherwise. Prices quoted are per night, double occupancy, with no additional charge for goose bumps.

Lodge on Lake Lure, Lake Lure, North Carolina

It was the summer of 1937 when highway patrolman George Penn lost his life while chasing two escaped convicts through this region of western North Carolina, 30 miles southeast of Asheville. The following year, a lodge in his memory was built as a recreation center for patrol officers and their families.

Years later, after the building became a bed-and-breakfast inn, strange stories began circulating. The owner at the time reported some odd occurrences — doors slamming unassisted and missing objects turning up under beds.

The Christmas after Robin and Jack Stanier bought the inn, their adult daughter Betsy casually mentioned that if there really were a ghost around, she wished he'd do something to make his presence known. Just a few minutes later, a goblet flew off the back of the buffet table in the dining room and shattered against a counter on the opposite side of the room. Months later, a plant flew off an end table in the library, although no one was standing near it at the time.

Even more eerie was that more than one guest reported awakening to see a man pacing about Room 4, although the door to the room was closed and locked. Is George Penn simply inspecting the lodge built in his memory? Or is the specter another unfortunate soul who can't seem to check out?

When not looking for clues, guests can enjoy the inn's cozy great room with its 20-foot native stone fireplace. The library houses a television and VCR, along with videos of "Dirty Dancing" and "Last of the Mohicans," both filmed in the area.

Overlooking the lake is a veranda with rocking chairs and a rope hammock. By the shore is a sun deck as well as a boathouse with canoes and paddleboats. Jack, accompanied by a lovable Labrador retriever named Muffin, takes guests on pontoon boat rides each evening.

Cost: From $95, including a full breakfast and wine each evening.

Information: Lodge on Lake Lure, Box 519, Lake Lure, NC 28746, (800) 733-2785.

Captain Lord Mansion, Kennebunkport, Maine

This romantic Federal-style home overlooking the Kennebunk River was built in 1812 by a successful shipbuilder, Nathaniel Lord. While Lord passed away long ago, his wife, Phebe, doesn't yet seem willing to leave her beautiful house, now a 16-room inn.

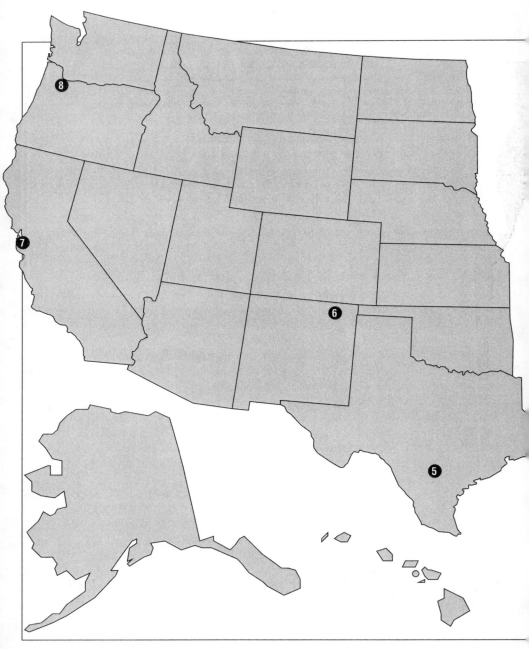

1 Lodge on Lake Lure, North Carolina
2 Captain Lord Mansion, Kennebunkport, Maine
3 Henry Ludlam Inn, Dennisville, New Jersey
4 The Myrtles Plantation, St. Francisville, Louisiana

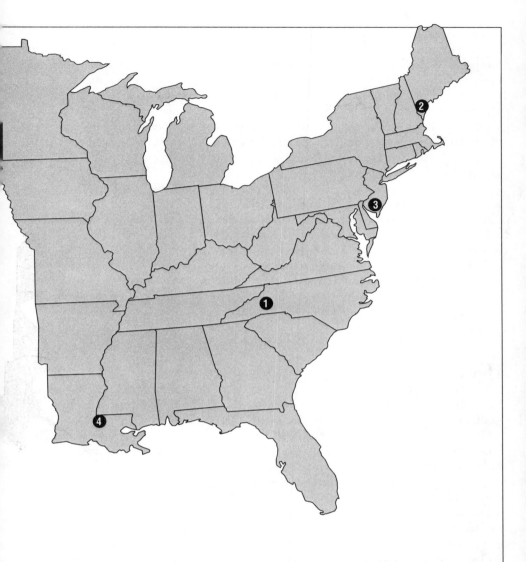

HAUNTED HIDEAWAYS

5 Menger Hotel, San Antonio, Texas
6 St. James Hotel, Cimarron, New Mexico

7 The Mansions, San Francisco, California
8 The John Palmer House, Portland, Oregon

It's said that Phebe occasionally appears in the master suite, currently named the Ship Lincoln Room. She allegedly has been spotted in nightclothes seated in a rocking chair. Some guests also have said they saw her rise from the chair and drift across the room, aging as she goes. Still other guests have awakened in the middle of the night with the unmistakable sensation that they were not alone.

Before one of Phebe's midnight appearances, one guest says he sensed movement in his darkened room and smelled perfume. Thinking his wife was getting ready for bed, he felt a hand touch his shoulder and turned. Expecting to see his wife, he instead found himself face to face with Phebe. As the ghost vanished, the guest saw that his wife was already asleep in bed.

Phebe's specter isn't the only unusual aspect of this inn. Nathaniel Lord designed several special features, such as an octagonal cupola with a four-story spiral staircase leading to it. The house, listed on the National Register of Historic Places, also boasts a three-story suspended elliptical staircase, *trompe l'oeil* hand-painted doors, an 18-foot bay window with curved sashes, a hand-pulled working elevator and a gold vault.

The mansion also has 14 working fireplaces, original handblown window glass and pumpkin pine floorboards. Each of the guest rooms offers an antique four-poster bed, many with lace canopies.

Cost: From $75-$329, including full breakfast and afternoon tea and sweets.

Information: Captain Lord Mansion, P.O. Box 800, Kennebunkport, ME 04046, (207) 967-3141.

Henry Ludlam Inn, Dennisville, New Jersey

The evening entertainment can become otherworldly indeed at this charming Cape May County inn, built around 1750 as a three-story home for the family of Henry Ludlam, one of whom, the rumor goes, was a pirate.

One guest is said to have awakened in the middle of the night to hear music from the floor below. The music traveled up the stairs and into his room, he claimed, where it was replaced by the sound of snare drums and a roll call. This, too, abruptly changed to a woman's voice singing opera. But when the guest climbed out of bed to investigate, the sounds stopped.

On another occasion, a guest said she awoke suddenly with a horrible chilling sensation, also felt by her 8-year-old daughter. Yet another guest woke to sounds of a wild windstorm inside the room, although the weather was quite calm.

Owners Ann and Marty Thurlow aren't immune to the odd sounds. They say they once awoke to the sound of smashing glass, although they later found nothing broken. And Ann's mother, Anna Lynch, believed she saw a small boy at the foot of her bed in the middle of the night.

As if this weren't enough, the Thurlows say they have witnessed lights that inexplicably go on and off, a television that turns itself on, and knocking sounds at the front door when no one was there.

Identity of the ghost is unknown, but it may have culinary talents. Ann, Marty and Anna all thought they smelled bacon or ham cooking one afternoon, but when they converged on the kitchen from three separate parts of the house, they discovered no one was cooking anything.

Mysterious occurrences aside, the inn is quite pleasant, with such homey touches as pineapple stenciling, rag rugs on the stairs and many antiques. Three of the five guest rooms have working fireplaces, and all have antique feather beds with feather pillows and handmade quilts.

Cost: From $85, including full breakfast and afternoon wine and sherry.

Information: Henry Ludlam Inn, Cape May County, 1336 Route 47, Dennisville, NJ 08270, (609) 861-5847.

The Myrtles Plantation, St. Francisville, Louisiana

This 1795 plantation that now is a 10-room bed-and-breakfast inn has been called the most haunted house in America. Dating from 1795, it has seen 10 violent deaths and has at least as many ghosts roaming its corridors, many guests say.

The first murders at the Myrtles occurred after the estate's second owner, Judge Clark Woodruffe, cut off the ear of his eavesdropping nanny, a slave named Cleo. In retaliation, Cleo reportedly mixed poisonous oleander flowers into a birthday cake that caused the death of the judge's two young daughters and wife.

Cleo was hanged on the grounds, and she now allegedly appears in her trademark green turban, which she wore to hide her disfigurement. The girls are said to make appearances, too, giggling and playing all over the estate and even showing up as ghostly images in photographs.

Another ghost is said to be a plantation owner who was shot in the gaming room. After he was wounded, he staggered up the grand stairway, making it to the 17th step before he died. Guests say they have heard 17 footfalls in the middle of the night coming from the direction of the staircase. Still another ghost is believed to be the spirit of a wounded Confederate soldier who deserted his troops and hid in the mansion's attic.

One ghost hails from an even older era, when the land was an ancient burial ground belonging to the Tunica Indians. A naked Indian woman is said to be seen sitting on an island in the estate's pond occasionally.

At least the ghosts have earned their keep. They attract plenty of curious guests, and one spirit reportedly put out a fire while another pushed a burglar down a flight of stairs. It is claimed they also have entertained guests with harpsichord music, singing and dancing.

When no such performances are in the offing, guests seem more than satisfied to stroll through the estate's 10 acres of gardens and admire the mansion's fine architectural features and antique furnishings, including a 120-foot veranda, marble mantels and a stained-glass entrance with a 300-pound Baccarat crystal chandelier.

Cost: From $75, including full breakfast and a tour of the home.

Information: The Myrtles Plantation, P.O. Box 1100, St. Francisville, LA 70775, (504) 635-6277.

Menger Hotel, San Antonio, Texas

As the Menger Hotel has expanded from a 50-room inn built in 1859 to the 350-room hotel complex it is today, its notable and sometimes grizzly history has expanded with it.

Confederate Gen. Robert E. Lee rode his horse into the lobby and Teddy Roosevelt recruited Rough Riders in the bar, an exact reproduction of the House of Lord's pub in London.

Several other guests, however, have left a different legacy. Cattle baron Richard King died in a suite here in 1885. The funeral was held at the Menger, and King's body lay in state in the lobby for a time. One night, a guard said he saw a bearded figure who resembled King, dressed in black and wearing high boots, walk down the hall and disappear through a wall.

Another guest committed suicide on the fourth floor, and today the tub in his room mysteriously empties and fills, the television sometimes loses its picture, and the lights flicker. Maids say they have seen a mysterious lady in blue with a blank expression seated in a chair by an upstairs window.

Perhaps the most-told Menger ghost tale involves a chambermaid named Sally White, who was shot in the hotel by her husband. She lingered several days but finally died at the Menger. Now it is said she appears in a third-floor wing, the area where she worked, wearing her bandanna and carrying a duster or broom.

Guests interested in conjuring up more pleasant images from the past can choose one of the authentically restored guest rooms in the hotel's original section, which still sports its Victorian lobby with a leaded skylight and decorative tile floor.

Cost: From $112, although some packages including full breakfast go for $99 per night, subject to availability.

Information: Menger Hotel, 204 Alamo Plaza, San Antonio, TX 78205, (800) 345-9285.

St. James Hotel, Cimarron, New Mexico

This elegant territorial-style hotel in northern New Mexico, built as a saloon in 1872, certainly has a right to be haunted. Some 28 people have died here — 26 in gunfights and two in stabbings.

The building's first owner, Henri Lambert, served as the personal chef to Union Gen. Ulysses Grant and President Abraham Lincoln. After Lambert converted the saloon to an inn in 1880, it was known as one of the most luxurious stops on the Santa Fe Trail. Famous and infamous guests included Billy the Kid, Doc Holliday, Buffalo Bill Cody, Annie Oakley, Wyatt Earp and Jesse James.

Notorious gunman Clay Allison reportedly danced naked on the bar in what now is an elegant dining room. The pressed-tin ceiling, installed in 1902, still sports 22 bullet holes. In this room, trays of food sometimes disappear from one spot and reappear across the room, the story goes, and glassware has shattered on the bar.

Room 18, a tiny unrefurbished room that no longer is used, is said to be haunted by the spirit of T. James Wright, who won the hotel in a poker game and was killed attempting to collect his booty. It's claimed that a white swirling mass rudely knocked the current owner's first wife to her knees in this room.

A decidedly more pleasant ghost is said to inhabit Room 17, also known as Mary's Room and distinguished by its unusual tufted muslin ceiling. Mary, Lambert's first wife, died in 1881, but her scent lives on. Guests sometimes smell her flowery, old-fashioned perfume hanging in the air.

For hauntingly historic decor, book one of the original 13 rooms, decorated with Victorian antiques, brocade wallpaper, velvet curtains and crystal chandeliers. A more modern annex offers 12 additional rooms.

Cost: From $55.

Information: St. James Hotel, Route 1, Box 2, Cimarron, NM 87714, (800) 748-2694.

The Mansions, San Francisco, California

It's hard to tell what's more scary in this 21-room luxury hotel, the ghostly spirits or the shenanigans that owner Bob Pritikin puts on nightly for his guests.

Magician Pritikin conjures up the spirit of a 19th-century o
who is said to have died in a freak accident involving blades. T.
Claudia's disembodied head appears on a silver tray and asks i
she then downs. Her spirit also plays the hotel's grand piano, r.
ivories to whatever tunes the guests call out.

The "real" ghost is not quite as showy but every bit as capti\
to be a constant complainer) was hit in the head by a heavy ba\
off its hinges. In the Josephine Room (where Barbra Streisand o\ ....onet seat
lid is said to have ripped loose and a crystal wine glass exploded without cause. Several
guests (including actor Vince Schiavelli of "One Flew Over the Cuckoo's Nest" and,
coincidentally, "Ghost") say they have seen or felt a female presence on the third floor.

Several psychics and the team of demonologists that exorcised the house made
famous by the movie "Amityville Horror" also have visited the hotel. They've identified
a spirit named Rachel, a maid who died a traumatic death at age 19, and another named
Henry who committed suicide in the house when he was 21.

The Mansions actually is two interconnected Victorian buildings, originally one
house built in 1887 and separated soon after the turn of the century. The decor includes
crystal chandeliers, crushed velvet upholstery, brocade trim, regal tapestries and $5
million worth of art and antiques, including a 9-foot by 32-foot stained-glass mural
originally designed for a villa in Barcelona, Spain.

In deference to Claudia, who reportedly loved swine and kept several as pets, one of
the common rooms is filled with a magnificent collection of pig-related items. It's hog
heaven.

Cost: From $129, including full breakfast.

Information: The Mansions Hotel, 2220 Sacramento St., San Francisco, CA 94115,
(800) 826-9398 or (415) 929-9444.

The John Palmer House, Portland, Oregon

The ghost inhabiting this 1890 house-turned-inn is a musical one. Lotta Hoch, a
professional opera singer, and her husband, Oskar, operated the Multnomah Conservatory of Music in this splendid Victorian house for 30 years after buying it in 1907.
The house was passed down through the family with no sign of spirited residents until
the current owners, opera fans Richard and Mary Sauter, purchased and renovated it
in 1968.

Mary believes she has heard Lotta walking up and down the stairs, and other family
members say they have seen her at the bottom of the basement stairs. Guests playing
the piano say they have had the distinct impression that someone was looking over their
shoulder, especially late at night, as though Lotta was conducting yet another music
lesson.

Between the main house (now a national landmark) and an adjacent Victorian jewel
called Grandma's Cottage, the inn offers eight guest rooms decked out in Victorian silk-
screened wallpaper, white lace and period antiques. The exterior is dripping with
gingerbread architectural details and includes an Italianate veranda and stained-glass
windows. The gazebo in the garden sports a Jacuzzi.

Cost: From $70.

Information: The John Palmer House, 4314 N. Mississippi Ave., Portland, OR
97217, (800) 518-5893 or (503) 284-5893.

FUN & FUNKY
FESTIVALS

Long ago in the sweet by-and-by, the most magical day of summer was when the elephants came to town and the greatest show on Earth was under the big top.

But if you yearn for the circuses of yesteryear, take heart. This is the age of the superfestival, the fastest-growing form of popular entertainment in the country today.

Festivals give vacationers a unique chance to sample the best a region has to offer in art, music, food and fun times — all without spending a lot of money.

Whether your tastes are jazz and blues, Shakespeare and Hemingway or folklife and football, festivals feature every type of entertainment. They're a great focal point for a vacation, a draw to explore new territories.

Nowadays, most festivals are organized and staged by local volunteers with help from professional fair planners. As a result, they run like clockwork — with top-notch entertainment and officially sanctioned sports events. Despite this trend, however, free family activities, home-cooked food and low-cost extras are the norm.

We've chosen this list to tempt you off the interstate and onto America's byways. But, a word to the wise: Unfold the road map and pencil in that detour now, then make hotel reservations. You aren't the only one who's discovered that the circus is back in town.

Rates for accommodations are per night for two people.

Clam Festival, Yarmouth, Maine

For clams, clams and more clams — fried, steamed, baked, in chowder and cakes or on linguine — the annual Clam Festival in Yarmouth, on the rocky Atlantic coast, is the place to be on the third weekend in July.

For three delicious days, the folks in Yarmouth, population 9,000, welcome visitors with a big helping of Down East hospitality, fixing clams any way you want them, along with lobster, crab, pasta, hamburgers, chicken and salads.

The whole town turns out, blocking off Main Street and setting up game booths, a carnival area, arts and craft stalls and food booths, with home-cooked dishes sold by local non-profit groups.

Two stages are the scene of spirited high jinks, with country, classical and jazz combos taking turns with clogging and contra dance groups.

"Maine's biggest and best parade" kicks off the festival Friday night. Firefighters display their skills in a muster competition, an old-fashioned clambake introduces newcomers to a venerable New England tradition and a gala fireworks show winds up the weekend.

If a bite here and there doesn't ruin your appetite, try the Sweet Adelines' famous "Shore Dinner." The gals sing barbershop harmony while they cook and serve a mouth-watering meal.

Accommodations: The Down East Village, $80-$95, 31 U.S. Route 1, Yarmouth, ME 04096, (207) 846-5161, or the Freeport Inn, $99, 335 U.S. Route 1, Freeport, ME 04032, (207) 865-3106.

Information: Yarmouth Chamber of Commerce, 16 U.S. Route 1, Yarmouth, ME 04096, (207) 846-3984.

Harborfest, Boston, Massachusetts

The Boston Tea Party of 1773 was this historic city's first famous party but not the last and certainly not the most fun. That honor goes to the annual Boston Harborfest, planned the first week in July at many venues in the center of old Boston.

Not surprisingly, the festival is built around the city's Revolutionary War history and its maritime heritage. Ships are Boston's lifeblood, and shipping remains an important industry.

During the festival, an estimated 1.2 million people choose among 125 activities, including concerts, clambakes, cooking contests, harbor cruises, whale-watching cruises, museum visits and discovery tours.

Chowderfest, $7 a ticket, judges chowder recipes as prepared by Boston's best restaurants on City Hall Plaza. Chowder-tasters sample each soup (as much as you want) and vote for their favorite. A similar event, Wingfest, was added in search of the tastiest fried-chicken wings.

Take advantage of Boston's small size and European flavor to explore on foot. Walking tours of the nation's birthplace, guided by national park historians, include stops at Bunker Hill Monument and Paul Revere's house.

To celebrate July 4 where the first spark was struck, take a blanket and a picnic supper down to the Esplanade for a memorable evening that includes a Boston Pops concert and a fireworks salute to independence.

Accommodations: The Lenox Hotel, $99 for a Harborfest package, 710 Boylston St., Boston, MA 02116, (800) 225-7676; Bostonian Hotel, $159, Faneuil Hall Market-place, Boston, MA 02109, (800) 343-0922; Midtown Hotel, near a subway line to downtown, $89 for a getaway package, 220 Huntington, Boston, MA 02115, (800) 343-1177. Or avoid crowds and traffic by staying in the suburbs and commuting via subway.

Information: Massachusetts Office of Travel & Tourism, 100 Cambridge St., 13th Floor, Boston, MA 02202, (617) 727-3201 or (800) 227-6277.

Sternwheeler Regatta, Charleston, West Virginia

When the hometown favorite, the P.A. Denny, steams up to the starting line beside the Haddad Riverfront Park on the Kanawha River in Charleston, the crowds roar their approval and the annual Sternwheeler Regatta is on.

Though the 115-foot paddlewheeler Denny, built in 1930, is the best-known steamer here, she's just one of 40 that cruise upriver from Pittsburgh and Cincinnati to relive the glorious days of riverboating.

The 10-day event, which began as a single race, has become the region's largest festival, drawing an estimated 1 million visitors from surrounding counties and from neighboring Kentucky, Ohio and Virginia.

Dozens of activities and sports events are scheduled, including a 15K run, hot air balloon races, volleyball tournament and book sale. At night the action moves down to the riverbank in the heart of Charleston, capital of West Virginia.

The boulevard is blocked off, and a raised stage is erected for a street party that lasts until the wee hours. Out on the river, revelers on private pleasure boats and sternwheeler dinner cruises catch the action on mammoth video screens.

Accommodations: Charleston House Holiday Inn, $90-$135, 600 Kanawha Blvd. E., Charleston, WV 25301, (304) 344-4092.

Information: Charleston Festival Commission, 2 Port Amherst, Charleston, WV

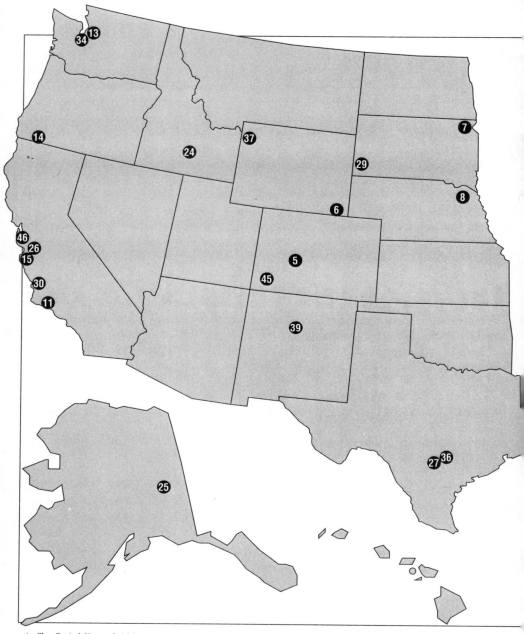

1 Clam Festival, Yarmouth, Maine

2 Harborfest, Boston, Massachusetts

3 Sternwheeler Regatta, Charleston, West Virginia

4 Fiddlers' Jamboree, Smithville, Tennessee

5 Music Festival, Aspen, Colorado

6 Frontier Days, Cheyenne, Wyoming

7 Fort Sisseton Historical Festival, Lake City, South Dakota

8 Chicken Show, Wayne, Nebraska

9 National Cherry Festival, Traverse City, Michigan

10 Maine Festival, Cumberland, Maine

11 Old Spanish Days Fiesta, Santa Barbara, California

12 Aquatennial, Minneapolis, Minnesota

13 Seafair, Seattle, Washington

14 Shakespeare Festival, Ashland, Oregon

15 Squid Festival, Monterey, California

16 Taste of Chicago, Chicago, Illinois

17 Smithsonian Festival of American Folklife, Washington, DC

18 Pro Football Hall of Fame Festival, Canton, Ohio

19 International Country Music Fan Fair, Nashville, Tennessee

20 Superman Celebration, Metropolis, Illinois

21 National Hollerin' Contest, Spivey's Corner, North Carolina

22 International Freedom Festival, Detroit, Michigan, and Windsor, Ontario

23 Mount Washington Auto Road Hill Climb,

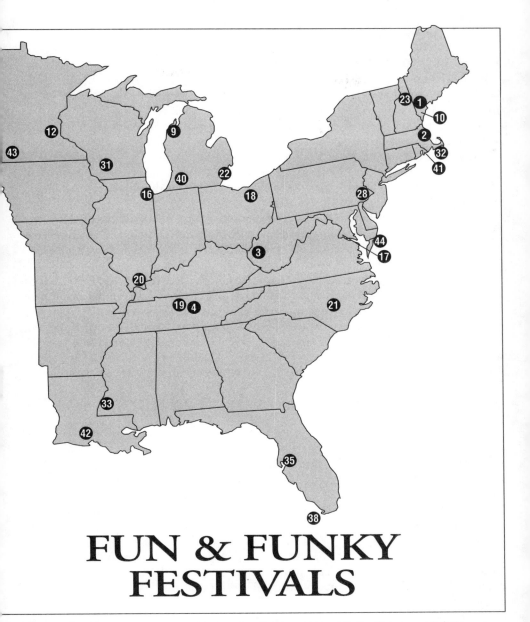

FUN & FUNKY
FESTIVALS

25306, (304) 348-6419.

Fiddlers' Jamboree, Smithville, Tennessee

Foot-tapping mountain tunes and old-time instruments are the soul of the Smithville Fiddlers' Jamboree, which takes place every year on the weekend closest to the 4th of July in the Tennessee countryside 70 miles east of Nashville.

A traditional banjo and fiddle contest, the jamboree is among the top-rated bluegrass, folk and Appalachian music competitions in the nation, drawing 50,000 visitors over two days and contestants from as far as Australia.

Beginning at 10 a.m. on Friday, junior and senior contestants perform in more than 25 categories, playing past midnight and all day Saturday as the audience crowds into the square with blankets and lawn chairs.

The fiddle music is followed by gospel singers, clogging and square dancing, bluegrass bands and performances on banjo, harmonica, dulcimer, guitar and mandolin. A "novelty event" for home-grown noise-makers includes the washboard bass, the tooting "corn-whiskey" jug, spoons, kazoo and the saw.

Food booths with tasty eats at low prices keep body and soul together. A 300-booth craft fair on the side streets offers authentic, handmade weavings, quilts, white-oak baskets, jewelry, carvings and furniture.

Accommodations: Bridgeway Motel (24 units in Smithville), $30, 713 W. Broad St., Smithville, TN 37166, (615) 597-4166; Days Inn (25 miles northeast on Interstate 40 in Cookeville), $36-$50, 1292 Bunker Hill Road, Cookeville, TN 38501, (800) 325-2525; Holiday Inn (Cookeville), from $77, Interstate 40 at Highway 136, Cookeville, TN 38501, (800) 465-4329.

Information: Smithville Chamber of Commerce, P.O. Box 64, Smithville, TN 37166, (615) 464-6444.

Music Festival, Aspen, Colorado

The Aspen Music Festival has grown from a hometown happening under the pines to a world-famous, monthlong summer fete with 150 musical events planned June through August.

For music lovers, the festival is a rhapsody come true. Concerts — classical and jazz — are scheduled every day by symphony or chamber orchestras, string quartets or jazz groups.

The best known venue is the huge music tent in Aspen Meadows, an old-time, open-air tent seating 1,700. In this shady mountain setting, with alpine breezes stirring the columbine and larkspur, concert-goers buy tickets for seats inside the tent or sit outside on the grass at no charge.

The meadow is an idyllic place to spread out a blanket, and hundreds do each Sunday, whiling away the hours with a jug of wine, a loaf of bread and a Beethoven concerto.

Other performances are held in and around Aspen. Distinguished guest performers headline the main concerts.

For a special treat, hike, bike or ride the gondola — the ski lift — to the top of Aspen Mountain for the famous "Music on the Mountain" concerts. Or for an in-depth look at the music-making process, attend rehearsals and master classes open to visitors. Ticket prices for concerts range from $8 to $40. In addition, twenty-five percent of all concerts are completely free.

Accommodations: Hotel Aspen, $99-$169, 110 W. Main St., Aspen, CO 81611,

(970) 925-3441; Aspen Bed & Breakfast, $89-$135, 311 W. Main St., Aspen, CO 81611, (970) 925-7650.

Information: Aspen Music Festival and School, 2 Music School Road, Aspen, CO 81611, (970) 925-3254.

Frontier Days, Cheyenne, Wyoming

For the rodeo treat of a lifetime (and the chance to put on your boots and feel like a real cowboy), nothing beats Cheyenne Frontier Days, held the last week of July in the heart of the Old West.

A Professional Rodeo Cowboys Association event that lasts 10 days, this humdinger of a rodeo is the biggest and the best in the United States. It's also the richest, with a total purse of more than $500,000, a prize that corrals North America's top-rated riders and ropers and 100,000 spectators.

Frontier Park arena is the hub of the rodeo, with timed qualifying events in the mornings at no charge, and a rodeo each afternoon. Ticket prices range from $8 to $12.

The evening events include chuck wagon races, barrel racing and traditional dance performances by American Indians from Southern Plains tribes. Also booked each night are top-rated country singers.

For a break from the heat and dust, check out the three free pancake breakfasts, a western art show and sale, a carnival and midway, a chili cook-off, and an air show and tours at Warren Air Force Base.

Accommodations: The Hitching Post (Best Western), $200, 1700 W. Lincoln Way, Cheyenne, WY 82001, (307) 638-3301.

Information: Cheyenne Frontier Days, P.O. Box 2477, Cheyenne, WY 82003, (307) 778-7200. For tickets, (800) 227-6336.

Fort Sisseton Historical Festival, Lake City, South Dakota

For most of the year, Fort Sisseton, built in 1864 by the Army to fight the Sioux on the plains of South Dakota, is a peaceful state park that is open for tours in the summer and for picnics year-round.

But on the first weekend in June, Fort Sisseton Historical Festival brings back the sights and sounds of the late 1800s in a re-enactment of life on the Great Plains in the years when the buffalo ran.

Dozens of events, including many American Indian cultural demonstrations, are staged by volunteers in period costumes — cavalry troops, mountain men, fur traders, Sioux warriors and pioneers — recapturing the flavor, hardship and occasional humor of those rough and tough times.

On one side is the military camp, with soldiers shooting muzzle loaders and Gatling guns. Nearby are frontiersmen in long beards and buckskin, trading knives, blankets and Indian beadwork for furs.

The pioneer folks show off their own survival skills, dipping candles, sharpening axes, carving wood, mending harnesses for draft horses and cooking up savory camp fare — fry bread, roast venison and wagon-train stew.

Popular events include a medicine show, square dance and a tour of Fort Sisseton, one of the few frontier forts to survive intact. Don't miss the chance to tour the original officers' mess hall, ammunition cache, guard house and field-stone barracks, now a visitors center.

Accommodations: Sunset Motel in nearby Britton, $30, Box 1074, Britton, SD

57430, (605) 448-2205.

Information: Fort Sisseton Historical Festival, Rural Route 2, Box 94, Lake City, SD 57247, (605) 448-5701.

Chicken Show, Wayne, Nebraska

Wayne, population 5,000, used to be just another sleepy farm town with a big old poultry plant. That was before chicken madness. Now each year on the second weekend in July, 20,000 feather-fanciers come home to roost at the Annual Wayne Chicken Show, an event featuring Nebraska's most bird-brained stunts and cheepest puns.

Two days of events are touted as "eggciting" and "a lot of cheep fun." At the egg-drop event, contestants try to catch raw eggs dropped from a cherry-picker, with smashing results.

"Those folks in Wayne are truly fowl," clucks hard-boiled Nebraska resident Todd Kirshenbaum, who endorses the festival but hesitates to recommend it to the chicken-hearted. "The motto of this 'eggstraordinary' event," he claims, "is that no pun is too terrible to use."

At the top of the pecking order is the annual cluck-off, a rooster sound-alike competition held in front of an unflappable but appreciative audience.

Accommodations: Super 8 Motel, from $43, 610 Tomar, P.O. Box 284, Wayne, NE 68787, (800) 800-8000; K.D. Inn, $35-$43, 311 E. Seventh, Wayne, NE 68787, (402) 375-1770.

Information: The Wayne Chicken Show, P.O. Box 262, Wayne, NE 68787, (402) 375-3729.

National Cherry Festival, Traverse City, Michigan

The next time you buy a can of cherries, read the fine print on the label. Chances are the fruit was grown in northwest Michigan, "cherry capital of the world." As the country's largest commercial cherry-growing region, the orchards here produce 250 millions pounds each year.

But why bother with canned cherries when you can eat them fresh off the trees? The annual Cherry Festival is planned around the first Saturday after the 4th of July in Traverse City, on the shores of Lake Michigan. Cherries sweet and sour are the center of the eight-day event attended by 500,000 people.

The festival began in 1926 when local cherry growers and state legislators decided that cherries jubilee deserved to be more than a dessert. For kids, there's a bike rodeo, pet contests, midway rides and a pie-eating competition that smears dozens of little faces with gooey, sugary filling and delights feature photographers. Adults compete in more serious events, like the pit-spitting contest.

A top draw is the Million Dollar Hole-In-One contest, where golfers compete in daily heats for vacation prizes and a place in the final competition, a 175-yard shoot-off at the nearby Grand Traverse Resort golf course.

Cherries take center stage, featured in pies, tarts, cakes, cookies, preserves, relish, salads, cherry butter, cherry jam and cherry fudge. A local favorite and big seller is Amon Orchard's tangy cherry mustard.

Accommodations: Park Place Hotel, a renovated 1890s Victorian with 300 rooms, close to the festival and the beach, $80-$95, 300 E. State St., Traverse City, MI 49484, (616) 946-5000.

Information: National Cherry Festival, 108 W. Grandview Parkway, Traverse City,

MI 49684, (616) 947-4230.

Maine Festival, Cumberland, Maine

During the first weekend in August, Maine's artistic community takes center stage at this event, outside Portland, showcasing top talent in both performing and visual arts.

The site has several performance and exhibition areas. Appearing on the festival stage are many well-known entertainers. The theater stage has a variety of shows featuring comedy and puppetry. The folk arts area has tents that include skill demonstrations, exhibits, dancing, storytelling and a children's area. There is a musical instrument makers tent and a literary arts cafe, with readings and discussions of contemporary American literature. Also featured are a crafts marketplace, both contemporary and traditional, and lots of great food.

Portland is a harbor city in the midst of revitalization; the waterfront now offers a variety of boutiques, pubs and restaurants along narrow cobblestone streets.

Accommodations: For seacoast atmosphere, try the Holiday Inn by the Bay, $138, 88 Spring St., Portland, ME 04101, (800) 465-4329 or (207) 775-2311; Coastline Inn, $75, 80 John Roberts Road, S. Portland, ME 04106, (800) 470-9494 or (207) 772-3838. Other hotels are as low as $40 a night; the area has many campgrounds, too.

Information: Maine Arts, 582 Congress St., Portland, ME 04101, (207) 772-9012 or (800) 639-4212. Group ticket rates are available.

Old Spanish Days Fiesta, Santa Barbara, California

This city's largest and oldest annual festival has celebrated the Spanish and Mexican heritage for 72 years. Fiesta is five August days of colorful, family-oriented activities.

The scene is set with two authentic Mexican marketplaces that feature Spanish, Mexican and early California foods plus booths of arts and crafts and free entertainment. The atmosphere continues with two big parades and a rodeo and horse show.

A popular tradition is evening entertainment by colorfully costumed dancers, singers and musicians in the sunken gardens of the county courthouse. Other activities include tours, concerts and ethnic performances.

Accommodations: For resorts, go north to Fess Parker's Red Lion Inn, $149, 633 E. Cabrillo Blvd., Santa Barbara, CA 93103, (800) 879-2929 or (805) 564-4333; the Four Seasons Biltmore, $259, 1260 Channel Drive, Santa Barbara, CA 93108, (805) 969-2261. Downtown, try the Harbor View Inn, $150, 28 W. Cabrillo Blvd., Santa Barbara, CA 93101, (800) 755-0222 or (805) 963-0780; Cathedral Oaks Lodge, $115 up, 4770 Calle Real, Santa Barbara, CA 93110, (800) 654-1965 or (805) 964-3511.

Information: Old Spanish Days Fiesta, P.O. Box 21557, Santa Barbara, CA 93121-1557, (805) 962-8101.

Aquatennial, Minneapolis, Minnesota

Minneapolis is known as the City of Lakes, boasting over 1,000 bodies of water.

For 57 years, the Aquatennial has celebrated the city's lakes, rivers, parks and neighborhoods. The event is held in mid-July each year.

Some 2 million people gather for 10 days of parades, competitions, races, art, music and food. Held at sites along the Mississippi, popular events include the milk-carton boat races, sand castle and sand sculpture contests, Arts on the Avenue (free music, dance drama and gallery displays), a variety of big-name entertainers, a river run, a canoe derby, baseball and volleyball tournaments and a big fireworks finale.

Accommodations: For a river view, try the Whitney Hotel in Minneapolis, $135 up, 150 Portland, Minneapolis, MN 55401, (800) 248-1879 or (612) 339-9300; or the Radisson St. Paul, $110 up, 11 E. Kellog Blvd., St. Paul, MN 55101, (800) 333-3333. In downtown Minneapolis, Radisson Plaza, $73 for a family, 35 S. Seventh St., Minneapolis, MN 55402, (800) 333-3333. Other prices are as low as $55 downtown, $30 in outlying vicinities.

Information: Minneapolis Aquatennial Association, Riverplace, 43 Main St. S.E., Ste. 145, Minneapolis, MN 55414, (612) 331-8371.

Seafair, Seattle, Washington

Seafair is three weeks of mostly free entertainment, with over 55 different events throughout Seattle's many communities and the Puget Sound. It begins in mid-July and continues through the first week in August.

Seafair's biggest events are a torchlight parade, hydroplane races and Blue Angels air show. Many events have a nautical theme, including the milk-carton derby, rowing regatta, yacht and sailboard races and the arrival of the U.S. Navy Pacific Fleet. A seafood fest, salmon derby and salmon bake celebrate the area's seafood industry; other activities honor its ethnic diversity.

Accommodations: At the center of waterfront action is the Alexis Hotel, $190, 1007 First Ave., Seattle, WA 98104, (800) 426-7033 or (206) 624-4844. Also, the Inn at the Market, a French country atmosphere, $140 up, 86 Pine St., Seattle, WA 98101, (800) 446-4484 or (206) 443-3600. Others downtown are as low as $65, in the outlying areas $45 up. Advance reservations are recommended.

Information: Seafair, The Westin Building, Suite 2800, 2001 Sixth Ave., Seattle, WA 98121, (206) 728-0123.

Shakespeare Festival, Ashland, Oregon

While this small community celebrates Shakespeare most of the year, summer is prime time for seeing the best of the bard. Ashland, in the heart of scenic Rogue River Valley, looks like an English village, the perfect setting for Shakespeare.

February through October, several of the master's plays, as well as works by other more contemporary playwrights, are performed on three stages: at the sophisticated Angus Bowmer Theatre, the experimental and intimate Black Swan and at the outdoor Elizabethan theater. In summer, hundreds are drawn to the outdoor dramas, staged against a backdrop of forests and hills.

Begun in 1935, this festival features the country's oldest and largest professional regional theater company. Besides daily performances, it offers a summer schedule of noontime lectures, backstage tours, educational programs, exhibits and concerts in Lithia Park.

For the serious Shakespeare enthusiast, "Wake Up With Shakespeare" combines day-long studies of the plays, led by a scholar, and backstage tours. The weeklong summer package costs $350.

Tickets for the plays are $19-$42 for adults, or $14.25 and up for children ages 5-17. Previews are slightly less. No one under age 5 is admitted.

Around Ashland, the Rogue River offers excellent rafting, fishing and boating, and Oregon's scenic southern coast is only two hours away.

Accommodations: Fadden's Inn, $50-$110, 326 N. Main, Ashland, OR 97520, (503) 488-0025; Quality Inn, $65-$118, 2520 Ashland St., Ashland, OR 97520, (800)

334-2330; Windmill's Ashland Hills Inn, $88-$118, 2525 Ashland St., Ashland, OR 97520, (800) 547-4747.

Information: Oregon Shakespeare Festival, P.O. Box 158, Ashland, OR 97520, (503) 482-2111 or (503) 482-4331 for tickets.

Squid Festival, Monterey, California

If you're squeamish about squid, this Memorial Day weekend event is sure to change your mind. A walk through the festival grounds offers tastes of fried, broiled, sauteed, marinated and barbecued squid, as well as squid pizza, chowder, ceviche, fajitas, empanadas and squid prepared with Sicilian, Cajun or Greek touches.

This festival is also a celebration of one of Monterey Bay's biggest industries. The cephalopod is the subject of films, videos, demonstrations and educational displays that will teach you everything you ever wanted to know about the marine creature.

Entertainment includes a variety of live music (jazz, rock, country/western, bluegrass) at several bandstands around the festival site, plus special features for the kids, such as strolling clowns, mimes, a touchtank with marine life, and wonderful octopus balloons. You can even have your picture taken with Mr. Squid!

Monterey is about two hours south of San Francisco on the Pacific coast. The marina offers some outstanding restaurants and views, and a visit to the Monterey Bay Aquarium is highly recommended. Just south is the quaint, upscale village of Carmel, and in between are some of the world's finest golf courses.

Accommodations: Best Western Monterey Inn, $73, 825 Abrego St., Monterey, CA 93940, (800) 528-1234; Pacific Grove Inn, a historical Victorian B&B, $70, 581 Pine Ave., Monterey, CA 93950, (800) 732-2825; Steinbeck Gardens Inn, $155, 443 Wave, Monterey, CA 93940, (800) 248-8442. Many lodgings offer multiday packages for festival-goers.

Information: Great Monterey Squid Festival, 2107 Del Monte, Monterey, CA 93940, (408) 649-6544.

Taste of Chicago, Chicago, Illinois

Summer brings out the best in Chicago — glorious sunny days by the lake and a week-long food fest.

More than 2 million people from around the world have discovered that the Taste of Chicago is the best way to sample the good food and fun times of this town.

For a week in late June/early July, Chicago's rib joints, pizza pubs, hot dog stands, ethnic eateries and finest restaurants all try to outdo each other. For lower prices, eat your way through the booths in Grant Park, fronting Lake Michigan, while local and national bands entertain. Youngsters can head to the Children's Oasis for fun, as adults seek out cooking demonstrations. The festival is capped by a 45-minute fireworks finale over the lake.

Accommodations: Numerous hotels are within walking distance of the festival. Along the river are the Hyatt Regency Chicago, $109 (festival special), 151 E. Wacker Drive, Chicago, IL 60601, (800) 233-1234; Comfort Inn, near Wrigley Field, $99, 601 W. Diversey, Chicago, IL 60614, (312) 348-2810; Chicago Marriott, $219, 540 N. Michigan, Chicago, IL 60611, (800) 228-9290. Other city hotels range from $80-$300 a night; in outlying areas, $45-$175.

Information: Chicago Mayor's Office of Special Events, 121 N. LaSalle, Room 703, Chicago, IL 60602, (312) 744-3315.

Smithsonian Festival of American Folklife, Washington, DC

Though scheduled around July 4th, this festival celebrates the nation's heritage more than its independence.

Each year the festival focuses on several subjects from the country's melting pot.

Each subject has its own section of the festival site (the grounds along the Mall), with workshops, panel discussions, booths of craft and food demonstrations as well as performances of music, dance and other entertainment. All events are free, and dance parties are featured each evening.

Accommodations: Within walking distance or a quick trip by Metro (subway), Ramada Inn Central, $109, 1430 Rhode Island Ave. N.W., Washington, DC 20005, (800) 368-5690; Omni Georgetown Hotel, $119, 2121 P St. N.W., Washington, DC 20037, (202) 293-3100; Embassy Square Suites, $89, 2000 N St. N.W., Washington, DC 20036, (800) 424-2999. The city offers a central reservations number, (800) 847-4832. Wherever you stay, use public transportation to the festival because parking is a problem.

Information: Smithsonian Institution Office of Public Affairs, 900 Jefferson Drive S.W., Room 2410, Washington, DC 20560, (202) 357-2700.

Pro Football Hall of Fame Festival, Canton, Ohio

This festival scores No. 1 with football fans. Begun in 1963 as a celebration of the annual induction of football's finest into the Hall of Fame, this week of festivities in late July now attracts hundreds of thousands of football faithful.

It has more than football, though. It kicks off with a Balloon Classic, 10K run, parade and concert. Other events include a drum corps competition and Ribs Burnoff, with more than 50 booths preparing their favorite versions of barbecued ribs to sample; fireworks accompanied by the Air Force Band; the enshrinees' dinner; and the enshrinement of the year's elected Hall of Famers.

Each year the festival is capped by the opening game of the exhibition season.

Save time to explore the Pro Football museum itself, which houses memorabilia of the game and has a movie and store. The Canton area has other attractions, including Cedar Point, an amusement park with a swimming beach in nearby Sandusky, and Sea World, in Aurora.

Many festival events are free; tickets to the football game are $15.

Accommodations: Red Roof Inn, $50, 5353 Inn Circle Court, N. Canton, OH 44720, (800) 843-7663 or (216) 499-1970; Sheraton Belden Inn, $89, 4375 Metro Circle N.W., Canton, OH 44720, (800) 325-3535 or (216) 494-6494; Newmarket Hilton, $109, 320 Market Ave. S., Canton, OH 44702, (800) 445-8667. Also check nearby Akron and Youngstown, as Canton hotels book quickly.

Information: Canton-Stark County Convention and Visitors Bureau, 229 Wells Ave. N.W., Canton, OH 44703, (800) 533-4302.

International Country Music Fan Fair, Nashville, Tennessee

If twang is your thang, this annual "lovefest" between country music artists and aficionados likely will strike a responsive chord.

For more than 20 years now, the Country Music Association and the Grand Ole Opry have harmonized to gather dozens of stars to meet, sign autographs and pose for snapshots with thousands of fans. The event occurs the second week in June.

At the first such event in 1972, 100 musical artists drew 5,000 persons to Nashville's

Municipal Auditorium. Now, more than 200 artists draw 24,000 fans to the Tennessee State Fairgrounds.

Even at $90 apiece, tickets can be scarce. But anybody who corrals one can expect to soak up more than 30 hours of live stage shows and come face-to-face with the likes of Garth Brooks, Billy Ray Cyrus, Wynonna Judd and Reba McEntire.

Accommodations: Opryland Hotel, $179, 2800 Opryland Drive, Nashville, TN 37214, (615) 889-1000; Shoney's Inn (Music Row), $89, 1521 Demonbreun St., Nashville, TN 37203, (800) 222-2222 or (615) 255-9977.

Information: Fan Fair Office, 2804 Opryland Drive, Nashville, TN 37214, (615) 889-7503.

Superman Celebration, Metropolis, Illinois

Since this is the only city in the United States named Metropolis, simple logic makes it natural to adopt the man of steel as its favorite son. Metropolis, you'll recall, is the name of the city in which the D.C. Comics superhero lived and worked under the guise of mild-mannered reporter Clark Kent.

During the second week in June, Superfans can wander among such events as a Lois Lane award presentation and Superman drama, a super dog contest and Little Miss Supergirl and Mr. Superboy pageants.

You can prowl the Super-Museum with its $2.5 million collection of original movie props, life-size figures, comic book exhibits and other Superman memorabilia.

You can munch on supersnacks, shop for supersouvenirs and rest in the shadow of the 15-foot Superman statue standing for truth, justice and the American way in front of the courthouse square.

And if Superman isn't enough for you, there is always the local burial site of the Birdman of Alcatraz. Metropolis is located at the southern tip of Illinois.

Accommodations: Metropolis Inn, $42-$48, Route 3, Box 668, Metropolis, IL 62960, (618) 524-3723.

Information: Massac County Chamber of Commerce and Tourism, P.O. Box 188, Metropolis, IL 62960, (800) 949-5740 or (618) 524-2714.

National Hollerin' Contest, Spivey's Corner, North Carolina

If you're looking for something to shout about, most likely this is it — a family event, sponsored by the Spivey's Corner Volunteer Fire Department and, as its brochure proclaims, aimed at "helping to revive the almost lost art of hollerin'." The event is held on the third Saturday in June.

Hollerin' involves a complex system of sounds, tones or rhythm patterns that predates the telephone as a means of rural communication. It conveys a clear pattern of sound over a distance of a mile or more.

"Hollerin' is not to be confused with screaming or yelling," says Ermon Godwin Jr., who founded the contest in 1969. "It is part of the heritage of North Carolina handed down from generation to generation. The Rebel Yell was a holler. My grandfather was a hollerin' man."

The nature of the event may rule out prospects of a conventional quiet getaway. But, in lieu of silence, visitors can examine crafts from toys to furniture and meet the artisans who created them, guffaw at a watermelon roll or a greasy pole climb and pig out on barbecue.

So come on over to Spivey's Corner (population 49) and find out what the yell's going on.

Accommodations: Shield House Bed & Breakfast in Clinton, $50-$75 including breakfast, 216 Sampson St., Spivey's Corner, NC 28334, (910) 592-2634.

Information: Ermon Godwin Jr., National Hollerin' Contest, 8101 Newton Grove Highway, Spivey's Corner, NC 28334, (910) 567-2156. North Carolina Travel & Tourism Division, 430 N. Salisbury St., Raleigh, NC 27611, (800) VISIT-NC.

International Freedom Festival, Detroit, Michigan, and Windsor, Ontario

This mammoth chain of events spans two cities in two countries over two national holidays. The locales are Detroit, MI, and adjacent Windsor, Ontario, Canada. The holidays are Canada Day (July 1) and U.S. Independence Day (July 4).

While not actually part of the celebration, two races — the Budweiser Gold Cup Grand Prix and the Big Boy Unlimited Hydroplanes — precede the festival opening.

The festival itself offers assorted events for several days leading up to the two holidays, including parades, games, pancake breakfasts, tugboat racing, rescue demonstrations by both U.S. and Canadian coast guards, concerts, band competitions, arts displays and boat tours. On July 4, a swearing-in ceremony is held for new U.S. citizens.

Highlights include a tug-of-war across the Detroit River and Hudson's Freedom Festival Fireworks, North America's largest fireworks display.

Accommodations: Westin Hotel, $120 per family, Renaissance Center, Detroit, MI 48243, (313) 568-8200.

Information: Parade Company, 9600 Mount Elliot, Detroit, MI 48211, (313) 923-8259.

Mount Washington Auto Road Hill Climb, Gorham, New Hampshire

As it has since 1904, excitement peaks in these parts with the Climb to the Clouds — the nation's oldest hill climb, which takes place the fourth weekend in June.

The international field of up to 60 auto racers will follow a 70-cornered course that alternates between pavement and gravel for 7.4 miles as it ascends 4700 feet in altitude. Vintage race cars representative of past contestants will participate in this event sanctioned by the Sports Car Club of America.

Festivities associated with the Sunday morning race include time trials on Friday and Saturday mornings, a "cruise night" and free concert Friday night.

Saturday will bring a motorsports parade, classic and vintage car show and fireworks. Spectators can purchase tickets for viewing from the base area, the halfway point or the summit.

Accommodations: Town & Country Motor Inn, $64, Route 2, Gorham, NH 03581, (800) 325-4386 or (603) 466-3315. Historic Mount Washington Hotel & Resort (Bretton Woods, NH), $225 (including breakfast and dinner) or $145 (room only), Route 302, Bretton Woods, NH 03575, (800) 258-0330 or (603) 278-1000.

Information: Mount Washington Auto Road, P.O. Box 278, Gorham, NH 03581, (603) 466-3988.

Music Festival, Sun Valley, Idaho

Superb artistic performances by humans and nature combine to entice visitors to the Sun Valley Music Festival in July and August each year.

The hills that amphitheatrically envelop Trail Creek Cabin grounds, for example, come alive with the sounds of classical music, jazz, rhythm and blues, country-western, soul and gospel. Makers of such music have included Stan Getz, Dizzy Gillespie, Miriam Makeba, Emmylou Harris, Herbie Mann, Los Lobos and the New York Chamber Soloists. Tickets are $15-$18 for adults, $6-$8 for children under 7.

The festival dovetails with Sun Valley's Saturday night ice shows, a summertime tradition at Idaho's legendary winter sports resort since 1937. Between a huge buffet and a starlit sky, skaters gather from mid-June through mid-September to show their fire on the ice of an outdoor rink. Adult admission may increase slightly from last year's price of $61 with buffet, $23-$33 without.

Another festival rolls around on Labor Day weekend. During Wagon Days, more than 100 museum-quality, animal-drawn vehicles compose the Northwest's largest non-motorized parade.

Celebrating the Wood River Valley's mining heritage before the railroad arrived, the parade showcases enormous ore wagons that hauled nine to 12 tons of cargo apiece in the 1880s. Mules or oxen originally drew the wagons, which today are pulled by teams of horses.

Accommodations: Sun Valley Resort, $104-$369, 1 Sun Valley Road, Sun Valley, ID 83353, (800) 786-8259.

Information: Sun Valley/Ketchum Chamber of Commerce, P.O. Box 2420, Sun Valley, ID 83353, (800) 634-3347; Sun Valley Center for the Arts and Humanities, P.O. Box 656, Sun Valley, ID 83353, (208) 726-9491; (208) 622-2231 for tickets to the ice show.

World Eskimo-Indian Olympics, Fairbanks, Alaska

Every summer, Alaskan Natives — Aleuts, Indians, Eskimos — gather to compete in what is known as the World Eskimo-Indian Olympics.

Yes, there are dances, storytelling and exhibitions of crafts and artwork. But most significant are the games themselves, more accurately described as feats of strength, stamina, endurance and determination.

These feats are based upon skills on which survival itself may depend — especially in the environments of frozen lands and frigid waters.

Accommodations: Alaska Motel, $60-$80, 1546 Cushman, Fairbanks, AK 99701, (907) 456-6393.

Information: Fairbanks Convention and Visitors Bureau, 550 First Ave., Fairbanks, AK 99701, (800) 327-5774.

Garlic Festival, Gilroy, California

Packing the purest, pre-eminently pungent punch of any perennial produce presentation, the Gilroy Garlic Festival will bowl you over, if not in fragrance or flavor, then surely in scope and imagination.

Starting eighteen years ago almost as a joke, arguably the most aromatic apotheosis in all kitchendom has grown into one of the world's most celebrated fetes of a single ingredient.

More than 135,000 people pour into the garlic capital of the world the last full weekend each July to pig out and otherwise participate in the lifestyles of the richly fragrant.

There are garlic braiding competitions and garlic souvenirs and all kinds of exhibitions and innovations. But mostly, garlic in prodigious amounts is used to flavor everything from scampi or mushrooms or rosemary-mopped pepper steak to chocolate candies (better than it sounds) or ice cream (worse than you can imagine).

Between the food booths, arts and crafts booths and the cooking competitions, use of fresh garlic can be measured in gastric tons. But the atmosphere, the alimentations and the fun — for the entire family — are truly, like garlic burps, irrepressible.

Accommodations: Leavesley Inn, $70 per night (two-night minimum during festival), 8430 Murray Ave., Gilroy, CA 95021, (800) 624-8225 or (408) 847-5500. Sixpence Motel, $45-$55, 6110 Monterey Highway, Gilroy, CA 95020, (408) 842-6061.

Information: Gilroy Garlic Festival Association, P.O. Box 2311, Gilroy, CA 95021, (408) 842-1625.

Texas Folklife Festival, San Antonio, Texas

Nearly everyone who has ever heard of Texas knows about its magnitude. But if anything has proven more important to the state than its ration of square miles, it has been the diversity of the people who inhabit them.

As it has for more than 20 years, the University of Texas Institute of Texan Cultures will celebrate that diversity with one of the state's most important events: the Texas Folklife Festival.

Some 10,000 participants representing 30 ethnic and cultural groups will share their heritages with more than 100,000 visitors.

The festival, usually held in early August, makes entertainment educational and education entertaining. Visitors can learn to braid a rope and swing a lasso, grind peanuts for peanut butter and carve on bone. They can nibble on such familiar elements of Texas cuisine as chili or pecan pralines, or experiment with calf fries, Alsatian dried sausage or Filipino skewered pork.

The concept of this festival fits neatly into the city of its venue, and the reason lies in a time-honored line of Texas lore.

Every Texan, goes the maxim, has two hometowns: his own and San Antonio. The Texas Folklife Festival has grown to make that saying truer than ever.

Accommodations: La Quinta Motor Inns-Market Square, $89 (includes breakfast), 900 Dolorosa, San Antonio, TX 78207, (210) 271-0001.

Information: San Antonio Convention & Visitors Bureau, P.O. Box 2277, San Antonio, TX 78298, (800) 447-3372 or (210) 270-8700; Institute of Texan Cultures, 801 S. Bowie, San Antonio, TX 78205, (210) 558-2300.

Autumn's Colors and Chrysanthemum Festival, Longwood Gardens, Pennsylvania

Two tandem events celebrate fall and its colors at one of the nation's loveliest, most historic gardens.

First comes Autumn's Colors, during the month of October, displayed by hundreds of varieties of trees, some of which have been gracing Longwood's nearly 1,100 acres since 1798. The day after Autumn's Colors ends, the Chrysanthemum Festival begins with more than 15,000 flowers featured in special displays, performances, demonstrations and children's activities through the month of November.

Longwood Gardens, long a major landmark on the American horticulture scene, was the estate of industrialist Pierre S. du Pont from its purchase in 1906 until his death in

1954. It is located on U.S. 1, about three miles northeast of Kennett Square and 30 miles west of Philadelphia.

The gardens are open daily year-round, from midmorning until early evening. Admission is $10 for adults ($6 on Tuesdays), $4 for youths ages 16-20, $2 for children ages 6-15 and free for children under 6.

Accommodations: Longwood Inn, $75 (includes continental breakfast), 815 E. Baltimore Pike, Kennett Square, PA 19348, (610) 444-3515.

Information: Longwood Gardens, P.O. Box 501, Kennett Square, PA 19348, (610) 388-1000.

Buffalo Roundup and Auction, Custer State Park, South Dakota

It's a perennial bison-tennial at the Buffalo Roundup at Custer State Park in South Dakota. You can make yourself at home where the buffalo roam for roundup festivities the first weekend in October and/or catch the auction about six weeks later.

About 1 percent of the 100,000 bison in North America roam free in 73,000-acre Custer State Park. "Bison," by the way, is the correct scientific name for what most Americans call "buffalo," a name derived from *les boeufs*, French for beeves or oxen.

Spring calving increases by 50 percent the nearly 1,000 such animals the park's grassland can support through winter. So each fall, wranglers round up the herd for branding, sorting, testing and vaccinating in corrals at the park's southern end. Visitors can observe from special elevated walkways or bleachers.

Starting Saturday, an arts festival and other events kick off the roundup activities, scheduled Monday through Wednesday.

Surplus animals are held for the auction and sold mainly to ranchers. The bulk of the herd is released into the park.

Accommodations: The Blue Bell Lodge and Resort and the State Game Lodge, each $65-$300, HC 83, Box 74, Custer, SD 57730, (800) 658-3530.

Information: Custer State Park, HC 83, Box 70, Custer, SD 57730, (605) 255-4515.

Harbor Festival, Morro Bay, California

If you think there is something fishy about the celebration of a working waterfront, you are right. The two-day series of events on California's Central Coast nets upwards of 40,000 visitors who get their hooks into more goodies than you can shake a squid at.

During the first weekend in October, The California Seafood Faire, launching National Seafood Month, tops a list of what's up at the docks with California-caught marine cuisine. Accompaniments include the commercial fishermen's Albacore & More barbecue, a Central Coast wine tasting, ship tours, maritime historical exhibits and oceans of other attractions and entertainments.

When festival gates close at 6 p.m. Saturday, the Festival After Dark lights up the rest of the town. Proceeds benefit more than 40 non-profit organizations in the area.

Admission is $4 for adults, free for children under age 12. Parking and shuttles are free.

Accommodations: Blue Sail Inn, $65-$115, 851 Market Ave,. Morro Bay, CA 93442, (805) 772-2766; El Morro Lodge, $60-$85, 1206 Main St., Morro Bay, CA 93442, (805) 772-5633.

Information: Morro Bay Harbor Festival, P.O. Box 1869, Morro Bay, CA 93443,

(805) 772-1155 or (800) 366-6043.

Mid-Continent Steam Train Autumn Color Tours, North Freedom, Wisconsin

New England and the Northeast may predominate as the best-known regions in the fall color department, but don't let anyone railroad you into thinking the rest of the country is just so much mulch. Rich seasonal color bursts from the branches of trees all over the Midwest.

Wisconsin offers some of the best fall viewing, including the scenic area north of Madison where a turn-of-the-century steam train runs. On the second and third weekends in October, the Mid-Continent Steam Train huffs and puffs its way through the leaf-drenched Baraboo River Valley for five special autumn color tours each date, adding a sixth train at dinner on Saturdays.

Regular tours do the seven-mile route in about an hour; dinner trains take about two hours. Fares, which are subject to change, are expected to be $8 for adults, $7 for seniors and $4.50 for children ages 3-12. First-class tickets are $18.50, and the Saturday dinner train costs $45.

Accommodations: In nearby Baraboo, Best Western Baraboo Inn, $58, 725 W. Pine, Baraboo, WI 53913, (800) 831-3881 or (608) 356-1100; Howard Johnson Inn, $58-$88, Highway 12 W., Baraboo, WI 53913, (800) 421-4748 or (608) 356-8366.

Information: Mid-Continent Railway Museum, P.O. Box 358, North Freedom, WI 53951, (608) 522-4261. Wisconsin Dells Visitor and Convention Bureau, 701 Superior St., Wisconsin Dells, WI 53965, (800) 223-3557.

Cranberry Harvest and Festival, Nantucket, Massachusetts

For fabulous fall color and flavor, this special weekend belongs to the berries. To the standard flame-hued foliage for which New England is renowned, Nantucket Island adds the plump, juicy brilliance of its top crop.

Visitors can view the harvesting of the tart, ripe berries, which involves flooding the bogs to float the crimson fruit, manually corralling the berries, then skimming them to bog's edge with floating wooden booms.

Nantucket has cultivated cranberries, named for the resemblance of the pink blossoms to a crane's head, since 1857. Until subdivided in 1959 to conserve water, the island's 234-acre Milestone Road bog was the largest contiguous natural cranberry bog in the world.

Events for the mid-October festival include a tour of inns and guest houses, some dating from Nantucket's whaling days, and a cranberry cookery contest, open to everyone, with fresh cranberries available to entrants at the chamber of commerce office. At Cranberry Harvest Marketplace, you can watch a cranberry wreath being crafted while you chomp cranberry pizza and slurp cranberry beverages.

Accommodations: Anchor Inn, $95-$155, 66 Centre St., P.O. Box 387, Nantucket, MA 02554, (508) 228-0072; Corner House, $95-$135, P.O. Box 1828, Nantucket, MA 02554, (508) 228-1530; India House, $85-$135, P.O. Box 576, Nantucket, MA 02554, (508) 228-9043.

Information: Nantucket Island Chamber of Commerce, 48 Main St., Nantucket, MA 02554, (508) 228-1700.

Fall Pilgrimage, Natchez, Mississippi

After this event, visitors understand why Natchez is synonymous with antebellum mansions. Old South architecture, dress and decor welcome visitors on tours of 24 pre-Civil War mansions and their grounds and gardens during the Natchez Fall Pilgrimage, during the month of October.

These great houses, built between the late 1700s and 1860, continue to exude charm and fascination. Some still are occupied by descendants of the original families, while others extend legendary hospitality as the Deep South answer to the New England inn.

Like a hoop-skirted Southern belle pausing regally at the head of a sweeping stairway, the city stands proudly on a bluff overlooking the Mississippi River. Founded by the Natchez Indians, it is the oldest continuous settlement on the Mississippi River.

During the annual fall pilgrimage, visitors can choose a three-home tour ($15) or a four-home tour ($18). Evening entertainment options include a plantation-style dinner or the music and comedy of a Mississippi medicine show.

While tours and bed-and-breakfast packages are available year-round, Fall Pilgrimage offers some of the best and broadest possibilities.

Accommodations: Best Western River Park, $79, 645 S. Canal, Natchez, MS 39120, (800) 274-5532; Natchez Eola Hotel, $70-$110, 110 N. Pearl St., Natchez, MS 39120, (800) 888-9140; Ramada Inn Hilltop, $66-$130, P.O. Box 1263, Natchez, MS 39121, (800) 256-6311. For information about bed-and-breakfast inns, contact Natchez Pilgrimage Tours.

Information: Natchez Pilgrimage Tours, P.O. Box 347, Natchez, MS 39121, (800) 647-6742.

Apple Squeeze, Steilacoom, Washington

On the shores of Puget Sound, just south of Tacoma, this sweet little settlement offers visitors one of autumn's most auspicious apple-tunities.

As the name suggests, locals and outlanders alike are invited to squeeze apples into a delicious cider. You can bring your own apples and containers for the cider or buy a sack of fruit and gallon jugs at the Squeeze.

Whether you bring or buy, squeeze or not, you still can sink your teeth into candied apples, donuts, apple pie and other goodies — all composed of, or compatible with, apples.

Cider is plentiful and comes hot and cold, spiced and plain. Demonstrations include apple identification experts, old-time fiddlers, manual apple presses and old-fashioned apple-peeling machines.

The festival takes place every year and is sponsored by the Steilacoom Historical Museum Association. Admission is free, but a donation is appreciated.

Accommodations: Best Western Executive Inn, Tacoma, $74-$79, 5700 Pacific Highway E., Tacoma, WA 98424, (800) 938-8500; Tacoma Travelodge, $40-$65, 8820 S. Hosmer, Tacoma, WA 98444, (800) 578-7878.

Information: Steilacoom Historical Museum Association, P.O. Box 88016, Steilacoom, WA 98388, (206) 584-4133. Washington State Tourism Division, P.O. Box 42500, Dept. 282, Olympia, WA 98504, (800) 544-1800.

Guavaween, Ybor City, Florida

The neat trick behind this celebration is the treat that spends much of the year soberly masked as a national historic landmark district.

More than 100 years ago, on 40 acres northeast of Tampa, Ybor City was built, ultimately employing 12,000 people in 200 cigar factories. Times and changing attitudes doused the city's fortunes, but determination keeps Ybor and its traditions alive and attractive.

Among its liveliest is Guavaween, a Latin-style Halloween festival that derives its name from neighboring Tampa's alias: The Big Guava. The festival, in late October, draws about 100,000 celebrants.

The zany celebration starts with family activities and entertainment in the morning. Evening events include the satirical Mama Guava Stumble parade that wraps up at the Guavaween Street Party.

Admission is $5, with tickets available from Ticketmaster. Parking is limited, and round-trip Guavaween bus transportation between Ybor City and downtown Tampa is available.

Accommodations: Amerisuites in Tampa, $85-$95, 4811 W. Main St., Tampa, FL 33607, (800) 833-1516; La Quinta Inn Tampa Busch Gardens, from $51, 2904 Melbourne Blvd., Tampa, FL 33605, (800) 531-5900.

Information: Ybor City Chamber of Commerce, 1800 E. Ninth Ave., Tampa, FL 33605, (813) 248-3712.

Wurstfest, New Braunfels, Texas

In New Braunfels, a historic German enclave that surrounds the tiny Comal River, Wurstfest first sizzled in 1961. The event barely filled a single Saturday, when maybe 2,000 mostly local folks gobbled up a few hundred pounds of sausage.

Steadily the celebration, usually starting in early November, has stretched into a 10-day showcase of German food, music, dance, heritage and fun, where 125,000 people from around the world pack away 27 tons of meat, mostly sausage, and down thousands of steins of beer.

Between bites of the best of the wurst — not to mention turkey legs, Bavarian pork chops, barbecued beef, fajitas, corn on the cob and countless other yummies — participants can listen to brass bands, dance the polka, check out heritage exhibits and cultural activities or work in some pre-emptive weight loss in walking, running or biking events. Admission is $6 for adults, free for children under 12.

Accommodations: Faust Hotel, $59-$79, 240 S. Seguin, New Braunfels, TX 78130, (210) 625-7791; Gruene Mansion Inn, $85-$125, 1275 Gruene Road, New Braunfels, TX 78130, (210) 629-2641; Holiday Inn, $68-$85, 1051 IH-35 E., New Braunfels, TX 78130, (800) 465-4329.

Information: Wurstfest Association of New Braunfels, P.O. Box 310309, New Braunfels, TX 78131, (800) 221-4369. Greater New Braunfels Chamber of Commerce, 390 S. Seguin St., New Braunfels, TX 78131, (800) 572-2626.

Grand Teton Music Festival, Teton Village, Wyoming

Breathtaking, majestic, inspiring — these are words that come to mind when describing the Grand Tetons. They also can be used to describe a renowned eight-week classical music festival held here each summer.

Begun in 1962 with a few concerts in the high school gym and on a church lawn, the festival today features 150 acclaimed classical musicians and more than 40 concerts presented in the 740-seat Walk Festival Hall at the foot of the Grand Tetons.

There is chamber music Tuesdays through Thursdays and performances by the

Festival Orchestra on Fridays and Saturdays. Tickets are $5-$30, depending on the event. Student tickets are 50 percent off.

Other activities during festival season include the Mountain Artists Rendezvous, Indian Art Show, Targhee Bluegrass Festival and the Teton County Fair.

Accommodations: In Teton Village, Crystal Springs Inn, $68, P.O. Box 250, Teton Village, WY 83025, (307) 733-4423; Village Center Inn, $72, P.O. Box 310, Teton Village, WY 83025, (307) 733-3155. Other area options include camping, cabin rentals, guest ranches and lodging in the town of Jackson. For information, call Jackson Hole Central Reservations, (800) 443-6931.

Information: Grand Teton Music Festival, P.O. Box 490, Teton Village, WY 83025, (307) 733-3050 or, to order tickets, (307) 733-1128.

Hemingway Days Festival, Key West, Florida

What would a festival devoted to the memory of Ernest Hemingway be without a spotlight on writing — particularly short stories? The backbone of this increasingly popular event is the Hemingway Writer's Workshop Conference where for three days writers from around the world focus on the styles and techniques of fiction and poetry, guided by some of today's leading writers.

The short-story competition attracts nearly 1,000 entries read by a panel of judges that in the past has included some of Hemingway's descendants. Other literary endeavors feature a walking tour (Key West long has been a haven for many well-known authors) and fiction and poetry readings.

But this festival is not just for writers — it is for anyone with an appreciation for Hemingway and his mystique. For seven days, usually in July, a variety of outdoor Hemingwayesque activities are featured, including a fish fry, Hemingway look-alike contest, regatta, arm-wrestling championships, a 5K run, Caribbean street fair and a fishing tournament.

Accommodations: Blue Marlin Motel, $79, 1320 Simonton St., Key West, FL 33040, (800) 523-1698, in Florida (800) 826-5303.

Information: Hemingway Days Festival, P.O. Box 4045, Key West, FL 33041, (305) 294-4440.

New Mexico Arts and Crafts Fair, Albuquerque, New Mexico

If one of your passions is Southwestern art, this festival is for you. Held the last weekend in June for more than 30 years, the four-day event showcases the finest of New Mexico's artists and craftspeople — and New Mexico is a haven for fine artists. Exhibits range from oils and watercolor paintings to sculpture, jewelry, furniture and tapestries — all with a distinct Southwestern flavor.

The festival kicks off with a preview where visitors can mingle with the artists over cocktails and catch a first glimpse of art to be displayed and sold during the show. Visitors also can enjoy live entertainment (mostly country and jazz) and Southwestern foods during the festival.

Accommodations: Best Western Inn at Rio Rancho, $64-$71, 1465 Rio Rancho, Albuquerque, NM 81724, (800) 528-1234.

Information: New Mexico Arts and Crafts Fair, 5500 San Mateo N.E., Suite 105, Albuquerque, NM 87109, (505) 884-9043.

World Balloon Invitational, Battle Creek, Michigan

All eyes turn skyward at dawn and dusk as hundreds of hot-air balloons launch, filling the horizon with a colorful array of all shapes and sizes. During this eight-day event, held the last weekend in June and the first weekend in July, some 150 balloons will compete for $32,000 in prize money, turning the town of Battle Creek — better known as the home of America's breakfast cereals — into the hot-air capital of the Midwest.

More than a million people turn out for this festival that also includes an air show featuring the Canadian Snowbirds, fireworks, an arts and crafts festival and carnival rides.

Admission is $2 per person each day (plus $4 for parking) or $7 for the official festival button, which guarantees admission for the entire festival.

Accommodations: The Comfort Inn, $69, 165 Capital S.W., Battle Creek, MI 49017, (800) 228-5150 or (616) 965-3976.

Information: Battle Creek Hot Air Balloon Championship, 3300 Sixth, Suite B, P.O. Box 2019, Battle Creek, MI 49015, (616) 962-0592.

JVC Jazz Festival/Ben & Jerry's Newport Folk Festival, Newport, Rhode Island

On two consecutive weekends at Newport's Fort Adams State Park, you can work on your tan while you enjoy some of the finest jazz and folk music offered anywhere in the United States.

Top rhythm-and-blues musicians kick off the festival during the last weekend in July against the backdrop of boats in Newport Harbor. The following weekend, fans can enjoy folk music in the same location.

Jazz concludes the festival the second weekend in August, beginning with a gala concert Friday at the historic Newport Casino in the International Tennis Hall of Fame — the site of the first Newport Jazz Festival. Saturday and Sunday, 10,000 jazz lovers fill the lawn at Fort Adams with blankets and picnic baskets and sit back to enjoy the music.

Past performers have included B.B. King, Pete Seeger, Leon Redbone, Emmylou Harris, Herbie Mann, Dizzy Gillespie and Mel Torme.

Accommodations: Journey's End Motel, $79, 936 W. Main Road, Newport, RI 02840, (800) 668-4200.

Information: Ben & Jerry's Newport Folk Festival/JVC Jazz Festival, P.O. Box 605, Newport, RI 02840, (401) 847-3700.

Crawfish Festival, Beaux Bridge, Louisiana

On the first full weekend in May, pole your pirogue to Beaux Bridge, LA, a sleepy little town on the banks of Bayou Teche. There you can eat your weight in the world's most succulent mud bug, known locally as "Monsieur Ecrevisse" and elsewhere as the crayfish.

Family entertainments combine with authentic Cajun music and food, including a crayfish etouffee cook-off. Samples are part of the deal.

Accommodations: Holiday Inn Central, P.O. Box 91807, Lafayette, LA 70509, (800) 942-4868 or (318) 233-6815.

Information: Lafayette Convention and Visitors Bureau, P.O. Box 52066, Lafayette, LA 70505, (800) 346-1958 in the United States, (800) 543-5340 in Canada, or (318) 232-3737.

Song of Hiawatha, Pipestone, Minnesota

Who says the classics are dead? Every summer more than 25,000 people find their way to tiny Pipestone on the western edge of Minnesota to attend a professional-quality outdoor pageant based on Henry Wadsworth Longfellow's "Song of Hiawatha."

The pageant is performed by a cast of 200 in a three-acre quarry-turned-amphitheater on the last two weekends of July and the first weekend of August.

Accommodations: Historic Calumet Inn, from $63, including continental breakfast, 104 W. Main, Pipestone, MN 56164, (800) 535-7610.

Information: Pipestone Area Chamber of Commerce, P.O. Box 8, Pipestone, MN 56164, (507) 825-4126.

Firemen's Carnival, Assateague, Virginia

You *can* have your own pony. Every summer on the last Wednesday of July, Assateague Island's wild ponies are rounded up and guided on a swim across the channel to Chincoteague Island. The next day they are auctioned — going price usually is around $525 — and on Friday the remaining ponies swim back to Assateague.

A giant Firemen's Carnival encompasses all events.

Accommodations: Anchor Inn, $59-$89, 3775 Main St., Chincoteague, VA 23336, (804) 336-6313.

Information: Chincoteague Chamber of Commerce, P.O. Box 258, Chincoteague, VA 23336, (804) 336-6161.

Summer Festivals, Telluride, Colorado

This mountain resort, sometimes called "the new Aspen" because it is attracting the Beautiful People, is a festival-crazy town.

From May to September, 30 to 35 festivals are staged in Telluride, an average of one a week. So many festivals crowd the calendar that the town council decreed that one summer week — the third in July — would be festival-less.

Biggest of Telluride's fetes is the annual Telluride Bluegrass Festival, held the third weekend in June. Next in importance are the Film Festival at Labor Day and the Jazz Festival in mid-August.

No festival in Telluride is very large because the bed base here is limited to 3,800 pillows. Still, room reservations usually are necessary only for the Bluegrass Festival.

Situated at 8,700 feet in a box canyon, Telluride offers grand opportunities for outdoor activities — hiking, horseback riding and fishing among them. And there is no lack of nightspots.

Accommodations: Telluride Accommodations, (800) 446-3192, offers a variety of lodging at rates of $65-$695 a night.

Information: Telluride Visitors Services, P.O. Box 653, Telluride, CO 81435, (800) 525-3455.

A la Carte, A la Park, San Francisco, California

What would a trip to San Francisco be without sampling some of the city's fabulous restaurants? At A la Carte, A la Park, you don't have to spend a fortune doing it — and no reservations are necessary.

Begun in 1985 as a fund-raiser for the San Francisco Shakespeare Festival, this event now features more than 50 Bay Area restaurants that offer tasty tidbits from their menus. The food ranges from American classics and California cuisine to Asian, Italian,

Indian and Latin dishes — and, of course, desserts galore. The festival also offers wine tastings.

Golden Gate Park is the site of this three-day event, held during Labor Day weekend. Booths are arranged around the entertainment area in one of the park's many large glades, so visitors won't miss any of the bands or Shakespearean performances as they wander from one taste treat to another. Musical entertainment is as diverse and upbeat as the food offerings, from rock and rhythm and blues to Latino jazz and steel drums. One of the highlights is the cooking demonstrations by top chefs.

Admission is $8, including entertainment. Restaurant specialties range from 50 cents to $5.

Accommodations: Stanyan Park Hotel, across from Golden Gate Park and within walking distance of the festival, $105, 750 Stanyan St., San Francisco, CA 94117, (415) 751-1000.

Information: Events West, 99 E. Blithedale Ave., Mill Valley, CA 94941, (415) 383-9378.

HISTORICAL PLACES

Seeing where important events occurred, learning how people lived in earlier days — that's what makes historical sites and museums so interesting. America is full of such places, and each has a different spin.

The historical places profiled here will take from one afternoon to 12 days to explore.

Titusville, Pennsylvania

In the Oil Creek valley a half-mile south of Titusville, the world's first successful oil well was drilled by Edwin L. Drake in 1859. Thus was born the oil industry — and today's oil-dependent way of life.

The Drake Well Museum in Titusville commemorates this historic event with indoor and outdoor exhibits, including drilling rigs, a full-scale replica of Drake's original derrick and a working oil well.

Accommodations: Cross Creek Resort, $65-$115, P.O. Box 432, Titusville, PA 16354, (814) 827-9611.

Information: Drake Well Museum, RD 3 Box 7, Titusville, PA 16354, (814) 827-2797.

Plymouth, Massachusetts

It lies there, surprisingly small, under what looks like a Greek portico. But Plymouth Rock — marking the spot where the Pilgrims landed in the Mayflower in 1620 — is one of the key sights in this historic port city.

We tend to associate Plymouth with Thanksgiving, and certainly autumn is a wonderful time to visit, but summer is pleasant and, indeed, probably busier.

A tour of Plimoth Plantation, the replicated village where interpreters play the roles of actual early settlers, helps visitors understand the Pilgrims' ordeal.

If history pales on you, step into nearby Cranberry World, where you can learn all about cranberries (a big crop here) and sample products made of the fruit.

Accommodations: John Carver Inn, from $59, 25 Summer St., Plymouth, MA 02360, (800) 274-1620.

Information: Plymouth County Development Council, Box 1620, Pembroke, MA 02359, (800) 231-1620.

Port Tobacco, Maryland

Looking at Port Tobacco today, you'd never suspect it played an important role in American history on two occasions.

Only a handful of buildings remain in the original town center, and the harbor on the Potomac, once one of the biggest ports on the East Coast, filled with silt many years ago.

Just after the Revolutionary War, meetings held in Port Tobacco, the home of many influential citizens, led to the Mount Vernon Compact and the decision to write the Constitution.

Shortly after the end of the Civil War, Port Tobacco, then in decline, became

1 Titusville, Pennsylvania
2 Plymouth, Massachusetts
3 Port Tobacco, Maryland
4 Gettysburg, Pennsylvania

5 Lexington, Virginia
6 Natchez, Mississippi
7 Guthrie, Oklahoma
8 The Oregon Trail*

9 Greenfield Village, Michigan
10 Edenton, North Carolina
11 Delta Queen Riverboats**
12 Navigating Erie Canal, Rhode

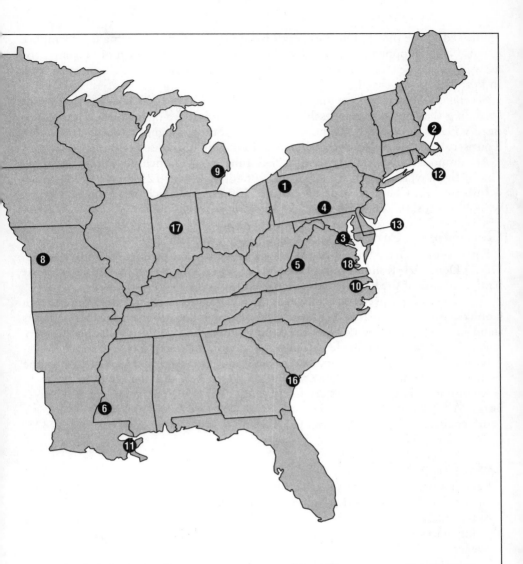

HISTORICAL PLACES

*Origination point is noted on map
**Based in New Orleans, with multiple departure
points on Mississippi and other rivers

embroiled in the plot to kill President Lincoln. John Wilkes Booth and accomplice David Herold stopped at the home of Mary Surratt 22 miles north of here after the assassination. Then they went on to Dr. Samuel Mudd's home for treatment and stayed in Port Tobacco overnight.

Several 18th-century structures in Port Tobacco have been restored or rebuilt, including the courthouse and schoolhouse. The latter are open to the public, as is nearby Havre de Venture, the home of Thomas Stone, a signer of the Constitution. Tourists also can visit the Surratt home and Dr. Mudd's house.

Accommodations: Best Western La Plata Inn, $55-$82, including breakfast, 6900 Crain Highway, Route 301, La Plata, MD 20646, (800) 528-1234 or (301) 934-4900.

Information: Charles County Tourism, 8190 Port Tobacco Road, Port Tobacco, MD 20677, (800) 766-3386.

Gettysburg, Pennsylvania

Battle sites at Gettysburg bring to life a tragic era of our history. Seminary Ridge, Devil's Den, Little Round Top and Cemetery Ridge all can be explored on a tour of the battlefield, site of the bloodiest confrontation of the Civil War.

You can look out over the field where Gen. George E. Pickett, under orders from Confederate Gen. Robert E. Lee, sent his troops on a disastrous charge. Monuments stand in cornfields to mark other important battles, and you can visit the cemetery where Abraham Lincoln made his famous 272-word address on Nov. 19, 1863.

Nearby is another historical place that has nothing to do with the Civil War — the modest retirement farm of Gen. Dwight D. Eisenhower, also open to the public.

Accommodations: Best Western Gettysburg, $74-$150, 1 Lincoln Square, Gettysburg, PA 17325, (800) 528-1234 or (717) 337-2000.

Information: Gettysburg Travel Council, 35 Carlysle St., Gettysburg, PA 17325, (717) 334-6274.

Lexington, Virginia

Four of America's greatest generals are linked to this pleasant Shenandoah Valley city. George Washington saved an impoverished college here and gave it his name.

Robert E. Lee came here after the Civil War to become president of that university, now known as Washington and Lee. Lee is buried here, and so is his famous horse, Traveller.

Stonewall Jackson, one of the Confederacy's greatest generals, founded a Sunday school for blacks in defiance of local custom and was a professor at Virginia Military Institute (VMI) for 10 years.

George C. Marshall, one of America's top generals in World War II and author of the Marshall Plan as secretary of state, graduated from VMI. A large museum here commemorates his brilliant service.

Aside from the military, Lexington offers hiking in wooded hills, motoring on the nearby Blue Ridge Parkway and summer theater.

Accommodations: Holiday Inn Lexington, $56-$80, P.O. Box 1108, Lexington, VA 24450, (800) 480-3043 or (540) 463-7351.

Information: Lexington Visitors Bureau, 106 E. Washington St., Lexington, VA 24450, (703) 463-3777.

Natchez, Mississippi

In the antebellum days when cotton was king, Natchez was the prime minister. Plantations sent their cotton to this Mississippi River port, where it was baled and loaded aboard steamships.

Cotton brokers and plantation owners built remarkable homes here, which luckily were spared during the Civil War. Although Natchez is best-known for pilgrimages in spring (March and early April) and fall (October), several of its magnificent antebellum homes are open for tours year-round, and some offer bed-and-breakfast accommodations.

Natchez also marks the southern end of the Natchez Trace Parkway, originally a 500-mile footpath used first by Indians and then by traders and settlers before the arrival of the steamboat on the Mississippi River.

Accommodations: Best Western River Park Hotel, $69, 645 S. Canal St., Natchez, MS 39120, (800) 528-1234 or (601) 446-6688.

Information: Natchez Convention and Visitors Bureau, P.O. Box 1485, Natchez, MS 39121, (800) 647-6724 or (800) 99-NATCHEZ.

Guthrie, Oklahoma

Imagine a city created in a day. At noon on April 22, 1889, when the first Oklahoma Land Run began, Guthrie did not exist. By 5 p.m., there were 15,000 homesteaders on the town site.

Guthrie went on to become the capital of Oklahoma when the state was admitted in 1907, but lost that honor three years later to Oklahoma City — a move that sent the city into economic decline.

Now, thanks in part to its long slumber, Guthrie boasts one of the largest collections of Victorian buildings in the nation — a total of 2,169 on 400 city blocks. Visitors can survey a downtown that is 80 percent restored, pop into Miss Lizzie's former bordello (now a boutique mall), take in a play at the historic Polland theater and visit the Bluebelle Bar, where Tom Mix dispensed drinks from 1902 to 1904.

Accommodations: Best Western Territorial Inn, $53-$59, P.O. Box 977, Guthrie, OK 73044, (800) 528-1234 or (405) 282-8831.

Information: Guthrie Chamber of Commerce, P.O. Box 995, Guthrie, OK 73044, (800) 299-1899.

The Oregon Trail

You can pick up the trail of pioneers almost anywhere between Independence, MO, and Oregon City, OR. Wagon ruts left 150 years ago still are visible in many places, and museums and parks along the route tell the story of the hardy thousands who went west to build a new life. All told, the Oregon Trail has 300 miles of discernible wagon ruts and 125 historic sites.

The best place to get an overview is at the National Historic Oregon Trail Interpretive Center in Baker City, OR, where, atop Flagstaff Hill, weary travelers in 1843 gained their first glimpse of the richness of Oregon. Dioramas, films, living history demonstrations and exhibits tell their stories. Other interpretive centers are found at Independence, MO; Scottsbluff, NE; Fort Laramie, WY; and Oregon City, OR.

Interesting sites on the route include Chimney Rock, a natural feature visible for miles in Nebraska; Independence Rock, the halfway point of the trail in Wyoming; Three Island Crossing in Idaho, the most dangerous river crossing; and the Blue

Mountains of Oregon, a difficult traverse.

Accommodations: Best Western Sunridge Inn, $58-$75, 1 Sunridge Lane, Baker, OR 97814, (800) 528-1234 or (503) 523-6444.

Information: National Historic Oregon Trail Interpretive Center, P.O. Box 987, Baker City, OR 97814, (503) 523-1843.

Greenfield Village, Michigan

Greenfield Village, in Dearborn, MI, a suburb of Detroit, is an amazing collection of genuine historical buildings — no replicas — from all over America.

Thomas Edison's laboratory, where he invented the electric light bulb, is there, moved from Menlo Park, NJ. The Wright brothers' bicycle store, where they developed plans for the first airplane, was brought from Dayton, OH. Noah Webster's home is there, and so is Henry Ford's birthplace.

The village is remarkable for its gathering at one site of so many authentic settings in which significant history took place.

Adjacent is the Henry Ford Museum, an enormous collection of Americana, from early refrigerators and radios to historical vehicles, including several presidential limousines. John F. Kennedy was riding in one of them when he was assassinated.

Accommodations: Courtyard by Marriott, from $89, 5200 Mercury Drive, Dearborn, MI 48126, (800) 321-2211 or (313) 271-1400.

Information: Henry Ford Museum and Greenfield Village, 20900 Oakwood Blvd., Dearborn, MI 48121, (800) 343-1929.

Edenton, North Carolina

Boston staged a famous "tea party" in December 1773 to protest taxation without representation, and Edenton followed suit a few months later when 51 women signed a resolution protesting such taxation. That symbolic act became known as Edenton's "tea party."

Then the capital of the colony of North Carolina, Edenton has survived splendidly to become an outstanding repository of historic structures, largely due to the active role played by its women then and since.

One house, the Cupola (1725), is considered the finest Jacobean-type house south of Connecticut. Another, the Chowan County Courthouse (1767), has been called the finest Georgian-style public building in the South. Three other structures on the National Register of Historic Places also are open for guided tours.

Accommodations: Lords Proprietor's Inn, $85-$145 ($155-$215 including dinner), 300 N. Broad St., Edenton, NC 27932, (800) 348-8933 or (919) 482-3641.

Information: Edenton Historical Commission, P.O. Box 474, Edenton, NC 27932, (919) 482-2637.

Delta Queen Riverboats

For an only-in-America luxury lodging, consider floating down one of the great mid-American rivers on a paddle-wheel steamboat that evokes the era of Mark Twain.

Delta Queen's three steamboats — the new American Queen joining the Delta Queen and Mississippi Queen — ply rivers from St. Paul to New Orleans and east to Pittsburgh. A Mark Twain impersonator is sometimes part of the entertainment, and a "riverlorian" shares the history of the waterways and the small towns where the boats dock. Some towns, like Vicksburg, MS, with its famous Civil War battlefield, can be explored for a day.

Cost: Lodging, meals and entertainment are included in prices that start at $330 a person in an inside cabin on a two-night cruise and range to $7,070 in a superior suite on a 12-night cruise. Airfare is extra.

Information: Delta Queen Steamboat Co., 30 Robin St. Wharf, New Orleans, LA 70130-1890, (800) 543-7637.

Navigating Erie Canal, Rhode Island to Quebec

Easygoing, informal and inexpensive as most cruises go, this 12-day voyage along some of North America's oldest maritime highways will delight sailors and historians alike.

Thanks to American Canadian Caribbean Line's shallow-draft vessels, you don't have to go to Europe to enjoy canal cruising. Passengers board in Warren, RI, and sail along the New England coast and up the Hudson River, past the mansions and manor houses of families like the Roosevelts and Vanderbilts. The heart of the voyage is navigating the historic Erie Canal and its many locks.

Following a traditional trade route, where scenery and history now overshadow commerce, you travel along the St. Lawrence Seaway to Montreal and Quebec City, then the scenic Saguenay River. Cruises operate June through mid-October.

Cost: Rates are $1,905-$2,415 per person, double occupancy.

Information: American Canadian Caribbean Line, P.O. Box 368, Warren, RI 02885, (800) 556-7450.

Oxford, Maryland

Founded in 1683, Oxford is one of the oldest towns in Maryland. Located midway on the Eastern shore of the Chesapeake at the end of Route 333, where the Choptank and Tred Avon rivers meet, the town has a prevailing look of Victorian Gothic. Few of the earlier buildings have survived.

Maritime history buffs will revel in this charming old port. It hosted an early Chesapeake sailing regatta in 1860, and that sailing history is documented in the Oxford Museum at Morris and Market streets. Some of the museum's sailboat models were constructed at the nearby Cutts and Case shipyards.

Along the riverbank is the Customs House, actually a bicentennial replica of the shed from which Jeremiah Banning, the first federal collector of customs, managed the traffic at this once-busy port.

Accommodations: Robert Morris Inn, from $90, is an 18th-century charmer overlooking the Tred Avon River, P.O. Box 70, Oxford, MD 21654, (410) 226-5111.

Information: Talbot County Chamber of Commerce, 210 Marlboro Ave., Suite 3, Easton, MD 21601, (410) 822-4606.

Dodge City, Kansas

Dodge City is a town forever associated with the Wild West. Named for nearby Fort Dodge and built by construction crews of the Santa Fe Railroad, the town drew hunters eager for buffalo hides.

The hunters are gone, and so are most of the buffalo. But as cattle were driven north to feed a hungry nation after the Civil War, Dodge City became the cowboy capital of the West. Peace-keeping residents like Bat Masterson and Wyatt Earp live on in legend.

Nowadays, visitors flock to historical Front Street, a two-block re-creation of the town in the 1870s. Highlights include Boot Hill Museum, on the site of the notorious cemetery, and Hardesty House, the restored mansion of an early cattle baron. At the Long Branch Saloon, there's a chuck wagon dinner, a variety show, a medicine show, stagecoach rides and re-enacted gunfights.

Accommodations: Best Western Silver Spur Lodge, from $49, P.O. Box 119, Dodge City, KS 67801, (316) 227-2125.

Information: Dodge City Convention & Visitors Department, P.O. Box 1474, Dodge City, KS 67801, (316) 225-8186 or (800) OLD-WEST.

Tuolumne County, California

Relive the colorful California gold rush days in Tuolumne County, east of San Francisco and adjacent to Yosemite National Park.

At Columbia State Historic Park, the restored gold rush town of Columbia has guided tours, museums, stagecoach rides, horseback riding, gold panning and even a saloon from the 1850s.

Stay in the park or in historic Jamestown, next door, which offers several bed-and-breakfasts and hotels, in addition to antique shops, art galleries and Railtown, a state park featuring steam train rides, a huge roundhouse and a train museum.

Other options include white-water rafting, cavern tours, winery visits and sightseeing at Yosemite.

Accommodations: In Jamestown, Royal Hotel, from $80 for Greenhouse Cottage, sleeping four to eight, including breakfast, P.O. Box 219, Jamestown, CA 95327, (209) 984-5271.

Information: Tuolumne County Visitors Bureau, P.O. Box 4020, Sonora, CA 95370, (209) 533-4420 or (800) 446-1333.

Savannah, Georgia

Strolling through Savannah, GA, brings to life three centuries of American history. On the Savannah River, this seaport was America's first planned city and the original settlement in Georgia, one of the original 13 colonies.

It's a gracious city, known for its small parks with fountains. Magnolias and moss-draped oaks line the streets, stately mansions stand as sentinels to the past, and cobblestone paths lead to Victorian neighborhood and Civil War sites.

The best way to experience old Savannah is to walk its historic downtown area. A walk to Forsyth Park passes by the city's most famous landmarks, including the Green-Meldrim House, where Gen. Sherman established his Union headquarters.

You also can enjoy sightseeing by horse-drawn carriage or riverboat. Museum buffs shouldn't miss the Ships of the Sea Maritime Museum.

Accommodations: Mulberry Holiday Inn, early Victorian structure, $125-$160, 601 E. Bay St., Savannah, GA 31401, (912) 238-1200 or (800) HOLIDAY. River Street Inn, $79-$139, 115 E. River St., Savannah, GA 31401, (800) 253-4229. Best Western Savannah Historic District, $65, 412 W. Bay St., Savannah, GA 31401, (912) 233-1011 or (800) 528-1234.

Information: Savannah Area Convention & Visitors Bureau, 222 W. Oglethorpe Ave., Savannah, GA 31499, (912) 944-0456 or (800) 444-2427.

Noblesville, Indiana

It's always 1836 at Conner Prairie Pioneer Settlement in Noblesville, just north of

Indianapolis. Costumed interpreters at the 39 buildings in this 250-acre museum make history come alive. Chat with Martha Zimmerman as she bakes gingerbread at the Golden Eagle Tavern, watch the blacksmith work and let the teacher grade your spelling at the one-room school house. At the Pioneer Adventure Area, a hands-on outdoor arena, children dip candles, try weaving and sample 19th-century games.

History is anything but boring here. In early summer, you can be a guest at a traditional 1836 wedding. On July 4, kick up your heels at an old-fashioned village celebration.

Admission is $9 for adults, $8.50 for seniors, $6.50 for children ages 6-12 and free for younger children.

Children also will enjoy the nearby Indiana Transportation Museum with its rolling stock including a trolley that runs on a one-mile track. The train collection is part of Forest Park, which has picnic facilities, a swimming pool, a nine-hole golf course, and miniature golf. Indianapolis, with its state capital, museums, a zoo and the Hall of Fame at the Indy 500 track, is less than a half hour away.

Accommodations: $69 a night Summer Fun package at the Quality Inn Castleton Suites, including lodging for up to four people, hot breakfast, afternoon snack and discount tickets to Conner Prairie. The hotel is in suburban Indianapolis six miles from Conner Prairie, at 8275 Craig, Indianapolis, IN 46250, (317) 841-9700.

Information: Conner Prairie, 13400 Allisonville Road, Fishers, IN 46038, (317) 776-6000 or (800) 966-1836. Hamilton County Convention & Visitors Bureau, 11601 Municipal Drive, Fishers, IN 46038, (317) 598-4444 or (800) 776-TOUR.

Williamsburg, Virginia

Summer is prime time for family visits to Colonial Williamsburg, the 173-acre, re-created Virginia capital that bred independent politics and fostered such revolutionaries as Thomas Jefferson and Patrick Henry.

The seasonlong military encampment, a favorite attraction, makes army folk out of tenderfoot visitors — kids included. After signing up with the 2nd Virginia Regiment, new recruits practice drills, learn the bayonet lunge, present arms (using sticks instead of muskets) and help clean and fire a cannon.

Take the family to the courthouse to participate as plaintiffs, defendants, witnesses and judges in 18th-century court cases. Teach your kids about folk art at the Abby Aldrich Rockefeller Folk Art Center. The whimsical quality of the weather vanes, carvings and paintings makes this place especially appealing to kids.

Be sure to stroll past the Palace Green to see if you can join a game of quoits (similar to horseshoes) or lawn bowling. For more history, visit Jamestown Settlement and Yorktown Battlefield Park, both easy day-trips from Colonial Williamsburg.

A basic admission ticket is $25 for adults and $15 for children ages 6-12.

Accommodations: The Williamsburg Woodlands, next to the Visitor Center, has a pool, tennis courts, miniature golf and rooms starting at $85, 102 Visitors Center Drive, Williamsburg, VA 23187, (804) 229-1000.

Information: For information and reservations in Colonial Williamsburg, call (800) HISTORY or write to The Colonial Williamsburg Foundation, P.O. Box 1776, Williamsburg, VA 23187-1776. For information about Williamsburg, Jamestown or Yorktown, contact the Williamsburg Area Convention and Visitors Bureau, 201 Penniman Road, Williamsburg, VA 23185, (800) 368-6511 or (804) 253-0192. For accommodations, call (800) 446-9244.

Santa Fe, New Mexico

With its multifaceted background, as an artists' colony, Spanish Colonial settlement and American Indian culture center, Santa Fe casts a unique ambience. It's the oldest capital city in the country, founded in 1610.

Painters, sculptors and other artisans sell more original work here than in any other location between the two coasts. Quick-sketch artists and purveyors of Indian-made jewelry and pottery display their wares on the 380-year-old Plaza.

The Santa Fe Opera company performs in an amphitheater.

A long weekend in Santa Fe should include a drive through the Rio Grande Valley to Taos, where some American Indians still live in a pueblo.

Accommodations: La Fonda, on the Plaza, from $169, 100 E. San Francisco St., Santa Fe, NM 87501, (800) 523-5002 or (505) 982-5511.

Information: Santa Fe Convention & Visitors Bureau, P.O. Box 909, Santa Fe, NM 87504, (800) 984-9984 or (505) 984-6760.

Lincoln, New Mexico

Strange as it may seem, there's a peaceful, quiet little town in the foothills of south-central New Mexico where one of the most violent episodes of Wild West history took place.

During its heyday in the 1860s and '70s, Lincoln was a rowdy but prosperous ranching and mercantile center. Then a battle between rival merchants and ranching factions for control of the county erupted in 1878.

When the smoke had cleared from a deadly five-day shootout, a hired gunslinger named Billy the Kid emerged to blaze a trail in Western lore. Some of Billy's misdeeds took place in Lincoln, including a much-chronicled 1881 escape from the county courthouse. Bullet holes in the old courthouse walls intrigue onlookers to this day.

Well-preserved territorial-era buildings with shady porches, sleeping dogs and showy gardens invite leisurely exploration. You can dine or stay at the Wortley Hotel; Sheriff Robert Ollinger is said to have rushed from the Wortley to his death at the hands of the escaping Kid. Or, bed down at the 1860 Casa de Patron B&B, where owners can legitimately claim — you guessed it — "Billy the Kid Slept Here."

Accommodations: Wortley Hotel, $55-$65, Box 98, Lincoln, NM 88338, (505) 653-4300. Casa de Patron, $79-$107, P.O. Box 27, Lincoln, NM 88338, (505) 653-4676.

Information: Lincoln County Heritage Trust, P.O. Box 98, Lincoln, NM 88338, (505) 653-4838.

ROMANTIC
INNS

A cross the country, in both urban and rural settings, small hostelries create the perfect atmosphere for romantic getaways.

Some have canopied beds, private hot tubs and fireplaces. Guests may be pampered with afternoon tea and cookies, evening wine and cheese and morning breakfast served on a silver tray.

What makes an inn truly romantic are the little extras, such as a hidden courtyard, a bed so high it has steps, an intimate bay window perfect for watching sunsets or a private deck with a view worth sharing with someone special.

Each of our selections offers such bonuses, as well as more surprises we left for you to discover on your own. They range from rustic to elegant, from seaside manor to mountain-top lodge. Each is different but they all share a special hospitable atmosphere, aesthetic beauty and an environment that inspires romance.

Costs given are for a double room for two.

Thunder Bay Inn, Big Bay, Michigan

Only one road leads to Big Bay on Michigan's Upper Peninsula, but it's a road well traveled. Henry Ford drove it back in the 1940s and became so taken with the Big Bay Hotel that he bought and restored it, mainly to have a place where he could invite his friends. Jimmy Stewart and Lee Remick came up that same road in 1959 to film "Anatomy of a Murder," the movie based on a murder that actually took place in this tiny settlement. The film company added a bar to the hotel and renamed it Thunder Bay Inn.

Now, restored under new owner Darryl Small, the inn is luring visitors up the same 28-mile road from Marquette to hang out in the inn's popular bar or to enjoy quiet moments on the shores of Lake Superior.

Cost: $55-$95, including continental breakfast.
Information: Thunder Bay Inn, Box 286, Big Bay, MI 49808, (800) 732-0714.

Harry Packer Mansion, Jim Thorpe, Pennsylvania

You might just kill to stay at this inn in the foothills of the Pocono Mountains of northeastern Pennsylvania. But you'd surely be caught; the establishment's guests usually are rather keen on solving bloody crimes. This inn, dating from 1874 and resembling something from the pages of a Gothic novel, is known for its murder-mystery weekends.

The decor is stately, with Victorian antique furnishings, original marble fireplace mantels, inlaid wooden floors, 10-foot gilt-framed mirrors and hand-painted ceilings. Details such as Minton tiles, Tiffany windows and carved walnut woodwork around the fireplaces make the mansion a showpiece that is open daily for guided tours.

The 13 guest rooms (including six in another building called the Carriage House) are furnished just as elegantly with antique beds and handmade quilts. The top of the line is the Harry Packer Suite, with a sitting room adjacent to the bedroom.

For those who want to wander, the Victorian village of Jim Thorpe offers historic

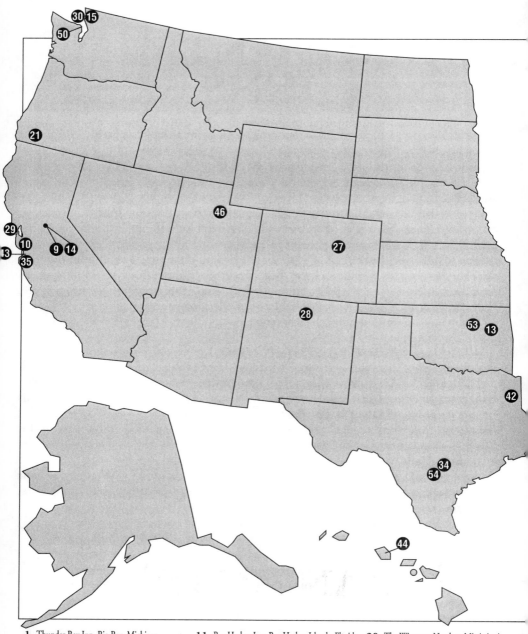

1 Thunder Bay Inn, Big Bay, Michigan
2 Harry Packer Mansion, Jim Thorpe, Pennsylvania
3 The Inn at Canoe Point, Bar Harbor, Maine
4 Griswold Inn, Essex, Connecticut
5 Angel of the Sea, Cape May, New Jersey
6 Strawberry Inn, New Market, Maryland
7 Balsam Mountain Inn, Balsam, North Carolina
8 Hale Springs Inn, Rogersville, Tennessee
9 Sutter Creek Inn, Sutter Creek, California
10 The Inn at Saratoga, Saratoga, California

11 Bay Harbor Inn, Bay Harbor Islands, Florida
12 Monmouth Plantation, Natchez, Mississippi
13 Graham-Carroll House, Muskogee, Oklahoma
14 Wedgewood Inn, Jackson, California
15 The Castle, Bellingham, Washington
16 Dusty's English Inn, Eaton Rapids, Michigan
17 White Hill Manor, Warsaw, Indiana
18 Potter House, Rock Island, Illinois
19 Victoria Inn, Cincinnati, Ohio

20 The Wigwam, Natchez, Mississippi
21 Buckhorn Springs, Ashland, Oregon
22 Westmoor Inn, Nantucket, Massachusetts
23 Thatcher Brook Inn, Waterbury, Vermont
24 Sweetwater Farm, Glen Mills, Pennsylvania
25 Foley House Inn, Savannah, Georgia
26 Inn at Cedar Crossing, Sturgeon Bay, Wisconsin
27 Queen Anne Inn, Denver, Colorado
28 Grant Corner Inn, Santa Fe, New Mexico
29 Blackthorne Inn, Inverness, California

ROMANTIC INNS

home and church tours, an excursion train, boutiques and museums.

Cost: Starting at $85, including full breakfast.

Information: Harry Packer Mansion, P.O. Box 458, Packer Hill, Jim Thorpe, PA 18229, (717) 325-8566.

The Inn at Canoe Point, Bar Harbor, Maine

Hidden away from the highway and set snugly amid pines on the rocky shore, this inn is a Bar Harbor favorite. Its ocean room, with a fireplace and comfortable seating, exudes friendly warmth, as does the living room, which has a piano as well as a fireplace. Outside, overlooking the water, is a deck for sunning. On nice summer days, breakfast is served on the deck.

A wealth of paintings, books and a Lalique collection reflect innkeeper Don Johnson's love of cultural expression. The inn is near the entrance to Acadia National Park.

Cost: $125-$225, including full breakfast.

Information: The Inn at Canoe Point, Box 216, Bar Harbor, ME 04609, (207) 288-9511.

Griswold Inn, Essex, Connecticut

When publications print photos of picturesque inns, the white clapboard Griswold and its wraparound veranda is often among them. Built in 1776, this historic hostelry looks like everybody's idea of a romantic inn.

Inside, paintings and prints of old riverboats and ocean liners decorate the walls, along with lanterns and other nautical items. Two oars hang from the arched wood ceiling of the bar, where live entertainers always draw a full crowd.

Essex, once a major shipping center, is a delightful historic town near the mouth of the Connecticut River. Train and boat excursions run up the river, an excellent marine museum tells the story of Essex, and classy boutiques on Main Street lure shoppers.

Cost: $90-$165, including continental breakfast.

Information: Griswold Inn, 36 Main St., Essex, CT 06426, (203) 767-1776.

Angel of the Sea, Cape May, New Jersey

In a town known for its Victorian ambiance, this is a standout. With gables and dormers, two levels of gingerbread balconies and violet and white decor, the 27-room Angel of the Sea is not simply this resort city's largest B&B. It's also one of Cape May's most striking inns.

In addition to a full breakfast, Angel of the Sea serves tea and sweets every afternoon at 4 and wine and cheese each evening from 5:30 to 7. In summertime, guests often enjoy their goodies on the veranda.

The beach is only a few steps away, and bicycles are available to pedal around flat Cape May.

Cost: $135-$285, including full breakfast, afternoon tea, evening wine and cheese, parking and beach passes.

Information: Angel of the Sea, 5 Trenton Ave., Cape May, NJ 08204, (800) 848-3369.

Strawberry Inn, New Market, Maryland

If you're into antiques, you'll love this charming five-room inn about an hour north of Washington, DC, near Frederick, MD — and not just because the place is furnished Victorian-style.

New Market is just six blocks long, but it has more than 40 antique shops, most housed in buildings that are antiques themselves. Whatever you're looking for in antiques, New Market probably has it.

The inn is a delightful place whose summer guests can take breakfast on the back porch under a trellis of grapevines. Behind spreads an expansive back yard with an enormous maple tree and a pretty gazebo. Owners Ellen and Mike Pierce live in a large 19th-century log cabin on the property.

Cost: $95, including full breakfast.

Information: Strawberry Inn, P.O. Box 237, New Market, MD 21774, (301) 865-3318.

Balsam Mountain Inn, Balsam, North Carolina

In 1990, Merrily Teasley bought the run-down, vacant Balsam Mountain Inn, determined to return the venerable hostelry to its turn-of-the-century charm.

It took her two years and $2 million, but today this grand old place is once again welcoming guests to this lovely sector of North Carolina. Many rooms have fireplaces and/or balconies, and the broad front porch, lined with rocking chairs, is perfect for reading and mountain-gazing.

In its heyday, guests of the Balsam Mountain Inn arrived by train at the Balsam depot, at 3,443 feet the highest rail station east of the Rockies. The tracks are still there, and Teasley is trying to convince the Great Smoky Mountains Railway to come a-calling again.

Cost: $90-$150, including full country breakfast.

Information: Balsam Mountain Inn, P.O. Box 40, Balsam, NC 28707, (800) 224-9498.

Hale Springs Inn, Rogersville, Tennessee

Restoring a historic inn is a lot bigger job than it looks, as Carl Netherland-Brown learned when he decided to restore the Hale Springs Inn.

Three presidents (Andrew Jackson, James Polk and Andrew Johnson) had stayed in the historic inn since its founding in 1824, but when Netherland-Brown bought it, time had taken its toll. Three of the four original chimneys were gone, all the fireplaces were sealed, the brick exterior was covered with paint, and walls and floors were in poor condition.

Today, the inn is a beauty, with new bathrooms, a working fireplace in every room, new wallpaper, brass and crystal chandeliers and antique furniture.

Rogersville has a wealth of historic buildings, and nearby Jonesborough is a charming historic town.

Cost: $40-$70, including continental breakfast.

Information: Hale Springs Inn, 110 W. Main St., Rogersville, TN 37857, (615) 272-5171.

Sutter Creek Inn, Sutter Creek, California

The rooms bear names like The Woodshed, Lower Washhouse and Miner's Cabin, but don't be put off by their rustic monikers. The 18-room Sutter Creek Inn, snug inside its honeysuckle-draped fence, is a place for romance to bloom.

Late afternoon is a time for lemonade in the parlor, and breakfast brings guests together for a family-style meal. For a swinging time, book one of four rooms furnished with beds hung from the ceiling.

This is gold country, and Sutter Creek is one of several charming villages that date back to the Gold Rush of '49. There still are mine tunnels beneath the town, and innkeeper Jane Way keeps a collection of nuggets she has found on her property over the years.

Cost: $60-$125 midweek, $88-$145 weekends, including full breakfast and afternoon refreshments.

Information: Sutter Creek Inn, P.O. Box 385, Sutter Creek, CA 95685, (209) 267-5606.

The Inn at Saratoga, Saratoga, California

When they were small, the two sisters played in Saratoga Creek in the shade of huge eucalyptus and sycamore trees. Both grew up to be movie stars, so when a classy new inn opened on the creek bank in Saratoga, a suburb of Silicon Valley's San Jose, it seemed natural to name its two suites after the town's most famous alumnae, Olivia de Haviland and Joan Fontaine.

Each room has a bay-window area that can be closed off by a curtain; this allows one occupant to read while another sleeps.

Cost: $145-$440 for single or double occupancy, including continental breakfast and afternoon tea, wine and hors d'oeuvres.

Information: The Inn at Saratoga, 20645 Fourth St., Saratoga, CA 95070, (800) 338-5020 or (408) 867-5020.

Bay Harbor Inn, Bay Harbor Islands, Florida

This inn incorporates the oldest building in town, but don't look for it on the National Register of Historic Places. Built in 1940, it's the only authentic waterfront inn in the Miami area.

The 36-room establishment has a split personality. Half is housed in the Townside building, offering turn-of-the-century antiques in two-room suites with king-sized four-poster beds. Grandfather clocks, hardwood floors and alcoves for reading enhance the ambience.

The inn's other half is across the street in the Creekside building, with tile floors and more contemporary decor in rooms with balconies overlooking Indian Creek. The downstairs area features a replica of a London pub, with a bar from the Vanderbilt mansion in London. There's a heated pool on the grounds.

Meals are a little out of the ordinary, with breakfast being served aboard the inn's yacht, Celeste. Other meals are served at the inn's Palm restaurant, sister of the famous Palm restaurant in New York.

Nearby you'll find fine shopping, golf, tennis, theater, museums, art galleries and, of course, the beach.

Cost: Starting at $60, including continental breakfast.

Information: Bay Harbor Inn, 9660 E. Bay Harbor Drive, Bay Harbor Islands, FL 33154, (305) 868-4141.

Monmouth Plantation, Natchez, Mississippi

The romance of the antebellum South is still very much alive at this stately inn, presiding over 26 landscaped acres in Natchez. Dating from 1818, Mon national historic landmark that is open during the day for public tours.

The South's legendary hospitality is at its warmest here, with pralines and a welco beverage served on arrival, a complimentary bottle of wine in your room, mint juleps and complimentary hors d'oeuvres offered at cocktail hour and chocolates placed on your pillow at night.

The decor includes such touches as lace runners on the tables, silver tea sets, globe chandeliers and antique silver and fine china in the dining room.

The 25 guest rooms are spread among the main house, the servants' quarters, individual cabins and the renovated carriage house. All are air conditioned and filled with period antiques.

Monmouth also is known for its five-course gourmet dinners ($35 per person, not including drinks, tax and gratuity), served by candlelight and featuring regional dishes.

On the grounds you can wander down pebble paths through flower gardens, cross an arched bridge over a pond and sit in the gazebo or on the wrought-iron furniture gracing a brick courtyard.

The charming town of Natchez offers historic home tours, carriage rides, antique shops and colorful Natchez-Under-the-Hill, a district of shops and restaurants on the banks of the Mississippi River.

Cost: Starting at $110, including full breakfast.

Information: Monmouth Plantation, 36 Melrose Ave., Natchez, MS 39120, (800) 828-4531.

Graham-Carroll House, Muskogee, Oklahoma

How can you go wrong at a Victorian Gothic inn that graces a road known by the locals for almost a century as Silk Stocking Avenue?

Built in 1935 by one of the founders of Texaco, this five-bedroom mansion 45 miles southeast of Tulsa is no stranger to the good life. The living room features an 1880s square grand piano, a marble fireplace, a Chinese rug and polished oak floors. The dining room furniture once belonged to none other than William Randolph Hearst.

The Silk Stocking Room, which has an antique stained-glass window and fireplace, opens onto a lovely rooftop garden. The Cedar Tower Room, with its sultan's bed and marble bath, also adjoins the garden. The inn also offers romantic suites. Access to the Honeymoon Suite (with an antique French bed) is by a private elevator.

After breakfasting in the solarium, with its three stained-glass windows and hand-cut marble floor, you may want to enjoy the Victorian gardens, sit on the patio or watch the Japanese carp swimming in the fish pond.

Farther afield, you'll find antique shopping, a few small museums, Muskogee's downtown historic district and the submarine U.S. Batfish (now in dry dock and open for tours). The pre-Civil War Fort Gibson also is just a few miles away.

Cost: Starting at $80, including full breakfast.

Information: Graham-Carroll House, 501 N. 16th St., Muskogee, OK 74401, (918) 683-0100.

Wedgewood Inn, Jackson, California

This Victorian inn on five wooded acres in the Sierra foothills, a few hours by car from the Bay Area, is bound to fool you. For all its old-fashioned architecture and gingerbread charm, it dates from the '80s — the 1980s. It's almost brand new.

don't give the secret away. In addition to the antiques, you'll
...ioned gems that look older than your great-grandmother. The
; were made by owner Vic Beltz, and the Victorian lace lamp-
f his wife, Jeannine, who made them from the train of her wedding

ques are a hand-carved grand piano, European tapestries and a
fabu.............-wheel collection from around the world. A 1921 Model T is on
display in its ... showroom.

The six guest rooms each have clawfoot tubs and pull-chain toilets. The Victorian
Rose Room has a balcony, a view of the rose garden and English carved furniture. The
Carriage House, a separate cottage with a country theme, canopied bed and wood stove,
is filled with four generations of family heirlooms.

You'll enjoy complimentary cheese and beverages each afternoon, and breakfast can
be served in your room.

The English country-style grounds include walking paths, a rose arbor, fountains and
a gazebo. For relaxing, plunk yourself down on a porch swing or snooze in a hammock.
Guests with more energy might want to play croquet and horseshoes or tussle with the
resident cocker spaniel, Lacey.

Cost: Starting at $90, including full breakfast.

Information: Wedgewood Inn, 11941 Narcissus Road, Jackson, CA 95642, (800)
933-4393.

The Castle, Bellingham, Washington

When you're staying at an inn with a name like The Castle, it's easy to imagine you're
royalty. This particular castle perches on a hill overlooking Bellingham Bay and the San
Juan Islands 90 miles north of Seattle.

Furnished in part with carved appointments from the Black Forest region of
Germany, the establishment lives up to its name. Guests can relax on a large front porch
or inspect a huge early electric lamp collection (the owners also run an antique shop
downtown) and a set of murals depicting the history of The Castle.

The four guest rooms are decorated in different fantasy themes; the most notable is
the Sultan's Tent in the turret, with its Arabian Nights decor and a 400-year-old bed.
Others include the King's Balcony, with marble-topped furniture and a Romeo-and-
Juliet balcony; the Oriental Cupola Room, with museum-quality Asian antiques and
artifacts; and the Bayview Honeymoon Suite, decorated in lavender and lace with its
own veranda and fireplace, not to mention great bay views.

The inn was built in 1890 by entrepreneur Jim Wardner, who made and lost several
fortunes in his lifetime. His castle has served as a teahouse, a fried-chicken restaurant
and even student housing before becoming a bed-and-breakfast inn.

A few blocks away is the historic Fairhaven District, with shops, entertainment and
restaurants.

Cost: Starting at $65, including full breakfast.

Information: The Castle, 1103 15th St., Bellingham, WA 98225, (360) 676-0974.

Dusty's English Inn, Eaton Rapids, Michigan

Here's an inn 13 miles south of Lansing that's suffering from a delusion — it thinks
it's in England. Built by Oldsmobile president Irving Reuter in 1927, the red brick and
stone Tudor mansion has wrought-iron gates, a slate roof and ivy-covered walls. It

seems as though it was plucked directly from the English countryside and comes complete with an authentic British pub.

The inn's public rooms include a library with fireplace and a Devonshire dining room with walnut paneling, huge fireplace and grand piano. In a rare bow to its true homeland, the inn offers American as well as continental cuisine.

For those interested in such classic English fare as shepherd's pie and fish and chips, pub grub is served in the paneled English pub. Ask the bartender about the pub's stint as a bishop's chapel when the first bishop of the Diocese of Lansing lived here.

The grounds are landscaped to resemble — what else? — a traditional English garden. A portion of the Grand River flows through the 15-acre estate. Croquet, canoeing, fishing, biking, hiking and cross-country skiing are available, and two golf courses are nearby.

Cost: Starting at $85, including full breakfast.

Information: Dusty's English Inn, 728 S. Michigan Road, Eaton Rapids, MI 48827, (800) 858-0598.

White Hill Manor, Warsaw, Indiana

This rather grand English Tudor mansion 40 miles northwest of Fort Wayne was built in 1934 at the height of the Depression. Yet with its stained-glass windows, arched entryways, crown molding and mullioned windows, you'd think it was constructed at the peak of national prosperity.

It is stately both inside and out, with burgundy leather couches and blue velvet wing chairs adorning the living room, and wicker chairs, glass-topped tables and the original slate floor gracing the porch.

Of the eight guest rooms, the Windsor Suite sports a Jacuzzi. The Buttery (with its yellow decor and clawfoot tub) is in what once was the kitchen. The guest room known as the Library once was just that and still has its original bookshelves.

Most guests spend an evening at the renowned Wagon Wheel Theatre next door. Outdoorsmen find recreational opportunities galore on Kosciusko County's nearly 100 lakes. The area also offers great antique shopping, and it's close to northeast Indiana's Amish country.

Cost: Starting at $70, including full breakfast and afternoon tea.

Information: White Hill Manor, 2513 E. Center St., Warsaw, IN 46580, (219) 269-6933.

Potter House, Rock Island, Illinois

The town of Rock Island, 165 miles west of Chicago, may have become rather famous recently for its riverboat gambling. But you won't be taking any chances by staying at Potter House, a 1907 colonial revival-style inn on the National Register of Historic Places.

The detailing includes embossed leather wallpaper, mahogany paneling, 13 stained-glass windows, six fireplaces and 24-karat gold embellishments on the beveled-glass entry doors — all original to the house. A 1924 player piano adorns the front parlor.

The five rooms and cottage suite have special touches. The Potter Room has a large fireplace, the Palladian Room has a stained-glass panel over a Palladian window, and the Guest Room's writing table once was an old sewing machine. Jenny's Suite has an antique wrought-iron bed and clawfoot tub, while Marguerite's Room has an unusual built-in hat cupboard.

Guests can borrow the inn's tandem bicycle to tool around town or ask the innkeepers to arrange a horse-and-carriage ride.

In the area you'll find museums, the Mississippi River Visitors Center, the Buffalo Bill Cody Homestead, the restored historic village of East Davenport and the Walnut Grove Pioneer Village.

Cost: Starting at $70, including full breakfast.

Information: Potter House, 1906 Seventh Ave., Rock Island, IL 61201, (800) 747-0339.

Victoria Inn, Cincinnati, Ohio

The Victoria Inn, with a history dating to 1909, was Cincinnati's first B&B inn. Located in fashionable Hyde Park, the inn offers a big front porch with wicker furniture and a swimming pool outside. Inside you'll find mahogany woodwork, stained-glass windows and brass chandeliers.

Of the inn's four guest rooms, the Victorian Suite is a favorite. It has a Jacuzzi, hand-carved 1880s furniture, feather bed and fireplace. Decorated in a floral motif, the English Garden Room is filled with antiques and has a clawfoot tub. The Country Room offers a private screened porch. Bathroom amenities in each include blow dryers and bathrobes — unusually plush for a B&B.

Complimentary beverages and snacks are available in the guest refrigerator. For breakfast, you can eat in your room, in the dining room or by the pool. Guests have free use of the Cincinnati Sports Club.

In addition to the upscale shops, restaurants and galleries of Hyde Park Square, just two blocks away, guests have all of Cincinnati to explore.

Cost: Starting at $79, including continental breakfast.

Information: Victoria Inn, 3567 Shaw Ave., Cincinnati, OH 45208, (513) 321-3567.

The Wigwam, Natchez, Mississippi

Lovers in an antebellum mood should head for Natchez and its fabulous mansions, some of which are now bed-and-breakfast lodgings.

This gracious Old South town sits on the bluffs of the Mississippi River. During the Civil War, Natchez capitulated rather than fight, a matter appreciated by admirers of her preserved mansions today.

Several mansions-turned-B&Bs recall the swirl of silk and satin, symbolic of the huge concentration of wealth that the cotton economy created. A prime example is The Wigwam, from 1836, one of the earlier grand houses. The Wigwam is full of antiques from the 1790s to the 1850s and was restored by a Southern belle, Estelle Mackey, who is steeped in the lore of the era.

The romantic thing to do in Natchez is tour the great mansions, sip iced drinks under the huge shade trees and contemplate the many lovers whose lives were disrupted by the Civil War.

Cost: Rates are $110 a night, including continental breakfast.

Information: The Wigwam, 307 Oak St., Natchez, MS 39120, (800) 862-1300 or (601) 442-2600.

Buckhorn Springs, Ashland, Oregon

Summer visitors pour into Ashland to savor Shakespeare and other theater, raft the

Rogue River, tour Crater Lake National Park and explore the history of the area, such as the Gold Rush village of Jacksonville.

Spas brought well-heeled patrons at the turn of the century. One of the grand old hostelries was Buckhorn Springs, east of Ashland. With changing times, Buckhorn fell to ruin until a young couple resurrected it in the 1980s.

Today Buckhorn is a popular lodging again, with reasonably priced rooms and creative cuisine. A large organic garden supplies the kitchen.

Cost: Rates are $80-$120 per unit, including breakfast. The inn is open July through September.

Information: Buckhorn Springs, 2200 Buckhorn Springs Road, Ashland, OR 97520, (503) 488-2200.

Westmoor Inn, Nantucket, Massachusetts

Once a Vanderbilt summer "cottage," this inn takes its name from the moors, the misty hills on the island of Nantucket, about a mile from its historic whaling town. From a warm yellow-and-white exterior to pastel chintz and country prints inside, the mood is one of an inviting seaside home.

A two-story foyer features a grand staircase and views of the island and sound. Wine and hors d'oeuvres are served in the large living room, where a grand piano awaits the touch of a musician.

A one-room suite on the first floor has a large bath with Jacuzzi and sliding doors onto the lawn. Upstairs, half of the original Vanderbilt master bedroom is a suite with fireplace, sitting area and a queen-size wicker bed. A third-floor suite has a cathedral ceiling and panoramic view. Antiques accent all 14 bedrooms.

The small library is a perfect hideaway for reading or watching television. The beach is about a block away; chairs and towels are provided. Bicycles are available for sightseeing around the island or riding to town.

For breakfast, serve yourself freshly baked breads, fruit and cereal. Breakfast is served at linen-covered tables for two or four in a bright sun room.

Cost: $120-$245 June through September; off-season rates $85-$175; closed December-March.

Information: Westmoor Inn, Cliff Road, Nantucket, MA 02544, (508) 228-0877.

Thatcher Brook Inn, Waterbury, Vermont

Here's a hideaway listed in the state's Register of Historic Buildings. Its twin gazebo front porch with tall-back rockers and white wooden railings evokes the romantic mood of a different era.

The 24 antique-filled guest rooms are decked out with Laura Ashley-print wallpaper, rose carpeting and lace balloon curtains, although each varies somewhat. The newer rooms have Jacuzzi tubs, and some also have fireplaces.

The dining room encompasses four separate areas, one candlelit and reserved for couples.

The inn also houses The Newsroom Bar & Grille, an authentic English-style country pub that seats 40. The bar is all cherry, and antique cast-iron lanterns light the room.

Cost: $75-$175.

Information: Thatcher Brook Inn, P.O. Box 490, Waterbury, VT 05676, (802) 244-5911 or (800) 292-5911.

Sweetwater Farm, Glen Mills, Pennsylvania

This 50-acre working farm in southeastern Pennsylvania's Brandywine Valley was a stop on the underground railroad transporting slaves in the Civil War. Even earlier, the Marquis de Lafayette slept here before the place was ransacked by British troops during the Revolutionary War.

Most of the six rooms in the refurbished Georgian-style mansion have working fireplaces and four-poster beds (some with canopies). Five cottages are also available — each having its own fireplace and living room.

Outside is a swimming pool, gardens (including a strawberry patch), a duck pond and a horse pasture. For quiet, try the back porch with wooden rockers and wicker chairs, the library with floor-to-ceiling bookshelves, Wyeth prints and fireplace and the parlor window seat, which faces west and is popular for both sunsets and deer-viewing.

Mozart and Beethoven playing in the background set a peaceful and elegant tone, especially for the afternoon wine and cheese (available by request), sweets and tea, and for the full country breakfast.

Cost: $175-$275, $25 off on weekdays.

Information: Sweetwater Farm, 50 Sweetwater Road, Glen Mills, PA 19342, (610) 459-4711 or (800) 793-3892.

Foley House Inn, Savannah, Georgia

This cozy 1896 Victorian townhouse is nestled in the heart of the historic district and is home to the city's most extensive antiques collection. Plenty of furniture and Oriental rugs are among the period pieces, as well as gargoyles guarding the parlor fireplace and candelabra from "Gone With the Wind."

Each of the 19 guest rooms is decorated differently, but most feature high ceilings, four-poster canopy beds and fireplaces. Four rooms also have balconies and Jacuzzis— bubble bath and candles are provided.

Outside, you will find an enclosed courtyard garden and a second patio garden accented with a fountain.

In the evenings, wine, sherry, port and amaretto are offered with fruit, cheese and paté.

If you sense unearthly company, remember that no inn in Savannah would be authentic without a few spirits. Those that live here are a friendly sort.

Cost: $85-$190.

Information: Foley House Inn, 14 W. Hull St., Chippewa Square, Savannah, GA 31401, (800) 647-3708, in Georgia (912) 232-6622.

Inn at Cedar Crossing, Sturgeon Bay, Wisconsin

A two-story brick building dating from 1884, this inn located downtown is on the National Register of Historic Places.

All the guest rooms are filled with elegant country antiques from the Midwest. Some rooms have exposed brick walls, and two have private porches overlooking rooftops and church steeples. The anniversary room has a king-size carved mahogany bed that's so high you must climb steps to scramble into it. The room also has a fireplace and a double whirlpool tub in its own alcove. Other rooms offer white iron beds or four-poster, canopied sleeping quarters.

Wood-burning fireplaces warm the common areas. The breakfast room has a 13-foot ceiling of pressed tin; many of the serving plates were made by local potters.

Don't miss the evening popcorn and cider, and rest assured that the cookie jar is always full of homemade goodies (decadent chocolate being the romantic's favorite).

Cost: $79-$138.

Information: Inn at Cedar Crossing, 336 Louisiana St., Sturgeon Bay, WI 54235, (414) 743-4200.

Queen Anne Inn, Denver, Colorado

In the shadow of Denver's skyscrapers, yet in a quiet historic neighborhood, this three-story Victorian home is a favorite retreat for urban romantics in all seasons.

It was built in 1879 and rescued from demolition a century later. Strains of classical music, fresh lemonade, sherry and wine invite guests to relax in the downstairs parlor. A grand oak staircase leads to rooms on the upper levels, all with views of the Rocky Mountains or the city.

No two rooms are alike in decor or size; each has a name, a special attraction and works by regional artists. The large Fountain Room, named for its bay-window view of an adjacent park with a fountain, is a favorite for honeymooners. It has a sunken tub and a white queen-size canopied bed, adorned with bride and groom teddy bears given by guests. The Skyline Room has an antique brass bed and window seat overlooking the garden, where breakfast is served in warm weather. If you like the outdoors, check the Aspen Room, where the ceiling is a hand-painted mural of an aspen grove.

Breakfast is homemade granola, freshly baked breads and fruits. The inn is within walking distance of shopping and sightseeing. The owners also will provide a map for a historic walking tour and direct guests to restaurants.

Cost: $75-$155.

Information: Queen Anne Inn, 2147 Tremont Place, Denver, CO 80205, (800) 432-4667 or (303) 296-6666.

Grant Corner Inn, Santa Fe, New Mexico

This three-story Colonial house with a wraparound front porch, white picket fence and gazebo sits in downtown Santa Fe. Among the furnishings are Indian works of art, such as pots, rugs, prints, dolls and other artifacts.

One of the inn's two deluxe rooms has an ornate, three-tiered white ceramic Austrian stove. The bed is white iron with brass trim and a lace dust ruffle. Other touches include Oriental rugs and a brass chest. French doors open onto a private balcony.

The other deluxe room has an Indian motif, with a chief's blanket, Navajo rug and pine pencil-post bed enclosed with draperies. It, too, has a private balcony, and a clawfoot tub in the bathroom.

All guests receive fruit baskets with personalized notes each day. A full breakfast is served in the dining room (or, if preferred, in bed). For a romantic lunch option, order a picnic basket. Each evening, wine and cheese is served in the living room.

Cost: $95-$155.

Information: Grant Corner Inn, 122 Grant Ave., Santa Fe, NM 87501, (505) 983-6678.

Blackthorne Inn, Inverness, California

Resembling a huge treehouse more than an inn, this multitiered building is tucked into a wooded canyon on the Point Reyes Peninsula, one hour north of San Francisco. Its creative design sports decks (one of them is 3,500 square feet) on four levels, bay windows and french doors, a solarium, skylights, an A-framed living room, private balconies, stained-glass windows and an outdoor hot tub.

The inn was built with planks of redwood, cedar and Douglas fir cut and milled on the site, plus recycled timbers from San Francisco wharves. Some barnacle-encrusted stones in the large living room are from nearby Tomales Bay.

Each guest room has a unique feel, but the most romantic is the Eagles Nest— the inn's highest. An octagonal room enclosed by windows, this spot is perfect for stargazing. By day, its roof becomes a private sundeck.

The menu for the full buffet-style breakfast varies each morning but has encompassed everything from African to Cajun cuisine.

Cost: $105-$195.

Information: Blackthorne Inn, P.O. Box 712, Inverness, CA 94937, (415) 663-8621.

Orcas Hotel, San Juan Islands, Washington

On this 56-square-mile piece of paradise in the northern Puget Sound, forested hills rise from pristine coastline. The town center is a Norman Rockwell painting come to life, with Victorian-style inns and quaint shops.

The historic Orcas Hotel is the town's grand dame, a Victorian heartbreaker surrounded by a white picket fence, with flowers lining steps to a long veranda. It's no surprise that the hotel is on the National Register of Historic Places.

The inn's old-fashioned parlor with rock fireplace is crammed with antiques and memorabilia. Upstairs, 12 bedrooms furnished with antiques and locally made quilts offer views of the tranquil harbor. As for the food, many visitors ferry across the sound just for dinner. The Orcas Island Ferry departs eight times daily during the summer from Anacortes, WA, two hours north of Seattle.

Because the inn sits directly across from the ferry landing, you may want to leave your car on the mainland and rent a bicycle or moped for exploring Orcas from the ground up. On a paradise this small, why miss an inch?

Cost: From $69 including full breakfast.

Information: Orcas Hotel, P.O. Box 155, Orcas, WA 98280, (360) 376-4300. San Juan Islands Visitor Information, P.O. Box 65, Lopez Island, WA 98261, (206) 468-3663. For fares and schedules of the Orcas Island Ferry, (206) 376-2134.

Sise Inn, Portsmouth, New Hampshire

This Victorian lady has quite a colorful past. The 1881 Queen Anne-style building started out as a private home before becoming an apartment building, a health center, business offices, a dress boutique and even a beauty parlor. Its latest owners have transformed it into an elegantly appointed inn in the heart of historic Portsmouth, one hour from Boston.

Its three-story lobby boasts teak banisters and Oriental rugs, with decor including museum prints, ceiling fans and period wall coverings and window treatments. The library houses a grand collection of paperback books for the borrowing.

The inn's 34 antique-filled guest rooms are spacious and elegant and include such non-Victorian touches as television, VCRs and cassette players (with which guests can play classical tapes borrowed from the inn). Some rooms also have whirlpool tubs and bay windows.

Activities in the area include beachcombing, fishing, whale watching, harbor cruises, golf, museums, historic buildings, theaters, antiquing and craft shops.

Cost: From $115, including breakfast as well as snacks and coffee available anytime.

Information: Sise Inn, 40 Court St., Portsmouth, NH 03801, (800) 267-0525 (reservations) or (603) 433-1200.

Nauset House Inn, East Orleans, Massachusetts

Leave it to a former duck farm to know just how a nest should be feathered. The rooms in this 1807 Cape Cod inn are furnished with antiques, handmade quilts and various forms of crewel work. Special accents like the stenciling on the walls and the stained glass decorations are creations of artist/owner Diane Johnson.

Take your pick of 14 guest rooms, nine in the clapboard farmhouse, four in the carriage house and a single unit (the Outermost House) in the apple orchard. Each room is named for a native wildflower or plant. Rosebud, the most popular, has a tiny balcony.

As lovely as the guest rooms are, the architectural highlight of the inn undoubtedly is its turn-of-the-century Victorian conservatory. Here, white wicker furniture is set among numerous flowering plants that surround a beautiful weeping cherry tree.

The low-beamed breakfast room, with its brick floor and huge open hearth, also is inviting, as is the living room, where guests gather around the fireplace to read or play games. This also is where you're likely to encounter the inn's two resident dogs, Roo and Winnie, who make it their business to mingle with the visitors. Be sure to read the book of guests' comments on local restaurants before setting off for dinner.

The beach is an easy half-mile walk away, and the quaint villages of Cape Cod — crammed full of art galleries, boutiques and antique and craft shops — make for more adventures.

Cost: From $65, including evening hors d'oeuvres.

Information: The Nauset House Inn, P.O. Box 774, East Orleans, MA 02643, (508) 255-2195.

Duval House, Key West, Florida

The Florida Keys provide the perfect tropical getaway in the continental United States — one made even more irresistible by this cozy 29-room inn.

The Duval House is a century-old pale peach Victorian structure sporting a double-decker front balcony with pristine white railings. Inside you'll find contemporary wicker and antique furnishings, each room offering both a ceiling fan and air conditioning.

The hibiscus blossom tucked in the towels left on each bed is typical of the gracious touches the inn provides. Local temperatures in guests' hometowns are tracked on a chalkboard that also may include cities in Europe as well as the United States.

The highlight of this inn undoubtedly is a beautifully landscaped wooden deck surrounding a small pool. Don't be surprised to hear acoustic jazz here during the day. The front porch is another popular spot for guests who like to sit and watch the comings and goings on Key West's main street.

The Duval House sits halfway between the Atlantic Ocean and the Gulf of Mexico, within walking distance of the beaches, galleries, shops, bars and restaurants that make Key West famous. The innkeeper also arranges excursions on a 30-foot sailboat upon request.

Cost: From $80, including breakfast.

Information: The Duval House, 815 Duval St., Key West, FL 33040, (305) 294-1666 or (800) 22-DUVAL.

Crystal River Inn, San Marcos, Texas

Here's a pleasant country inn that can't decide if it's a cooking school, a rafting outfitter, a theater or a historic Victorian hideaway. Fortunately for its guests, it's a little of each.

The 100-year-old building with Greek columns and double-decker front porches was the first bed-and-breakfast establishment in this Texas Hill Country town.

Although guests are welcome to come simply to sleep, eat and relax, the inn offers several special theme weekends, such as murder mysteries, river trips, romance packages and gourmet cooking lessons.

Its twelve rooms, each distinctively different, are named after Texas rivers. Five are in the main house, including Frio (with its fireplace and wicker sitting area), Pedernales (with an antique canopied bed and fireplace) and Colorado (with Indian rugs and a rope-design canopied bed).

Three additional rooms are in the Young House, a restored 1885 building across the street. Its offerings include Guadalupe, featuring a wood stove and a clawfoot tub, and Sabinal, with its unusual lacy white iron bed and bay window.

The inn's common areas include the library (don't miss the vintage magazines here), the wide, wicker-filled veranda and the magical courtyard, decked out with twinkle lights, a fountain and whimsical topiary sculptures.

Activities in San Marcos, home to the Aquarena Springs theme park and a commercial cave called Wonder World, include canoeing, rafting, hiking and antiquing. San Antonio is a 45-minute drive, and Austin is 30 minutes away.

Cost: From $65, including breakfast.

Information: The Crystal River Inn, 326 W. Hopkins St., San Marcos, TX 78666, (512) 396-3739.

Tickle Pink Inn, Carmel, California

Despite its amusing moniker, the 35-room inn on the Monterey Peninsula has a rich, luxurious atmosphere that's no laughing matter.

For starters, the views from atop the rugged cliffs overlooking the ocean are magnificent. What you'll encounter indoors is equally arresting. Furnishings include rough-hewn night tables, hand-crafted armoires and wrought-iron beds. Each room offers a VCR, terry-cloth robes and fresh-ground coffee service.

Most rooms have private balconies, and some also have stone fireplaces and whirlpool tubs. Look for the garden's many pink flowers — including varieties of geranium, impatiens, begonia and petunia.

Service at the Tickle Pink is top-notch. Each afternoon, the owners offer fresh-baked chocolate chip cookies. Guests gather on the Cliffside Deck at sunset as they sip Monterey County wines served with cheese, breads and fruit.

More than a few famous names have graced the inn's register. Doris Day used to stay here every year until she moved to the Monterey Peninsula herself, and Robert Wagner and Natalie Wood spent *both* their honeymoons here.

Nearby sights include an aquarium, Fisherman's Wharf, Carmel-by-the-Sea, Pebble Beach and Cannery Row. Activities include boating, whale-watching, fishing, golfing, shopping in the many art galleries and studios and, at night, local theater productions and symphony concerts.

Cost: $139, including breakfast and an evening wine and cheese reception.

Information: Tickle Pink Inn, 155 Highland Drive, Carmel, CA 93923, (800) 635-4774.

Washington House Inn, Cedarburg, Wisconsin

At this amiable inn dating from 1884, you can have your history in your choice of two styles. The 34 guest rooms are divided between two wings — one with high Victorian decor (lots of brass, marble and carved oak) and the other in historic country style (with patchwork quilts, plank floors, four-poster beds and braided rugs).

Either way, most of the antique-filled rooms have whirlpool baths, and 14 also have fireplaces. A sauna is open to all guests.

As you explore the building, which is on the National Register of Historic Places, look for such atmospheric features as tin ceilings, reproduction wainscoting (copies from the original discovered during restoration) and English embossed-tissue wallpaper, which simulates tin.

The inn is located in the center of Cedarburg's historic district, three blocks from Cedar Creek Settlement (a historic shopping village) and the Cedar Creek Winery. Other nearby attractions include a racing car museum, the last remaining covered bridge in the state, a marina and a nature center. Lake Michigan is a mere four-mile drive, and Milwaukee is 15 miles away.

Cost: From $59, including breakfast and afternoon hors d'oeuvres.

Information: The Washington House Inn, W62 N573 Washington Ave., Cedarburg, WI 53012, (800) 554-4717.

Big Bay Point Lighthouse, Big Bay, Michigan

It may seem unlikely that this peaceful little inn on the shoreline of Lake Superior could be connected with a cold-blooded murder, a Hollywood movie and a lightkeeper's ghost. Rest assured, however, that these rumors are true. If only the five-brick-thick walls of this bed-and-breakfast inn could talk.

The two-story building and 60-foot square tower that make up the working lighthouse were built in 1896 and are now on the National Register of Historic Places. The spirit of the inn's first lightkeeper (William Pryor, who hanged himself in 1901) is said to make rare but friendly appearances.

Each of the seven guest rooms has a beautiful view of the lake or its shoreline. Creations by local artists adorn the walls, and the furnishings include weathered chests and hand-carved beds. Common rooms include the living room with its brick fireplace, the dining room and a library.

You'll even find a sauna in the tower. At the top of this five-story structure, you can see the 1,500-pound lantern and enjoy a 360-degree panorama.

The inn is surrounded by wilderness, including a rock beach, 19 waterfalls, several scenic lakes, fishing streams and lots of hiking and biking trails that lead into the Huron Mountains. The innkeepers can arrange jeep tours or hiking trips for guests who want a guide. If you awaken early enough, you won't even have to leave the inn to see deer, raccoon, rabbit, fox or wild turkey, all of which have been sighted in the meadow near dawn.

Three miles away in the village of Big Bay (population 250) is the infamous Lumberjack Tavern, the site of a brutal 1952 shooting that inspired the movie

"Anatomy of a Murder." The film, starring Jimmy Stewart and Lee Remick, also was shot here. You can still see bullet holes in the wall behind the bar and read framed press clippings about both the murder and the filming of the movie.

Cost: From $115, including breakfast.

Information: Big Bay Point Lighthouse, 3 Lighthouse Road, Big Bay, MI 49808, (906) 345-9957.

Two Meeting Street Inn, Charleston, South Carolina

In a historic city such as Charleston, being the oldest inn in town is a boast worth claiming. Two Meeting Street Inn (named for its address) is the oldest and among the most charming inns in the city.

The nine-room Queen Anne-style inn is located in the heart of the historic district, facing the waterfront. The exterior looks like a wedding cake, with two stories of piazzas with grand white pillars and archways. The image is appropriate; the house originally was built in 1890 as a wedding gift from the bride's father. (The happy couple took a long honeymoon in Europe while the house was under construction.)

Inside, decor features original antiques, carved oak paneling, Tiffany stained-glass windows and Oriental rugs. The inn reputedly is haunted but, fortunately, the spirit seems to be friendly.

Cost: $90-$150, including continental breakfast, afternoon tea and evening Sherry.

Information: Two Meeting Street Inn, 2 Meeting St., Charleston, SC 29401, (803) 723-7322.

Juniper Hill Inn, Windsor, Vermont

Outside the town of Windsor, snuggled next to the Connecticut River, a driveway winds through a tunnel of pine trees to the top of Juniper Hill. There sits a stately white mansion built in 1902 as the private home of a prominent lawyer.

The three-story house was restored in 1984 and furnished with antiques. Today it's Juniper Hill Inn, listed on the National Register of Historic Places.

The 16 high-ceilinged guest rooms have either canopy, sleigh, brass or four-poster beds. Many rooms have fireplaces, faced by comfortable sofas.

Downstairs, guests relax in the huge great room or the cozier library. Hot cider is always brewing, and refreshments are served from 3 to 5 p.m. Breakfast is served in a gracious, informal dining room. Also, guests may opt for an elegant candlelight dinner at the inn, by special reservation.

The grounds sprawl over 14 acres of manicured lawns, formal gardens and forested hillsides with hiking trails. You can relax by the pool or sit on the patio and view Mount Ascutney, Lake Runneymeade and the church spires of Windsor. Antique shops and the longest covered bridge in America are nearby.

Cost: $90-$140, including breakfast. Closed in April.

Information: Juniper Hill Inn, Rural Route 1, Box 79, Windsor, VT 05089, (800) 359-2541.

The Gastonian, Savannah, Georgia

The setting is historic Savannah, a two-square-mile living museum designated as a National Historical Landmark. Composed of two connecting 1860s mansions and a carriage house, the Gastonian is luxuriously elegant — and intensely romantic.

Furnished in Italianate, French, Victorian and Colonial American styles, the 13 high-ceilinged guest rooms have canopied beds, Persian rugs, fireplaces and whirlpool or soak tubs. The Carriage House features a canopied Oriental wedding bed, a scarlet bathroom embellished with gold-plated faucets and a private balcony.

But the Caracalla Suite, named for a sybaritic Roman emperor, is the creme de la creme. Its room-size bathroom is centered with an eight-foot-long Jacuzzi tub draped with ceiling-to-floor sheer curtains. To one side is a fireplace, topped with brass candlesticks. Nearby is a chaise lounge and a mirrored wet bar. Double sliding doors lead to the peach-and-cream bedroom, which has a canopied Charleston Rice Bed (named for sheaves of rice carved on the bed posts), fireplace, reclining couch and Oriental rug.

Whatever room guests choose, they have fresh flowers, fruit and wine upon arrival, and bed turndown service with sweets and cordials. Southern hospitality permeates the house, beginning with breakfast served in the parlor, courtyard or bedroom.

Cost: $125-$200, extra for suites, including breakfast.

Information: The Gastonian, 220 E. Gaston St., Savannah, GA 31401, (912) 232-2869 or (800) 322-6603.

St. Croix River Inn, Osceola, Wisconsin

High on a wooded bluff overlooking the St. Croix River, this romantic inn offers breakfast in bed, whirlpool baths and spectacular views from its seven elegantly decorated guest rooms.

Recalling the area's riverboat history, every room is named for a steamboat built in Osceola.

Special rooms include the Jennie Hays, featuring a river view through floor-to-ceiling Palladian windows, a riverfront balcony and a four-poster canopy bed. All rooms have Jacuzzi tubs and antique reproduction furniture; some rooms also have fireplaces and decks or porches.

Built in the early 1900s of limestone quarried south of Osceola, the inn was a family home until it was converted into a hostelry in 1984.

Nearby Taylor Falls, MN, has paddleboat cruises and historic homes to tour, and canoeing and fishing in the St. Croix National Scenic Riverway are options.

Cost: $85-$200, including breakfast.

Information: St. Croix River Inn, P.O. Box 356, Osceola, WI 54020, (715) 294-4248 or (800) 645-8820.

McKay House, Jefferson, Texas

Near the northeast corner of Texas is an Old South town with antebellum homes, surrey rides and moonlight serenade cruises. Once the fifth largest city in Texas, Jefferson now has 3,000 residents, many of whom have historical markers at their front doors, lace curtains at their windows and antiques in their parlors.

McKay House is a pristine 1850s cottage with a front porch swing and white wicker rockers. Owner Peggy Taylor often greets guests with lemonade and tea cakes, or perhaps a fireside cup of coffee. In the bedrooms, Victorian nightgowns and sleep-shirts hang in the armoire in place of terry robes. A "Gentleman's Breakfast," a hearty affair, is served by a hostess in period dress.

Each guest room, accented with such furnishings as canopied beds and antique armoires, has a unique personality. The Garden Suite has His and Hers footed tubs, a skylight and exquisite stained glass, while the Grand Gable Suite has a cozy step-down sitting area. Both open onto a balcony overlooking the garden. Many rooms have fireplaces.

A frontier cabin behind the main house has two guest rooms furnished pioneer-style. A blackened pot hangs over a stone fireplace, as if awaiting the return of the family.

Cost: $90-$125, extra for suites, including breakfast.

Information: McKay House, 306 E. Delta St., Jefferson, TX 75657, (903) 665-7322. Book-A-Bed Ahead reservation service, (800) 468-2627.

The Martine Inn, Pacific Grove, California

The setting is a cliff-side pink palace on the famed Monterey Peninsula. In your room, you find a fresh rose, a silver Victorian bridal basket filled with fruit and a canopied bed draped with curtains. And outside your window, sea otters play in the ocean and waves crash against the rocky coastline.

Built in 1899, today's inn was once the home of Laura and James Parke of Parke Davis Pharmaceuticals. Innkeepers Marion and Don Martine seek to re-create the atmosphere of the home when the Parkes entertained guests at the turn of the century.

Avid collectors, the Martines have paid great attention to detail in decorating the 10,000-square-foot palace with museum-quality antique furniture, Sheffield silver, Victorian china and antique pewter.

Guests are pampered with gourmet breakfasts, Godiva chocolates on their pillow and gracious service. And they're left to themselves to sunbathe in the walled courtyard, relax in the 1870s oak steam bath and modern-day hot tub, play pool on an 1890s oak table, read in the library, or watch whales, sailboat races and fishing boats through huge picture windows.

Incidentally, the inn is so romantic that the Martines chose it as the site for their own wedding, exchanging vows in the courtyard.

Cost: $125-$230, including breakfast.

Information: The Martine Inn, 255 Oceanview Blvd., Pacific Grove, CA 93950, (800) 852-5588 or (408) 373-3388.

Manoa Valley Inn, Honolulu, Hawaii

In a quiet neighborhood just two miles from Waikiki is an unexpected surprise — a plantation-style inn in the lush Manoa Valley, held sacred by the ancient Hawaiians. Beautiful University of Hawaii is one block away. Manoa Marketplace, home of Castagnola's Italian Restaurant (one of the most popular restaurants on Oahu), is close, and so are arboretums abounding in exotic flowers and hiking trails leading to mountain pools.

The inn, built in 1915, was the home of John Guild, vice president of one of Hawaii's biggest sugar companies. Meticulously renovated in recent years, the mansion has ornately buttressed eaves, an abundance of gables and sprawling porches. Decorated in sumptuous fabrics and Victorian antiques, it's a true Hawaiian treasure, with tropical flowers in the guest rooms, a bounty of fresh fruits for breakfast, flowering trees and gardens and tropical birds.

From the lanai, you can look down on action-packed Waikiki and Honolulu and savor the inn as a tranquil oasis. Guests gather on the lanai for fruit, cheese and wine in the afternoon, play croquet on the lawn, and enjoy the Nickelodeon, antique Victrola, piano and pool table.

Cost: $99-$190, extra for suites, including breakfast.

Information: Manoa Valley Inn, 2001 Vancouver Drive, Honolulu, HI 96822, (800) 634-5115.

The Buckhorn Inn, Gatlinburg, Tennessee

This Smoky Mountains country inn, established in 1938, has only six guest rooms, four cottages and a guest house, giving it a genuinely secluded, romantic feel.

The main building (and most guest rooms) faces Mount LeConte, the highest mountain in the Smokies, and is surrounded by 30 wooded acres. Outdoor wanderers will find a fishing pond and resident ducks and geese. Inside, public areas include a huge stone fireplace, dining room and library/sitting area with a Steinway grand piano.

Just down the road is the Great Smoky Arts & Crafts Community, a rich collection of shops selling fine quality, handmade Appalachian crafts. The boundary of the Great Smoky Mountains National Park, the most visited in the country, is only a mile away. Also conveniently close (yet far enough that it isn't intrusive) is bustling downtown Gatlinburg and its plethora of shops, haunted-house attractions, miniature golf courses and restaurants.

Cost: $105-$130 (more for cottages), including full breakfast.

Information: The Buckhorn Inn, 2140 Tudor Mountain Road, Gatlinburg, TN 37738, (615) 436-4668.

Washington School Inn, Park City, Utah

Here's one school where you won't mind taking a detention. This 12-room, three-suite inn in the heart of Park City's historic Main Street district was the mining town's schoolhouse in the late 1880s. Listed on the National Register of Historic Places, the building retains its original bell tower and flagpole, along with three brick-faced chimneys.

Inside, classical music plays in the background, and you'll find hardwood floors, historic photos and Victorian furnishings. The main level shows off a huge fireplace, and the lower level offers whirlpools and saunas. The mezzanine includes a library and game room.

Park City may be known as prime ski country, but the town has plenty of summer charms, too, including golf, tennis, fly-fishing, windsurfing, mountain biking, horseback riding, hot-air ballooning and incredible hiking.

Cost: $100-$175, including full breakfast, appetizers and wine and tea in the afternoons.

Information: Washington School Inn, P.O. Box 536, Park City, UT 84060, (800) 824-1672.

Harbor Light Inn, Marblehead, Massachusetts

Marblehead may bill itself as the yachting capital of the world, but even folks who get seasick in the bathtub will fall in love with this quaint seaside community and its Harbor Light Inn.

The 21-room hotel — which has hosted Walter Cronkite, among other celebrities — dates from 1712. Oriental carpeting over wide-board pine floors, mahogany furniture, chandeliers, four-poster beds, brass and porcelain doorknobs and limited-edition prints make its atmosphere elegant. Several rooms have fireplaces, and some also have private decks.

The rooftop walk (with a great view of the harbor and its light) is one of the most romantic spots in town. Another is the Harbor Light guest room with private sunken Jacuzzi under a skylight.

If you somehow manage to exhaust the charms of Marblehead — visiting historic buildings, poking around its narrow, winding streets and watching the lobster boats — Salem is only a few miles away, and Boston a mere 35-mile drive.

Cost: $95-$150 ($160-$225 for suites), including continental breakfast.

Information: Harbor Light Inn, 58 Washington St., Marblehead, MA 01945, (617) 631-2186.

Cliffside Inn, Newport, Rhode Island

One of the most unusual characters in Newport's history inhabited the home that later became the Cliffside Inn, built in 1880 by the first post-Civil War governor of Maryland.

Cliffside was the residence of reclusive artist Beatrice Turner, who lived at the turn of the century. Pulled from art school as a girl when her parents discovered nude models were part of the program, Beatrice was more or less sequestered in the house and told to use herself as a model.

She followed orders well. Upon her death in the 1940s, more than 1,000 self-portraits (including many nudes) were found throughout the estate. Although most of her work was destroyed, you will find a painting of Beatrice and her mother in the inn's parlor. The curious also can view a video about Beatrice and her unusual life.

Fortunately, the inn's mood these days is much less gloomy. There's a wide front porch filled with wicker furniture, and the high-ceiling, Victorian-furnished parlor features tables for games and puzzles, large bay windows and unusual antiques. In front of the fireplace, guests mingle each afternoon for drinks and hors d'oeuvres.

Many of the inn's 13 guest rooms have views of Narragansett Bay. Features include fireplaces, whirlpools and bay windows with cozy window seats. The Turner Suite has a sitting room with its own library, and the Governor's Suite sports an antique Victorian bird cage shower. The Attic is the most romantic room, with its four skylights, cathedral ceilings and king-size bed.

The inn is just one block from Newport's famous 3.5-mile Cliff Walk, where you can watch the waves battering the shore on one side and contemplate the splendor of Newport's famous historic mansions (some open for tours) on the other. The beach is a two-block walk away, or you can go into town for some antiquing on Thames and Spring streets.

Cost: Starting at $155, including full breakfast.

Information: Cliffside Inn, 2 Seaview Ave., Newport, RI 02840, (800) 845-1811.

Du Pre House, Georgetown, South Carolina

This cozy bed-and-breakfast inn on the southernmost end of South Carolina's Grand Strand may boast beautifully decorated rooms with fireplaces, generous verandas, an outdoor pool and a convenient location just one block from the waterfront. But the best of its many amenities is its unusually friendly innkeeper, Mike Streppone.

Mike makes a scrumptious breakfast each morning, complete with friendly commentary. He serves afternoon tea and evening refreshments, puts candy on each pillow with evening turn-down service, gives detailed sightseeing and restaurant recommendations and makes dinner reservations for you. He will even arrange a delightful tour of Georgetown in a horse-drawn carriage, which is housed at the inn.

He also offers the ultimate luxury — massages for a modest
frequently throwing in an extra 15 minutes or so. And, he a
elementary school principal, gladly pull baby-sitting duty for p
evening out without their kids.

The inn's four guest rooms all include high poster beds and fi
romantic is the Caine Room on the second floor, thanks to its
complete with rocking chairs.

The Elisha Screven Place, a fireplace lounge on the first floor, is a good setting to curl
up with a book. Guests wanting more activity can borrow a bicycle, play horseshoes,
bocce or basketball or take a dip in the inn's outdoor pool or hot tub.

Downtown Georgetown offers historic home tours, the Rice Museum, a small but
pleasant harbor walk with shops and restaurants along the water's edge and a seaport
tram tour. Don't miss the delightful Kudzu Bakery; it advertises "creative Southern
foods" and delivers on the promise. Brookgreen Gardens, home of the world's largest
permanent outdoor exhibition of American figurative sculpture, is 15 minutes away,
and action-packed Myrtle Beach is a half-hour drive.

Cost: Starting at $70, including continental breakfast.

Information: Du Pre House, P.O. Box 2931, Georgetown, SC 29442, (800) 921-
3877.

Ann Starrett Mansion, Port Townsend, Washington

This inn on an Olympic Peninsula bluff overlooking Puget Sound has a ceiling with
a secret. Built in 1889 by wealthy contractor George Starrett as a wedding present for
his bride Ann, the inn has a reputation for its extraordinary architectural features.

The free-hung, three-tiered antique spiral staircase would be cause enough to make
this building a national historic landmark, but above the staircase is an even more
notable eight-sided domed ceiling. The eight sections depict the four seasons and the
four virtues (charity, chastity, hope and faith). On the first day of each season, the sun
strikes one of several adjacent dormer windows in the inn's tower in such a way that a
ruby red beam of sunlight points toward the panel depicting the appropriate season.

Elsewhere, architectural details are more apparent. You'll find moldings with carved
animals and plants as well as Victorian gingerbread trim. The 11 guest rooms are each
different, with sitting alcoves, brick walls, balconies, antique tin bathtubs, wicker
furnishings and wonderful views of the sound and the mountains. The innkeepers are
not without a sense of humor; the Carriage Room, for example, features a sleigh bed.

In addition to its lovely atmosphere, the inn also offers a host of spa treatments, such
as massage, reflexology, acupuncture, biofeedback and facials.

In the immediate area, you'll find lots of opportunities for water sports and wildlife
viewing. In fact, one highly recommended option is a wildlife sea kayak tour, which
promises excellent chances for sightings of sea birds, seals, sea otters and often bald
eagles.

Cost: Starting at $65, including full breakfast.

Information: Ann Starrett Mansion, 744 Clay St., Port Townsend, WA 98368,
(800) 321-0644.

Live Oak Inn, Daytona Beach, Florida

This highly decorated inn one hour from Orlando sits on the site of an 18th-century
plantation home built by the founder of Daytona Beach, Mathias Day. While Day's

...onger exists, the two buildings now rising from its foundations date from ...nd 1881, and both are listed on the National Register of Historic Places.

...he Pope House, dating from 1881, is the inn's main building. Its 19th-century furnishings, fireplaces and pine floors give it a warm ambience. The dining room, added in 1926, features wood walls and high windows (so built because the owner didn't want anyone looking at him while he dined).

This building houses the inn's first four guest rooms, each named for a person or event from Florida's (and often Daytona's) history. They feature memorabilia and furnishings from the period, including oak furniture originally used by Daytona settlers. Most rooms have Jacuzzis or Victorian soaking tubs and all overlook the historical gardens or the Halifax Harbor Marina.

The Rogers Room has an iron bed, an oak buffet now serving as a dresser and a foot-driven sewing machine used as a television stand. The Audubon Room has the most antiques, including a wicker chaise lounge, a 1930s radio cabinet and pieces from innkeeper Vin Fisher's family.

The Foster Room has a men's shaving stand, a mandolin, an iron-post bed and wicker tables. Its enclosed porch overlooks the inn's calamondin orange tree (lighted at night) from which the Fishers make the inn's unusual marmalade. The Pope Room offers a sleigh bed, another pedal sewing machine and, in the bathroom, a heart-shaped Jacuzzi tub.

The second building, called the 1871 House, has 12 additional rooms, including the Jackie Robinson Room, the France Room and the extra-spacious Halifax Room (featuring a private balcony).

All rooms come with a complimentary beverage. Guests have the use of a nearby pool, health club, golf course and the inn's slips at the Halifax Harbor Marina.

Cost: Starting at $80, including continental breakfast and afternoon tea and cocktails.

Information: Live Oak Inn, 444-448 S. Beach St., Daytona Beach, FL 32114, (904) 252-4667.

Jailer's Inn, Bardstown, Kentucky

Now that the building known for 53 years as the Nelson County Jail accepts guests strictly on a volunteer basis, the beds, food and comments from those spending the night have improved markedly.

The main building of this six-room bed-and-breakfast inn 35 miles south of Louisville operated as a jail from 1819 until 1874. In that year, the new jail was built next to the first building, which was then converted into the jailer's residence. When the buildings were sold at public auction in 1987, the complex was the oldest operating jail in Kentucky. It's now listed on the National Register of Historic Places.

The owners, Fran and Challen McCoy, both had connections to the place before they bought it — albeit respectable ones. Challen is the town's prosecuting attorney and was responsible for putting many people in the jail before it became a B&B. Fran's great-great-uncle built the jail — a fact the McCoys didn't uncover until they started researching the property after they bought it.

Five guest rooms are in the main building. They've been completely remodeled, with floral wallpaper, antiques, Oriental rugs, fireplaces, ceiling fans, stenciling, patchwork quilts and lace curtains. One room even features an extra-large Jacuzzi tub. The only clue to the building's initial purpose is its 30-inch-thick limestone walls.

The sixth (and most popular) room is unmistakably a former cell located in the "new" jail out back. It was the women's cell and still sports its original metal door along with bunk beds and black-and-white decor (including checkered sheets and a patterned floor). The waterbed, however, is a decidedly modern addition.

Pictures of James Dean and Elvis Presley, along with copies of poems written on jail walls by inmates, add whimsy. Potential prisoners take note: Be sure to reserve this room about a month in advance during summer and a few weeks in advance during the off-season.

The rest of the cells in this building have been left empty and serve as a museum, with the original iron rings still bolted to the floor and, courtesy of former inmates, the writing still on the walls.

Nearby attractions include My Old Kentucky Home, the Stephen Foster Outdoor Drama and several whiskey distilleries.

Cost: Starting at $55, including continental breakfast.

Information: Jailer's Inn, 111 W. Stephen Foster Ave., Bardstown, KY 40004, (800) 948-5551 or (502) 348-5551.

Harrison House, Guthrie, Oklahoma

This inn, spread over five historic buildings (each with its own story to tell), is the largest bed-and-breakfast inn in Oklahoma, with 30 guest rooms.

The entrance and main building is the Eager-Hirzel Building, which dates from 1902, when it served as the home of the Guthrie Savings Bank. Telltale artifacts include inch-square tiles on the front doorstep that spell out "bank" and the original vault door in the lobby.

The Victor Building (the oldest of the five structures) dates from 1893 and originally housed a ballroom, several retail businesses and some apartments. The Freeman Building was a pharmacy, and the Silvers Building was a clothing store. The inn also takes over part of the Pollard Theatre building (originally a furniture store), dating from around the turn of the century.

Throughout, you'll find period wallpaper and curtains, brass doorknobs, crochet cloths covering antique tables, old-fashioned lamps and antique quilts strung on clotheslines. The lobby's brass light fixtures and ornately carved front desk originally were installed in Guthrie's post office.

Each room is named for someone from Guthrie's past, including Tom Mix, Carrie Nation, Will Rogers, Lon Chaney and O. Henry. Look for appropriate detailing in each. Every room also has a diary where guests have written humorous poems and surprisingly personal notes.

Guthrie, 28 miles from Oklahoma City, was the state's first capital. It's a delight to explore, with its brick-paved sidewalks and turn-of-the-century trolleys. It boasts the largest commercial historic district on the National Register of Historic Places, including 100 Victorian business buildings and 2,300 Victorian homes.

Nearby, you'll find horseback riding, hayrides and western cookouts at the 5 W's Sunrise Ranch (by reservation only), three museums (including the Oklahoma Territorial Museum), golf and lots of opportunities for antiquing.

Cost: Starting at $60, including continental-plus breakfast.

Information: Harrison House, 124 W. Harrison, Guthrie, OK 73044, (800) 375-1001.

Terrell Castle Bed & Breakfast, San Antonio, Texas

If you've always dreamed of being Cinderella or Prince Charming, here's your castle — glass slipper optional.

This 10-room inn near downtown San Antonio resembles a stone fortress, complete with turrets, arches and balconies. It was built in 1894 by an English architect for a U.S. ambassador to Belgium who was charmed by the castles and chateaus he encountered in Europe. Its one concession to American (and Southern) style is a large front porch, complete with antique porch swing.

The decor is heavy on Victorian woodwork, family heirloom antiques, lace curtains and floral prints. One of the highlights is the central hall staircase with its carved, harp-shaped newel posts. Each guest room has a gas fireplace, and one has a working pot-bellied stove. A few have bay windows with window seats or unusual curved-glass windows.

San Antonio's many attractions include the charming downtown River Walk, Sea World, Fiesta Texas amusement park, El Mercado (a Mexican market), La Villita (the city's original settlement) and, of course, the Alamo.

Cost: $85-$136, including full breakfast.

Information: Terrell Castle Bed & Breakfast, 950 E. Grayson St., San Antonio, TX 78208, (800) 356-1605.

The Whistling Swan, Fish Creek, Wisconsin

The history of this Door County inn is quite moving, in a very literal sense. Originally constructed in 1887 in Marinette, WI, the building was moved (in pieces) at the turn of the century across ice-covered Green Bay and rebuilt on its present site in Fish Creek.

The five guest rooms and two suites are appointed with antique reproductions, floral print wallpaper, fresh flowers and potpourri. The common area's sitting room includes a fireplace, lots of books and a baby grand piano. Guests have breakfast on the wicker-filled veranda overlooking the harbor village of Fish Creek. During the winter, breakfast is served at the White Gull Inn.

Fish Creek's amusements include beaches, golf, biking, hiking and the Peninsula Players, America's oldest professional summer stock theater.

Cost: $98-$134, including continental breakfast.

Information: The Whistling Swan, P.O. Box 193, Fish Creek, WI 54212, (414) 868-3442.

Cheat Mountain Club, Durbin, West Virginia

This rustic, three-story lodge seven miles west of Durbin, WV, has one heck of a back yard. It sits on 187 wooded acres and is surrounded by the 900,000-acre Monongahela National Forest in the Allegheny Mountains.

Cheat Mountain Club also has quite a history. A Pennsylvania hunting and fishing club built the 60- by 40-foot lodge with square, hand-hewn spruce logs more than 100 years ago. Operated as a private club until 1988, its guests have included Henry Ford, Thomas Edison and Harvey Firestone.

Its large living room with exposed log beams, called the Great Hall, is a homey gathering place, decorated with bear skins and mounted caribou antlers and boar heads. You'll find a fire burning in the huge stone fireplace year-round, comfortable cherry furniture for lounging and lots of books, cards and board games as well as foosball and table tennis. Upstairs are nine bedrooms and a third-floor children's bunk room.

The innkeepers serve three hearty, family-style meals a day on the lodge's original china. For those who want to explore the surrounding wilderness, box lunches are available on request. Snackers will find the pantry filled with fresh fruit and cookies, ripe for raiding.

Outdoors, guests can enjoy a hammock, a pond and Shaver's Fork River, known for its trout fishing. Hunters can stalk grouse, turkey and deer in the surrounding wilderness (although not on club grounds). Hikers will enjoy more than 150 miles of abandoned railroad grades and logging roads in the area, and downhill skiers can choose among three nearby ski resorts.

The innkeepers also turn into outfitters when needed, equipping guests with cross-country skis (for the lodge's five miles of groomed trails), snowshoes and ice skates in winter and kayaks, canoes, mountain bikes and fishing rods in warmer weather. Nearby attractions include the Cass Scenic Railroad, the Swiss village of Helvetia and the Pearl S. Buck birthplace.

Cost: Starting at $80, including three full meals a day.

Information: Cheat Mountain Club, P.O. Box 28, Durbin, WV 26274, (304) 456-4627.

HOTELS, LODGES & RESORTS

With well over 20,000 hotels and motels dotting the American landscape, there's no shortage of lodging options. Large chains of cookie-cutter hotels dominate the market, and their economies of scale and professional management ensure a clean room, a consistent level of service and a reasonable value. In this chapter, however, we stray far from the familiar and the predictable. Many of our top lodging picks are vacation destinations in themselves, resorts so fascinating, varied and enjoyable that you won't want to leave the premises once you've arrived. Most are set in spectacularly scenic surroundings, and all are known for delivering a richly memorable vacation experience.

Fisherman Island, Boothbay Harbor, Maine

Fisherman Island is a private, 68-acre island estate three miles offshore in Boothbay Harbor, and its classy, 6,000-square-foot stone house sleeps up to 15 guests.

Available by the week or month to one group at a time, rates include use of the six-bedroom Tudor manor house (built in 1928 and refurbished in 1994) and all meals (including fresh lobster, salads, freshly baked breads — raid the refrigerator at midnight if you like).

Activities include swimming on two beaches and in various private coves and a lagoon, plus use of a heated saltwater pool, sauna and steam bath. Fishing and sailing opportunities abound with unlimited use of the island's 26-foot boat.

Cost: Rates starting at $8,000 a week (up to 10 guests, $800 for each extra person) sound steep, but that's an average of $114 a day per person for everything, ideal for family or friends willing to pool resources.

Information: Fisherman Island, Cherokee Station, P.O. Box 20692, New York, NY 10021-0073, (212) 288-0804.

McKinley Chalet Resort, Denali National Park, Alaska

McKinley Chalet Resort, at the entrance to Denali National Park, puts you close to the most astonishing display of wildlife in North America.

The lodge is a handsome structure, with a log exterior and steep chalet-type roof, overlooking the Nenana River. Anticipate a crackling fireplace and cozy rooms.

At 5 a.m. be ready to plunge into the vast wilderness of Denali. No cars are allowed to tour the park, so you explore the interior in ancient school buses on roads that at points are like washboards. The driver and guide keep a watch for the Big Four — elk, moose, bear and Dall sheep. If you're lucky, the sky will be clear and you'll see the great mountain, McKinley, rising to 20,300 feet.

After a full-day excursion, the comforts of McKinley Chalet await you again. Ironically, moose like to live near the lodge and give birth to their calves there. Why? Because the predator of the calf, the dreaded grizzly, will not venture close to human habitation.

The lodge is open from mid-May to late September.

Cost: $122-$189 a night, varying by dates within the season.

Information: McKinley Chalet Resort, 241 W. Ship Creek Ave., Anchorage, AK

99501, (800) 276-7234.

El Tovar, Grand Canyon, Arizona

From those classic days when the venerable Fred Harvey set up restaurants and lodgings along the great American train routes, El Tovar Lodge on the South Rim of the Grand Canyon has had a special cachet.

El Tovar is the oldest and most elegant of the seven lodgings at the Grand Canyon. It was built in 1905, followed by Bright Angel Lodge in 1935. The El Tovar dining room is famous for elegant presentation in this rustic setting. Try the specialty, a sliced steak sandwich.

The setting, of course, is world-class. From El Tovar you stroll out to glance over the South Rim and read various visual chapters in the geologic history of the world. At sunrise and sunset, you can amble around the South Rim or take a shuttle to scenic points.

Cost: Lodge rates start at $111 a night.

Information: Grand Canyon National Park Lodges, P.O. Box 699, Grand Canyon, AZ 86023, (520) 638-2543.

Old Faithful Inn, Yellowstone National Park, Wyoming

If you want ringside seats for the Old Faithful geyser, especially in early morning and late evening when crowds are thin, Old Faithful Inn is the best Yellowstone lodging.

The historic log structure, built in 1904, welcomes guests in a soaring lobby with a huge fireplace and five tiers of balconies overlooking it. Many of the rooms have Victorian furniture.

From an outside balcony you can sit and watch Old Faithful spout into the air. On moonlit nights, it's fun to follow trails from the inn to see thermal wonders in their eerie natural state. You also may catch a glimpse of elk, buffalo and other wildlife.

Reservations should be made months ahead of a visit.

Cost: Rates start at $50 for the simplest room (without bath) in the original building and range up to $350 for suites.

Information: TWR Services, Box 165, Yellowstone National Park, WY 82190, (307) 344-7311.

Queen Wilhelmina State Park Lodge, Mena, Arkansas

Arkansas boasts some of the loveliest state parks in the country, complete with their own lodgings. One choice example is Queen Wilhelmina State Park and Lodge, named for the Dutch queen.

It's located in western Arkansas, on the 55-mile Talimena Scenic Drive, which connects Mena, AR, to Talihina, OK. Both the drive and the sturdy rock lodge have sweeping views of the gentle, heavily forested Ouachita Mountains.

The drive offers seasonal changes in color, with summer painting the undulating terrain a rich green.

Cost: Lodge rates are $55-$85 a night.

Information: Queen Wilhelmina State Park Lodge, 3877 Highway 88 W., Mena, AR 71953, (800) 264-2477 or (501) 394-2863.

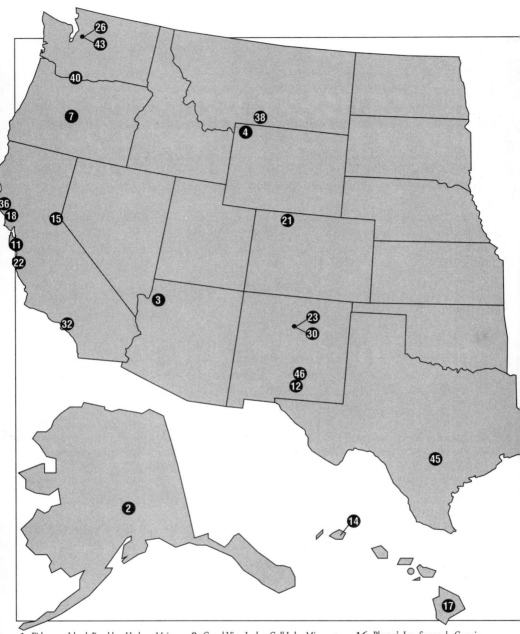

1 Fisherman Island, Boothbay Harbor, Maine

2 McKinley Chalet Resort, Denali National Park, Alaska

3 El Tovar, Grand Canyon, Arizona

4 Old Faithful Inn, Yellowstone National Park, Wyoming

5 Queen Wilhelmina State Park Lodge, Mena, Arkansas

6 Rock Harbor Lodge, Isle Royale National Park, Michigan

7 Inn of the Seventh Mountain, Bend, Oregon

8 Grand View Lodge, Gull Lake, Minnesota

9 The Balsams, Dixville Notch, New Hampshire

10 Opryland Hotel, Nashville, Tennessee

11 Hotel Monaco, San Francisco, California

12 The Lodge in Cloudcroft, Cloudcroft, New Mexico

13 Renaissance Vinoy Resort, St. Petersburg, Florida

14 Waimea Plantation Cottages, Kauai, Hawaii

15 Sorensen's Cabins, Lake Tahoe, California

16 Planter's Inn, Savannah, Georgia

17 Mauna Lani Bay Hotel, The Big Island, Hawaii

18 Heritage House, Little River, California

19 Algonquin Hotel, New York City, New York

20 Hotel Willard Inter-Continental, Washington, DC

21 Home Ranch, Clark, Colorado

22 Ventana Country Inn, Big Sur, California

23 Bishop's Lodge, Santa Fe, New Mexico

HOTELS, LODGES
& RESORTS

Rock Harbor Lodge, Isle Royale National Park, Michigan

Michigan's Isle Royale National Park and Rock Harbor Lodge promise a true get-away-from-it-all vacation — with no phones, no televisions and no cars. It's a wonderful place for relaxed isolation.

It's an adventure just to get there — a 4.5-hour, 45-mile boat trip from Copper Harbor to this island in the middle of Lake Superior. Once safely billeted at the Rock Harbor Lodge, there is an exciting nature story to behold — the equilibrium in the park between moose and wolves, which keep each other in balance.

Rock Harbor Lodge, open from late May into September, offers lodge rooms and housekeeping cabins, a restaurant, camp store and rental of canoes and fishing boats. On a lodge excursion boat, the Sandy, visitors are accompanied by a park naturalist. For the hiker, there are 170 miles of trails on Isle Royale.

Cost: Rates are $183 a day for two people in the lodge, including three meals, and $119 for two in a cabin, without meals. Reservations should be made early and must be coordinated with ferry schedules; ferries run from Michigan and Minnesota.

Information: Rock Harbor Lodge, National Park Concessions, Inc., P.O. Box 405, Houghton, MI 49931, (906) 337-4993. During the off-season, reservations can be made through National Park Concessions, General Offices, P.O. Box 27, Mammoth Cave, KY 42259, (502) 773-2191.

Inn of the Seventh Mountain, Bend, Oregon

The inland high desert around Bend, OR, has become a favorite destination because of its ample sun and warmth, scenic drives (such as the Cascade Lakes Highway), fishing and an excellent interpretive museum called the High Desert Museum.

With its mountains, lakes, rivers and forests, this area is a paradise for those who enjoy outdoor recreation, in the summer or winter. One of the best lodgings for all ages and all activities is the Inn of the Seventh Mountain, about 15 miles from Mount Bachelor, popular for both downhill and cross-country skiing in the winter. Besides offering pools, hot tubs, miniature golf, a championship golf course and horseback riding, the inn can arrange for white-water rafting, float trips and mountain biking. The low-rise cedar inn has a variety of accommodations, including fireside studio apartments.

Cost: Prices range from $59 a night for a basic bedroom to $99-$299 a night for condominiums.

Information: Inn of the Seventh Mountain, 18575 S.W. Century Drive, Bend, OR 97702, (800) 452-6810.

Grand View Lodge, Gull Lake, Minnesota

In the upper Midwest, nothing beats a relaxing family vacation at a North Woods lakefront lodge — such as Grand View on Gull Lake, two hours from Minneapolis.

The grounds encompass elaborate flower gardens, a historic log lodge and many detached cabins on a pine-studded lakefront. Some families like to kick back and relax, while others prefer active days of volleyball, fishing, swimming, golf, tennis and canoeing. Kids enjoy their own planned activities — and seeing the Paul Bunyan and Babe the Blue Ox statues in nearby Brainerd. Many families come to Grand View for weeklong stays.

Cost: The all-inclusive cost, covering lodging in a two-bedroom cabin, meals and activities, is about $400 a day for a family of four.

Information: Grand View Lodge, S. 134 Nokomis, Nisswa, MN 56468, (800) 432-

3788 or (218) 963-2234.

The Balsams, Dixville Notch, New Hampshire

Since the 1860s, the White Mountains of New Hampshire have been a favorite family retreat at palatial lodges that are worlds unto themselves.

Today the Balsams, at Dixville Notch, remains the most viable example of this genteel tradition. It's a drive to get there, but families come year after year for the serenity, fine dining, pleasant hiking, canoeing and the scenic White Mountains.

Summer visitors enjoy scenic drives in the mountains, through glacially carved "notches," as passes are called in the area.

Cost: All-inclusive price per couple, including lodging, activities and meals, is $308-$388 a night. The price for kids per day is $7 multiplied by their age.

Information: The Balsams, Route 26, Dixville Notch, NH 03570, (800) 255-0600.

Opryland Hotel, Nashville, Tennessee

If you want to immerse yourself in country music, Nashville is the cultural capital and the Opryland Hotel is the place to stay.

As you watch an evening performance at the nearby Grand Ole Opry, one aspect of the experience is striking. Fans have an especially close relationship with the stars — they run up with their cameras to take photos during the performance, something considered gauche at other music venues but encouraged here.

The Opryland Hotel is a giant, glass-enclosed affair with greenhouselike restaurants whose air-conditioning seems merciful on hot, muggy days.

Cost: Room rates for a family of four run $209-$249.

Information: Opryland Hotel, 2800 Opryland Drive, Nashville, TN 37214, (615) 889-1000.

Hotel Monaco, San Francisco, California

San Francisco ranks high on the list of many romantics looking for a getaway.

A good lodging choice is the art deco Hotel Monaco, created with a designer's touch in the theater district. The hotel also boasts an adjacent restaurant, the Grand Cafe, which features Mediterranean cuisine with California touches. Amenities include a wine reception each evening and a fitness center.

The concierge can help you select romantic outings, such as renting a car and driving to the promontories on the Marin headlands to view the Golden Gate Bridge and the city skyline, preferably at sunset with a bottle of Chardonnay.

Cost: Room rates are $160-$355 a night.

Information: Hotel Monaco, 501 Geary St., San Francisco, CA 94102, (800) 214-4220.

The Lodge in Cloudcroft, Cloudcroft, New Mexico

High in the pine-filled New Mexico mountains, west of Ruidoso and north of El Paso, lies a Southwestern escape for romantics, appropriately named The Lodge in Cloudcroft.

Perched in the mountains at 9,200 feet, Cloudcroft often is bathed in fog or clouds. The lodge is Victorian, built in the railroad era of the 1890s, complete with gourmet dining room and resident ghosts. Cloudcroft boasts a Scottish-style golf course, heated pool and sauna.

On a moonlit night, drive down to nearby White Sands National Monument and stroll on the huge white dunes.

Cost: Room rates are $79-$129 a night.

Information: The Lodge in Cloudcroft, P.O. Box 497, Cloudcroft, NM 88317, (800) 395-6343 or (505) 682-2566.

Renaissance Vinoy Resort, St. Petersburg, Florida

Roaring '20s seaside charm is the specialty at the lovingly restored Renaissance Vinoy Resort in St. Petersburg, FL.

The salmon-pink stucco structure and its opulent lobby project the grandeur of an earlier era for this romantic spot, now on the National Register of Historic Places.

St. Petersburg was among the first Florida cities to envision tourism as the state's main industry. When Aymer Vinoy Laughner opened his Vinoy Park Hotel in 1925, the railroad swells and land boomers who patronized it helped turn Florida tourism sites into cities of gold.

Visitors can take day excursions to sugar-white beaches or sail to nearby islands, such as Egmont Key, complete with a historic fort.

Cost: Rates start at $129.

Information: Renaissance Vinoy Resort, 501 Fifth Ave. NE, St. Petersburg, FL 33701, (800) HOTELS1 or (813) 894-1000.

Waimea Plantation Cottages, Kauai, Hawaii

Waimea Plantation Cottages consist of a cluster of turn-of-the-century houses on an authentic former sugar cane plantation.

The houses, updated with modern amenities, are spaced comfortably under coconut palms adjacent to the beach. A main lodge building includes a restaurant, The Grove Dining Room, with Hawaiian specialties.

Watching the sunset from the deserted beach at Waimea Plantation Cottages takes you back to turn-of-the-century Hawaii, before the era of mass tourism and megaresorts.

The place is a good base for adventure activities, such as hiking the Kalalau Trail, walking Waimea Canyon, catamaran sailing along the Na Pali Coast, sea kayaking, horseback riding along the beach, snorkeling and diving, and helicopter flightseeing over the island.

Cost: Rates start at $160 for a one-bedroom cottage with full kitchen.

Information: Waimea Plantation Cottages, P.O. Box 367, Waimea, Kauai, HI 96796, (800) 9-WAIMEA.

Sorensen's Cabins, Lake Tahoe, California

Mark Twain, who was not often given to superlatives, made an exception for California's Lake Tahoe. He called the lake "the fairest picture the whole Earth affords."

An appealing lodging from which to explore the area is Sorensen's, a cluster of cabins south of the lake in Hope Valley. Sorensen's puts you in a rustic setting noted for its scenery, fishing and hiking in summer.

The complex contains 29 cabins and a restaurant. The cabins range from small units that sleep just two to rather grand places that could host a family reunion. Most have kitchens, allowing for economical travel. The site is casual, and even the family dog is welcome (in some cabins).

Cost: Rates run from $65-$275.
Information: Sorensen's Cabins, 14255 Highway 88, Hope Valley, CA 96120, (800) 423-9949.

Planter's Inn, Savannah, Georgia

A discerning traveler can live like a cotton king on a modest budget in Savannah, one of the gracious cities of the South.

One choice lodging is the Planter's Inn near the downtown waterfront on prestigious Reynolds Square, one of 22 scenic squares in the city.

May is a delightful month here, when gardens are flourishing and the heat of summer has not yet hit with force. Stately oak trees strewn with Spanish moss shade the square in front of Planter's Inn and provide a home for squirrels and birds. Monumental statuary honors military heroes and religious luminaries.

You'll find service with a personal touch at Planter's Inn. Afternoon tea is complimentary, and you're welcome to a glass of wine for a small fee at the honor bar.

Cost: Budget rooms in this posh hostelry start at $99, including an enhanced continental breakfast.

Information: Planter's Inn, 29 Abercorn, Savannah, GA 31401, (800) 554-1187 or (912) 232-5678.

Mauna Lani Bay Hotel, The Big Island, Hawaii

Royalty has a way of choosing the best places to live. On the island of Hawaii, generations of kings left no doubt concerning their judgment about the choicest site. They favored the sunny west side of the island, the Kona and Kohala coasts, and their abodes remain important historic shrines today.

You, too, can live royally. It's no accident that some of the grandest Hawaiian hostelries are located here. The warmth, beaches and clear sky are all attractions.

Mauna Lani, carved out of lava rock, typifies these lodgings. Located by a royal fish pond, the resort has a marbled atrium, an enticing beach and a renowned golf course amidst the lava rock, with roughs that are indeed rough.

Cost: Summer rates start at $225, but check with a travel agent for cost-cutting packages that include airfare, hotel and sometimes a rental car or golfing.

Information: Mauna Lani Bay Hotel, 68-1400 Mauna Lani Drive, Kohala Coast, HI 96743, (800) 367-2323.

Heritage House, Little River, California

The crashing surf along the Mendocino coast, north of San Francisco, is one of the primal experiences in the Golden State.

Heritage House at Little River is a sumptuous lodging located on this choice coast. Luxury rooms and separate houses are scattered over a bluff above the sea. The dining room is famous for its lavish dinners and ample breakfasts, which are included in room rates.

You can walk down to a gazebo on a bluff over the ocean and watch the sunset. Nearby is the artsy town of Mendocino and some rugged state parks to explore, especially Russian Gulch and Van Damme.

Cost: Rooms with meals are $190-$350 per couple.
Information: Heritage House, 5200 N. Highway One, Little River, CA 95456, (800) 235-5885.

Algonquin Hotel, New York City, New York

The cultural pleasures of New York City have perennial appeal, and one fitting lodging for such an adventure is the historic literary hotel, the Algonquin.

You can sip a sherry in the stately lobby and recall an earlier era when the hotel was the literary meeting place in New York. Since the 1920s, when the famous Round Table literary wits met for lunch here, the Algonquin has been an index of subdued civility.

The lobby is a collection of sofas and chairs in a warm wood-paneled room that invites conversation. As a signature of the hotel's sense of style, you ring a small bell on the lounge tables to alert waiters that you want their attention, replacing ineffectual gestures.

Close to the theater district and museums, the Algonquin is an inviting big-city lodging that retains a small-scale, intimate feel.

Cost: Room rates are $220-$400.

Information: The Algonquin Hotel, 59 W. 44th, New York, NY 10036, (800) 548-0345 or (212) 840-6800.

Hotel Willard Inter-Continental, Washington, DC

Whether you want to keep your eye on the White House or indulge in visits to the Smithsonian, the Hotel Willard Inter-Continental Washington is the place to be.

There is no lodging more centrally located in the nation's capital. You dine with politicos, walk to the Smithsonian and sleep a shout away from the tourable White House. On weekend evenings, you can catch some jazz in its restaurant/bar, The Nest.

Cost: The best prices are on weekends, with rooms starting at $179.

Information: Hotel Willard Inter-Continental Washington, 1401 Pennsylvania Ave. NW, Washington, D.C. 20004, (800) 327-0200 or (202) 628-9100.

Home Ranch, Clark, Colorado

Clark, CO, is little more than a wide spot in the road, 18 miles northwest of Steamboat Springs, but its reputation as home to one of the West's finest guest ranches far exceeds its size.

A rustic 586-acre spread bounded by the Elk River and Routt National Forest, Home Ranch is a splendid combination of a working ranch and sophisticated wilderness resort.

Scattered in an aspen glen behind the timber-and-stone two-story main house are eight private guest cabins of rough-hewn log but featuring such refinements as hot tubs, wood stoves, antique furnishings, Indian rugs, robes and coffee makers. A sauna and lap pool add to the luxury list of extras.

During summer, hiking, horseback riding, fly-fishing for trophy trout, hayrides and barbecues are popular activities.

Cost: This choice is a splurge, starting at $3,010 for two for a minimum weeklong stay. Rates include meals and all activities.

Information: Home Ranch, P.O. Box 822, Clark, CO 80428, (970) 879-1780.

Ventana Country Inn, Big Sur, California

On three ridges jutting 1,200 feet above the Pacific Ocean sits Ventana Country Inn Resort, about 28 miles south of Carmel. The inn's 13 guest buildings are spread over a mountain meadow and nestled between oaks, redwoods and cedar trees, giving the feeling of a quiet retreat.

Each room has a private deck overlooking the majestic mountains, canyons or ocean. Walking paths wind through the resort and into the hills. Most rooms have fireplaces, and some come with hot tubs. Some feature window seats with great views and wonderful reading nooks. The beds are all king- and queen-size, some with draperies.

Guests can use the Japanese hot baths, fitness room, two swimming pools and saunas; massages and full-body treatments can be arranged by appointment.

Don't miss the promontory view from the library on top of the hill.

Cost: $195-$260 for rooms, $440-$970 for suites.

Information: Ventana Country Inn Resort, Highway 1, Big Sur, CA 93920, (408) 667-2331 or (800) 628-6500.

Bishop's Lodge, Santa Fe, New Mexico

Enchanted family weekend? Isn't that an oxymoron? Not when you're headed to Bishop's Lodge, a four-star adobe-style retreat in the pink and orange foothills of the Sangre de Cristo Mountains near Santa Fe.

The 1,000-acre oasis offers peace, quiet, starry skies, mountain views and an all-day supervised children's program so you can enjoy it all.

When you're not collapsing by the pool or hot tub, you can enjoy golf, tennis, guided horseback rides into the Santa Fe National Forest and Pecos Wilderness Area or white water rafting and kayaking on the Rio Grande.

Drives to Taos and Carson National Forest offer a wealth of cultural, historic and scenic attractions, including American Indian pueblos and crafts. The fascinating ancient cliff dwellings at Bandelier National Monument are less than an hour away, and you can visit Los Alamos Atomic Research Center Museum and learn all about the late, great bomb.

But don't worry. The only thing that glows around here now is the sun.

Cost: From $65.

Information: Bishop's Lodge, P.O. Box 2367, Santa Fe, NM 87504, (800) 732-2240 or (505) 983-6377. Santa Fe Convention and Visitors Bureau, P.O. Box 909, Santa Fe, NM 87504-0909, (800) 777-2489.

Osceola Mill Country Inn, Steele's Tavern, Virginia

You won't hear any gears grinding or see any dusty white clouds hanging in the air here, but with its 27-foot waterwheel and the original 5,000-pound millstone now in use as a coffee table, this country inn certainly doesn't try to hide its history.

From 1849 through 1969, the mill ground countless tons of Flavo flour. The property also includes the mill store and the miller's house — all now part of the inn.

The main building is the mill, with its exposed hand-hewn poplar beams lending a rustic ambiance. It offers five guest rooms, a living room (featuring the aforementioned coffee table), a dining room and a study.

The converted mill store now is a private cottage perfect for honeymooners, with vaulted ceilings and a whirlpool tub next to the stone fireplace.

The third accommodation option is the miller's residence, known as Mangus House, an elegant antique-filled Victorian farmhouse dating from 1873. This building has seven guest rooms, a parlor, a music room, a game room and four porches that together provide 100 feet of space for sitting and rocking.

Grounds include a swimming pool, a babbling brook, walking paths and a playground. Area activities include biking, hiking, antiquing, golfing, hunting and fishing.

The Blue Ridge Parkway is four miles away, and Lexington is a 17-mile drive.

Cost: From $89, including breakfast.

Information: The Osceola Mill Country Inn, Steele's Tavern, VA 24476, (800) 242-7352.

Bavarian Inn & Lodge, Shepherdstown, West Virginia

Watch the Appalachians turn into the Alps when you stay at this 72-room Bavarian-style inn reminiscent of a European mountain getaway. The inn sits on a secluded 11-acre estate overlooking the Potomac River — just an hour and a half outside Washington, DC.

Three of the guest rooms are in the gray stone mansion that serves as the main building, constructed in 1930 as a private residence. The other rooms are in four Alpine-motif chalets built along the river.

Each room has a canopied queen-size bed, antique reproduction furniture and a balcony with spectacular river views. Some rooms also have tiled fireplaces, whirlpool baths and stained-glass windows. The decor is distinctively Alpine, thanks to the native Bavarian owner, Erwin Asam, whose four-diamond AAA and four-star Mobil ratings are well-deserved.

The inn's well-known restaurant is one of the finest in the state and serves such German and American specialties as sauerbraten and Maine lobster.

The inn also boasts a heated pool, lighted tennis courts and bicycle rentals, with golf, white-water rafting and canoeing all nearby. In addition to excursions into the nation's capital, guests can browse in the area's antique shops and boutiques or explore nearby Harpers Ferry and the Antietam Battlefield. Horse racing, outlet malls and the Berkeley Springs Spa also are within easy driving distance.

Cost: From $95.

Information: Bavarian Inn & Lodge, Route 1, Box 30, Shepherdstown, WV 25443, (304) 876-2551.

The Challenger, Seattle, Washington

This 96-foot World War II tugboat may be retired, but it is enjoying a successful second career as a floating bunk-and-breakfast.

The Challenger, permanently moored on the south shore of Lake Union, is surprisingly plush. You'll find the former cargo hold transformed into a sunken conversation pit, with a fireplace surrounded by comfy couches and gleaming brass railings. The stern has been enclosed to make a solarium, which doubles as a dining room.

Nautical maps serve as wallpaper, and ship instruments and other equipment make for interesting decor. The curious can request a below-decks tour, but sitting outside and enjoying the view of the lake, downtown Seattle and the Olympic Mountains in the distance is even more compelling.

The tug offers eight cabins, including three with queen beds and four with televisions and VCRs for viewing selections from the boat's film library. The Master's Cabin is a favorite, with its private entrance and deck.

Provisions are as abundant as the on-board charm. Guests find M&Ms on the pillows at night and feast on a breakfast of crab omelets, sausage, fresh fruit compotes, pancakes and french toast the next morning.

Feel free to take a ride in the dinghy and spend the day on the water, or opt to walk the 10 blocks to downtown Seattle for urban explorations.

Cost: From $75, including breakfast.

Information: MV Challenger, 1001 Fairview Ave. N., Seattle, WA 98109, (206) 340-1201.

High Hampton Inn, Cashiers, North Carolina

Hidden away in the mountains of North Carolina is a sprawling lodge-style resort with a history dating back to the Confederacy. Its 1,200 acres, draped with centuries-old trees, have the atmosphere of an estate, for this was once the summer home of Wade Hampton, Confederate general, South Carolina governor and U.S. senator.

The rustic main inn is the center of activity. Guests enjoy rocking chairs on porches overlooking the mountains and board games in the family-room-style lobby with a four-sided fireplace. They also play golf, on the resort's scenic 18-hole course, and tennis (seven courts), or go hiking, canoeing, fishing or swimming in the resort lake.

Accommodations are comforting and homey, with furniture and quilts made locally. Choose rooms in the lodge or in multilevel cabins (many with porches), or book the secluded honeymoon cottage, set on its own lake.

Three meals a day, served buffet-style, are included in a stay at High Hampton. Guests are assigned their own table, decorated with dahlias from the gardens, and at dinner, everyone dresses up, bringing an air of sophistication to this unpretentious yet genteel inn.

Cost: $72-$93, extra for honeymoon cottage, all including three meals. Closed December-March.

Information: High Hampton Inn, P.O. Box 338, Cashiers, NC 28717, (800) 334-2551.

Hotel Maison de Ville, New Orleans, Louisiana

Deep in the heart of the French Quarter, Maison de Ville immerses you in the spirit of New Orleans. Outside its doors is all the revelry of the Big Easy — Dixieland jazz, Creole restaurants, the antique shops of Royal Street and the bars on Bourbon Street.

Staying at the hotel is like visiting a New Orleans relative. Knock on the front door to enter, walk down the entry hall to an antique-studded living room, then step onto a large landscaped courtyard. The home's intimate "dining room," Bistro at Maison de Ville, is one of the city's highest rated restaurants.

The hotel is actually three distinct types of lodging, each representative of New Orleans history. The main house is more than 250 years old. Its 16 guest rooms are furnished with antique four-poster beds, marble basins and period art works. Behind the main house, and opening onto the courtyard, are the 1700s slave quarters, a two-story wing with four rooms. These have beamed ceilings, brick walls and small mock fireplaces. (Tennessee Williams finished writing "A Streetcar named Desire" in Room Nine.)

A block and a half away are seven cottages, some dating back to 1788, named for American naturalist John James Audubon. In 1821, Audubon and his family moved into Cottage One. Set behind a high stucco wall, the tiny houses cluster around a brick-bordered swimming pool, open to all hotel guests.

In all the lodging, guests awaken to continental breakfast served on a silver tray, accompanied by a rose.

Cost: $185-$205, extra for suites or cottages, including continental breakfast.

Information: Hotel Maison de Ville, 727 Rue Toulouse, New Orleans, LA 70130, (800) 634-1600.

Little Palm Island, Little Torch Key, Florida

The name of the shuttle boat says it all: Escape. Little Palm Island, a five-acre dot of palm-fringed tranquillity 2 1/2 hours by car southwest of Miami and 15 minutes offshore by schooner, is the way to drop out first class. Just 30 luxury suites in 14 ocean-front thatched cottages — with a rope hammock for two swinging between coconut palms on the grassy front lawn — make this about as uncrowded as a retreat can get unless you happen to own your own island.

Meals are gourmet, but you never have to get dressed up. Guests get free use of kayaks, small sailboats and kickboards. Most popular excursion is the two-hour snorkel trip to Looe Key Marine Sanctuary. The 5.3-square-mile reef, just a 20-minute boat ride from the resort, offers some of the best snorkeling in American waters. At dusk, guests go down to the resort's sandy beach to watch the spectacular Keys sunset.

Cost: It's quite a splurge at $290 per day per couple, but Little Palm Island makes for a perfect romantic weekend. The price includes all water sports and a villa suite.

Information: Little Palm Island, 28500 Overseas Highway, Little Torch Key, FL 33042, (800) 343-8567.

La Posada de Santa Fe, Santa Fe, New Mexico

The only authentic Southwestern touch lacking at La Posada de Santa Fe may be a wild coyote or two wandering the grounds. This 119-room historic complex in downtown Santa Fe actually is a village of 1930s adobe cottages surrounding a European-style mansion dating from the late 1880s.

The inn sits on six landscaped acres, giving it a certain oasis quality. In architecture and furnishings, the cottages evoke a Southwestern feeling, with beamed ceilings and wood or flagstone floors. Some also offer private patios and traditional American Indian kiva fireplaces.

In contrast, the five guest rooms in the main building share its elegant Victorian decor. The Staab House, a renowned restaurant and bar in the mansion, also offers a Victorian ambience with its deep red carpets and leather chairs. It's a favorite with the locals, so don't be surprised to find it hopping at night.

The inn is only a three-minute walk from Santa Fe's plaza and many downtown attractions, including art museums, galleries, shops and historic houses.

Cost: $110-$397 per night.

Information: La Posada de Santa Fe, 330 E. Palace Ave., Santa Fe, NM 87501, (800) 727-5276.

Chalet Suzanne, Lake Wales, Florida

You may think you took a wrong turn and ended up at Disney World when you arrive at this remarkable central Florida hotel. Its through-the-looking-glass quality can be attributed to sloping floors on at least 14 different levels, slightly crooked walls and more odd knickknacks than you're likely to find in the attics of 100 grandmothers.

The inn dates from the early 1930s, when Bertha Hinshaw opened it. Later she added rooms one at a time and filled them with treasures collected on her 18 trips around the world. The result: 30 guest rooms of different colors, shapes, sizes and styles, each with its own front door, but built touching one another in one mammoth structure.

The food at the inn's Mobil four-star restaurant is so good that astronaut James Irwin took several cans of Chalet Suzanne soup to the moon with him in 1973. (Ask to tour the soup canning plant.) House specialties include homemade potato rolls and rum pie.

The inn is a 40-minute drive from Orlando and its many attractions.

Cost: $135-$195, including full breakfast.

Information: Chalet Suzanne, 3800 Chalet Suzanne Drive, Lake Wales, FL 33853-7060, (800) 433-6011.

Regent Beverly Wilshire Hotel, Los Angeles, California

Shoppers who want to indulge in a "Pretty Woman" fantasy trip might first check into Los Angeles' Regent Beverly Wilshire Hotel, one of the main settings for the popular film. All the gilt and lavish decor is there to see (sans Richard Gere, alas). Right across the street is Rodeo Drive, home of Gucci, Pucci, Versace and many other shops that can separate you from your dollars for a sampling of high-tone stuff. You can even get custom-baked dog food for your pet.

Price tags are high, but it's free to look. Stop for lunch in one of the sidewalk cafes and enjoy great people-watching.

Cost: Rates at the Regent Beverly Wilshire start at $275 a night for a double room, $450 for a suite; check about special packages.

Information: Regent Beverly Wilshire, 9500 Wilshire Blvd., Beverly Hills, CA 90212, (800) 545-4000. Los Angeles Convention and Visitors Bureau, 633 W. 5th St., Suite 6000, Los Angeles, CA 90071, (213) 624-7300.

The Crown Hotel, Inverness, Florida

This hotel is fit for a king — and it has the British Crown Jewels to prove it. The Crown Hotel also has brass beds, leaded glass doors, rubbed mahogany banisters, a real pub and the ambiance of a genteel English inn. Outside is parked a 1908 red double-decker bus.

All of this makes its location in this small central Florida town something of a puzzle. The twin-gabled hotel is the creation of a British entrepreneur who bought a dilapidated, 90-year-old hotel and transformed it into this imposing inn.

The crown jewels? Actually very good replicas, they're the hotel's crowning glory. You can see them in a lobby display case.

Cost: $60 for one person, $70 for two, including continental breakfast.

Information: The Crown Hotel, 109 N. Seminole Ave., Inverness, FL 34450, (904) 344-5555.

Jekyll Island Club Hotel, Jekyll Island, Georgia

Here's a seaside inn with a past, and a grand one at that. The Jekyll Island Club Hotel dates from 1886, when a group of millionaires bought Jekyll, a barrier island off the Georgia coast, and turned it into their personal playground.

For more than half a century, families with names like Vanderbilt, Morgan, Rockefeller and Astor came here each winter to swim, play croquet, bicycle and bask in the Georgia sunshine. The club disbanded in 1942, in part because of World War II, and the state eventually purchased the seven-mile-long island and what was left of the community.

The former clubhouse now is a beautiful 134-room inn (operated by Radisson Resorts) with rocker-strewn wraparound porches, Victorian trim and a turret.

Inside, you'll find the original pinewood flooring, floor-to-ceiling mirrors lining the hallways, crystal chandeliers, Oriental vases, huge floral arrangements, stained-glass transoms and an impressive five-story lobby staircase.

In the Riverview Lounge, where Victorian high tea is served every afternoon, look for old-fashioned photographs of the millionaires hamming it up on the beach and drinking tea on the lawn.

Guest rooms are richly appointed with Queen Anne mahogany reproduction furniture. Some rooms have fireplaces, balconies and whirlpool tubs. You won't find any sea views here (the hotel faces the Jekyll River and the marshes that separate the island from the mainland), but many rooms overlook croquet courts on the expansive grassy lawns that surround the inn.

The inn's Grand Dining Room (which serves a mean Sunday brunch) sports two rows of white Corinthian columns running down its middle and a massive fireplace with ornate woodwork. A baby grand piano sets a romantic tone.

Jekyll Island has plenty to offer, including a hard-packed sand beach that is perfect for bike riding. Visitors can take a self-guided walking tour or a 90-minute trolley tour of Jekyll's 240-acre historic district, a national historic landmark. Many homes once owned by the millionaires now are open for touring.

You'll also find excellent golf courses, clay tennis courts, 20 miles of level trails for biking or walking, fishing excursions, sunset cruises and dolphin watches.

Cost: Starting at $109.

Information: The Jekyll Island Club Hotel, 371 Riverview Drive, Jekyll Island, GA 31527, (800) 333-3333.

Admiral Semmes Hotel, Mobile, Alabama

This historic Gulf Coast inn, named for a rather admirable admiral, has a cool history. Not only was it Mobile's first luxury-class hotel when it opened in 1940, it also was one of the first air-conditioned hotels east of the Mississippi River.

On the National Trust for Historic Preservation's list of Historic Hotels of America, the inn is named for Raphael Semmes, who commanded the Confederate battleship Alabama. Like its namesake, the hotel is both distinguished and tough. While hurricane damage forced its closing in 1979, it recently has been returned to its original splendor.

On the outside, it is stately yet rather plain. Its interior, however, is surprisingly lavish. The circular lobby is palatial, with its original polished marble floor, Oriental carpet, ornate stairs and large central chandelier. The mezzanine's mirrored walls and balconies overlooking the lobby add to the glitz, as do the art deco-style elevator doors.

The 170 guest rooms are decorated in Chippendale and Queen Anne furnishings with designer wall coverings and tile and marble baths. The rooms with the best views overlook the harbor. Service is tops here, with complimentary coffee brought with your wake-up call and fresh-baked cookies left each evening.

The Admiral's Corner, the hotel's bar and a local watering hole, can claim some history of its own. This is where singer Jimmy Buffett got his start. Oliver's Restaurant features seven colorful murals depicting scenes from the history of Mobile's much-celebrated Mardi Gras.

The hotel also offers an outdoor swimming pool and whirlpool in a landscaped courtyard that's complete with gazebo. Guests also enjoy privileges at the nearby downtown YMCA.

Since the Admiral Semmes is nestled in the heart of historic downtown, you'll find the neighborhood makes for wonderful wanderings. Opportunities for tennis, golf, sailing and sunning on the beach are all nearby. Fishermen take note: The hotel will store your catch and package your fish for you when you leave.

Nearby sights also include the USS Alabama (open for touring), Bellingrath Gardens and Home (a famous 65-acre garden) and the Oakleigh Complex, the official antebellum mansion of Mobile (with an interesting display of Mardi Gras memorabilia).

Cost: Starting at $103.

Information: Radisson Admiral Semmes Hotel, 251 Government St., Mobile, AL 36602, (800) 333-3333.

Howard Creek Ranch, Westport, California

Snuggled in a valley along the scenic Mendocino Coast, this 1871 New England-style farmhouse may seem like it's on the wrong side of the country. But upon closer inspection, the unmistakably Californian wood-heated hot tub, sauna and solar heated swimming pool (not to mention massage service) give that illusion away.

The antique-strewn inn still has its original parlor fireplace and even the home's original bathtub. Rooms include some with separate entrances, skylights and private decks. One, Lucy's Room, features a century-old windowpane with "Lucy Howard" etched in the glass.

The accommodations here also include separate redwood cabins, the most unusual being the Boat House, built around the hull and galley of a boat. This cabin also features a night-lighted creek.

Horses and cows still graze in the pasture, once part of a sheep and cattle ranch with a sawmill, a blacksmith shop and a dairy. You can stroll through award-winning gardens, and a sandy beach is a mere 200 yards away. A paved lane through 10 miles of sand dunes offers still more opportunities for exploration, and the 75-foot-long swinging footbridge over adjacent Howard Creek is guaranteed to bring out the adventurer in any guest.

In addition to beachcombing, whale-watching and swimming from the ranch, visitors can explore the Cape Cod-style seaside village of Mendocino, visit the Mendocino Coast Botanical Gardens in nearby Fort Bragg or ride the Skunk Train, a 40-mile journey on a historic logging line into the redwood forest.

Cost: Starting at $55, including full breakfast.

Information: Howard Creek Ranch, P.O. Box 121, Westport, CA 95488, (707) 964-6725.

Great Southern Hotel, Columbus, Ohio

"Great" in this hotel's name is not an adjective used loosely. This grand establishment began life in 1897 as the Great Southern Fireproof Building and Opera House, boasting 222 guest rooms, several grand parlor rooms, a ballroom with magnificent stained-glass windows, an opera house/theater, several restaurants, residential space, a barber shop, a sauna (said to be Teddy Roosevelt's favorite) and a rooftop garden.

Stars such as Lillian Russell, Sarah Bernhardt and John Barrymore once signed the register. One of the first buildings in Columbus to have electricity, the hotel drew its own water from three wells in the basement. Its theater had a cooling system that was most unusual for its day — ice was packed into a bin in the basement, and a belt-driven fan blew the cold air it produced into the theater through ventilation holes in the floor.

Its heyday was, unfortunately, short-lived. At the turn of the century, the company that owned the hotel was forced into receivership and the property was auctioned. Everything went downhill, until a restoration in 1982, which earned the building a spot on the National Register of Historic Places.

During the renovation, the workers found such signs of quality workmanship as four-foot-thick walls. Today the hotel is every bit as elegant as it was at the start, with a fabulous stained-glass ceiling in the lobby, a polished white marble floor, gleaming brass fixtures, tall white pillars and intricate plaster work.

The 196 guest rooms are decorated in rich fabrics and fine cherry furniture. Only the theater, also once an opera house, is not yet completed; it's scheduled to reopen in 1998.

Located in downtown Columbus, the hotel is near the Columbus Museum of Art, the State Capitol, the zoo, the Brewery District and the city's intriguing German Village area.

Cost: Starting at $89. The "romance package" (including champagne, fresh flowers, chocolates and breakfast in bed) is $109.

Information: The Great Southern Hotel, 310 S. High St., Columbus, OH 43215, (614) 228-3800.

The Pollard, Red Lodge, Montana

If a man known as Jeremiah Liver Eatin' Johnson frequents a hotel, you know it's bound to be a colorful place. And indeed, the Pollard's strange and wonderful history does not disappoint.

This southern Montana hostelry on the National Register of Historic Places opened in 1893 as the Spofford Hotel. It was Red Lodge's first brick building and attracted such guests as Buffalo Bill Cody, William Jennings Bryan, Civil War General Nelson A. Miles and even Calamity Jane. Renamed The Pollard in 1902, the building also has housed a post office, a barber shop and a dry goods store in its lifetime.

Its 36 newly renovated guest rooms are filled with Victorian cherry and oak furniture, including sleigh beds and ornately carved headboards. Some rooms have mountain views, some come with private hot tubs and steam cabinets and still others feature balconies overlooking the inn's tranquil atrium gallery (an uncommon common area featuring stained-glass windows and a wood-burning fireplace).

The lounge, called the History Room, offers huge windows looking onto Red Lodge's historic Main Street. The room is filled with historical pieces from the Pollard family, including silver ladles, swords and a family portrait from the '40s. A decidedly modern addition is the hotel's health club, with hot tub, saunas and two racquetball courts.

The Red Lodge Mountain ski area is seven miles away, and summer activities include fishing, white-water rafting, horseback riding and golf. The scenic Beartooth Highway takes you to Yellowstone National Park, 69 miles away.

Cost: Starting at $50.

Information: The Pollard, 2 N. Broadway, P.O. Box 650, Red Lodge, MT 59068, (800) POLLARD.

Soniat House, New Orleans, Louisiana

Giving and getting *lagniappe* (Creole French for "bonus") is an established tradition in New Orleans. It means a little something extra that's quite unexpected. But guests have come to expect the unexpected at the Soniat House, a historic inn in a quiet residential corner of the French Quarter.

For example, many paintings that adorn the walls here are on loan from the New Orleans Museum of Art. Breakfast in the courtyard is served on Villeroy & Boch porcelain with linen napkins. And the elaborate balconies that adorn the front of the building — erected in 1829 as a three-story, red brick town home for a sugar plantation owner — make up some of the most elaborate cast iron in the French Quarter.

The inn's architecture is an unusual combination of Creole style with classic Greek Revival elements. A flagstone carriageway leads to the peaceful herringbone brick courtyard, filled with tropical plants, magnolia trees, hibiscus bushes, wisteria vines, fountains and a lily pond.

Inside, you'll find French, English and Louisiana antiques, some original to the house. The 31 guest rooms feature brass and four-poster beds (some with canopies), as well as bedsteads hand-carved by the finest cabinetmaker in town.

Some of the rooms are former slave quarters, now overflowing with luxurious touches including telephones by the bathtub, goose-down pillows and Jacuzzis. Some rooms have decorative fireplaces, exposed brick walls, polished hardwood floors with antique Oriental carpeting and beautiful leaded glass transoms. Most offer balconies facing the courtyard, and one suite even has its own elevator.

The inn is centrally located, just two blocks from the French Market and three blocks from Jackson Square. Wander aimlessly on your own or ask the concierge to help you arrange your sightseeing, from jazz performances to horse-drawn carriage rides.

Cost: Starting at $145.

Information: Soniat House, 1133 Chartres St., New Orleans, LA 70116, (800) 544-8808 or (504) 522-0570.

Columbia Gorge Hotel, Hood River, Oregon

This inn provides dramatic views no matter which direction you gaze. Looking down from the high bluff the inn sits on, you'll see the powerful Columbia River rushing to sea. Looking up, you'll see 11,245-foot Mount Hood, perpetually snow-covered and presiding over all. It's impossible to decide which view is more magnificent.

The 41-room, Mediterranean villa-style inn, a registered national historic landmark built in 1921 by lumber baron Simon Benson, has hosted such notables as Calvin Coolidge, Franklin Delano Roosevelt, Clara Bow, Myrna Loy and Jane Powell.

Rudolph Valentino was such a frequent guest that the inn's Valentino Lounge was named for the actor. With its piano, roaring fireplace and picture window overlooking the gorge, the lounge is one of the most popular spots in town. So, too, is Columbia River Court, the inn's renowned restaurant.

The inn's elegant lobby features sculpted floral carpeting, a plush circular settee, fresh flower arrangements and dainty lace curtains.

The guest rooms are spacious and warm with high ceilings, French doors and windows and antique furnishings, including polished brass and canopy beds. Some have fireplaces, but each has a view of either the gardens or the gorge. Turn-down service includes a fresh rose along with cookies to inspire sweet dreams, but don't spoil your appetite for the inn's notable five-course country farm breakfast.

The hotel's 13 acres include walking paths through exquisite gardens and an outdoor amphitheater offering concerts, plays and other performing arts. Phelphs Creek flows through the grounds and cascades over the bluff to form a 200-foot waterfall.

The area offers lots of outdoor activities (including skiing, mountain biking, white-water rafting, fishing and hiking) and is famous for its windsurfing. You also can opt to tour the Bonneville Dam and visit several regional wineries.

Cost: Starting at $150, including full breakfast.

Information: Columbia Gorge Hotel, 4000 Westcliff Drive, Hood River, OR 97031, (800) 345-1921.

Tanyard Springs, Morrilton, Arkansas

If you like your romance with a touch of fantasy, don't miss this inn on top of Petit Jean Mountain just outside Little Rock.

Spread among its 40 wooded acres are 13 unusual cabins, each constructed and decorated in a special theme. Each has a fireplace, cedar closets, a porch swing or rocking chairs and custom-made pieces of furniture that are truly unique.

In the Stagecoach Cabin, for example, one bed is an authentic stagecoach from the 1800s. The Cattle Rancher uses branding irons for door handles, and a wagon (complete with wheels) serves as a bed. An unusual staircase carved out of the 35-foot trunk of a cedar tree is the focal point of the Mountaineer Cabin.

Tree branches form towel racks and clothes hooks in the Pioneer. In the Gambler, a roulette wheel graces the bathroom door. The bathroom in the Settler's Cabin is an "indoor outhouse," with a telltale crescent moon on the door.

The more feminine Adrienne DuMont Cabin (a favorite with honeymooners) features a diamond-shaped fleur-de-lis stained-glass window, a walnut swing suspended from a cedar beam and symbols of each wedding anniversary from one through 75.

All the cabins have kitchens, but if you're not in the mood to cook, you can arrange to have breakfast brought to you. Spring water is piped into each cottage.

Guests can play miniature golf on the grounds and ogle the view at Sunrise Point, a private scenic overlook. You also can explore neighboring Petit Jean State Park, where you can hike to 100-foot Cedar Falls, attend a nature talk, fish in four stocked lakes or tour the Museum of Automobiles.

Cost: Starting at $75.

Information: Tanyard Springs, Petit Jean Mountain, 144 Tanyard Springs Road, Morrilton, AR 72110, (800) 533-1450.

Whitney Hotel, Minneapolis, Minnesota

Was turning a 19th-century flour mill on the banks of the Mississippi River into a romantic eight-story hotel a half-baked idea? One glance at the Whitney's lobby — with its brass chandeliers, gleaming white Spanish marble floor, African mahogany trim and sweeping staircase — immediately suggests otherwise.

Expect the service to match the rich ambience. The Whitney boasts more than one staff member for each of its 97 rooms and amenities such as complimentary newspapers on weekday mornings, free coffee served in the lobby and a chocolate on your pillow each evening.

Accommodations include single-level rooms with high ceilings and bilevel rooms with a spiral staircase connecting each floor. Ask for a room with a view of the Mississippi's scenic St. Anthony Falls. Guests feeling particularly flush may want to reserve the three-bedroom penthouse suite, with its two living rooms, a baby grand piano, fireplaces, whirlpool tubs and private terrace.

In good weather, eat at the outdoor Garden Plaza, a landscaped courtyard restaurant with a central fountain and colorful flowers. The more formal Whitney Grille, with its tapestry chairs and cherry paneling, or Richard's, featuring mahogany paneling and fine art, are also options.

Fitness-minded guests can walk or jog along the Great River Road, a two-mile stretch running past the hotel and along the river. Downtown Minneapolis is just blocks away. If you aren't up for the short walk, The Whitney will gladly whisk you to any downtown destination you choose.

Cost: Starting at $115.

Information: Whitney Hotel, 150 Portland Ave., Minneapolis, MN 55401, (800) 248-1879 or (612) 339-9300.

Inn at the Market, Seattle, Washington

Nearby vendors can provide a bouquet of flowers or a pound of chocolates to add romance to your stay at this small luxury inn in the midst of Seattle's 87-year-old Pike Place Market.

The seven-acre-plus, open-air market that surrounds the modern-day brick inn is chock-full of produce, meat, fish and flower vendors, not to mention boutiques and restaurants.

The inn, however, is a haven from the downtown hustle and bustle. The peaceful inner courtyard, complete with fountain, was built to accommodate a beautiful 50-year-old cherry tree. And the landscaped fifth-floor sun deck offers plenty of pristine white Adirondack chairs from which to enjoy a panoramic view of both the market and Puget Sound.

The lobby is resplendent with overstuffed red chairs, a floral carpet, French country antiques and a wood-burning fireplace, providing a comfortable yet elegant atmosphere.

The inn's 65 guest rooms also are decorated with overstuffed furniture, and custom-designed pickled pine pieces. Rooms offer splendid views; the floor-to-ceiling bay windows open, so you can enjoy fresh air and sea breezes.

In the bathrooms, you'll find terry-cloth bathrobes and a special line of Seattle-made toiletries. Expect Dilettante chocolates with evening turn-down service and your choice of newspapers delivered in the morning. All rooms have refrigerators, and some have microwave ovens and wet bars, too.

Each also has a coffee maker, with freshly ground coffee delivered to your room daily. The gesture is appropriate, since more mocha is consumed per capita in Seattle than in any other U.S. city. (Is it any wonder they made a movie called "Sleepless in Seattle"?)

The inn serves cider during the holidays and fruit in the lobby each afternoon and offers free shuttle service to downtown locations and the use of a nearby health club.

The Seattle Aquarium, the Seattle Art Museum, Post Alley's antique shops and cafes and plenty of art galleries all are within easy walking distance.

Cost: Starting at $130.

Information: Inn at the Market, 86 Pine St., Seattle, WA 98101, (800) 446-4484.

Big Cedar Lodge, Branson, Missouri

Big Cedar Lodge certainly is big, with 75 buildings offering 215 accommodations on 250 wooded acres. But this resort by the shores of Table Rock Lake in the Ozarks has been cleverly designed to guarantee guests the experience of staying at a smaller, more intimate inn.

Take your pick of lodges, cabins and private cottages sprinkled about the grounds and separated by pine groves and cold mountain streams crossed by wooden footbridges.

The 51-room, four-story main Valley View Lodge sports log beams and handrails. Rooms here have pine furnishings, and some offer kitchenettes and balconies.

The 17-room, three-story Spring View Lodge looks like a turn-of-the-century Adirondack hunting lodge, with mounted animal heads, stone fireplaces, cathedral ceilings and wood paneling. Falls Lodge is a deluxe 65-room lodge.

More deluxe lodging is available in two private cottages — the Tudor-style Carriage House and Truman Cottage — dating from the 1920s.

The 10 informal Knotty Pine Cabins all have native wood paneling, tongue-and-groove pine floors and overstuffed furniture. Some have stone fireplaces and Jacuzzi tubs. The Cedar Trail Cabins and the Devil's Pool Cabins sit on a separate wooded ridge and all feature hand-peeled logs, limestone fireplaces, full kitchens, Jacuzzi tubs and private decks. Rooms here are decorated with handcrafted wood furniture, wrought-iron beds made by local craftsmen and hand-woven rugs on hardwood floors.

Big Cedar's rustic charm extends to Devil's Pool Restaurant, with its huge fireplaces at each end of the room, pine posts and beams with the bark intact, a 100-year-old mahogany bar and oak plank floors.

Resort activities include hayrides, horse-drawn carriage rides, chuck-wagon trips, tennis and miniature golf. Try the one-mile jogging trail, the two-mile nature trail or the weight machines at the fitness center. Guests also will find the full-service marina handy for explorations of 43,000-acre Table Rock Lake. Still more fishing and hiking are available at Dogwood Canyon, a private wilderness refuge for resort guests that's a 20-minute drive away.

After you've had your fill of wilderness, the country-music mecca of Branson — with its live entertainment, outlet shopping, amusement parks and mountain craft shops — is a short drive away.

Cost: Starting at $79.

Information: Big Cedar Lodge, 612 Devil's Pool Road, Ridgedale, MO 65739, (417) 335-2777.

Hyatt Regency Hill Country Resort, San Antonio, Texas

Although Hyatt's resort on the edge of San Antonio is large, with 500 rooms, it's low-rise and rambling, creating the feeling that you've pulled up to someone's ranch in the country.

The buildings are traditional Hill Country design, made of native limestone with wood porches. You can sit and rock a spell on Aunt Mary's Porch overlooking tree-covered grounds and on cool evenings, slip inside to warm up by two huge stone fireplaces. Rooms have a homey look but with all the expected amenities of Hyatt. Dining ranges from a fine restaurant featuring regional cuisine to a family-oriented cafe and a general store with snacks.

Of the many activities — including golf, tennis, a health club, jogging track, hiking and biking trails — the crowd-pleaser is the Ramblin' River, a man-made stream that flows through the grounds. On hot summer days, do what Texans do to cool off — hop in an inner tube and float on the cool, lazy river, as it's often called.

Cost: Rates start at $185 December through February and $230 March through November.

Information: Hyatt Regency Hill Country Resort, 9800 Hyatt Resort Drive, San Antonio, TX 78251, (800) 233-1234.

Inn of the Mountain Gods, Mescalero, New Mexico

Set beneath 12,003-foot Sierra Blanca, the Inn of the Mountain Gods commands a sweeping view of mountains, forests and Lake Mescalero, named for the Apache Indian Reservation that owns this lodging in southern New Mexico.

Outside the small resort town of Ruidoso, the inn is a popular retreat for residents in the Southwest, who appreciate the area's cool summers and winter sports at nearby Ski Apache. It's a casual, rustic-looking resort with Southwestern decor and spectacular views through tall picture windows in the lobby. Spacious rooms have balconies, and there's a choice of restaurants, from snacks by the pool to fine dining.

In summer, you can cast a line for trout or rent a canoe or rowboat to explore the lake. The resort has a large pool, tennis courts, horseback riding and a golf course that's challenging as well as scenic.

If that's not enough action, you can explore Ruidoso's galleries, crafts shops and museums or try your luck at the Ruidoso Downs Race Track (horse racing in the summer) or gamble at Casino Apache, also run by the reservation.

Cost: Rates range from $80 to $120 a night, depending on the season.

Information: Inn of the Mountain Gods, P.O. Box 269, Carrizo Canyon Road, Mescalero, NM 88340, (800) 545-9011.

Grove Park Inn, Asheville, North Carolina

You, too, can vacation like Henry Ford and Harvey Firestone — at the Grove Park Inn today. Once for the wealthy who came to enjoy the clean air and serene views of the Blue Ridge Mountains, this historic resort still is a popular escape — but now for all types of vacationers, golfers in particular.

Made of massive stones, the hotel has the feel of a lodge and, indeed, was inspired by Old Faithful Inn at Yellowstone National Park. Guests mingle in the high-ceilinged Great Hall with its massive fireplaces and stroll onto the terrace, which overlooks the golf course and mountains on the edge of Asheville.

Several wings of rooms and a sports complex have been added, turning this into a large resort with numerous activities and restaurants to suit different tastes. As you stroll down the halls, though, look at the pictures, which have captured the visits by many dignitaries and tell the rich history of this 1913 masterpiece.

Cost: Rates are $125-$155 January to mid-April, then $175-$215 the remainder of the year.

Information: Grove Park Inn, 290 Macon Ave., Asheville, NC 28804, (800) 438-5800.

STREETS
OF DREAMS

Some streets, through history or happenstance, have achieved a special cachet in America. On them are situated the most important sites, the busiest entertainment sectors or the grandest residences. Those that follow have gained national prominence.

Fifth Avenue, New York City, New York

"New York doesn't have many streets that inspire dreams, but Fifth Avenue can intoxicate us," Ronda Wist writes in her book, "Fifth Avenue."

New York's toniest stores claim Fifth Avenue as their address. So do some of the city's finest hotels and museums, not to mention such famous sites as St. Patrick's Cathedral, Rockefeller Center, the Plaza Hotel and the Empire State Building. Grand mansions once lined the street, grand parades still march there.

After a period of decline, Fifth Avenue has undergone a renaissance in the past few years. New, classy stores have moved in, less-desirable ones have lost their leases and push-cart vendors and scam artists have been driven away. Now visitors can shop in stores like Fendi, Bulgari, Bally, Cartier, Dior and Armani. Saks and Bergdorf Goodman have upgraded.

Probably the most celebrated site on Fifth Avenue is the Promenade at Rockefeller Center, a mecca for out-of-towners.

Accommodations: The Sherry-Netherland Hotel, $265-$440, 781 Fifth Ave. at 59th St., New York, NY 10022, (800) 247-4377 or (212) 355-2800.

Information: New York Convention and Visitors Bureau, 2 Columbus Circle, New York, NY 10019, (800) NYC-VISIT.

Pennsylvania Avenue, Washington, DC

In Pennsylvania Avenue, America has vested its national dreams. It is on this broad street that inaugural parades mark the beginning of presidential dreams — but it's also here, sadly, that presidential funeral corteges mark their end.

The White House anchors one end of downtown Pennsylvania Avenue, the Capitol the other end. On the mile between them are some of Washington's most important institutions — the National Archives, the National Gallery of Art, the Old Post Office, the Justice Department, the FBI Building, the U.S. Navy Memorial, the Commerce Department.

At Western Plaza, the original L'Enfant design for the city of Washington is imbedded in a block-long concrete mosaic. Many other important sites lie close to the avenue. If any street could be called the national street, this is it.

Accommodations: Wyndam Bristol, $89-$199, 2430 Pennsylvania Ave., Washington, DC 20037, (800) 822-4200 or (202) 955-6400.

Information: Washington, DC, Visitor Information Center, 1212 New York Ave. NW, Suite 1600, Washington, DC 20005, (202) 789-7000.

Michigan Avenue, Chicago, Illinois

While the song "Chicago" defines State Street as its great street, that honor really belongs to Michigan Avenue.

Sometimes called the Magnificent Mile, that part of Michigan Avenue from the Chicago River to Oak Street is the home of such noted buildings as the Tribune Tower, the Wrigley Building, the Water Tower Place mall and the 110-story John Hancock Center, the world's tallest office building, where a top-floor observatory offers fine views of the city.

Classy shops and upscale hotels also front Michigan Avenue.

Accommodations: Radisson Plaza Hotel, $114-$225, 160 E. Huron St., Chicago, IL 60611, (800) 325-3535 or (312) 787-2900.

Information: Chicago Convention and Tourism Bureau, 2301 S. Lakeshore Drive, Chicago, IL 60616, (800) 487-2446.

Bourbon Street, New Orleans, Louisiana

Just about anything goes on New Orleans' most famous street. Bars advertise nude table-top dancing and mud wrestling. Sidewalk stands offer beer in a plastic cup for a buck. Souvenir shops showcase T-shirts with obscene messages.

But Bourbon Street isn't all booze and raunch. You can listen to good jazz on the street and elsewhere in the French Quarter, dine in superb restaurants and shop for antiques. And that's why Bourbon Street attracts so many visitors — its appeal covers the gamut.

Accommodations: Best Western Inn on Bourbon, $79-$245, 541 Bourbon St., New Orleans, LA 70130, (800) 535-7891 or (504) 524-7611.

Information: New Orleans Metropolitan Convention and Visitors Bureau, 1520 Sugar Bowl Drive, New Orleans, LA 70112, (504) 566-5011.

Ocean Drive, Miami Beach, Florida

Ten years ago, Ocean Drive was a street of rundown hotels across from the beach. Today, thanks to the preservation and restoration of its art deco structures, Ocean Drive is one of the hottest tourist destinations in the country.

Visitors from all over the world flock here, admiring its distinctive art deco buildings by day and filling the outdoor cafes and late-hour spots at night.

Ocean Drive is a favored roosting spot for models and celebrities, some of whom even own homes or businesses here. Fashion designer Gianni Versace, for instance, converted an apartment house on Ocean Drive into a multimillion-dollar home. Singer Gloria Estefan owns Lorio's restaurant.

Accommodations: Park Central Hotel, $65-$175, 640 Ocean Drive, Old Miami Beach, FL 33139, (800) PARK CENTRAL or (305) 538-1611.

Information: Greater Miami Convention and Visitors Bureau, 701 Brickell Ave., Suite 2700, Miami, FL 33134, (800) 283-2707.

Rodeo Drive, Beverly Hills, California

Some of the world's most exclusive shops front on Rodeo Drive. Factory outlet stores are nowhere to be seen, and the only mall, the Rodeo Collection, has glitz galore.

Anchored by the svelte Beverly Wilshire Hotel, Rodeo Drive lures the well-heeled to shops like Chanel, Ferragamo, Cartier, Ungaro, Gucci, Armani and Giorgio, whose yellow-striped awnings are a Rodeo Drive landmark.

If you're curious about the famous folks who live in Beverly Hills, several companies offer van tours.

Accommodations: The Beverly Rodeo Hotel, $150, including continental breakfast,

1 Fifth Avenue, New York City, New York
2 Pennsylvania Avenue, Washington, DC

3 Michigan Avenue, Chicago, Illinois
4 Bourbon Street, New Orleans, Louisiana

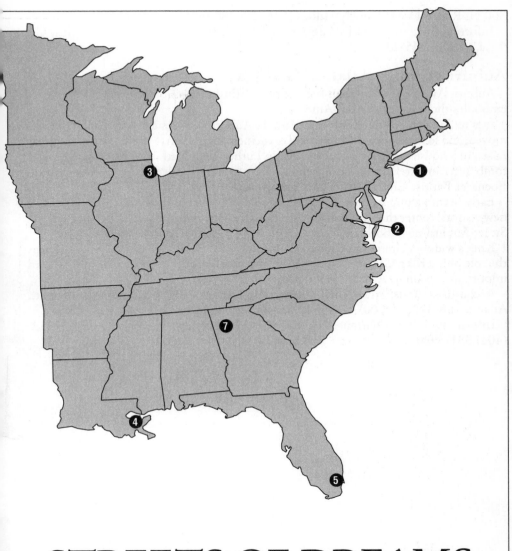

STREETS OF DREAMS

5 Ocean Drive, Miami Beach, Florida
6 Rodeo Drive, Beverly Hills, California

7 Auburn Avenue, Atlanta, Georgia

360 N. Rodeo Drive, Beverly Hills, CA 90210, (800) 356-7575 or (310) 273-0300.

Information: Beverly Hills Info Center, 239 S. Beverly Drive, Beverly Hills, CA 90212, (800) 345-2210.

Auburn Avenue, Atlanta, Georgia

Auburn Avenue is more than the site of Martin Luther King's birthplace home. It embodies the spirit of African-Americans.

It is to Auburn Avenue (known as "Sweet Auburn") that successful Atlanta blacks moved, and so it has become the symbol of their emancipation. Martin Luther King was raised in a house that now is part of Martin Luther King National Historical Site. His tomb rests in a reflecting pool behind the privately funded King Center next to Ebenezer Baptist Church, where his father preached.

Early homes along Auburn have been restored. Now the Park Service is building a new visitors' center that will house exhibits on the civil rights movement, King and the Sweet Auburn neighborhood.

King's widow Coretta has registered objections to the new facility, saying it usurps the role of the King Center. Whatever the outcome, Auburn Avenue will always be an important beacon to African-Americans.

Accommodations: Suite Hotel Underground Atlanta, $89-$250, 54 Peachtree St., Atlanta, GA 30303, (800) 477-5549 or (404) 223-5555.

Information: King National Historic Site, 526 Auburn Ave., Atlanta, GA 30312, (404) 331-3920.